THE FACTS ON FILE
BIOLOGY
HANDBOOK

Revised Edition

THE FACTS ON FILE BIOLOGY HANDBOOK

Revised Edition

THE DIAGRAM GROUP

Facts On File
An imprint of Infobase Publishing

The Facts On File Biology Handbook, Revised Edition

Diagram Visual Information Ltd

Editorial directors	David Harding, Moira Johnston
Science editor	Eleanora von Dehsen
Editors	Nancy Bailey, Jean Brady, Paul Copperwaite, Eve Daintith, Bridget Giles, Jane Johnson, Reet Nelis, Jamie Stokes
Design	Richard Hummerstone, Edward Kinsey
Design production	Anthony Atherton, Carole Dease, Oscar Lobban, Lee Lawrence
Artists	Susan Kinsey, Lee Lawrence, Kathleen McDougall
Research	Peter Dease, Catherine & Neil McKenna
Contributors	Michael Allaby, Martyn Bramwell, John Daintith, Trevor Day, John Haywood, Jim Henderson, David Lambert, Catherine Riches, Dr Robert Youngson

Facts On File, Inc.
An imprint of Infobase Publishing
132 West 31st Street
New York, NY 10001

For Library of Congress Cataloging-in-Publication Data,
please contact Facts On File, Inc.

ISBN 0-8160-5877-6

Cover design by Cathy Rincon

Printed in the United States of America

VB DIAG 10 9 8 7 6 5 4 3 2 1

This book is printed on acid-free paper.

INTRODUCTION

THE FACTS ON FILE BIOLOGY HANDBOOK, Revised Edition offers students a full view of this vital branch of science, in the form of a one-stop reference.

The Revised Edition expands greatly on the information available in the previous edition, with the inclusion of four new sections—an A–Z of key advances in the field of biology; a list of Nobel Prize winners in physiology or medicine; listings for important science and biology associations; and key science and biology Web sites. The biography and chronology sections have been updated and the glossary expanded to include charts and graphs illustrating important concepts. Finally, the index has been extended and completely revised to make searching even easier. THE BIOLOGY HANDBOOK, Revised Edition features the following components:

GLOSSARY
More than 1,700 entries are provided, many of them accompanied by illustrations, and now with 21 new large diagrams and charts, to aid students' understanding of the specialized terminology of the biological sciences.

BIOGRAPHIES
Biographies of more than 400 people are given here, including not only the giants of biological science, such as Charles Darwin, but also many whose achievements may have gone unnoticed, yet whose discoveries have nevertheless pushed forward the world's understanding of biology. Updated to 2005.

CHRONOLOGY
The chronology covers 2,500 years of events in the history of the biological sciences that have influenced our lives more than wars, political changes, and world rulers. Now extended to 2005.

KEY ADVANCES
This entirely new A–Z list of 125 important advances in the biological sciences enables students to find quick information on who invented or discovered what and when.

NOBEL PRIZE WINNERS
This newly added list of Nobel Prize winners in physiology or medicine is complete to 2005. Each entry includes the award citation as well as the nationality and dates of birth and death of the winners.

CHARTS & TABLES
This section brings together charts and tables on key areas of biology, for easy reference. Four pages have been added in the Revised Edition.

ASSOCIATIONS
Another new section, providing the names, addresses, telephone numbers, and Web addresses of 30 important associations in biology, and in science generally.

WEB SITES
A new guide to 50 selected Web sites for students, teachers, and library patrons.

CONTENTS

SECTION ONE
GLOSSARY

abdomen The part of the vertebrate body that contains all the internal organs except for the heart and lungs. In most arthropods, the hind region of the body.

Abomasum

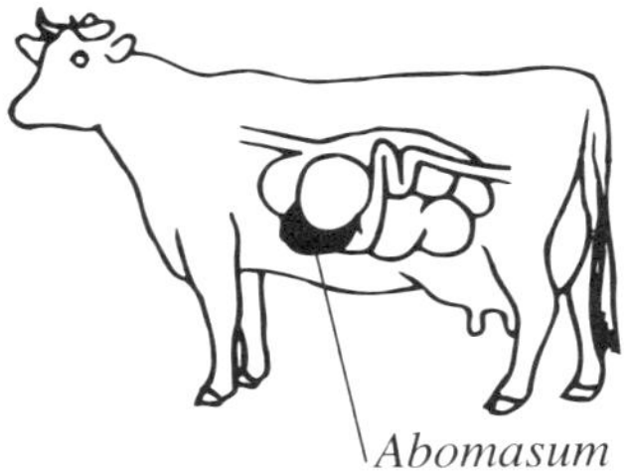

abductor muscle A muscle that pulls a limb or other structure (such as the shell of a bivalve mollusk) away from the center of the body.

abomasum The fourth and final region of the stomach of a ruminant.

aboral The side of an animal opposite the mouth.

absorption The uptake of dissolved substances into cells.

absorption spectrum The relative amounts of different wavelengths of light that are absorbed by an organism or structure.

acarinum In some bees, a small pouch that provides protection for symbiotic mites.

acellular Not divided into separate cells.

acephalous Lacking a clearly defined head.

acetabulum The socket in the ball-and-socket joint by which the femur is attached to the pelvis.

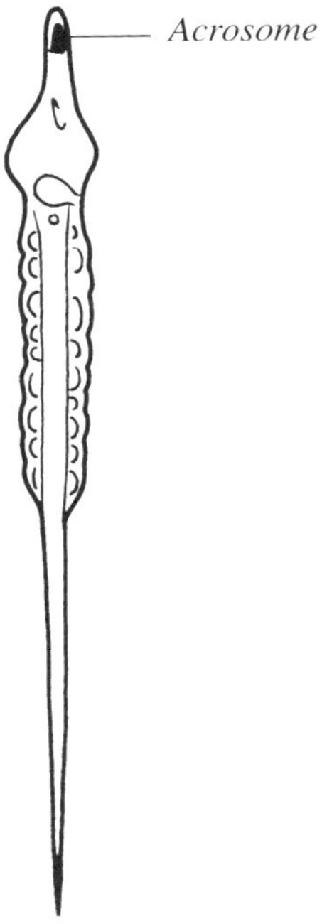

Acrosome

acetylcholine The most common chemical substance (neurotransmitter) involved in transmitting nerve impulses across a synapse and across a nerve-muscle junction.

acetylglucosamine A derivative of the amino sugar glucosamine and a common constituent of glycoproteins and glycolipids.

achene A one-seeded dry fruit formed from a single carpel.

Achilles tendon The tendon that attaches the gastrocnemius muscle to the heel.

acid A chemical compound that releases hydrogen ions (H^+) when dissolved in water and yields a solution with a pH value below 7.

acoelomate Without a coelom (refers to certain lower animal phyla).

acoustico-lateralis system The sensory system in a fish that comprises the inner ear and the organs of the lateral line.

acrodont Having the teeth fused to the jaw bone.

acromion An extension of the scapula in mammals; if the animal has a clavicle the acromion articulates with it.

acrosome A region at the anterior of a sperm that contains enzymes that dissolve the zona pellucida of an ovum.

ACTH *See* adrenocorticotrophic hormone.

action spectrum The relative amounts of different wavelengths of light that are absorbed by an organism or structure and are actively used in promoting a biochemical reaction, such as photosynthesis.

active site The small region of an enzyme molecule that combines with the substrate. It determines the enzyme's substrate specificity.

active transport The cellular process that actively transports dissolved substances across a membrane. It involves carrier proteins and requires ATP.

adambulacral At the outer edges of the plates of an echinoderm.

adaptive radiation The evolution of several divergent forms from a single ancestral form.

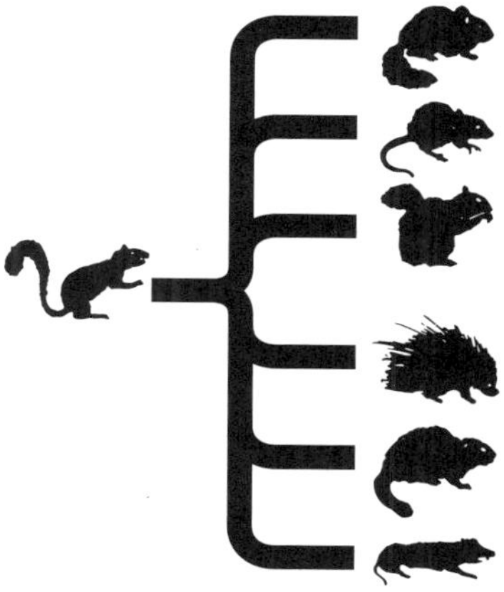

Adaptive radiation

adductor A muscle that draws an appendage toward the mid-line of an organism. In mollusks, it refers to the muscle that draws the two valves of a shell together.

adenohypophysis Part of the pituitary gland, comprising the anterior and part of the posterior lobes.

adenosine diphosphate (ADP) The chemical formed when a phosphate group is removed from ATP.

adenosine triphosphate (ATP) The main chemical-energy carrier common to all organisms. When ATP is hydrolyzed to ADP, energy is released and is used to power enzyme-catalyzed reactions.

ADH *See* vasopressin.

adipose Pertaining to fat.

adipose eyelid A thick, transparent eyelid possessed by some animals. It can cover most of the eye, except for a small central aperture.

adipose fin In some fish (including catfish and salmon), a second dorsal fin made from a flap of fatty tissue, containing rays and covered with skin.

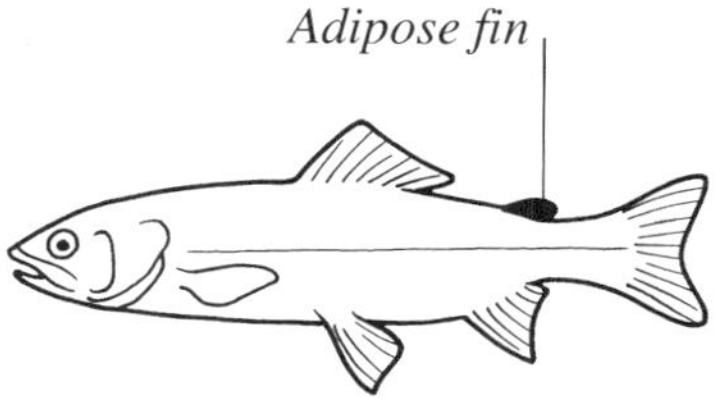

Adipose fin

ADP *See* adenosine diphosphate.

adrenal cortex The structurally distinct outer region of the adrenal gland.

adrenal gland A gland that secretes a range of hormones associated with fighting or fleeing (epinephrine [adrenaline] and norepinephrine [noradrenaline]), reproduction, and the regulation of water and salt balances. Mammals have two adrenal glands, one located near each kidney.

adrenaline *See* epinephrine.

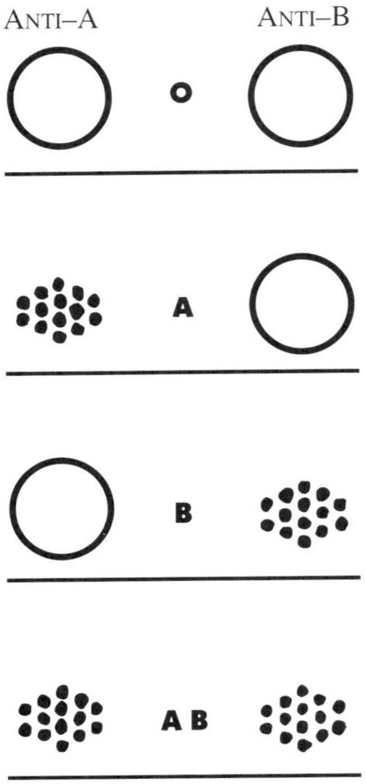

Agglutination
Antibody A agglutinates groups A and B; antibody B agglutinates groups B and AB.

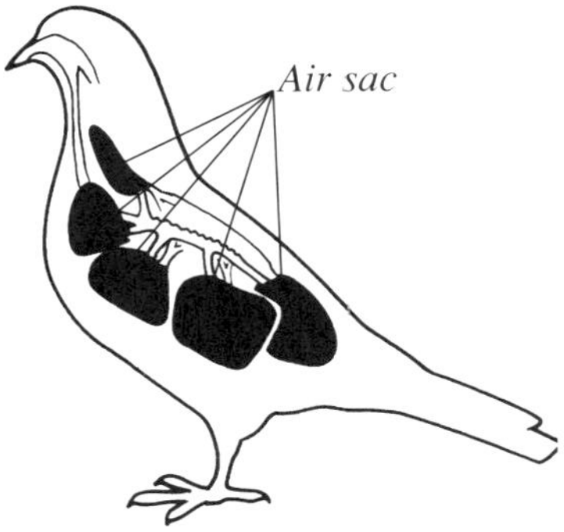

Air sac

adrenocorticotrophic hormone (**ACTH**) A hormone secreted by the anterior pituitary gland that stimulates the growth and secretory activity of the adrenal cortex.

adsorption The attraction and accumulation of a substance on the surface of a solid or liquid. *See also* absorption.

adventitious In plants, refers to tissues, organs, or structures that arise from unusual locations, e.g., small roots that arise from the stem rather than from the root system.

aedeagus The intromittent organ (penis) in most insects.

aerobic Respiration requiring gaseous oxygen.

afferent nerve A nerve that conducts signals from a sensory organ to the brain. *See* efferent nerve.

agar Gel-like substance extracted from seaweeds. It is used as a support medium on which to grow bacteria and other microbes.

agglutination The clumping or sticking together of cells. The term is applied to bacteria (when attacked by specific types of antibody) and red blood cells (when incompatible blood groups are mixed).

Agnatha The vertebrate class that comprises the jawless fish (lampreys, etc.).

air sac An extension of the lung of a bird that penetrates the body cavity and enters bones, giving them a very lightweight structure.

ala (pl. **alae**) A winglike projection on the shell of a bivalve mollusk.

alary muscle The wing muscle of an insect.

alate Having wings or structures resembling wings.

albino The term is usually applied to mammals. An individual who has very pale skin and pink eyes caused by the genetically controlled absence of skin pigments.

albumen A solution of a protein and water in the eggs of birds and some reptiles.

aldosterone A hormone secreted by the adrenal gland that acts on the kidneys to regulate the body's salt/water balance.

algae A loose grouping of plantlike organisms, including many single-celled forms and multicellular forms such as seaweeds. (*See also* illustration on page 11.)

alimentary canal (gut) A tube running through an animal's body into which food is delivered and then processed. Inside the intestines, food is broken down (digested), and from it, useful dissolved substances are absorbed and waste material is ejected.

Algae (see entry on page 10)

Characteristics

- Algae vary in size and complexity from microscopic single-celled organisms, through simple colonies consisting of filaments or sheets of cells, to large multicellular organisms, such as seaweeds.
- They live in seas, rivers, lakes, and other aquatic or moist habitats.
- Most obtain their food by photosynthesis.
- Algae are prominent members of the phytoplankton (plant-like plankton), and as such are an important part of aquatic food chains.

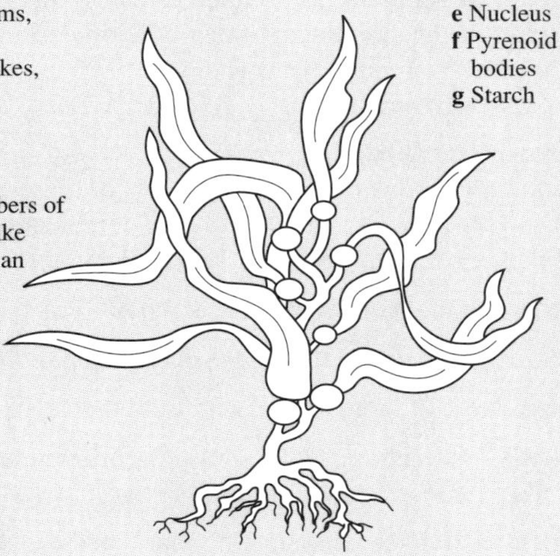

Structure of a freshwater green alga
a Cell wall
b Cytoplasm
c Surface of chloroplast
d Nucleolus
e Nucleus
f Pyrenoid (starch-producing) bodies
g Starch

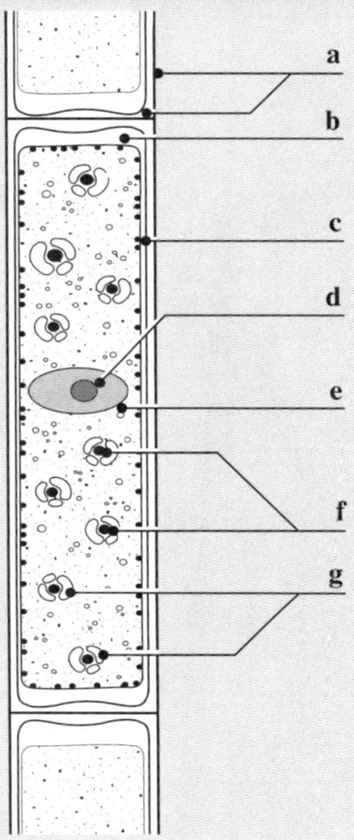

alisphenoid A bone forming part of the wall of the skull.

allantois A sac that forms from an outgrowth of the gut of vertebrate embryos. In birds and reptiles, blood vessels in its walls provide the means of respiration, and its cavity is used to store metabolic wastes. In placental mammals the allantois forms part of the placenta.

alleles or **allelomorphs** Different forms of the same gene.

allosteric Refers to an enzyme that has a site—other than the active site—to which a chemical may attach and regulate the activity of the enzyme molecule.

alternation of generations The life cycle of bryophytes, pteridophytes, and spermatophytes, during which a haploid, gamete-forming generation, the gametophyte, alternates with a diploid, spore-forming generation, the sporophyte. Alternation of generations also occurs in some animal phyla, particularly Cnidaria, but without any change in chromosome number.

alula (pl. **alulae**) A false wing comprising a few feathers attached to the thumb of a bird.

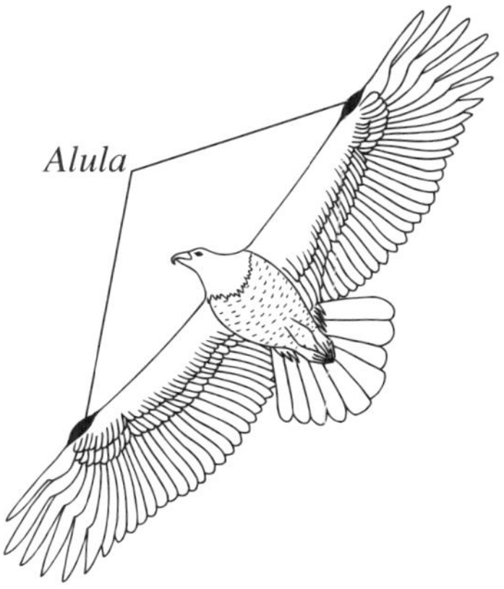

Alula

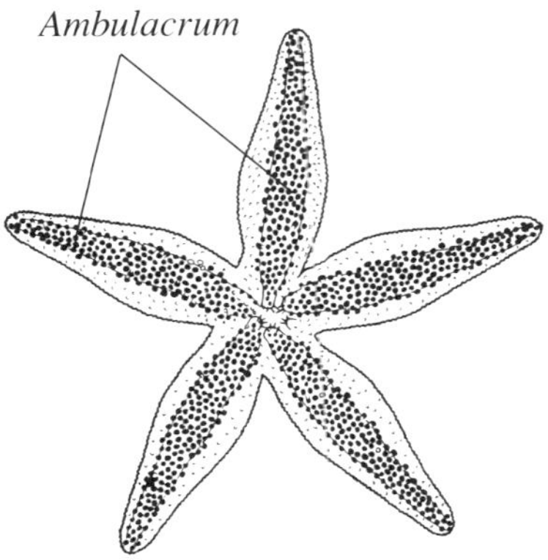

Ambulacrum

alveolus (1) A thin-walled compartment in the lung through the wall of which gas exchange occurs.
(2) A sac at the end of a duct leading from a gland.
(3) The socket in the jaw bone into which a tooth fits.

ambulacral groove A deep linear depression in an echinoderm's ambulacrum.

ambulacral ridge Raised plates (called ossicles) that run radially along the center of the ambulacra of echinoderms. They form a lattice bound together by connective tissue, together comprising the skeleton of the animal.

ambulacrum (pl. **ambulacra**) An area of the body surface of an echinoderm, lying above one of the radial canals of the water vascular system, that bears the tube feet. In most echinoderms ambulacra are covered by plates made from calcium carbonate.

amebocyte An animal cell capable of ameboid (amoebalike) movement.

amino acid An organic acid that is the chemical building block of a protein.

amino group The part of an amino acid with the chemical configuration $-NH_2$.

amniocentesis The withdrawal of amniotic fluid containing suspended fetal cells. These are tested for the presence of congenital abnormalities.

amnion A fluid-filled sac that grows around and eventually encloses the embryo of a reptile, bird, or mammal. It acts as a protective cushion and also provides the container for the fluid environment that the embryo needs.

amniotic fluid The fluid enclosed by the amnion. It provides a protective fluid environment for the fetus.

Amoeba A genus of animal-like protists with the ability to continuously change shape by the formation and withdrawal of pseudopodia.

Amphibia The class of vertebrates comprising three groups: the salamanders and newts (Urodela), frogs and toads (Anura), and the caecelians (Apoda). They are poikilotherms, most of which dwell on land but lay externally fertilized eggs in water from which aquatic larvae develop. The skin of adults is soft, rich in mucus and poison glands, and used in cutaneous respiration. There are about 3,000 species alive today.

amphicoelous vertebra A vertebra in which both faces of the central part are concave.

ampulla (pl. **ampullae**) A membrane-lined enclosure or bulge. Ampullae are found in the inner ear of mammals and in the water vascular system of echinoderms.

anaerobic Respiration without gaseous oxygen.

analogous When applied to the evolutionary origin of life-forms, refers to body parts that are similar in function but are fundamentally different in origin and structure. *See also* homologous.

anaphase The third stage of mitosis or meiosis. The chromatids have separated and are moving to opposite poles of the cell.

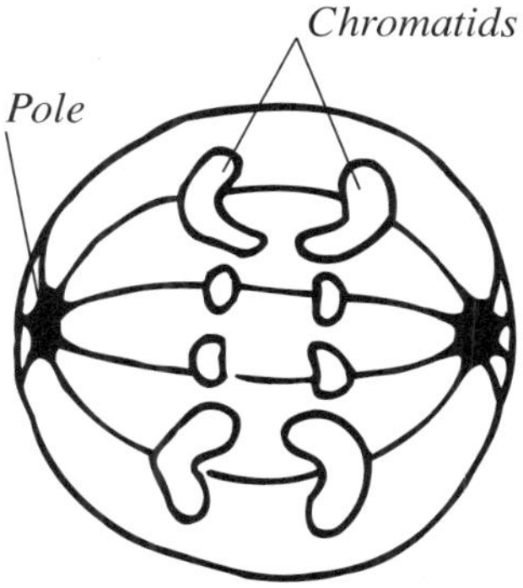

Anaphase

anastomosis Growing together and fusing to form interconnecting loops, as in blood capillaries.

anatomy The study of the structure of an animal or plant body by dissection.

angular A bone that forms part of the lower jaw in bony fish, reptiles, and birds. In mammals it has become separated and forms the tympanic bone.

animal A member of the kingdom Animalia. Animals are eukaryotic, heterotrophic, lack cell wall material, move from place to place, and react rapidly to stimuli.

Annelida (leeches, worms) A phylum of worms in which the body has a colon and is metamerically segmented, each segment bearing chaetae. The vascular, respiratory, and nervous systems of this phylum are well developed.

Annelida

annulus (pl. **annuli**) (1) A layer of cells that opens a moss or fern sporangium to release spores.
(2) One of the series of bands or concentric rings found in the scales of bony fish.

anogenital Pertaining to the genital organs and anus.

ANS *See* autonomic nervous system.

antagonistic muscles Sets of muscles that act in opposition to one another. When one muscle set contracts, the other relaxes.

antenna (pl. **antennae**) An appendage (paired) on the head of some arthropods. In insects and millipedes they are primarily used for touch and smell. In some crustacea they are used for swimming or attachment.

anteriad Pointing forward.

anterior The forward part; in most animals, the part nearest the head. *See also* posterior.

anther The tip of the stamen in a flowering plant that, when ripe, splits to release pollen.

antheridium The organ that produces male gametes in fungi and non-seed-bearing plants.

STRUCTURE OF AN ANTIBODY

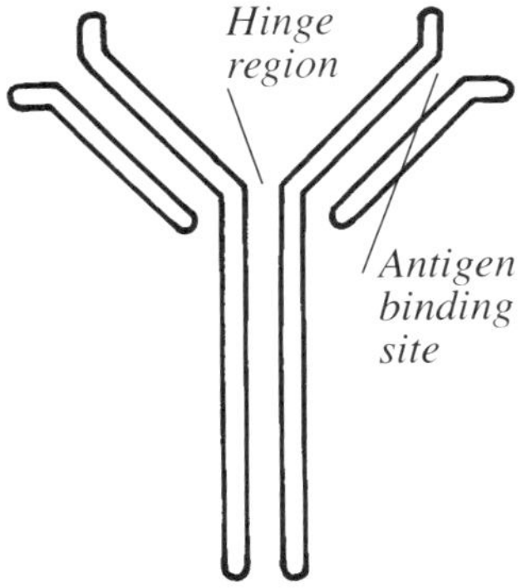

Antibody

Anthophyta The plant division containing flowering plants (angiosperms).

antibiotic A substance produced by living organisms, particularly fungi and bacteria, that, when released into their surroundings, is toxic to other species. Antibiotics have been harnessed for medical use in combating bacterial infections.

antibody A protein found in animal blood, particularly that of vertebrates. It attaches to antigens (specific foreign substances) and in so doing may help immobilize an invading organism.

anticodon Three adjacent nucleotides of transfer RNA that encode for a particular amino acid. *See also* codon.

antidiuretic hormone *See* vasopressin.

antigen A substance, usually protein or glycoprotein, that stimulates the production of an antibody.

antitragus The lower, posterior part of the external ear of a mammal.

antler One of the pair of branched horns carried by deer. In most species they are grown and shed each year. They are carried only by stags (males), except for *Rangifer* (caribou or reindeer) in which they are borne by both sexes.

anus The alimentary canal's exit through which undigested food passes.

anvil *See* incus.

aorta Known as the great artery in mammals. Arteries that branch out from it distribute oxygenated blood to all parts of the body except to the lungs.

aortic arch One of a series of paired arteries that join the dorsal and ventral aorta in vertebrates. There are up to six pairs in some fish, but fewer in other animals. In fish they form the branchial arteries; in other vertebrates they make up the carotid, pulmonary, and systemic arteries.

aperture The open end of a mollusk shell through which the soft body of the animal protrudes.

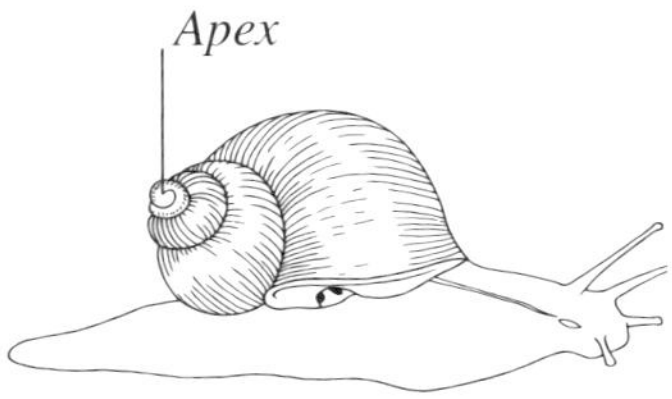

Apex

apex The tip of the spiral shell of a gastropod. It is the first part of the shell to grow.

apocrine gland A gland that releases a secretion containing material produced by the breakdown of its own cells. *See also* merocrine gland.

apodeme An inward projection from the exoskeleton of an arthropod, providing a site of attachment for a muscle.

apodous Lacking legs.

apophysis In vertebrates, a projection from a bone, commonly forming the site at which a muscle, ligament, or tendon is attached. In echinoderms, an inward projection from an ambulacral plate.

appendage In animals, a large functional projection from the body, such as a limb or antenna.

appendicular skeleton The part of the vertebrate skeleton that is attached to the vertebral column. *See also* axial skeleton.

appendix A small, vermiform (worm-shaped) extension to the cecum in the gut of mammals. In herbivores the appendix contains bacteria that assist in the digestion of cellulose. In nonherbivores, including humans, the appendix has no function.

apterous Without wings, as in some insect species.

aqueous humor In vertebrates, the fluid filling the space between the cornea and vitreous humor in the eye.

Arachnida A class of Arthropoda that contains spiders, scorpions, harvestmen, mites, pseudoscorpions, king crabs, and a few other smaller groups. Most have four pairs of walking legs and lack antennae. Except in mites, the body is divided into two sections: the prosoma, bearing the legs, eyes, and feeding apparatus; and the opisthosoma, containing most of the glands and internal organs.

Arachnida

archegonium The flask-shaped female sex organ of liverworts and mosses (bryophytes), ferns and related plants (pterophytes), and most gymnosperms.

archipterygium One of a pair of fins, leaf-shaped and with a narrow base, found in some fish.

arista (pl. **aristae**) In some flies, an extension to the third segment of each antenna, resembling a bristle.

Aristotle's lantern In sea urchins (echinoderms), the jaw apparatus, comprising five jaws, each with one tooth, forming a structure shaped like a lantern.

arteriole A small artery that delivers blood to a capillary network.

artery A blood vessel that carries blood away from the heart.

Arthropoda A phylum of animals that have jointed limbs and an exoskeleton. It includes arachnids, insects, crustaceans, centipedes, millipedes, and others. In terms of the number of species, it is by far the largest of all animal phyla. (*See also* illustration on page 16)

articular bone In fish, amphibians, reptiles, and birds, the bone of the lower

Arthropoda (see entry on page 15)

Class and common names	External appearance	Body sections	Antennae	Mouth parts	Number of walking legs	Gas exchange
1 Chilopoda Centipedes	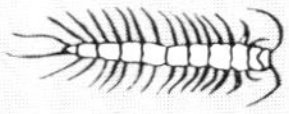	Head and body segments	1 pair 	Mandibles	1 pair per segment 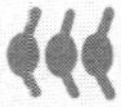	Tracheae
2 Diplopoda Millipedes		Head and body segments	1 pair 	Mandibles	2 pairs per segment 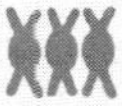	Tracheae
3 Crustacea Crabs, lobsters, water fleas		Cephalothorax and abdomen	2 pairs 	Mandibles	5 pairs in most forms 	Gills
4 Insecta Grasshoppers, butterflies, fleas		Head, thorax, and abdomen	1 pair 	Mandibles	3 pairs 	Tracheae
5 Arachnida Scorpions, ticks, spiders		Cephalothorax and abdomen	None 	First pair of legs adapted to hold prey	4 pairs 	Tracheae, lungs

jaw that articulates with the quadrate bone of the skull. In mammals, the articular has become the malleus of the inner ear.

artiodactyl A mammal that belongs to the order Artiodactyla. The even-toed hoofed mammals, which include camels, deer, pigs, cattle, sheep, and goats. The first digit is missing, the second and fifth often reduced or missing, and the third and fourth are of equal size. The digits end in hoofs. *See also* perissodactyl.

ascon The body of a sponge (Porifera) if it comprises a single chamber.

aseptate Lacking partitions (septa).

asexual reproduction Reproduction in which the organism produces new individuals without the fusion of gametes or the mixing of genetic material from two different sources.

assimilation The absorption and subsequent conversion of simple molecules into complex ones for use in the body, such as the building up of amino acids into proteins.

association neuron In vertebrates, a neuron that connects a sensory neuron with a motor neuron.

astomatous Lacking a mouth.

astralagus The ankle bone.

atom The smallest particle of an element that has all the properties of that element. It comprises a nucleus plus one or more orbiting electrons.

ATP *See* adenosine triphosphate.

ATPase The enzyme that catalyzes the hydrolysis of ATP to ADP.

atrioventricular (AV) node A mass of modified heart muscle that transmits the impulse to contract from atria to ventricles.

atrium (pl. **atria**) A chamber in the body, especially one of the chambers in the heart that receive blood from the body. It was formerly called an auricle.

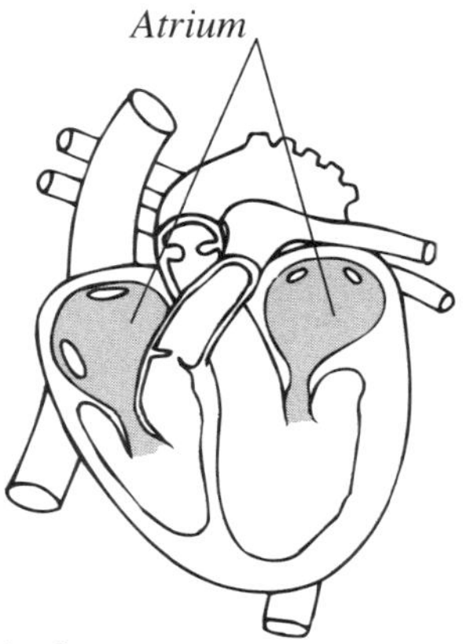

Atrium

auditory meatus A canal that leads from the external ear to the eardrum.

auditory (vestibulocochlear) nerve In vertebrates, the cranial nerve that supplies the inner ear.

auricle (1) The name formerly given to the atrium.
(2) An alternative name for the pinna (external ear).
(3) In echinoderms, an internal projection from one of the ambulacral plates that provides a point of attachment for muscles holding the Aristotle's lantern.

autolysis The digestion of cells or tissues by their own enzymes.

autonomic nervous system (ANS) Part of the nervous system of vertebrates. It controls visceral activities under involuntary (autonomic) control. It is subdivided into sympathetic and parasympathetic systems.

autophagy The digestion of cellular organelles by lysosomes.

autopolyploidy Polyploidy (cells with more than two sets of chromosomes) in which all sets of chromosomes come from the same individual.

autosome A chromosome other than a sex chromosome.

autotrophic Refers to an organism that is able to manufacture its own organic nutrients from inorganic raw materials. Blue-green algae, most green plants, and some bacteria are autotrophic.

Aves (birds) The vertebrate class that includes all the birds. They are endotherms in which the forelimbs are modified to form wings, the skin bears feathers, the mouth comprises a bill (beak) and there are no teeth, fertilization is internal, and the young hatch from shelled eggs incubated outside the body.

axial skeleton The part of the vertebrate skeleton that consists of the skull and vertebral column. *See also* appendicular skeleton.

axillary bud A bud formed at the point where the upper side of the petiole (leaf stalk) joins the stem.

axillary nerve A nerve in the upper arm of humans.

axon A long extension from the body of a nerve cell along which nerve impulses are conducted away from the cell body.

bacteriology The study of bacteria.

bacteriophage A virus that parasitizes bacteria.

bacterium (pl. **bacteria**) Prokaryotic microorganisms that are members of the kingdom Monera.

Bacteria

Types of bacteria

- Bacteria are classified according to their shape.

a Bacilli are rod-shaped bacteria.
b Vibrios resemble bent rods.
c Cocci are spherical bacteria.
d Spirilla are spiral-shaped bacteria.

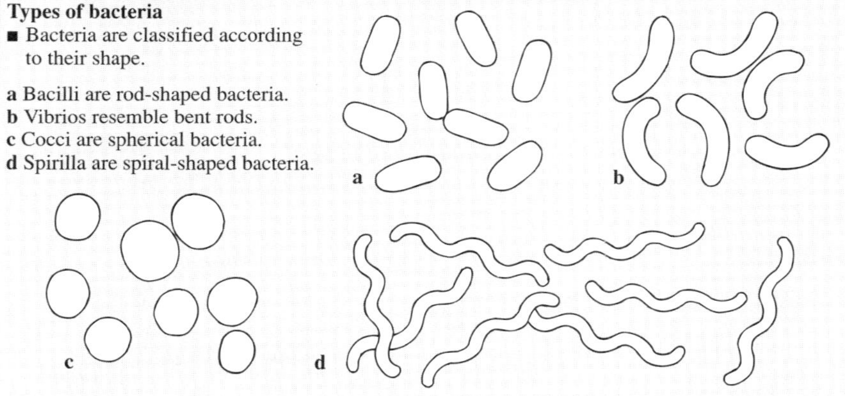

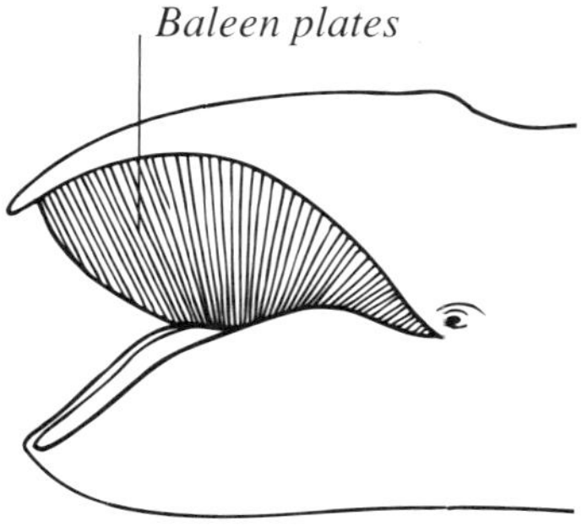

Baleen plates

baculum A name sometimes given to the penis bone found in some mammals.

baleen plates Sheets of keratin, the lower edges of which are fringed with hairs, forming a structure resembling a comb. They hang from the roof of the mouth of baleen whales and are used to trap food by filtering water forced through them by the tongue of the animal.

ball-and-socket joint A joint found in vertebrates where the ball-shaped end of one bone fits into the cuplike socket of another bone, as in the joint between femur and pelvic girdle.

barb One of the lateral projections from the quill of a feather that together form the vane.

barbel A fleshy, fingerlike protuberance that grows near the mouth of some fish. It is richly supplied with nerves and is used to locate food.

barbule A hooklike structure by which one barb of a feather is attached to another.

bark A protective covering of dead tissue found on the outside of the stems and roots of woody plants.

barrel The lower part of the side of a cow, between the fore- and hindlimbs.

basal bristle A small, modified feather at the base of the bill of a bird.

basal disk The structure at the base of *Hydra*, by which it is attached to the surface on which it rests.

base A substance that readily accepts hydrogen ions (H^+) when dissolved in water and gives a solution with a pH value above 7.

base pairing The linking, by hydrogen bonds, of purine and primidine bases in complementary strands of DNA or RNA. Adenine always pairs with thymine or uracil; guanine always pairs with cytosine.

base triplet The three bases comprising a codon or anticodon.

basilar membrane The basal membrane of the organ of Corti in the inner ear.

basipterygoid A bone forming part of the side of the skull of a snake, attached to the pterygoid bone.

basitarsus The first segment of the tarsus of an insect, articulating with the tibia.

basitibial Located at the base of the tibia.

beak (1) The bill of a bird.
(2) The oldest part of the shell of a bivalve mollusk, located near the hinge.

berry A succulent fruit, usually many-seeded, formed from a single flower with fused carpels.

biceps The muscles in the upper forelimbs of tetrapods that flex the elbow.

bicuspid valve (mitral valve) In birds and mammals, the heart valve lying between the left atrium and left ventricle.

Bidder's organ A rudimentary ovary found in males of some species of frogs and toads.

bilateral symmetry The arrangement of the parts of an animal's body in such a way that the body could be divided along a plane, with one-half being an approximate mirror image of the other.

bile A secretion of the vertebrate liver. A mixture of bile salts (which emulsify fats) and bile pigments, the alkaline fluid is stored in the gall bladder and is released, via the bile duct, into the duodenum.

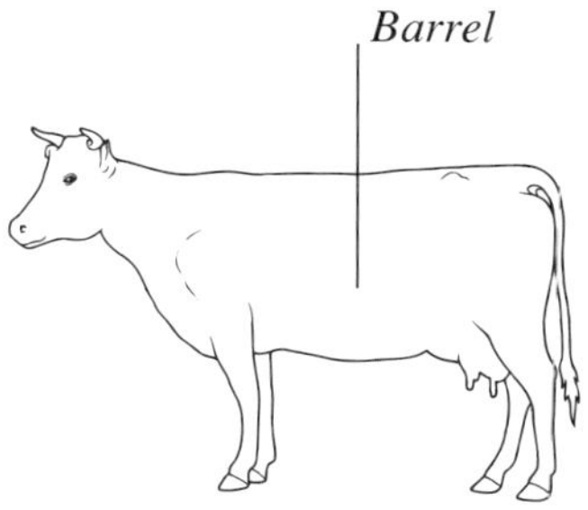

Barrel

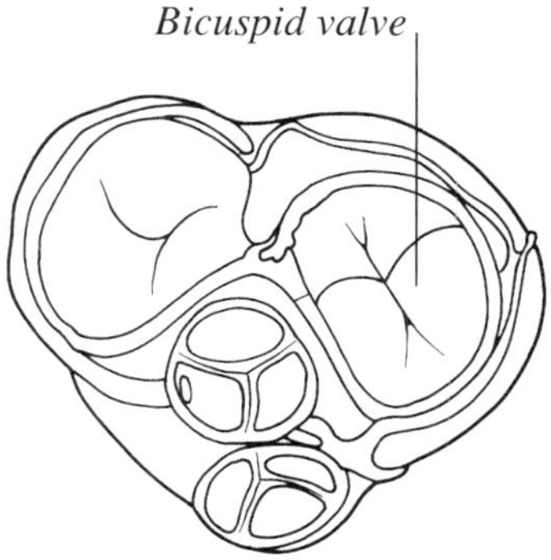

Bicuspid valve

Bill

bile duct The duct conveying bile from the liver to the duodenum in vertebrates.

bill The beak of a bird or turtle. It comprises the jaws and their covering of hornlike material.

binary fission Division into two. It is a common form of asexual reproduction in unicellular organisms such as *Amoeba*.

biochemistry The study of the chemistry of living organisms.

biology The scientific study of living organisms.

biomass The weight of living organisms in a given area or at a particular trophic level (usually expressed in terms of wet or dry weight).

biome A major ecological region with characteristic climate and vegetation, such as rainforest, tundra, desert, grassland.

biotechnology The industrial use of microorganisms, plants or animals to manufacture substances or produce effects of use to humans.

bipectinate Having toothlike projections on both sides of a central axis.

biradial symmetry An arrangement of the parts of an animal's body in which each of four equal parts of the body contains structures similar to those on the opposite side but different from those on the same side.

bird *See* Aves.

bivalent Two homologous chromosomes while pairing during the prophase of meiosis.

Bivalvia A class of mollusks that have two oval or long shells (called valves) joined at a hinge. All bivalve mollusks are aquatic. There are more than 20,000 species, including oysters, mussels, and scallops.

bladder (urinary bladder) In vertebrates and some arthropods, a sac for storing urine before it is excreted.

blastostyle An outgrowth that develops in the angle between the main stem and one of the branches of certain hydrozoa when the hydrozoan has reached a certain size. The blastostyle is enclosed in a vase-shaped sac called a gonotheca. Buds form inside it, develop into small medusae, and escape through the opening at the top of the gonotheca.

blastula In many animals, an early embryological stage usually consisting of a hollow ball of cells.

blind spot In the vertebrate eye, the region of the retina where the optic nerve enters the eyeball. This region lacks light-sensitive cells.

blood A fluid circulated through the body of an animal that transports oxygen by means of respiratory pigments and contains food,

Blood

Blood components
1 Erythrocytes (red blood corpusles)
2 Thrombocytes (platelets)
3 Leukocytes (white blood corpuscles)
3a Neutrophil (granulocyte)
3b Eosinophil (granulocyte)
3c Basophil (granulocyte)
3d Monocyte
3e Small lymphocyte
3f Large lymphocyte

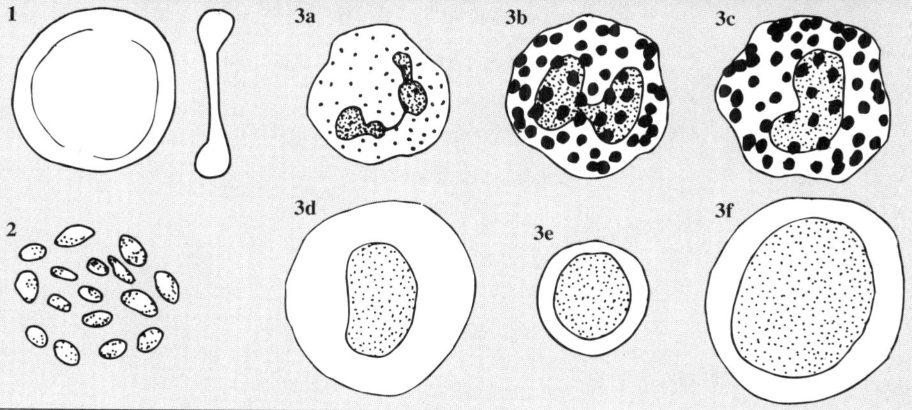

metabolic wastes, and cells that produce antibodies and attack invading particles or molecules.

blood group In humans, classification of blood into groups. The blood from individuals of the same group can be mixed without incompatibility (agglutination). In the ABO system there are four major groups—A, B, AB, and O—based on the presence of specific antigens on the surface of the person's red blood cells.

blood plasma *See* plasma.

blowhole The external opening of the nostrils in whales, porpoises, and dolphins.

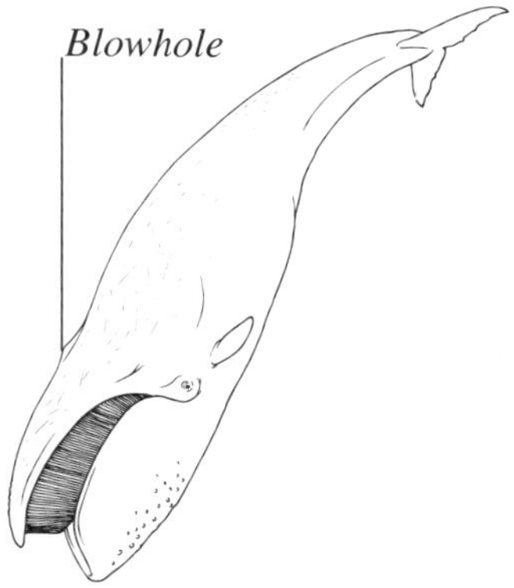

Blowhole

body coverts The small feathers that cover the body of a bird.

bone The material from which the skeleton of vertebrates is made. It consists of cells set in a matrix of collagen fibers with calcium and phosphate salts (called bone salt) and supplied with nerves and blood vessels.

book lungs Respiratory organs found in spiders. They are located in the abdomen and consist of many fine leaves, like the pages of a book, providing a large surface area where oxygen can be absorbed into the blood.

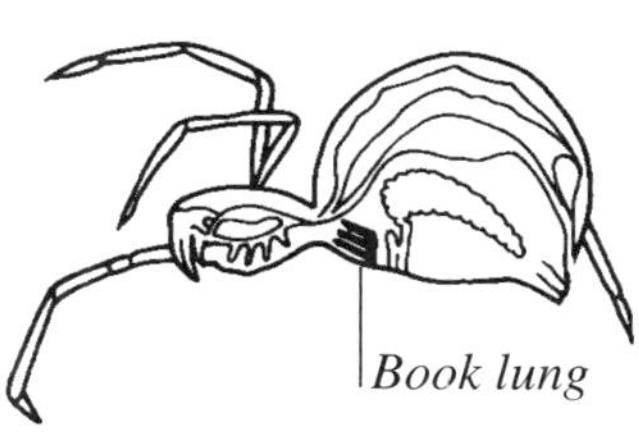

Book lungs

botany The scientific study of plants.

Bowman's capsule A capsule at the end of each of the nephrons in the vertebrate kidney where fluid is filtered.

brachial Referring to the forelimb of tetrapod vertebrates.

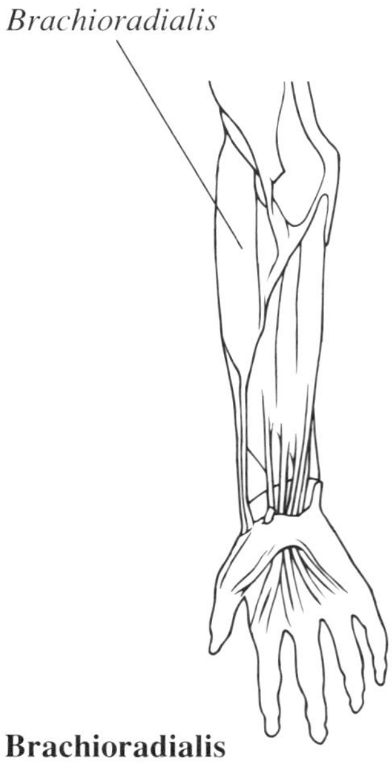

Brachioradialis

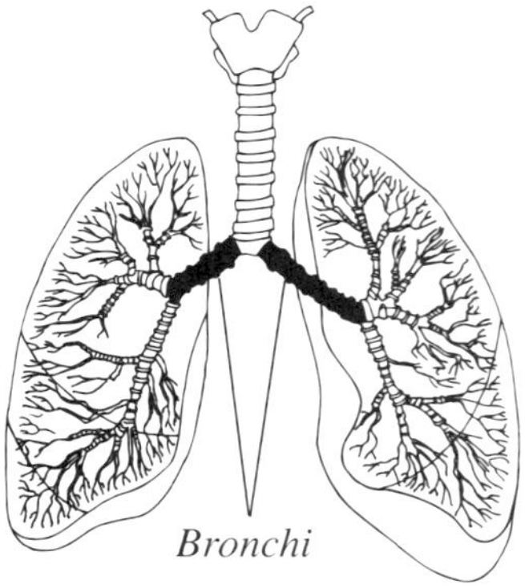

Bronchus

brachialis A muscle in the upper forelimb of mammals.

brachial plexus A nerve leading into the shoulder and arm of mammals.

brachiocephalicus One of a pair of muscles in the neck of mammals, extending from the head to the arms.

brachiole An echinoderm arm that gathers food.

brachioradialis A muscle extending from the upper forelimb to the wrist of mammals.

brachypterous Describes an insect in which both pairs of wings are reduced.

brain An enlarged part of the central nervous system of animals, located in the head and concerned with the processing of information received by sense organs and the coordination of bodily functions.

branchial Relating to the gills.

branchial arch or **branchial basket** The part of the vertebrate skeleton that supports the gills.

branchial artery One of the arteries in fish that carry blood to the gills.

branchial basket *See* branchial arch.

branchiostegal One of the folds of tissue that cover the gill chambers of a fish.

breast (1) One of the mammary glands of a female human.
(2) The underside of the body of a bird, comprising the large flight muscles.

brisket The lower part of the chest of a cow, between the forelegs.

bronchiole In the lungs of land vertebrates, the small tubular branches that connect bronchi with alveoli.

bronchus (pl. **bronchi**) One of two large air tubes that emerge from the trachea in land vertebrates. Within a lung, each bronchus divides into numerous smaller bronchi, which in turn finally divide into bronchioles.

brood gland *See* hypopharyngeal gland.

brood pouch A cavity in which eggs or young are contained and protected.

Bryophyta A division of the plant kingdom. It includes liverworts and mosses.

buccal cavity The mouth cavity at the anterior end of the alimentary canal.

buccal force pump A method of breathing, typical of amphibians, in which the nostrils are closed and the floor of the mouth raised, forcing air into the lungs.

buccal incubation The incubation of eggs in the mouth of one or other parent.

budding (1) A form of asexual reproduction in which new miniature individuals arise as an outgrowth of existing individuals.
(2) A form of artificial propagation in plants in which a bud is grafted.

bulla A projection from the skull that encloses the middle ear in most mammals.

bundle of His In the vertebrate heart, a bundle of nerve and muscle fibers that conveys electrical impulses from atrial muscle to the ventricular muscle.

bunodont Describes teeth that have rounded cusps.

bunolophodont Describes teeth that have rounded cusps linked by ridges.

buttock One of the protruding, fleshy pads that cover the dorsal part of the pelvis in many primates, including humans.

byssus One of the strands of strong tissue by which many bivalve mollusks are securely attached to the surface on which they rest.

calamistrum A row of bristles on the legs of some spiders, used to comb out silk.

calcaneum or **fibulare** The heel bone.

calcar A spur of hollow bone. In bats it provides attachment for the skin forming the "wing" between the hindlimbs (the uropatagium).

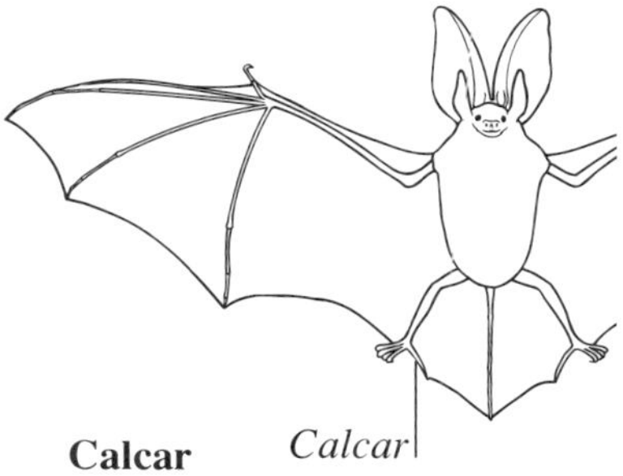

Calcar

Calcarea A class of sponges (Porifera) that have skeletons made from small splinters (spicules) of calcium carbonate.

Calvin cycle The cyclic pathway in photosynthesis by which carbon dioxide is fixed by ribulose diphosphate to produce two molecules of a three-carbon compound, phosphoglyceric acid (PGA). The cycle is named after Melvin Calvin.

cambium Meristematic tissue in a plant stem that gives rise to xylem and phloem. In woody perennial plants, the cambium is responsible for secondary thickening.

camera One of the chambers inside a chambered mollusk, such as a nautilus.

campanulate Bell shaped.

canine (1) Related to a dog (family Canidae).
(2) A pointed, conical tooth between the incisors and the premolars, found in many mammals.

cannon bone A bone formed by the fusion of the third and fourth tarsals in artiodactyls and by the enlargement of the third tarsal in horses.

capillary A tiny blood vessel, one of many linking arterioles with venules. The main exchange of substances between the blood and body tissues occurs across capillary walls.

Capillary

Structure
Capillaries are microscopic blood vessels whose walls are made of especially thin cells called endothelial cells (**a**). There are several different types, classified according to their structure.

- Continuous capillaries are abundant in the skin and muscles. Their cell walls contain intercellular clefts (gaps) (**b**) that allow the passage of fluids and some substances.
- Fenestrated capillaries have endothelial cells riddled with fenestrations (pores).
- Sinusoidal capillaries are modified to allow large molecules to pass between their walls. They are found only in the liver, bone marrow, lymphoid tissue, and some endocrine organs.

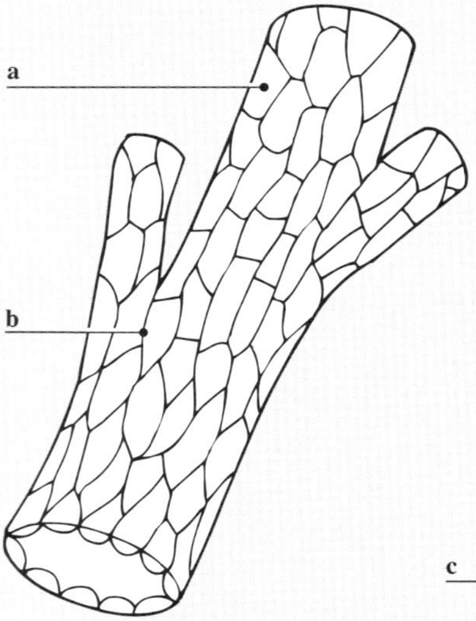

The capillary network
The networks of capillaries linking arteries and veins are known as capillary beds. Each capillary bed (**c**) provides a link between many arterioles (tiny arteries) (**d**) and venules (tiny veins) (**e**).

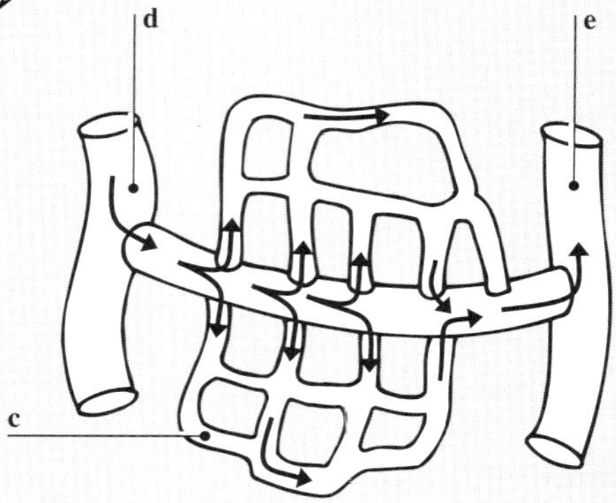

capitulum In king crabs, sea spiders, and Arachnida, the part of the body that bears the mouthparts. In goose barnacles, it is the main part of the body, including the shell.

carapace A protective shield of exoskeleton. It covers (1) the cephalothorax of some arthropods, e.g., crabs, or (2) the dorsal surface of some vertebrates, e.g., tortoises.

carboxyl group The part of an amino acid with the chemical configuration (–COOH).

cardiac stomach (1) The part of the stomach nearest to the duodenum of a vertebrate.
(2) The larger of the two stomachs of an echinoderm. *See also* pyloric stomach.

cardinal In bivalve mollusks, the region around the hinge.

cardinal tooth In some bivalve mollusks, a large hinge tooth below the umbo. There may be more than one.

cardinal vein One of a pair of veins that run longitudinally through the body of fish and the embryos of other vertebrates. The veins collect blood from most parts of the body and convey it to the heart.

carnassial A modification of the premolar or molar teeth found in many carnivorous mammals that gives teeth in the upper and lower jaws a shearing action, used to cut flesh. The teeth most commonly modified are the upper last premolar and lower first molar.

carotenoid Brown, orange, or yellow pigments, non-protein in nature, that are found in photosynthetic organisms. They commonly form accessory pigments to help in the utilization of a broad range of wavelengths of light.

carotid artery One of the pair of arteries in vertebrates that convey blood to the head.

carpal One of the eight small bones of the wrist.

carpal spur A sharp bone, covered in horn, on the carpus of some birds. It is used in combat.

carpel The female reproductive organ of a flowering plant. A flower may contain one or more carpels, collectively comprising the gynecium.

carpus The wrist joint. In birds it is the outer joint of the wing.

cartilage Vertebrate tissue consisting of rounded cells surrounded by a matrix of chondrin that contains collagen fibers. Cartilage forms most of the skeleton of embryos and is retained in some parts of the adult body, including the outer ear (pinna) and the ends of bones. In cartilaginous fish, cartilage comprises the whole of the skeleton throughout the life of the animal.

caruncle A projecting, fleshy structure, such as the wattles of some birds.

casque A helmet. In some animals, a bony growth on the top of the head.

caste A group of individuals that perform a particular function within a colony of social insects, such as the drones or workers in a hive of bees.

catarrhine In primates, describes nostrils that are close together and open downwards. *See also* platyrrhine.

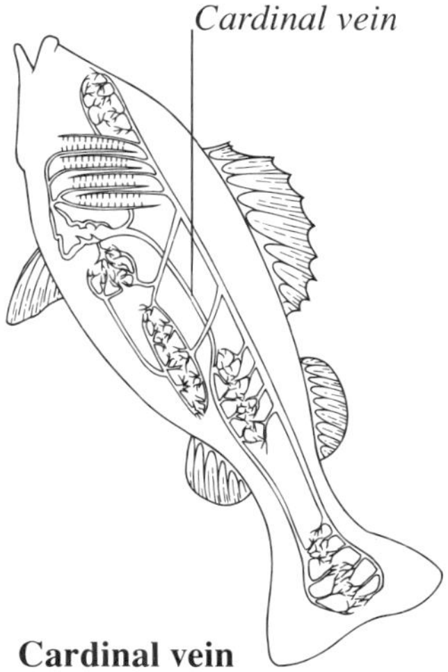

Cardinal vein

Caruncle

caterpillar The larva or grub of some insects, notably butterflies and moths. The wormlike larva has three pairs of jointed legs on its thorax and short prolegs on its abdomen.

caudal Referring to the tail of an animal.

caudal artery In vertebrates, the artery conveying blood to the tail.

caudal furca A forked extension of the final abdominal segment found in some crustaceans.

caudal peduncle The "stalk" behind the anal fin of a fish linking the body to the tail fin.

caudal vein In vertebrates, the vein conveying blood away from the tail.

cecum A blindly ending branch of the alimentary canal or other organ. In some mammals, particularly herbivores, the cecum is important in cellulose digestion.

celiac artery One of the arteries in vertebrates that branches from the aorta and then divides into three branches, supplying blood to the stomach, liver, and spleen.

cell The basic structural unit of living organisms. At minimum, a cell contains protoplasm surrounded by a membrane.

cell membrane *See* plasma membrane.

cellulose A polysaccharide that forms the main constituent of cell walls in some fungi, algae, and all green plants.

cell wall In prokaryotes and plant cells it is a rigid or semi-rigid layer outside of the cell membrane. It is absent in animal cells.

cement A substance resembling bone that forms a coat around the part of the tooth of a mammal that is embedded in the jaw. It helps hold the tooth in its socket. In some mammals cement also covers some of the exposed part of the teeth.

cenosarc Material linking the individual polyps in a colony.

centipede An arthropod belonging to the class Chilopoda. Each segment of the body possesses one pair of legs; the head bears long antennae; and there is a large pair of claws beneath the mouthparts (the claws inject poison). All centipedes are believed to be predators.

Centipede

central nervous system (**CNS**) The central mass of nervous tissue that coordinates the activities of more complex animals. In vertebrates, the CNS comprises the brain and spinal cord.

centrifugation Separating substances using a centrifuge—a device that spins samples at high speed to separate out their constituents according to size and density.

centriole A hollow, cylindrical structure lying just outside the nucleus in all animal cells. Usually there are two centrioles at right angles to one another. Each contains three sets of three microtubules (nine in all). Centrioles are self-replicating and play a part in cell division.

centromere The point of attachment between the two chromatids of a chromosome during cell division.

centrum The main part of a vertebra.

cephalon The front part of the body of some arthropods, composed of segments fused together.

cephalopedal sinus A space between the head and foot of a gastropod mollusk through which blood circulates.

Cephalopoda A class of mollusks that includes the squids, octopuses, nautilus, and cuttlefish. They are predators; all possess tentacles by which they capture prey.

cephalothorax The fused head and thorax forming the forward part of the body in some arthropods. *See also* prosoma.

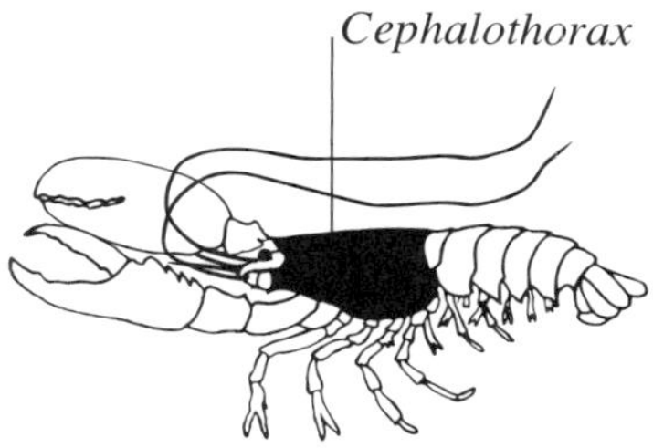

Cephalothorax

cercaria One of the swimming larval forms of flukes (phylum Platyhelminthes, class Trematoda). They develop from redia larvae.

cerci (pl. **cercus**) A pair of appendages at the end of the abdomen of many insects.

cere The area of skin around the base of the upper bill in birds.

cerebellum An outgrowth of the hindbrain in vertebrates. It coordinates complex muscular movements and is involved in maintaining balance.

cerebral Relating to the cerebrum.

cerebral hemisphere One of the pair of large lobes at the anterior end of the vertebrate forebrain. In fish and amphibians they are small and concerned mainly with the sense of smell. In mammals they form the largest part of the brain and are concerned with analyzing sensory information and coordinating responses to it.

cerebrum The part of the vertebrate forebrain from which the cerebral hemispheres develop.

cervical (1) Relating to the neck region.
(2) Relating to the cervix.

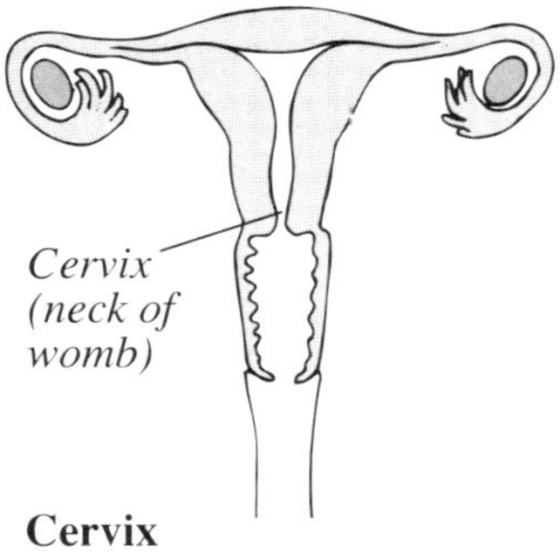

Cervix

cervical plexus The set of nerves, located near the upper four cervical vertebrae, that arise from the branching of the upper four cervical nerves and lead to various parts of the head and face.

cervix The neck of the uterus (womb) in mammals. It protrudes into the vagina.

chaetae (sing. **chaeta**) Bristles borne by some worms.

cheek teeth Molar and premolar teeth.

chela (pl. **chelae**) A claw or pincer that can seize objects.

chelicera (pl. **chelicerae**) One of a pair of appendages on the prosoma of an arachnid. The chelicerae are the first of six pairs of appendages. Their use varies among different groups of arachnids, but they are often used to seize prey, and in spiders they inject venom.

cheliped One of a pair of the most anterior legs found in most crustaceans. They are pincerlike and are specialized for seizing and crushing.

chemiosmotic mechanism A means of producing ATP by allowing hydrogen ions (H^+) to pass down a concentration gradient through a membrane.

chemoautotrophic or **chemosynthetic** Relates to autotrophic bacteria that use inorganic substances as a source of energy rather than sunlight.

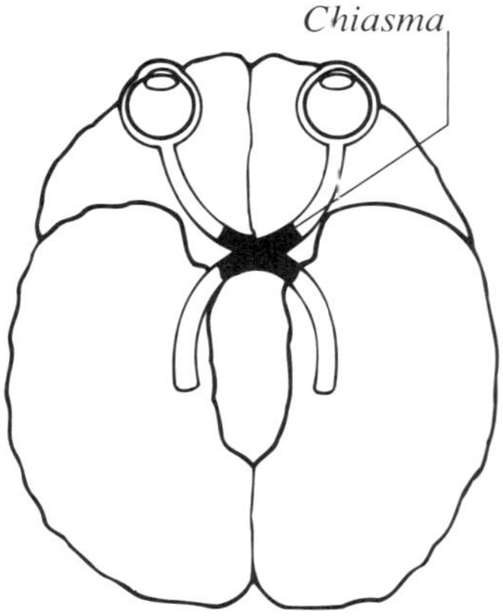

Chiasma *(optic nerves cross)*

chevron A projection from the dorsal side of the caudal vertebrae of whales.

chewing the cud Part of the digestive process in ruminant mammals in which food is chewed thoroughly after it has been partially digested in the rumen, made into pellets in the reticulum, and then regurgitated. When it is swallowed for the second time the food passes to the omasum and abomasum, where digestion is completed.

chiasma (1) A crossed shape formed by chromatids during crossing over in meiosis.
(2) The point at which the optic nerves cross in vertebrates, whereby each eye is connected to the optic lobe on the opposite side of the brain.

Chilopoda Centipedes. A class of the phylum Arthropoda.

chin The anterior edge of the mandible in humans.

chitin A nitrogen-containing polysaccharide that offers great structural support and resistance to chemical attack. It is a constituent of the cuticle of insects and the cell walls of many fungi.

chlorophyll A green pigment found in all green plants and photosynthetic prokaryotes. Chlorophyll is involved in light capture and the conversion of light energy to chemical energy in the initial reactions (light reactions) of photosynthesis.

chloroplast A plastid with chlorophyll found in photosynthetic eukaryotes.

choanae (sing. **choana**) Internal nostrils.

choanocyte or **collar cell** a cell bearing a flagellum, found lining the cavities and canals of sponges.

cholesterol A sterol found in animals; an important constituent of biological membranes and a precursor of bile salts and many steroid hormones.

Chondrichthyes The vertebrate class that comprises the cartilaginous fish, including the sharks, rays, and ghostfish (Holocephali).

Chordata A major phylum of animals that includes the subphylum Vertebrata. Its members have a notochord, hollow dorsal nerve cord, and gill slits at some stage in their lives.

choroid A layer of tissue containing blood vessels and pigment that lies immediately outside the retina in the eye of a vertebrate.

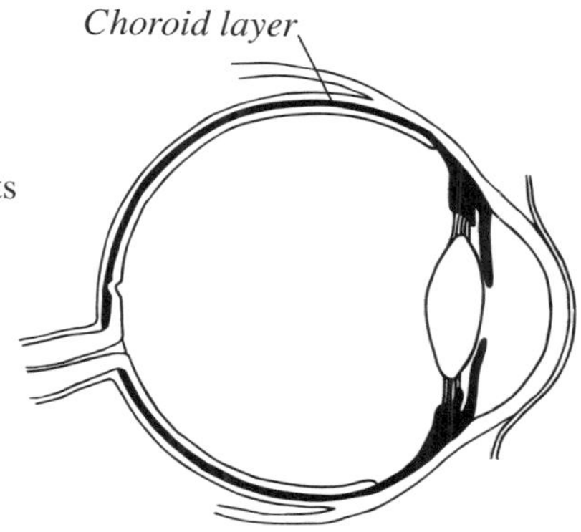

Choroid

chromatid One of two strands formed when a chromosome splits longitudinally during prophase of mitosis or meiosis. The two chromatids remain attached at the centromere. They later separate to form daughter chromosomes.

chromatin The substance from which chromosomes are made.

chromosome In eukaryotic cells, one of many threadlike structures seen in the nucleus during or just prior to cell division. A chromosome is composed of DNA and protein. DNA is the cell's genetic material and comprises a linear sequence of genes along the length of the chromosome. (*See also* illustration on page 30.)

chrysalis *See* pupa.

ciliary body In the vertebrate eye, a thickened rim of the choroid to which the suspensory ligaments are attached. It contains ciliary muscles that contract and relax to alter the curvature of the lens for focusing. It also secretes aqueous humor.

cilium (pl. **cilia**) One of many fine threadlike structures extending from a cell surface. Cilia are similar to flagella, but shorter and more numerous. Their coordinated beating action transports liquid or particles, or can propel the cell. *See also* flagellum.

cirrus (1) In some flatworms and flukes (trematodes), an eversible copulatory organ, equivalent to a penis.
(2) In many invertebrates, a slender projection from the body resembling a tentacle.

Chromosome (see entry on page 29)

Structure

- A small beadlike structure called a centromere divides the chromosome into arms.
- Each chromosome is made up of a chain of nucleosomes. These are histone proteins with deoxyribonucleic acid (DNA) wrapped around them.

Formation of chromosomes
Just before cell division occurs, the threadlike chromosomes become more tightly coiled. They condense to form the shorter, thicker, rod-shaped chromosomes.

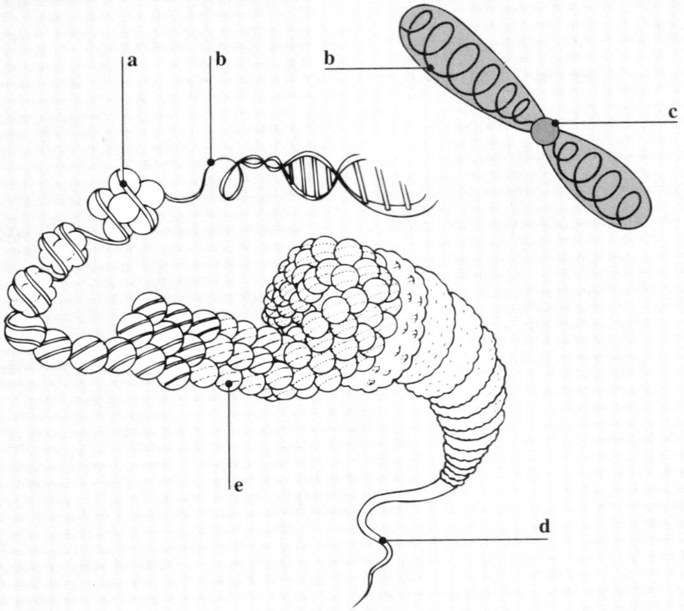

a Histones
b DNA strand
c Centromere
d Threadlike chromosome
e Chain of nucleosomes

citric acid cycle *See* Krebs cycle.

clasper (1) In some insects, extensions on the male's abdomen that are used to grasp the female during copulation.
(2) In some fish, an extension of the pelvic fin in males that aids the transfer of sperm.

classification The organization of living organisms into a hierarchical system of groups based on their degree of similarity.

clavate Club-shaped.

clavicle In many vertebrates, one of two bones on the ventral side of the shoulder girdle. In humans, the collarbone.

clitellum (or saddle). A structure shaped like a saddle around the anterior of the body of some annelids. It contains glands that secrete mucus, assisting two mating worms to bond and form a cocoon around the eggs.

clitoris In female mammals, a small, highly sensitive erectile structure found near the opening of the urethra. It is homologous with the male penis.

cloaca (1) In some invertebrates, the terminal part of the alimentary canal that may also serve respiratory, excretory, or reproductive functions.

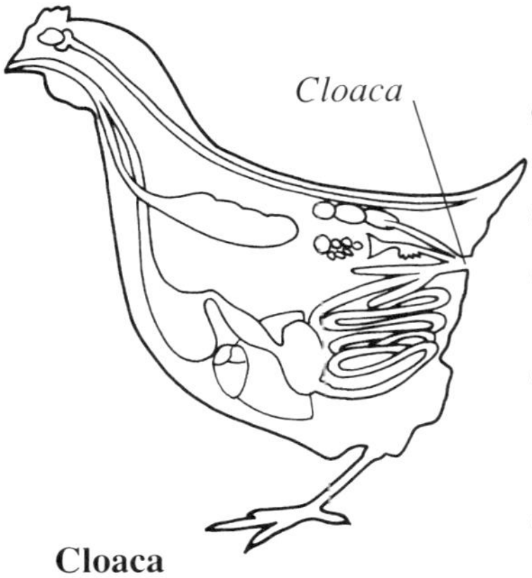

Cloaca

(2) In many vertebrates, but not mammals, a small chamber into which the alimentary canal, kidneys, and reproductive ducts empty.

cloacal chamber An open area adjacent to the opening of the cloaca.

clypeus An area of cuticle on the head of an insect, between the frons and labrum.

Cnidaria The animal phylum that includes corals, comb jellies, hydroids, jellyfish, and sea anemones.

cnidoblast (or nematoblast). A cell that contains nematocysts.

cnidocil A sensory bristle in a cnidoblast. When stimulated, it causes the nematocyst to be expelled.

cnidosac In some sea slugs (Nudibranchia), one of a number of sacs located near the dorsal projections of the body. Each sac contains a nematocyst captured from the slug's prey.

CNS *See* central nervous system.

coccygeal nerve One of the two nerves in the region of the coccyx.

coccygeomesenteric vein A vein in birds carrying blood from the tail region, through the abdominal cavity, and joining the femoral artery.

coccyx A bone formed from the fusion of posterior vertebrae. In humans, it comprises three to five vertebrae and is the remnant of a tail. The name is the Greek for "cuckoo," because of a supposed resemblance between the coccyx and a cuckoo's bill.

cochlea Part of the inner ear of mammals, birds, and some reptiles. It is used for analyzing the pitch of sounds that the ear receives.

codon In messenger RNA, a sequence of three adjacent nucleotides that encodes for a particular amino acid. *See* anticodon.

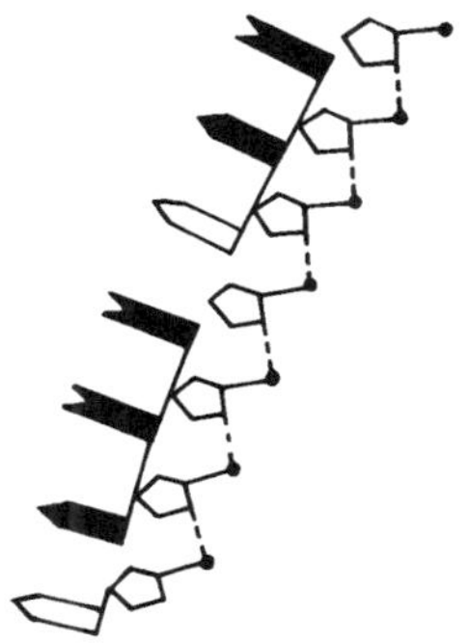

Codon

coelenterate An animal that possesses a coelenteron. Formerly all such animals were classed as a phylum, Coelenterata, but they are now separated into two phyla, Cnidaria (jellyfish, sea anemones, and corals) and Ctenophora (comb jellies).

coelenteron (or enteron). The body cavity, with only one opening, the mouth, found in coelenterates. The cavity comprises a highly branched system of digestive and circulatory canals.

coelom The main body cavity in higher animal phyla—those with three body layers (triploblastic).

coelomoduct A duct, found in invertebrates, connecting the coelom with the exterior. In some animals it carries metabolic wastes, in others gametes.

coenzyme A nonprotein organic molecule that activates an enzyme. Examples include coenzyme A (in Krebs cycle) and riboflavin.

colchicine A chemical that inhibits mitosis beyond metaphase. It disrupts spindle formation.

coleoptile In grasses, a protective sheath around the plumule in a seedling.

collagen A fibrous protein that is the main ingredient of connective tissue and the organic material in bone.

collar cell *See* choanocyte.

colloblast An adhesive cell on the tentacle of a comb jelly. It is used to capture prey.

colon The large intestine of vertebrates, concerned mainly with the absorption of water from the contents of the intestine. In some animals it contains bacteria involved in the digestion of cellulose and with the synthesis of vitamins.

columella A rod or column.

columella auris In birds, reptiles, and some amphibians, a rod of bone or cartilage that connects the eardrum to the inner ear and transmits sound.

columnar cells Cells, particularly epithelial cells, that are elongated and rectangular in profile.

comb The fleshy crest on the head of some birds, such as chickens.

commissure A bundle of nerve fibers linking ganglia in some invertebrates and the left and right sides of the central nervous system and brain in vertebrates.

companion cell In flowering plants, a small specialized parenchyma cell associated with a sieve element in the phloem.

competitive inhibitor A substance that inhibits enzyme action by competing with the substrate for the active site of the enzyme.

compound eye An eye that consists of individual units, called ommatidia. Many insects, crustaceans, and some members of other groups have compound eyes.

condensation A chemical reaction in which a molecule of water is liberated when two molecules are chemically combined.

condyle A knob of bone that fits into a socket on an adjacent bone to form a joint.

condylobasal length The length of a skull. It is measured from the anterior point of the premaxilla (the upper jaw) to the occipital condyle (the

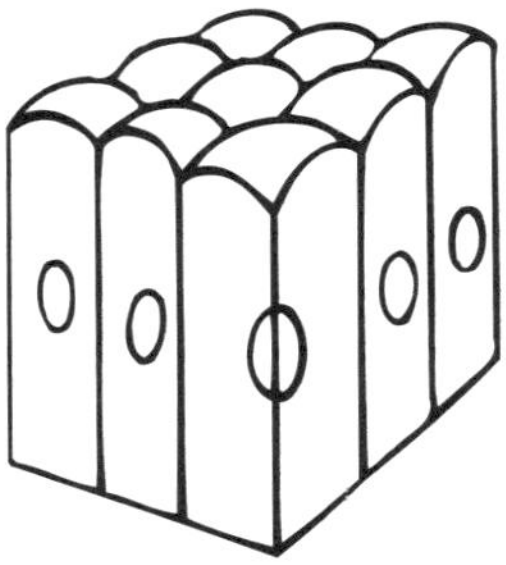

Columnar cells

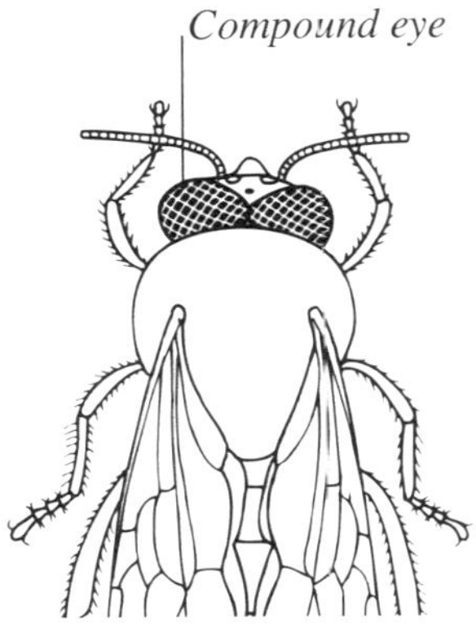

Compound eye

knob at the base of the back of the skull that articulates with the first vertebra).

cone (1) In gymnosperms and many pterophytes, the reproductive structure containing a group of sporophylls.
(2) In vertebrate animals, one type of light-sensitive cell in the retina of the eye. Cones are only sensitive to moderately high light levels but they can discriminate color and fine detail. *See* rod.

Coniferophyta Conifers (including cedars, firs, pines, and redwoods). Cone-bearing plants with naked ovules and seeds (not enclosed by an ovary) and lacking true flowers.

conjugation In bacteria and certain protozoa, the temporary union of two individuals when they are exchanging genetic material.

conjunctiva In the vertebrate eye, the transparent layer of protective cells covering the cornea. It also forms the opaque layer that lines the eyelids.

connective tissue Animal tissue found in vertebrates that provides support or fills spaces. Most is fibrous, but blood is also connective tissue.

consumer An organism or population that obtains its food and energy from the producer.

continuous variation Variation between individuals of a species that shows a continuous range of expression for a particular characteristic, e.g., height and weight in humans.

contraception Methods of preventing conception and pregnancy.

contractile vacuole In the cells of freshwater protists and sponges, a cavity that fills with water and then discharges into the surroundings. Its function is to remove excess water entering by osmosis.

convergent evolution The evolution of similar features by distantly related organisms as responses to similar selection pressures.

convoluted tubule In vertebrates, the highly folded regions of a kidney tubule where much salt and water uptake occurs.

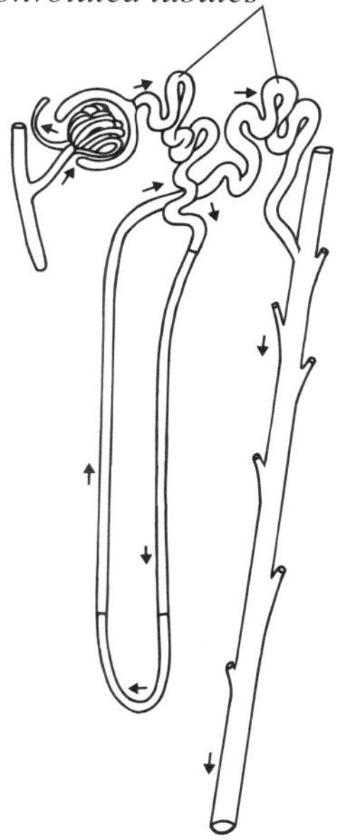

Convoluted tubule

coordination In the body of an organism, the harmonious combining of biological activities in space and time.

copulation (mating, coitus) Union of sex organs by which sperm are transferred from the male to the female.

copulatory bursa In female insects, a depression near the genital aperture that receives the intromittent organ of the male during copulation.

coracoid A bone on the ventral side of the shoulder girdle of vertebrates. It extends from the scapula to the glenoid cavity.

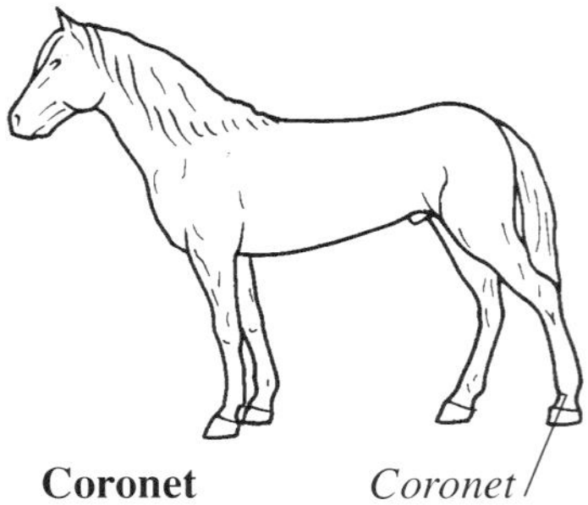

Coronet

coracoradialis A muscle in the upper forelimb of frogs.

corallite or **corallum** The skeleton of an individual coral polyp.

corbiculum *See* pollen basket.

cork The protective layer of dead cells found on the outside of woody plants and forming part of the bark. It prevents excessive loss of water. *See also* lenticel.

cornea In vertebrates, the transparent layer at the front of the eye covered by the conjunctiva. It refracts light to aid focusing.

coronary Referring to the heart.

coronet The part of the foot of a horse immediately above the hoof.

corpus allatum (pl. **corpora allata**) One of the glands found on either side of the esophagus in most insects, but in some, including flies, it is fused to form a single gland. It releases juvenile hormone, which maintains larval characteristics.

corpus callosum (pl. **corpora callosa**) In mammals, the broad tract of nerve fibers connecting the two cerebral hemispheres.

corpus luteum (pl. **corpora lutea**) In mammals, the "yellow body" that forms in an ovarian follicle after the ovum has been released.

cortex An outer layer. (1) In plants, the outer layer of parenchyma tissue in a stem or root.
(2) In animals, the outer region of an organ or structure.

corticosterone A steroid hormone produced by the adrenal cortex. It influences carbohydrate, lipid, and protein metabolism and is an immunosuppressant.

cortisol or **hydrocortisone** A steroid hormone produced by the adrenal cortex. It influences carbohydrate metabolism and suppresses inflammation.

cosmine A type of dentine that is perforated by canals.

costa (pl. **costae**) One of the main veins running along the wing of an insect. It often forms the leading edge of the wing.

costal respiration Breathing that involves moving the ribs.

cotyledon (seed leaf) The leaflike part of the developing plant embryo that is a reservoir of food. The first leaf or leaves to form. *See* dicotyledon and monocotyledon.

covert feather One of the small feathers found on the upper and lower sides of the wings and tail region of a bird.

Cowper's gland (bulbo-urethral gland) In humans, one of a pair of small glands that empty into the urethra at the base of the penis. Their secretions contribute to seminal fluid.

coxa The uppermost part of the leg of an insect, that articulates with the thorax.

coxal gland An excretory gland, found in arachnids, that opens near the coxa.

coxopodite The part of a biramous (two-branched) abdominal limb of a crustacean.

cranial Referring to the cranium.

cranium The skull of a vertebrate.

crenate Having a scalloped or notched edge.

crenulate Finely scalloped.

crest The part of a horse's back between the top of the head between the ears and the withers.

cribellum A structure resembling a sieve located anterior to the spinnerets of some spiders.

cristae (sing. **crista**) The folds of the inner membrane of a mitochondrion.

crop (1) In birds, an expanded part of the esophagus where food is temporarily stored.
(2) In some invertebrates, an expanded part of the gut toward the head end where food may be stored and partially digested.

crossing over In diploid organisms, the process of exchanging genetic material (recombination) between homologous chromosomes during meiosis.

croup The back of a horse's body immediately anterior to the root of the tail.

crown (1) In humans and other primates, the top of the head.
(2) The part of a tooth above the gum.

crura cerebri (sing. **crus cerebrum**) Two bands of nerve fibers linking the cerebrum and cerebellum in the brain of a vertebrate.

Crustacea A class of the phylum Arthropoda. It includes crabs, lobsters, shrimps, and water fleas.

crypt of Lieberkühn In vertebrates, pits in the lining of the intestine that are associated with mucus-secreting glands and digestive enzyme-secreting glands.

ctenidium (pl. **ctenidia**) A comb-like gill located in the mantle of some aquatic mollusks.

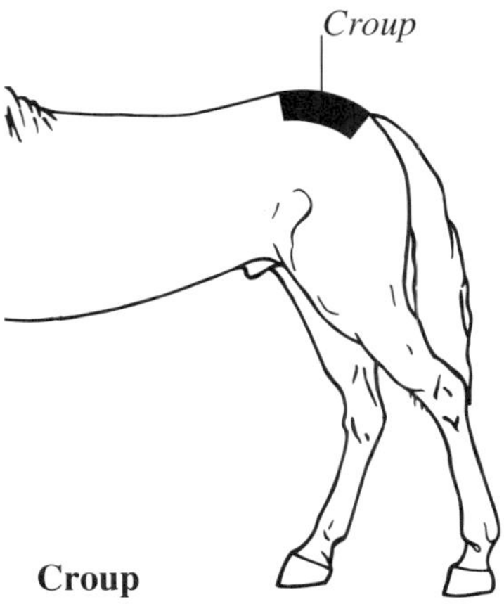

Croup

ctenoid scale A type of scale found in bony fish. It has many tiny "teeth" in its outer segment. *See also* cycloid scale.

cuboid bone A bone in the foot alongside the tarsus.

culmen A ridge along the upper bill of a bird.

cupulate Shaped like a cup.

cutaneous Referring to the skin.

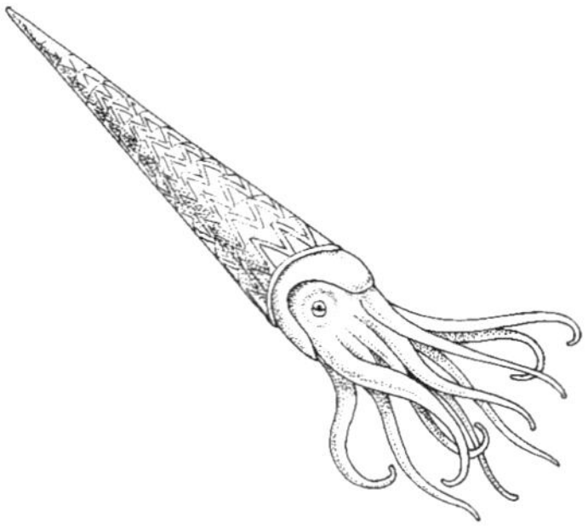

Cyrtoconic

cutaneous respiration The exchange of oxygen and carbon dioxide through the skin. This type of respiration is especially important in amphibians and soft-shelled turtles.

cuticle A layer covering and made from material secreted by the epidermis. In many arthropods it forms part of the exoskeleton.

cycloid scale A type of scale found in bony fish. It has a smooth outer edge, with no "teeth." *See also* ctenoid scale.

cyrtoconic Shaped as a curved, tapering cone, e.g., in a cephalopod shell.

cytochrome One of several electron carrier molecules that contain protein combined with a metallic ion in a porphyrin ring. They are components of the electron carrier system in photosynthesis and aerobic respiration.

cytology The microscopic study of cells.

cytoplasm The living parts of the cell enclosed within the plasma membrane but outside the nucleus.

dactylozooid A defensive or protective polyp, found in some colonial species.

dark reactions The photosynthetic pathway that is not directly dependent on light. It receives energy and reduced power from light reactions to fix carbon dioxide and convert it to carbohydrate. *See* light reactions.

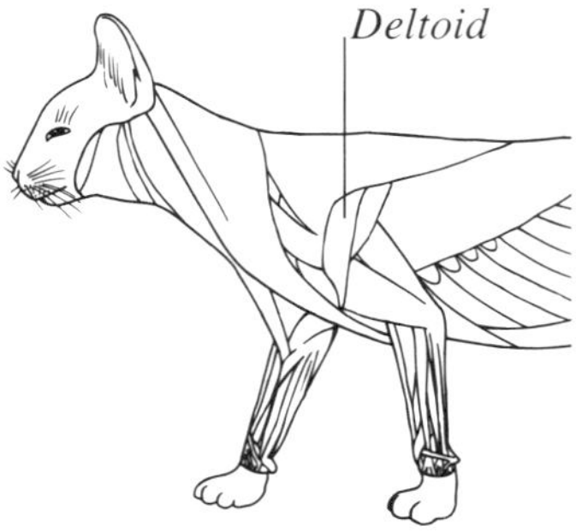

Deltoid

deciduous Refers to plants that shed their leaves at least once a year and remain leafless for a period of weeks or months.

decomposer An organism, such as a fungus, bacterium, or earthworm, that breaks down organic matter in the environment.

degenerate Describes a part of the body or stage in the life cycle that has become greatly reduced in size or importance in the course of evolution.

dehiscence Referring to fruits or anthers that split along a line of weakness to release their seeds or pollen.

dehydration The loss or removal of water.

deltoid The large, thick, triangular muscle that surrounds the shoulder joint.

demibranch The type of gills found in bivalve mollusks. These comprise two sheets of tissue joined in a V-shape. Two demibranches are joined along the ctenidial axis, giving the complete gill a W-shape.

dendrite A branched process extending from a nerve cell and connecting with other nerve cells.

dendritic With many branches, like a tree.

dendron An elongated extension of a neuron that carries nerve impulses towards the cell body. It commonly receives nerve impulses from several dendrites.

denitrifying bacteria Soil bacteria that break down nitrates and nitrites to release nitrogen gas, so depleting the soil of nitrogen supplies.

dentary The part of the lower jaw bone of vertebrates that bears the teeth. In mammals, it forms all of the lower jaw.

dentate Having teeth or serrations.

denticle A fish scale made from dentine and resembling a tooth.

dentine The main constituent of teeth. It is bone-like, contains no cells, and is covered in enamel.

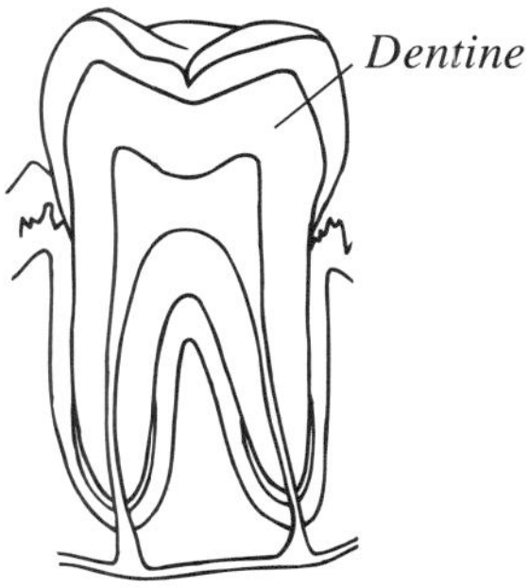

Dentine

deoxyribonucleic acid (DNA) A very large nucleic acid molecule that forms the genetic (hereditary) material of most living organisms. Typically, it comprises two complementary polynucleotide strands arranged in a so-called double helix. (*See also* illustration on page 38.)

deoxyribose The pentose (5-carbon) sugar found in DNA.

depolarization A reduction in electrical potential difference across a membrane. This accompanies, for example, the propagation of a nerve impulse.

dermal denticle *See* placoid scale.

dermis The layer immediately below the outer skin (epidermis).

desmodont Describes a type of hinge found in bivalve mollusks. The hinge teeth are very small or missing, and ridges may take their place.

desmognathous Describes the palate of some families of birds, including geese, swans, ducks, and parrots, in which the bones are fused.

detorsion The straightening out of the body that occurs during the development of some gastropods.

dewlap A loose flap of skin that hangs from the throat of certain animals.

dextrorse Growing in a right-handed spiral.

Deoxyribonucleic acid (DNA) (see entry on page 37)

The double helix model of DNA
The structure of DNA consists of two chains of nucleotides intertwined to form a double helix, or spiral.

- Each nucleotide consists of a sugar (deoxyribose), a phosphate group, and a base unit.
- The DNA base might be a purine, such as adenine (A) or guanine (G), or a pyrimidine, such as thymine (T) or cytosine (C).
- The sugar and phosphate groups link to form the "backbone" of each chain, while the bases project into the center of the helix.
- The two strands run in opposite directions, and are held together by bonds between pairs of bases.
- The base pairing is highly specific: adenine always pairs with thymine, and guanine with cytosine.

Spiral ladder arrangement of double helix
a Paired bases forming crossbonds.
b Strands forming backbone.
c Direction of sugar-phosphate backbone.

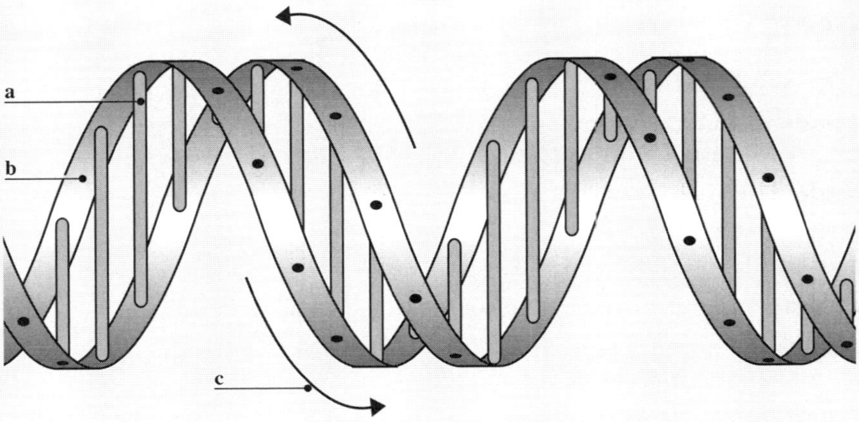

diadematoid Describes an ambulacral plate in echinoderms that bears three pairs of pores.

diaphragm (1) In mammals, a sheet of tissue, part muscle, part tendon, that separates the thoracic cavity from the abdominal cavity. Its contraction and relaxation helps facilitate breathing.
(2) A type of barrier contraceptive that covers the cervix.

diaphysis The main part of a bone.

diapsid An arrangement of the bones of the skull found in some reptiles. The postorbital and squamosal bones form a bar across each temple, so the temple has two openings, one above the other.

diastema A gap in a row of teeth that occurs naturally, not because a tooth has been lost. Usually it is between the incisors and first premolar.

diastole In vertebrates, the phase of the heartbeat when heart muscle relaxes and the heart fills with blood from the veins. *See* systole.

dibranchiate Describes the gills of some mollusks in which the ctenidia are paired. *See* ctenidium.

dicondylar Having a double articulation.

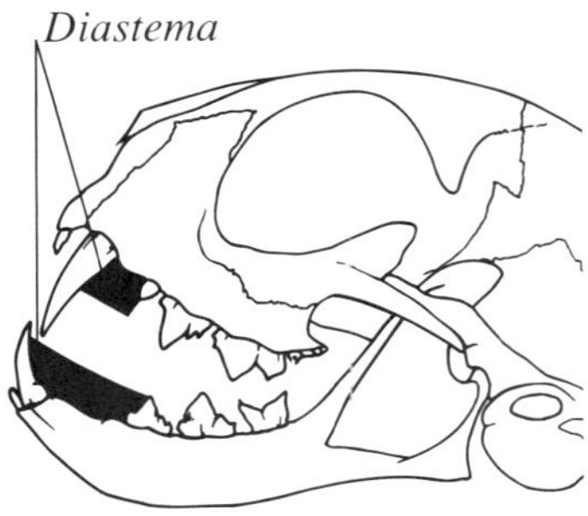

Diastema

dicotyledon A member of class Dicotyledonae within the division Anthophyta. Members are characterized by several features, including the presence of two seed leaves (cotyledons) in the embryo. *See also* monocotyledon.

didactylous Describes the condition in marsupials in which the second and third digits of the hindlimbs are not united in a single sheath.

digestion The breakdown of complex foodstuffs into simple molecules that can then be absorbed by the organism.

digestive system The organ system used to digest and absorb foods. In vertebrates and some invertebrates, it comprises the alimentary canal and associated structures, such as the liver and pancreas.

digit A finger or toe.

digital nerve A nerve serving a finger or toe.

digitigrade Describes a gait in which only the digits make contact with the ground. The animal walks on its toes. Cats and dogs walk in this fashion.

dihybrid cross In genetics, breeding from parents that differ in two simple, genetically controlled characteristics.

dimidiate Divided in two.

dimyarian Describes the condition, found in some bivalve mollusks, of having two adductor muscles.

dipeptide Two amino acids linked by a peptide bond.

diphycercal tail A fish tail in which the dorsal and ventral fins are of equal size.

diphyodont Describes the type of vertebrate dentition in which the first set of teeth is shed and replaced by a second, permanent set.

diploblastic Having a body derived from two layers of cells in the embryo.

diploid Describing a nucleus, cell, or organism having two sets of chromosomes. *See also* haploid.

Diplopoda Millipedes. A class of the phylum Arthropoda.

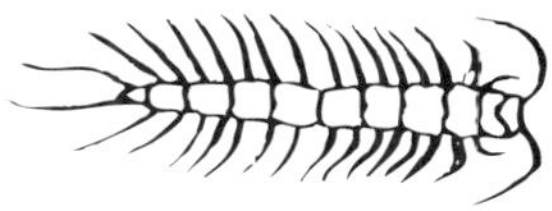

Diplopoda

diprotodont Describes the possession of enlarged first incisor teeth by marsupials.

direct flight muscle Muscle that is attached directly to the wing of an insect.

disaccharide A sugar formed from the condensation of two monosaccharides.

discontinuous variation Variation between individuals of a species that shows a discontinuous range of expression for a particular characteristic. Separate types are clearly distinguishable, such as eye color in humans.

dissepiment One of the small, domed plates that enclose the edges of corallites but do not enclose the entire corallite.

distichous Arranged in two rows.

diverticulum A pouch, sac, or closed tube leading from the wall of an organ.

dizygotic Refers to twins that are fraternal. They arise as a result of two separate fertilization events and are thus no more alike genetically than other siblings.

DNA *See* deoxyribonucleic acid.

dock The base of a horse's tail.

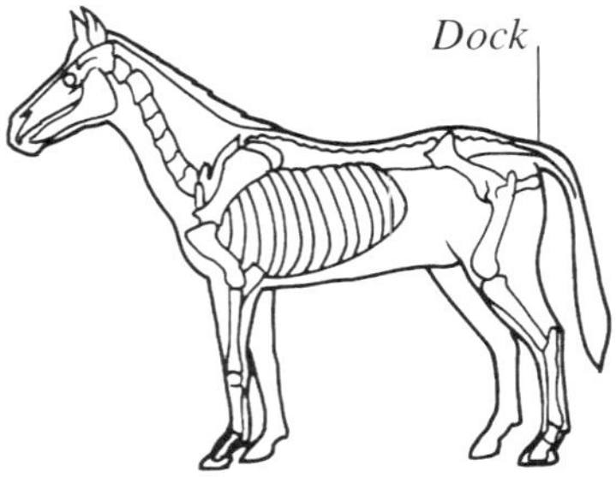

Dock

doliform Shaped like a jar or barrel.

dominant In genetics, refers to an allele that is expressed in both the heterozygous and homozygous condition. *See* recessive.

dorsal Describes the part of an animal closest to the back or spinal column.

dorsiventral Having upper and lower sides that differ from each other.

dorsobronchus One of the tubes linking the dorsal side of the laterobronchus of a bird to the lung.

dorsum The inside of the shell of an invertebrate.

Down's syndrome In humans, a congenital disorder (previously called mongolism) caused by the presence of an additional chromosome 21.

drone A male ant, bee, or wasp. Its only function is to mate with fertile females.

Drosophila The fruit fly. An important experimental animal in genetics.

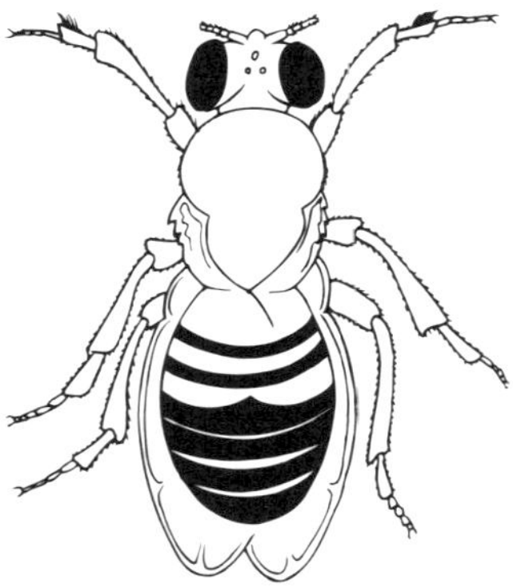

Drosophila

drupe A succulent fruit formed from one carpel and enclosing a single seed.

duct A fluid-carrying tube in animals or plants.

ductless gland *See* endocrine gland.

Dufour's gland A gland in the abdomen of most female ants, bees, and wasps. It discharges at the base of the ovipositor, or stinger, and has various functions in different insects.

duodenum The part of the alimentary canal of vertebrates into which the stomach discharges. It forms the first part of the intestine.

duplicidentate Describes the incisors of rabbits and hares. The central incisors are large and grow throughout the life of the animal, and those to either side of them are small.

duplivincular Describes a ligament consisting of alternating bands of soft and hard tissue.

dynein A protein with ATPase activity that is attached to microtubules in eukaryotic cilia and powers their movement.

dysodont Describes a type of hinge, found in some bivalve mollusks, that has simple, small teeth located close to the dorsal edges of the valves.

eardrum (or tympanic membrane or tympanum). A layer of connective tissue located between two layers of epidermis and located at the base of the external ear of a vertebrate. It transmits sound to the middle ear.

ear stone *See* otolith.

ecdysis Molting. In arthropods, it involves the periodic shedding of the cuticle in immature individuals to allow for growth. In most reptiles, it occurs periodically throughout life.

echinoderm An animal belonging to the phylum Echinodermata of marine invertebrates that have "spiny" skins. They have five-sided symmetry, an internal skeleton of porous plates, a water vascular system, and tube feet. The phylum includes starfish, brittle stars, sea urchins, sand dollars, heart urchins, and sea cucumbers.

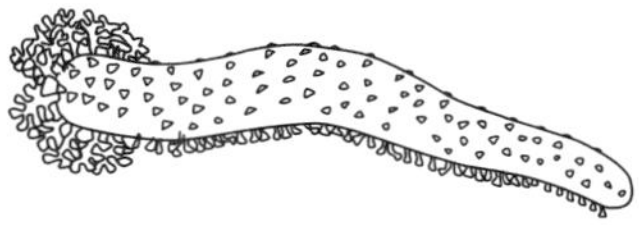

Echinoderm (Sea Cucumber)

Echinodermata The phylum of "spiny-skinned" animals that includes starfish, brittle stars, feather stars, sea lilies, sea urchins, and sea cucumbers.

echinoid An order of echinoderms that includes the sea urchins, sand dollars, and heart urchins. The body is enclosed in interlocking plates bearing moveable appendages.

echinulate Covered with spines.

ecology The study of organisms in relation to their physical, chemical, and biological environment.

ectoderm The outermost layer of cells in a vertebrate embryo. It gives rise to the epidermis, nerve tissue, and nephridia. *See* nephridium.

ectognathous Describes the mouthparts of an insect that are well developed and project forward from the head.

ectoplasm The outer cytoplasm of the cell found close to the plasma membrane. It is usually in a gel-like state and contains few if any organelles. *See* endoplasm.

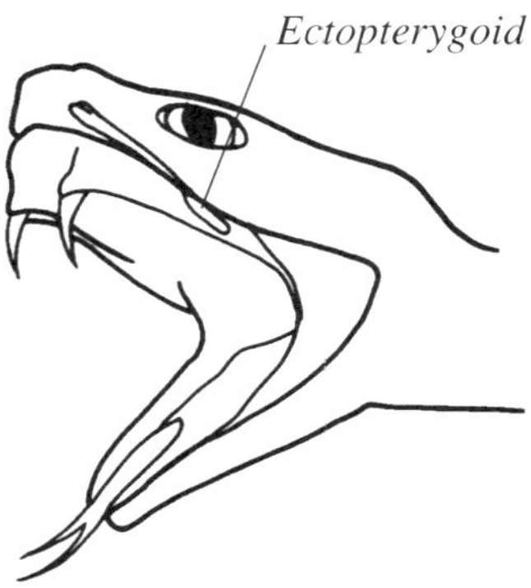

Ectopterygoid

ectopterygoid A bone, forming part of the upper jaw of a snake, above but joined to the palatine.

ectotherm An animal that maintains a fairly constant body temperature by behavioral means, such as basking and seeking shade.

edentulous Describes those bivalve mollusks that have no hinge teeth.

effector A muscle, organ, or any other structure that responds to a stimulus.

efferent nerve Describes a nerve that carries impulses away from the central nervous system. *See* afferent nerve.

effused Spreading irregularly or loosely.

egg burster A tooth or spine on the exoskeleton of an insect larva with which it breaks out of its egg. The egg burster is lost when the larva sheds its first exoskeleton.

ejaculation The expulsion of semen from the penis by means of strong muscular contractions.

electron carrier chain or **electron transport chain** (1) A series of enzyme-catalyzed ATP-generating redox reactions in the light reactions of photosynthesis.
(2) A similar series of enzyme-catalyzed ATP-generating redox reactions in aerobic respiration.

electron transport chain *See* electron carrier chain.

elicitor A stimulus that triggers the hypersensitive response in a plant.

elytron The hardened forewing of a beetle or earwig.

emarginate Having one or more notches at the edge.

Embden-Meyerhoff pathway *See* glycolysis.

embryo (1) In plants, the young individual that develops from the fertilized egg cell. In seed-bearing plants it is enclosed within the seed.
(2) In animals, the early stage in development that arises from the fertilized ovum. (*See also* illustration on page 43.)

embryology The study of the development of animals from fertilization to birth.

embryo sac In flowering plants, the large oval cell in which fertilization takes place. It is contained inside the ovule.

enamel The tough coating of teeth and denticles. It is made from crystals of a calcium phosphate-carbonate salt bound together by keratin.

endo- A prefix meaning "inner" or "on the inside."

Embryo (see entry on page 42)

Examples of embryos in three different animals: a mammal, a bird, and a reptile.

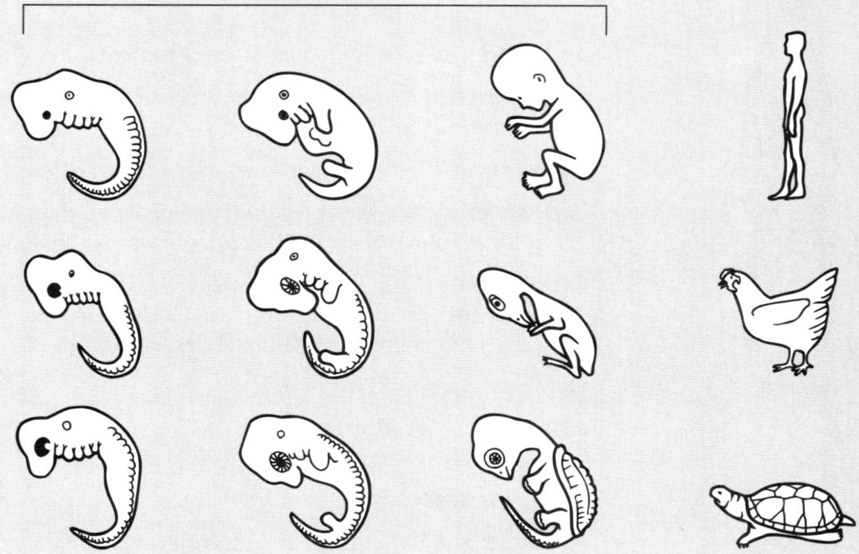

endocrine gland (or ductless gland). A gland secreting hormones that are discharged directly into the blood.

endocytosis The engulfing of fluid (pinocytosis) or solid matter (phagocytosis) that is then ingested by the cell.

endoderm The innermost layer of cells in an embryo. It gives rise to the gut and its associated glands.

endolymph In vertebrates, the protective and vibration-transmitting fluid associated with the inner ear.

endometrium (pl. **endometria**) In mammals, the glandular mucous membrane lining the uterus.

endophallus The inner wall of the intromittent organ (penis) of an insect.

endophragmal skeleton A scaffolding on the ventral side of a crayfish, produced in the thorax by ingrowths of the cuticle.

endoplasm The inner cytoplasm of the cell, found close to the nucleus. It is usually in a near-liquid state and contains many suspended organelles. *See also* ectoplasm.

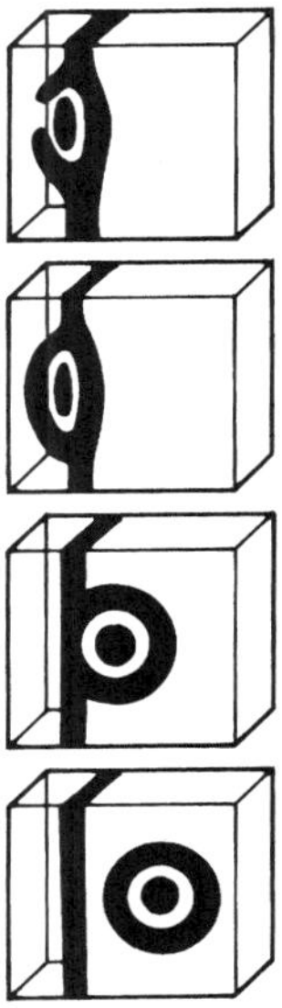

Endocytosis

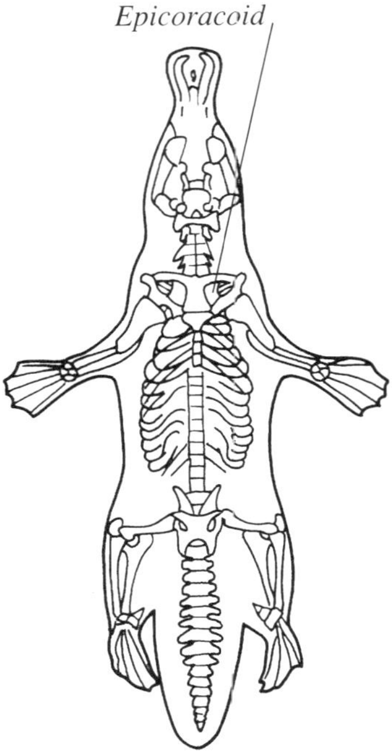

Epicoracoid

endoplasmic reticulum (**ER**) A complex network of sacs and tubules found in most cells. It is involved in the synthesis, storage, and transport of cell products. ER bearing ribosomes is called *rough ER*, that without ribosomes is *smooth ER*.

endopod The section of a crustacean limb that lies closest to the body.

endoskeleton A skeleton that lies within the body tissues of an animal. *See also* exoskeleton.

endosperm The tissue that surrounds and nourishes the embryo of seed plants.

endostracum A layer of calcium carbonate on the internal surface of some molluskan shells. It is often nacreous (like mother of pearl).

endotherm An animal that maintains a fairly constant body temperature by internal mechanisms, such as shivering, sweating, and the dilation and contraction of blood vessels.

ensiform Shaped like a sword.

enteron (1) *See* alimentary canal.
(2) *See* coelenteron.

entognathous Contained in a small pouch and eversible.

environment The collective term for the surroundings in which an organism lives. The environment has physical, chemical, and biological components.

enzyme A protein that acts as a catalyst. An organism typically contains several thousand different enzymes that control its metabolism.

enzyme-substrate complex The temporary combination of enzyme and substrate prior to the substrate being chemically changed to one or more products.

Eocene A geological epoch, part of the Tertiary period, lasting from about 55–34 million years before the present.

epibranchial artery In a fish, one of the arteries that conveys blood to the gills.

epicoracoid A bone adjoining the clavicle in a duck-billed platypus, forming part of the shoulder girdle.

epidermis The outer protective layer of cells in a plant or animal.

epididymis In mammals and some other vertebrates, a long, narrow, coiled tube between the testis and the vas deferens. It stores sperm.

epigeal Refers to a form of seed germination in which the seed leaves (cotyledons) appear above the ground. *See* hypogeal.

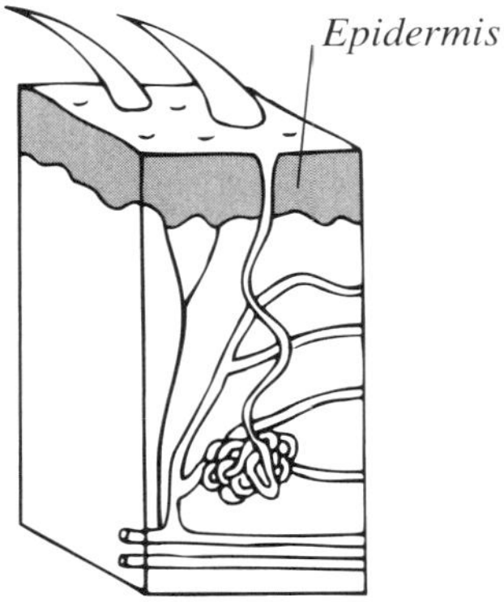

Epidermis

epiglottis A flap of cartilage in the larynx of mammals, near the base of the tongue.

epigyne A sexual opening on the ventral surface of the abdomen of an insect.

epinephrine (adrenaline) In vertebrates, a hormone secreted by the adrenal medulla together with the related hormone norepinephrine (noradrenaline). Both are secreted under conditions of physiological stress to mobilize the body for action.

epiotic Describes the region around the ear.

epiphysis (1) A cap of bone at the joints of mammalian vertebrae and limbs. (2) *See* pineal gland.

epipodite In some crustaceans, an appendage on the limb segment nearest the body.

epipubic bone In both male and female marsupials and monotremes (duck-billed platypus and echidnas), a bone resembling a rod that projects forward from the pelvis.

epistome A plate in front of the mouth on the ventral side of crustaceans.

epithelium A sheet or tube of tissue, made from tightly packed cells often one cell thick, and with an excretory function that covers internal surfaces of the body.

equid A member of the family Equidae, which includes horses, asses, and zebras.

ER *See* endoplasmic reticulum.

ergatogyne An ant that is intermediate in form between a worker and a queen and can function as a reproductive.

eruciform Shaped like a caterpillar.

erythrocyte (red blood corpuscle) The red blood cell found in vertebrates. It is densely packed with the oxygen-carrying pigment hemoglobin.

escutcheon A depression in the shell of a bivalve mollusk.

esophagus The muscular tube that conveys food from the pharynx to the stomach by peristalsis. It is part of the alimentary canal.

estradiol-17ß In vertebrates, the natural estrogenic hormone produced by the ovary. It has many physiological and developmental effects, including controlling the maturation of the female reproductive system and the development of female secondary sexual characteristics.

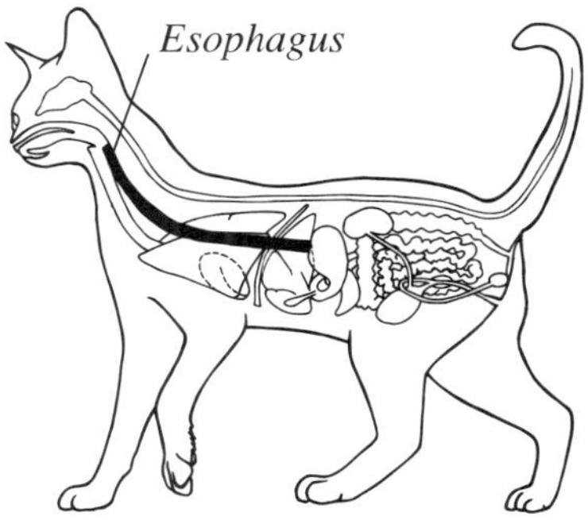

Esophagus

ethmoid A light, spongy bone at the anterior of the skull of a vertebrate, between the orbits and, in humans, at the base of the nose.

ethology The scientific study of animal behavior, particularly in relation to evolutionary theory.

Euglena A genus of photosynthetic or part-photosynthetic protists.

eukaryotes Higher organisms (animals, plants, and fungi) whose cells characteristically contain a true nucleus (with chromosomes enclosed by a nuclear membrane) and membrane-bound organelles. *Compare* prokaryotes.

Eukaryotes

Eukaryotic cells are those found in all cellular organisms other than bacteria and cyanobacteria. These organisms comprise unicellular organisms and the multicellular fungi, plants, and animals.

- Eukaryotic cells are larger than prokaryotic cells (*see* prokaryotes);
- have a true nucleus (**a**); and
- contain membrane-bound organelles (**b**).
- A cytoskeleton is present and might be extensive.
- Some eukaryotic cells also have cilia (**c**) and flagella (**d**).

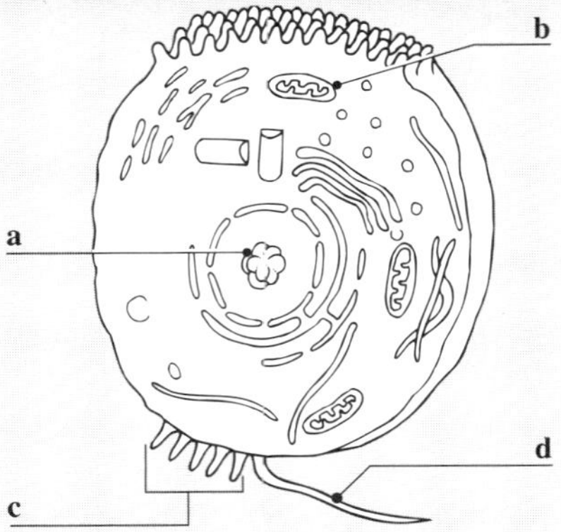

eulamellibranchiate Describes gills that are divided into vertical tubes, found in some bivalve mollusks.

Eustachian tube The tube that connects the pharynx and middle ear in tetrapods. It equalizes pressure between the two, thus preventing distortion of the eardrum (tympanic membrane).

evagination Turning inside out.

eversible Able to be turned inside out (everted).

evolute Describes the coiled shell of a cephalopod, all the whorls of which are exposed.

evolution Organic evolution refers to the cumulative genetic change of populations of organisms over generations.

exarate Describes an insect pupa in which the limbs are free to move.

excretion The removal from the body of the waste products of metabolism.

excurrent In an aquatic animal that feeds by filtering particles from a current of water, applied to structures involved in expelling water from the animal.

exo- A prefix meaning "outer," "out of," or "on the outside of."

exoccipital One of the bones located on either side of the foramen magnum of a vertebrate skull.

exocytosis The removal of liquids or solids from the inside of a cell via vesicles or vacuoles.

exopod The section of a crustacean limb that is furthest from the body.

exopterygote An insect that does not undergo metamorphosis from the larval to adult form and in which the wings develop slowly and externally. The young of such insects are called nymphs.

exoskeleton A skeleton covering the outside of the body or embedded in the skin. *See also* endoskeleton.

exotherm *See* poikilotherm.

extensor A muscle that extends a limb.

extra- A prefix meaning "on the outside of."

exuvium An empty arthropod exoskeleton left behind after the animal has molted.

eye An organ sensitive to light.

eyespot A marking on the wing of an insect, most commonly a moth or butterfly, that resembles an eye and serves to alarm predators.

facet A cup-shaped depression on the side of a vertebra, to which a rib is attached.

Fallopian tube The tube connecting the uterus with the peritoneal cavity of a female mammal. Fertilization occurs in the upper part of the tube. In animals other than mammals, it is known as an oviduct.

fang A needle-like process by which a spider or scorpion injects venom. A hollow tooth through which a venomous snake injects venom.

farinose Like powder or flour in appearance or texture.

fasciole A groove on the test of an echinoderm that bears no large spines or other projections.

fatty acids Long-chain carboxylic acids that are the major components in the formation of natural fats, oils, and waxes. *See* carboxyl group.

feather A light, flat structure grown from the skin of a bird, different types of which are adapted for insulation, display, and flight.

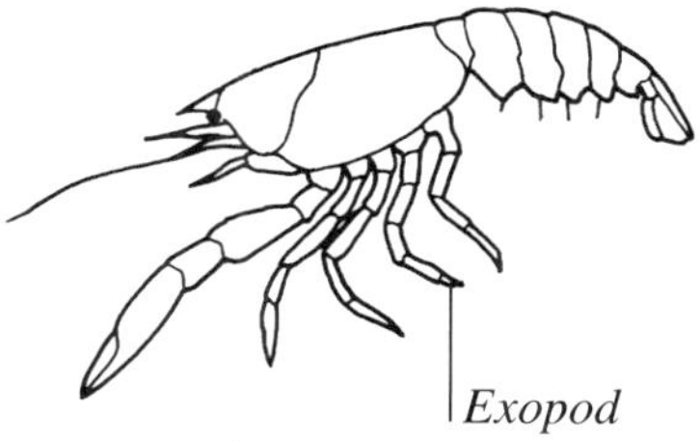

Exopod

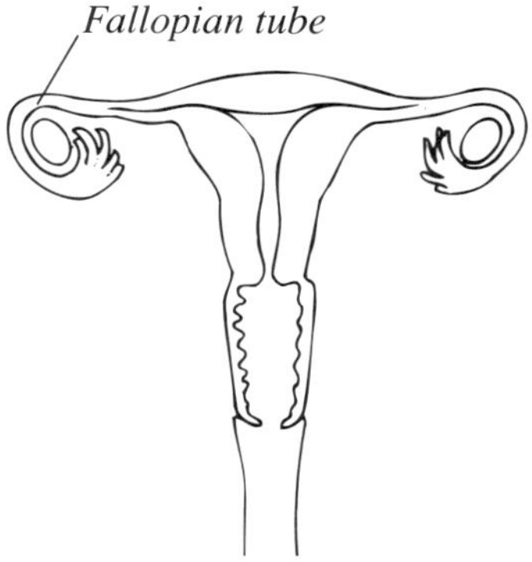

Fallopian tube

Feathers

feces Waste material, consisting of the indigestible components of food mixed with bacteria, dead cells, and bilirubin from the liver, that is evacuated through the anus of mammals (except monotremes).

femoral artery The artery conveying blood to the hindlimbs of a vertebrate.

femoral nerve A nerve in the upper part of the hindlimb of a vertebrate.

femur The long bone of the upper hindlimb of a vertebrate. In humans, it is the thigh bone.

fenestrated Having small openings or perforations, like windows.

fermentation (1) The breakdown of carbohydrates by anaerobic respiration. (2) More generally, the growth of microbes in large vessels to produce useful substances or processes.

fertilization The fusion of male and female gametes to form a zygote that will develop into a new individual.

fetlock The part of a horse's foreleg between the pastern and the shank.

fetus A mammalian embryo from the time its adult features are recognizable until its birth.

Fetus

Fetus development

- After twelve weeks, the embryo is called a fetus. By this time all of its structural parts have formed.
- From then until it is born, the fetus grows bigger and its organs mature.

1 14 weeks – fetus weighs about 5 oz (135 g)
2 24 weeks – fetus weighs about 25 oz (700 g)
3 36 weeks – fetus weighs about 7.5 lb (3.4 kg)

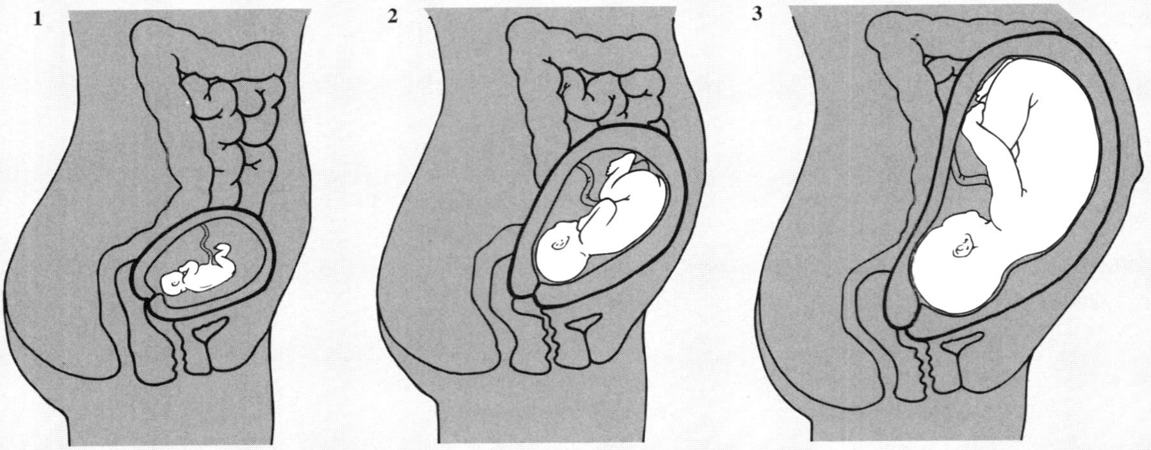

fibrous protein Refers to those proteins that form fibers—elongated molecular arrangements that are insoluble in water.

fibula The smaller of two bones in the lower part of the hindlimb of tetrapods. The long, slim bone at the outer side of the lower leg.

fibulare *See* calcaneum.

fibularis longus A muscle on the anterior side of the lower hindlimb.

filibranchiate Describes a type of gill, found in many bivalve mollusks, composed of sheets of filaments.

filiform Long and thin, like a thread.

fimbriate Having a fringe, usually of hairs.

fin A flattened limb possessed by a fish or other aquatic animal and used for propulsion, steering, or maintaining balance.

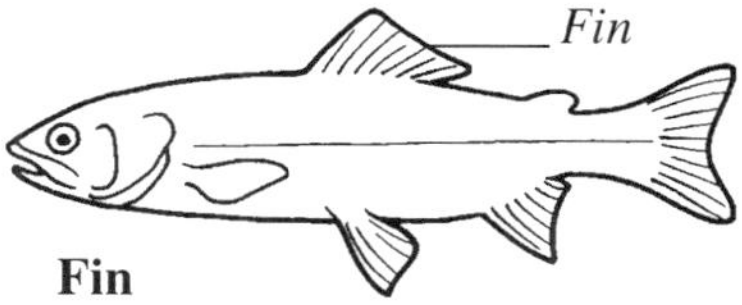

Fin

finlet A small fin, separate from other fins, comprising a single spine covered with its own membrane or a membrane with no spine.

fin ray A rod of bone or cartilage that supports the fin of a fish.

fish An aquatic vertebrate that is poikilothermic, lacks legs, breathes by means of gills, has a two-chambered heart, no internal nostrils, a tail fin, and at least one other fin.

flabelliform Fan-shaped.

flabellum A structure shaped like a fan, for example, on the tongue of bees.

flaccid In plants, refers to cells that have lost their turgidity due to lack of water. The cell contents no longer press firmly against the cell wall.

flagellum (pl. **flagella**) A long, threadlike structure extending from a cell surface. It incorporates a series of parallel microtubules, and its lashing movements propel the cell. *See also* cilium.

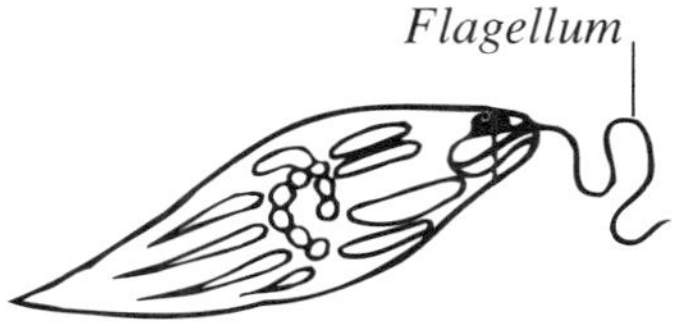

Flagellum

flame cell One or more cells making up a bulb-shaped structure involved in excretion and osmoregulation in several invertebrate phyla.

flank The side of a horse's body immediately anterior to the hind leg.

flatworm *See* Platyhelminthes.

flavoprotein Comprising several coenzymes based on riboflavin (vitamin B_2). They are hydrogen carriers in the redox reactions of the electron carrier chain.

flexor A muscle that causes a limb to bend at a joint.

flexuous Wavy.

flipper A paddle-like limb, a highly modified vertebrate leg that is found in aquatic mammals, such as seals, sea lions, dolphins, and whales.

floccose Covered in fine, down-like fibers.

flower The specialized reproductive shoot of an angiosperm. It comprises a receptacle on which are borne four kinds of organs: sepals, petals, stamens, and carpels.

fluid mosaic model A model for membrane structure that depicts globular proteins floating in a phospholipid and glycolipid bilayer.

fluke (1) A parasitic flatworm of the class Trematoda.
(2) The tail of a whale or dolphin.

follicle A small gland or cavity.

follicle-stimulating hormone (**FSH**) In vertebrates, a hormone secreted by the anterior pituitary gland. It stimulates the growth of follicles in the ovary and the development of sperm in the testis.

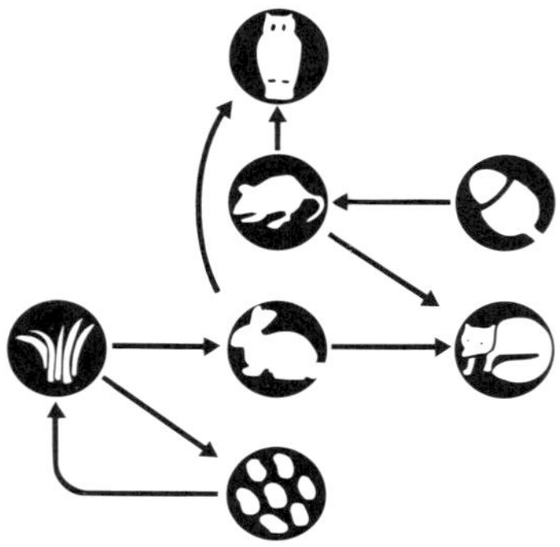

Food web

food chain Organisms in a biological community that are depicted as a straight-line series based on their feeding relationships. At the base of a food chain are producers—plants or bacteria—while higher levels of the food chain are consumers.

food web Organisms in a biological community that are depicted as a web of connections based on their feeding relationships. A food web typically incorporates many food chains.

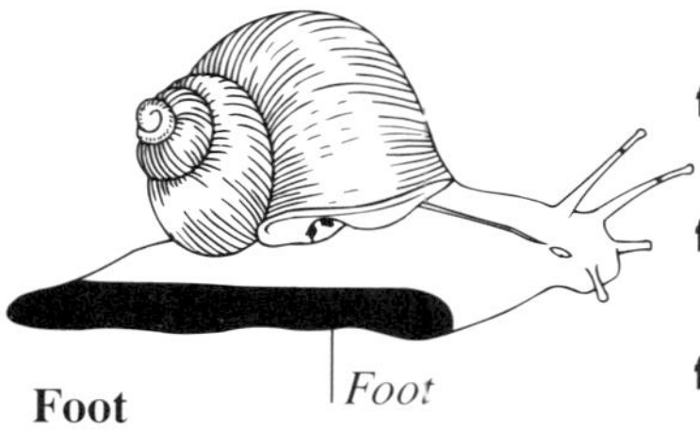

Foot

foot (in gastropods) The muscular organ by which an invertebrate, such as a snail, moves across a surface.

foramen magnum The posterior opening of a vertebrate skull, through which the spinal cord passes.

forceps (1) Modified cerci with which earwigs and a few insects grasp prey.
(2) Part of the corpus callosum in the vertebrate brain.

forehead The front of the head of a mammal, above the eyes.

foretop The front of a horse's head between the forehead and ears.

fossil The remains of an organism, or evidence of its presence such as tracks or feces, preserved in rocks. (*See also* illustration on page 51.)

fovea (pl. **foveae**) A shallow depression in the retina of most diurnal vertebrates. It contains cones but no rods or blood vessels. Light focused onto the fovea produces a sharp image.

foveate With small pits or depressions.

fraternal Refers to twins that are dizygotic.

Fossil (see entry on page 50)

Fossil formation and exposure
1 A fish lives in the sea.
2 A fish that has just died lies on the seabed.
3 Flesh rots revealing bones that are soon covered by a layer of sediment (**a**).
4 Layers of mud and sand cover the bones, preventing decay.
5 Layers of mud and sand harden into rocks, burying the bones, which are now reinforced and fossilized by minerals. Uplift (**b**) from Earth's crust raises the rocks and fossil above sea level.
6 Weather exposes the fossil bones by eroding the layered rocks above.

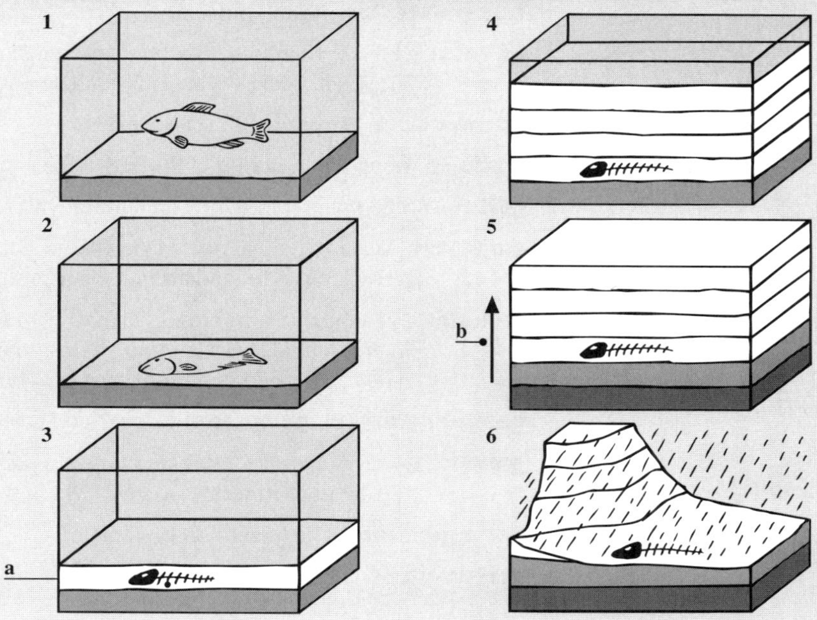

frenulum (pl. **frenula**) A hair or spine on the hindwing of an insect. It engages with a hook on the forewing, locking the wings together.

frons The front part of the head of an invertebrate.

frontal One of the pair of bones that form the front part of certain vertebrate skulls.

frontalis One of the pair of muscles that extend across the top of the human skull, ending above the orbits. They allow the eyebrows to be raised.

frontoparietal Pertaining to the frontal and parietal bones of the skull of a vertebrate.

fructose A hexose (6-carbon) sugar widely distributed in plants.

fruit The ripened ovary of a flower. It encloses seeds.

FSH *See* follicle-stimulating hormone.

fungus (pl. **fungi**) A member of the kingdom Fungi, which includes yeasts, molds, mushrooms, and toadstools.

funnel (or hyponome). The tube through which a cephalopod expels water as a means of "jet-propelled" swimming.

Furcula

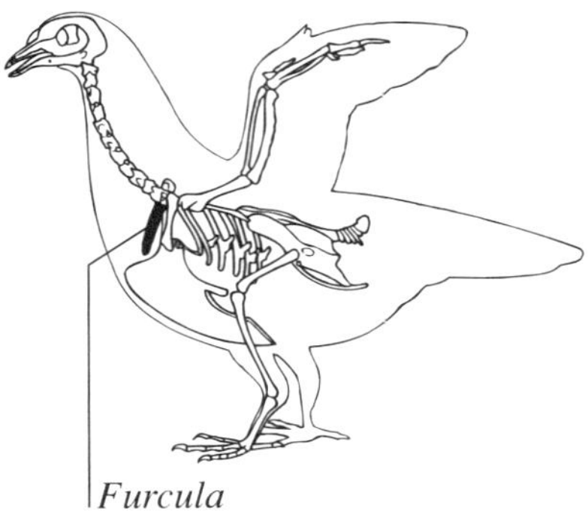

fur The body covering composed of hairs and found only in mammals.

furcipulate Resembling pincers.

furcula (1) The wishbone of a bird, formed from the fused clavicles. (2) A springing organ found in some insects, such as springtails.

furfuraceous Covered with small scales.

fusiform Long and tapering at the ends, like a spindle.

gait The manner in which an animal walks.

galactose A hexose (6-carbon) sugar that is a common constituent of plant polysaccharides and animal glycoproteins.

gall bladder In many vertebrates, a small gland found between the lobes of the liver. The gall bladder stores bile and expels it into the duodenum when fatty food is present. *See also* bile, bile duct.

gametangium (pl. **gametangia**) In plants, any organ that produces gametes.

gamete A reproductive cell in animals and plants. Two gametes fuse at fertilization to form a zygote, which becomes a new individual.

gametogenesis The formation of gametes.

gametophyte In plants that show alternation of generations, it is the haploid generation. It gives rise to gametes. *See* sporophyte.

ganglion (pl. **ganglia**) The swollen region of a nerve cord in invertebrates, or a nerve region in vertebrates that contains many cell bodies of neurons.

ganoid scale A fish scale that is rhomboid in shape and consists of a surface layer of ganoine, a substance resembling enamel, a middle layer of dentine, and a base layer of bony tissue.

gape The extent to which the mouth of an animal can open.

gas exchange The exchange of carbon dioxide and oxygen between an organism and its surroundings.

gas gland A gland found in the wall of the swim bladder of bony fish that releases gas into the swim bladder. This maintains the shape of the swim bladder against pressure when the fish descends to greater depths.

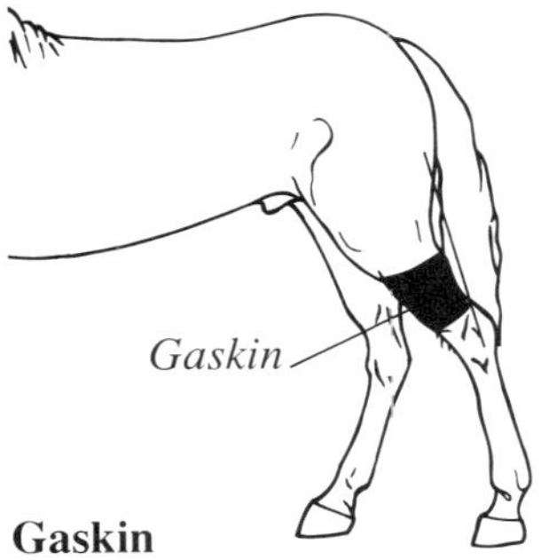

Gaskin

gaskin The anterior of the upper hind leg of a horse.

gaster The abdomen of a bee, wasp, ant, or sawfly (Hymenoptera). The first abdominal segment forms part of the thorax and is separated from the gaster by the petiole. *See* petiole.

gastric Pertaining to the stomach.

gastric mucosa The mucus membrane that lines the pyloric stomach (pylorus) and secretes gastrin, a hormone that stimulates the secretion of gastric juices.

gastrocnemius The muscle that arises on the posterior part of the femur of a vertebrate and runs behind the knee down the lower hindlimb, just below the skin. In humans it comprises most of the calf muscle.

Gastropoda A class of mollusks that includes slugs and snails. They have a true head and a broad, flat foot. Most have shells. The body undergoes torsion, at least during the development of the animal.

gastrovascular cavity A body cavity that has developed into a system of circulatory and digestive canals.

gastrozooid A member of a colony of polyps that is specialized for feeding.

gene A unit of inherited material. Specifically, it is a short section of a chromosome that determines an inherited characteristic. It is usually made of DNA.

genetic engineering or **gene splicing** (or recombinant DNA technology). The artificial removal of a section of DNA from a donor organism or tissue and its incorporation into the genetic material of another organism or tissue.

genetics The study of the mechanisms by which the characteristics of living organisms are inherited and expressed.

geniculate Able to bend like a knee, or resembling a knee in some other way.

genital In animals, particularly tetrapod vertebrates, relating to the genital organs (genitalia), the organs involved in sexual reproduction.

genital capsule Those organs and their associated structures that are used by a male insect to transfer sperm.

genital plate One of the five large plates of an echinoderm. These surround the anus, and each one bears a gonopore. One is porous and serves as the madreporite. *See* gonopore, madreporite.

genital pore *See* gonopore.

genotype The genetic constitution of an individual. It refers to the particular set of alleles present in each cell of the organism. *See also* phenotype.

geotropism In plants, a tropic response (tropism) to gravity.

germ cell Another name for a gamete.

germinate Refers to the first stage in the growth of a seed or spore into a young plant.

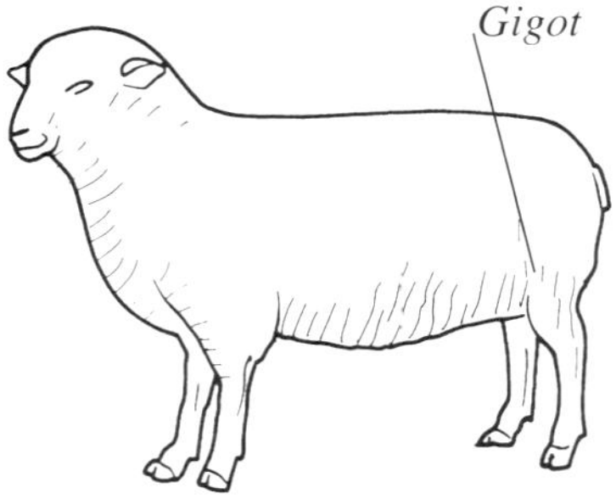

Gigot

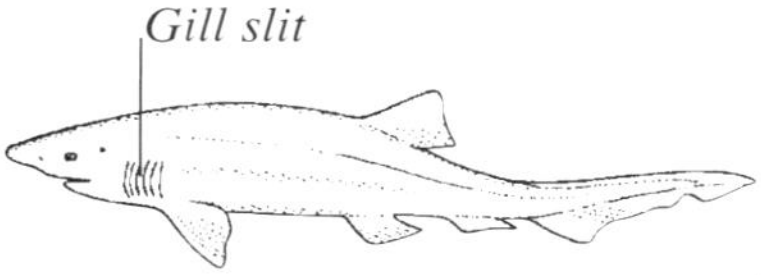

Gill slit

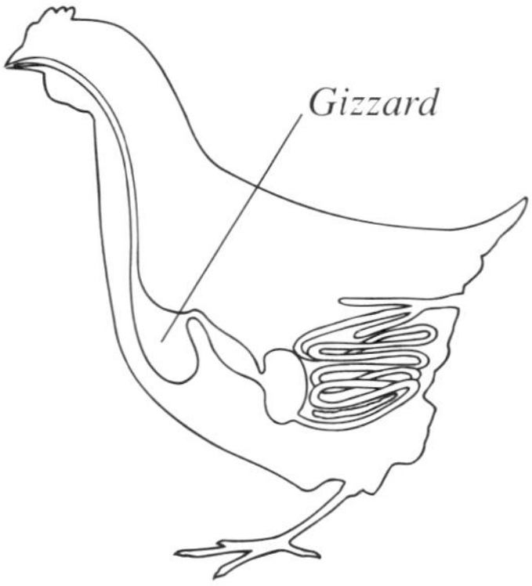

Gizzard

gigot The thigh of a sheep.

gill (1) A spore-releasing lamella on the underside of the cup of a toadstool or mushroom.
(2) The specialized respiratory (gas exchange) organ of an aquatic animal.

gill arch The bony or cartilaginous arc supporting the tissues of the gill.

gill cleft *See* gill slit.

gill filament One of many fine lateral extensions of the gill surface that increase the gill's surface area.

gill lamella *See* gill plate.

gill plate or **gill lamella** One of many platelike projections on a gill filament that further increase the gill's surface area.

gill pouch A muscular sac with gills on its inner walls. Lampreys and hagfish have a row of gill pouches on either side of the head. In vertebrate embryos, gill pouches form from outgrowths of the pharynx. In fish and amphibians they develop into gills. In land-dwelling animals they disappear.

gill raker One of a set of structures found in most bony fish. They are fairly rigid, located on the inside of the gill arches, and filter the water flowing through the gills.

gill slit or **gill cleft** A pocket formed by the meeting of a depression of the skin and outgrowth from the pharynx, which develops in all chordate embryos. In fish and amphibians it holds the gills.

gizzard In all birds and some invertebrates, a muscular region of the gut where food is mixed and crushed. It is located beyond the crop.

glabella The smooth, usually hairless, front of the head above the eyes.

gland (1) In plants, a cell or small organ that secretes substances to the exterior of the plant.
(2) In animals, a cell or organ that secretes substances internally or externally.

glenoid Relating to a socket.

glenoid cavity The socket in the vertebrate shoulder girdle in which the head of the humerus sits.

glenoid fossa The depression in the skull into which the jaw bone fits.

globose Spherical.

globular Refers to proteins that are approximately spherical and are fully or partially soluble in water.

glomerulus (pl. **glomeruli**) A mass of fine tubes located in the nephron of a vertebrate kidney. Waste products and water pass from it into the Bowman's capsule, and from there to the loop of Henle.

glossa (pl. **glossae**) Part of the mouthparts of an insect. In bees, fused glossae form the proboscis.

glossopharyngeal nerve The ninth cranial nerve of vertebrates, passing from the skull to the tongue and pharynx. It is concerned with the swallowing reflex and the sense of taste from those parts of the tongue it reaches.

glottis In vertebrates, the opening of the trachea into the pharynx. In mammals, vocal cords are stretched across it.

glucose In animals and plants, the most widely distributed hexose (6-carbon) sugar and the most common energy source in respiration.

gluteal nerves Two nerves arising from the spinal cord and passing to the gluteus muscles.

gluteus muscles Three muscles (gluteus maximus, medius, and minimus) on the side of the pelvis and upper part of the hindlimb.

glycerol A 3-carbon organic molecule that combines with fatty acids to form certain lipids (particularly fats and oils).

glycogen The carbohydrate used for storage in animals and some fungi. It is a partially soluble polysaccharide composed of branched chains of glucose.

glycolipid An organic molecule that is part-lipid, part-carbohydrate.

glycolysis (or Embden-Meyerhoff pathway). The anaerobic sequence of reactions in respiration. In it, glucose is broken down to pyruvic acid, with the liberation of some energy stored as ATP.

glycoprotein An organic molecule that is part-protein, part-carbohydrate.

glycosidic bond The chemical bond linking two sugar units, e.g., the bond between two hexose sugars.

Golgi apparatus A cell organelle that consists of a stack of smooth, flat, membrane-lined sacs called cisternae. The apparatus is involved in the assembling of simple molecules into more complex compounds and in the storage of metabolic substances.

Golgi vesicle A small, roughly spherical sac of packaged material released from the Golgi apparatus.

gonad Either the ovary or testes, an organ that produces ova or sperm.

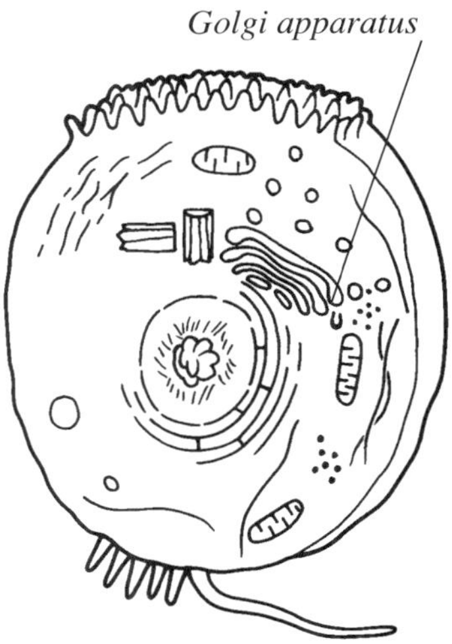

Golgi apparatus

gonadotrophic hormone In vertebrates, several polypeptide hormones that are secreted by the anterior pituitary and influence the activity of the gamete-producing organs (gonads). *See* follicle-stimulating hormone, luteinizing hormone.

gonophore A structure bearing gonads. In colonial coelenterates, a specialized polyp (gonozooid) that bears gonads.

gonopodium An organ formed from a modified anal fin and used in copulation by adult males of some families of fish.

gonopore or **genital pore** An external opening (a pore) to a reproductive system. *See* genital plate.

gonotheca A capsule containing a reproductive polyp (gonozooid), found in some colonial coelenterates.

gonozooid A reproductive polyp.

G-protein Any of the class of proteins that play an important role in relaying signals from mammalian cells.

Graafian follicle In mammals, the fluid-filled vesicle within the ovary that contains the oocyte prior to its release.

Granum

gracilis muscles Two muscles (gracilis major and minor) on the inside of the upper hindlimb of a vertebrate; in humans, on the inside of the thigh.

grafting The artificially bringing together of two tissues that are normally separate. The graft is a small part of a plant or animal that is merged with the body tissue of the same or a different individual.

granulocyte In vertebrates, a type of white blood cell with a granular cytoplasm that is phagocytic (engulfs and ingests foreign particles).

granum (pl. **grana**) In chloroplasts, a stack of flat, disk-shaped vesicles arranged like coins in a pile. The membranes (lamellae) of a granum contain photosynthetic pigments.

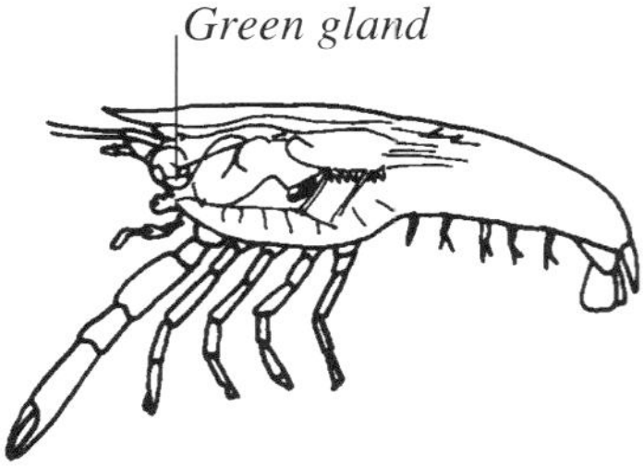

Green gland

gray matter In vertebrates, tissue of the central nervous system (cerebral cortex and interor of the spinal chord) that is rich in cell bodies and synapses and hence is where much coordination of nervous activity occurs. The tissue has a gray appearance.

green gland A gland located immediately behind each of the antennae of a crustacean. Part of it is green in color. The gland has an excretory function, rather like that of the vertebrate kidney.

gressorial Describes legs that are adapted for running.

growth Increase in size as a result of increase in cell size and/or number.

growth hormone (or somatotrophic hormone). In vertebrates, a polypeptide hormone secreted by the anterior pituitary. Among its various functions, it controls overall body growth.

guard cell In plants, one of two crescent-shaped epidermal cells found bordering a stoma. Changes in turgidity cause the guard cells to change shape and open or close the stomatal pore in order to control evaporation and the exchange of gases.

gular plate A plate extending forward from the gill covers of some bony fish and covering part of the lower jaw and throat.

gular pouch The large, elastic pouch on the lower mandible of a pelican, used in scooping up fish. Some birds related to pelicans also have gular pouches, although they are smaller.

gut Another name for the alimentary canal.

Gymnospermae A plant division (recently replaced by several divisions, including Coniferophyta) that contains seed-bearing plants that do not produce flowers but have reproductive structures like cones.

gynandromorph An animal that has a body of which one part is male and the other female.

gynecium *See* pistil.

gyroconic Loosely coiled, as in the shell of some cephalopods.

gyrose Curved or marked with wavy lines.

hackles The feathers covering the throat of some birds, such as chickens.

hair Fine, hollow filaments made from epidermal cells and grown in hair follicles in the skin. True hair is found only in mammals.

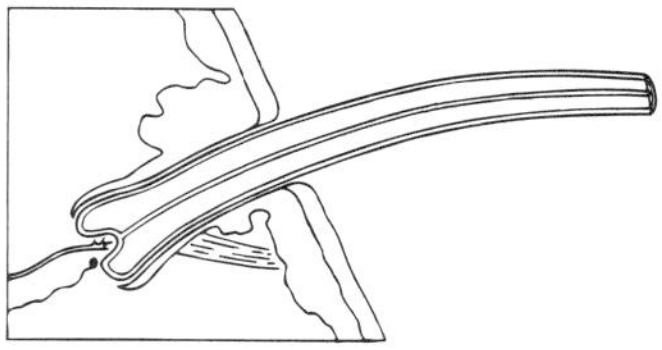
Hair

hallux The first digit of the hind foot of a pentadactyl limb. In humans it is the great toe.

haltere The modified hindwing of a fly, shaped like a drumstick and used to maintain balance.

ham The muscle at the posterior of a pig's hind leg and pelvis.

hammer *See* malleus.

hamstring The muscles behind the hindlimb that flex the femur. The tendons behind the knee, between the upper and lower leg.

hamula A structure on the ventral side of the abdomen of some insects. It supports the springing organ.

hamulus A row of hooks along the edge of the hindwing of bees, wasps, ants, and sawflies. The hooks attach to a fold in the forewing.

haploid Describing a nucleus, cell, or organism having a single set of chromosomes. *See also* diploid.

head The front (or in humans upper) part of the body, bearing sensory organs and enclosing the brain.

heart A muscular pump that causes blood to circulate through the body. In birds and mammals, the circulatory system is double, the blood supply to the lungs being separate from that of the rest of the body.

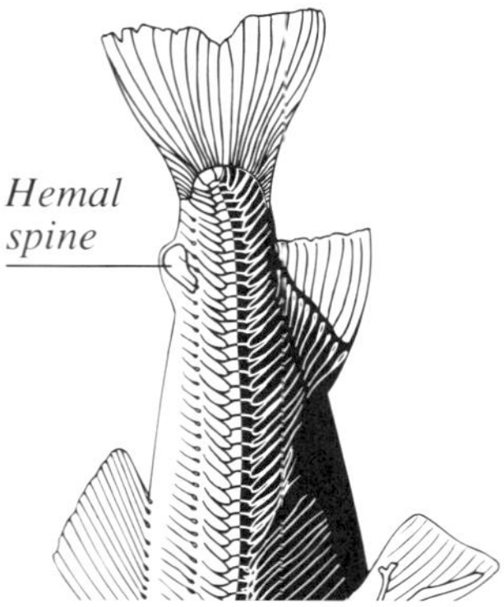

Hemal spine

hectocotylized arm A specialized cephalopod tentacle used as an intromittent organ for the transfer of sperm.

hemal spine A process growing from a posterior vertebra of a bony or cartilaginous fish.

hemielytron A leathery type of forewing, found in some bugs.

hemimetabolous Describes an insect that grows to its mature form by a series of molts. Metamorphosis is incomplete. The larvae of such insects are called nymphs.

hemipenis One half of the pair of penises possessed by a male snake. The erect penises protrude through the cloaca. Only one is inserted into the body of the female.

hemocoel In arthropods and mollusks, the main body cavity, which is bathed in blood.

hemoglobin A red oxygen-carrying pigment found in the red blood cells of vertebrates and in the blood plasma of some invertebrates.

hemolymph In some invertebrates, the fluid found in the coelom or hemocoel. It corresponds to the blood or lymph of higher forms.

hemophilia In humans, a hereditary disease that results in excessive bleeding caused by defective blood clotting.

hepatic Pertaining to the liver.

hepatic artery and vein Blood vessels supplying the liver.

hepatic portal vein A vein that carries blood from the alimentary canal through the liver before returning it to the heart. While in the liver, some substances are removed, to be stored or excreted.

hepatopancreatic duct One of the ducts that link the many short tubes of the hepatopancreas, the part of the digestive system of crustaceans where food is absorbed and some is stored.

heredity The transmission of genetic characteristics through generations. (*See also* illustration on page 59.)

Heredity (see entry on page 58)

Inheritance of facial characters

- The most obvious inherited characters are usually facial ones, such as hair color, eye color, shape of the nose, etc.
- The inheritance of facial characters can often be traced back over several generations of ancestors by looking at old family photographs, for example.

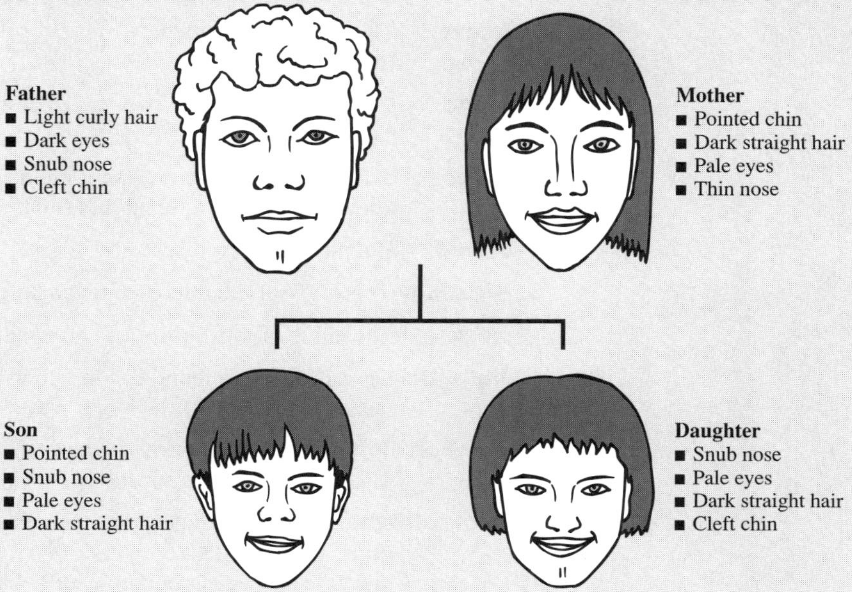

hermaphrodite An individual animal that possesses both male and female reproductive organs.

hermatypic Describes corals that contain single-celled organisms called zooxanthellae and that form reefs.

heterocercal tail A fish tail, found in sharks and some bony fish, in which the end of the vertebral column curves upward into the dorsal lobe of the tail fin. This often makes the dorsal lobe larger than the ventral lobe.

heterodont Having teeth of different types, for example, incisors, canines, premolars, and molars.

heteromerous Made from units, such as segments, that are different from each other.

heterotrophic Referring to an organism that requires ready-made organic molecules as a source of energy and raw material. All animals and fungi, and a few flowering plants, are heterotrophic.

hexacanth *See* onchosphere.

Hexactinellida A class of deep-water sponges (Porifera) in which the skeleton is made mainly from six-rayed spicules.

hexaster Describes one of the spicules of a sponge if it is fleshy and has six rays emanating from a central point.

hilum The scar on a seed where it was formerly attached to the funicle (ovule stalk).

hinge The region where the two valves of a bivalve mollusk are attached to each other.

hinge joint A joint allowing movement in one plane only, e.g., in humans, the knee joint between femur and tibia.

hispid Having bristles or short, stiff hairs.

histology The study of the microscopic anatomy of plant or animal tissues.

hock The ankle of most birds and mammals.

holoptic Describes a compound eye in which the facets of the upper part are bigger than those of the lower part.

holozoic Referring to organisms with animal-like feeding involving the ingestion of organic substances.

homeotherm An animal whose body temperature varies only within narrow limits. The constant temperature may be maintained by internal mechanisms (*see* endotherm) or behaviorally (*see* ectotherm). *See also* poikilotherm.

homocercal tail A symmetrical fish tail in which the fin rays are supported by bony structures from the final vertebra.

homodont Having teeth that are all similar.

homogenate Material that is ground up in a homogenizer to dissolve or suspend its components in liquid.

homologous Describing organs or parts that have a similar structure and evolutionary origin but do not necessarily perform the same functions, e.g., a human arm and a bird's wing. *See also* analogous.

homologous chromosomes In diploid organisms, two near-identical chromosomes that pair with each other during the prophase of meiosis.

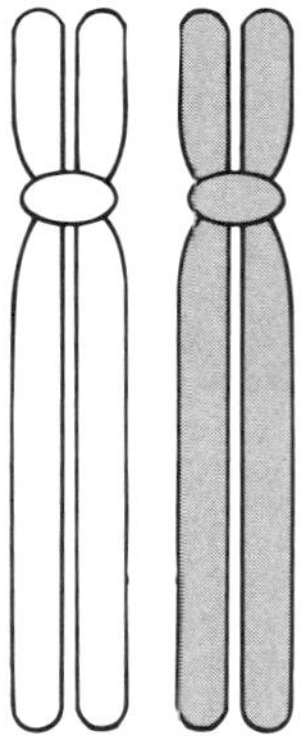

Homologous chromosomes

hoof A casing that covers the toe of a horse or ruminant. It is made from keratin.

hook bone The hip (pelvis) of a sheep.

hormone (1) In animals, an organic substance that, in minute quantities, controls bodily functions. A hormone is produced by an endocrine

gland and exerts its effect on a target organ or tissue elsewhere in the body.
(2) In plants, an organic substance that, in very small amounts, controls the growth and development of plant tissue.

horn A sharp, straight, or curved structure borne as a pair on the head of a ruminant animal. Horns grow from the skin and are made mainly of keratin.

host (1) An organism that harbors a parasite and provides it with food and protection.
(2) An organism whose body provides a place of attachment or protection for another organism.
(3) An animal that receives a graft from another individual.

humerus In tetrapod vertebrates, the long bone found in the upper forelimb.

hyaloplasm Another name for endoplasm or cytosol.

hybrid An individual or strain produced by crossing parents that are genetically dissimilar.

Hydra A genus of freshwater cnidarians. Members are widespread.

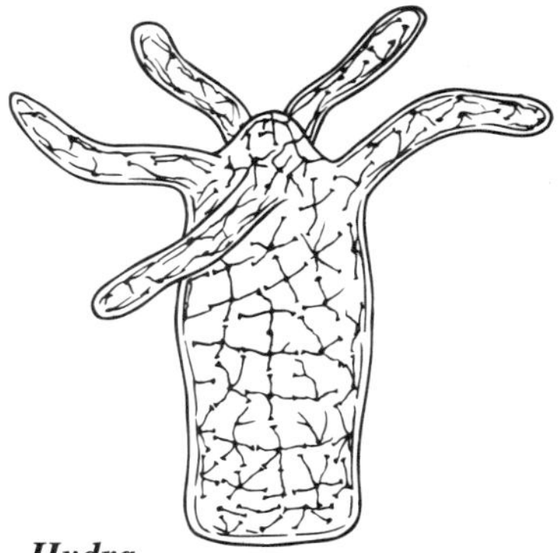

Hydra

hydrocarbon A chemical compound containing only hydrogen and carbon.

hydrocortisone *See* cortisol.

hydrofuge Water-repellent.

hydrogen bond A weak form of ionic bond that is important in maintaining the overall conformation of biologically important molecules, particularly proteins and nucleic acids.

hydrolysis The breakdown of a substance involving the chemical incorporation of water.

hydrophilic Water-loving. In solution, it refers to a chemical or part of a chemical that is highly attracted to water.

hydrophobic Refers to a chemical or part of a chemical that repels water.

hydrostatic skeleton Fluid held under pressure in the coelom of a soft-bodied invertebrate. It holds the body's shape and provides a support against which muscles can contract.

hydrotheca In a coelenterate colony, one of the cup-shaped structures that surrounds and protects an individual polyp.

hyoid A bone derived from the visceral arch, immediately behind the hyomandibular arch. In vertebrates, one or more hyoid bones support the floor of the mouth.

hyomandibular An arch composed of bone or cartilage that connects the cranium to the jaw in fish. It forms the columella auris in some amphibians and in birds and reptiles. In mammals it forms the stapes, part of the inner ear.

hypha (pl. **hyphae**) In fungi, a tube-like branching filament. Hyphae comprise the vegetative body of a fungus and form a network called a mycelium.

hypocercal tail A fish tail in which the lower lobe is larger than the upper lobe.

hypocone The inside posterior cusp of the upper molar tooth of a mammal.

hypoconid The outside posterior cusp of the upper molar tooth of a mammal.

hypocotyl The part of a seedling stem that is below the cotyledons and above the radicle.

hypogeal Refers to a form of seed germination in which the seed leaves (cotyledons) remain below the ground. *See also* epigeal.

hyponome *See* funnel.

hypopharyngeal gland (or brood gland). A gland in the head of bees, associated with the mouthparts.

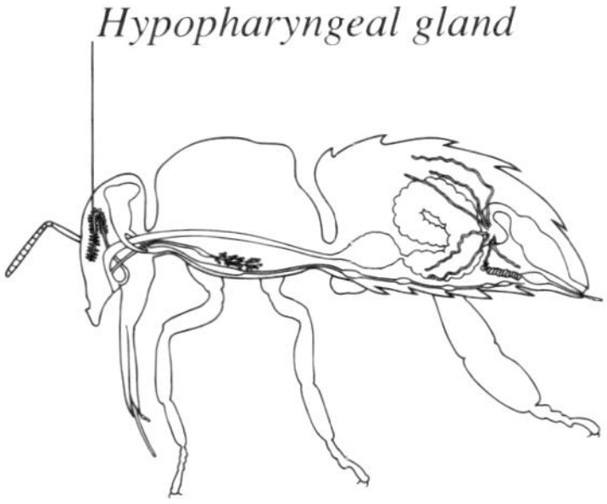

Hypopharyngeal gland

hypopharynx Part of the mouth of an insect. It usually carries the apertures through which saliva is released, but in some insects it extends into the proboscis.

hypophysial sac (or Rathke's pouch). A pit in the middle of the roof of the mouth of vertebrates.

hypophysis A pouch that forms at the front of the buccal cavity in a vertebrate embryo. It meets and merges with the infundibulum, loses its connection with the mouth, and, with the infundibulum, forms the pituitary body.

hypopleural bristles Two rows of bristles on the sides of the thorax of flies.

hypostome A conical mound around the mouth of *Hydra*.

hypothalamus In vertebrates, a small structure associated with the forebrain. In higher mammals, it is found just above the pituitary gland and is the main coordinating center for visceral functions, in part, by its action on the pituitary gland.

hypsodont Describes teeth with high crowns and open roots. They continue to grow as they are worn down.

hypurals Enlarged ventral ribs that support the tail fin in some fish.

ICSH *See* luteinizing hormone.

ileum In mammals, the last part of the small intestine.

iliac arteries and veins The arteries into which the aorta divides in the abdomen. They supply blood to the pelvic region, reproductive and other organs, and the upper part of the hindlimb. The iliac veins join one another and eventually unite with the vena cava.

iliofibularis A muscle in the upper hindlimb of a frog.

iliohypogastric nerve A branch from the first lumbar nerve in the posterior part of the vertebrate abdomen, near the ilium.

iliolingual nerve A branch from the first lumbar nerve that passes close to the iliohypogastric nerve.

iliolumbar artery and vein An artery that branches from the iliac artery to supply blood to muscles of the posterior abdomen. The veins collect abdominal blood.

iliopsoas The blood vessels, derived from the iliac vessels, supplying the psoas muscle of the posterior abdomen.

ilium The upper and widest of the bones making up the hip bone.

illicium The "fishing pole" lure used by angler fish to attract prey. It is the first fin ray of the dorsal fin with a flap of skin at the end.

imago The adult form of an insect.

imbricate Overlapping, like roof tiles.

immunity An organism's ability to resist infection by the use of active and passive defenses.

immunology The study of immune reactions, in particular antigens, antibodies, and their interactions.

incisor In mammals, a chisel-shaped tooth at the front of the mouth. It is commonly used for gnawing, nibbling, biting, or cutting. In humans and most mammals there are three on either side of both jaws.

incurrent In an aquatic animal that feeds by filtering particles from a current of water, applied to structures involved in drawing water into the animal.

incus (or anvil). In mammals, one of three ossicles in the middle ear.

indirect flight muscle Muscle that compresses the thorax of an insect, to which the wings are attached, causing the wings to move up and down.

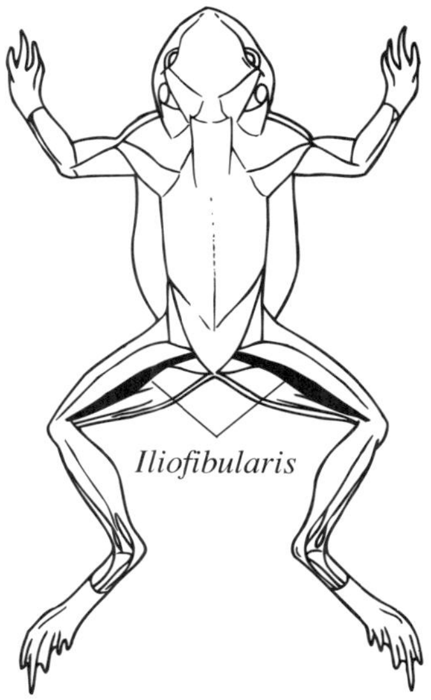

Iliofibularis

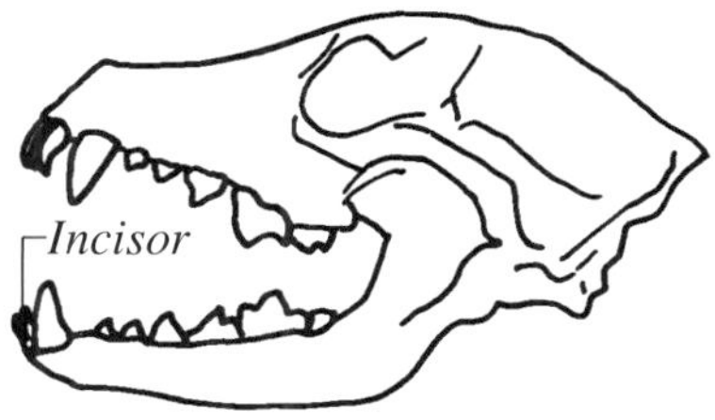

Incisor

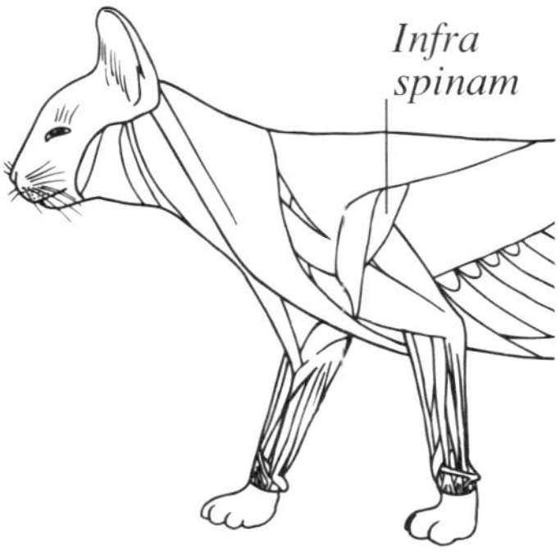

Infra spinam

indusium In ferns, a thin outgrowth that protects developing sporangia in a sorus.

infra spinam A muscle in the shoulder of a cat.

infraspinatus A thick, triangular muscle in the shoulder of a mammal.

infundibulum Part of the pituitary gland in vertebrates. It develops in an embryo from the downward growth of the posterior of the floor of the forebrain and the hypophysis.

ingestion The process of taking in solid or liquid material for use as a food source.

inhibitor A substance that prevents or slows a chemical reaction.

innominate artery An artery that branches from the aorta and with further branching becomes the subclavian and carotid arteries.

Insecta Insects, a class of arthropods that have three pairs of legs and, in most cases, two pairs of wings borne on the thorax. Most insects have one pair of antennae and one pair of compound eyes.

instar An insect larva that is between molts.

insulin In vertebrates, a hormone secreted by the pancreas and involved in the control of blood glucose level.

interclavicle A median bone on the ventral side of the shoulder girdle, between the clavicles. It is present in all tetrapods, including monotremes (duck-billed platypus and echidnas), but not in other mammals.

intercostal muscle In tetrapod vertebrates, muscles connecting adjacent ribs. Their contraction produces breathing movements.

intercostal nerve One of 12 nerves on each side of the body of a vertebrate. They arise from the spinal column and are distributed to various parts of the thorax and abdomen.

interna Feeding "roots" produced by certain parasitic barnacles. They penetrate and invade all parts of the body of the host.

internode In plants, the region of a stem between two nodes (points from which leaves grow).

interparietal A small bone on the posterior of the top of the skull, between the parietals. It is present in rodents and some other small mammals, but not in all mammals.

interphase In cells, the period between one cell division and the next.

interstitial cell *See* Leydig cell.

interstitial cell-stimulating hormone (ICSH) *See* luteinizing hormone.

intestine In vertebrates and some invertebrates, the region of the alimentary canal between stomach and anus or cloaca. It is where food is digested, water absorbed, and feces produced.

intra- A prefix denoting "within" or "inside."

invagination The infolding of a sheet of cells to form a pouch or pocket.

involute Having edges that are rolled over.

iris In vertebrates, a colored ring of muscular tissue toward the front of the eye. By altering the size of its central opening, the pupil, it controls the amount of light passing to the retina.

ischium A bone in the pelvic girdle. It lies on the ventral side and, in primates, supports the weight of the sitting animal.

isocercal tail A fish tail that is symmetrical, the dorsal and ventral fin rays being supported equally by arches developed from the vertebrae. Cod have isocercal tails.

isomyarian Describes bivalve mollusks in which the two adductor muscles are the same size.

jaw The structures forming the upper and lower parts of the mouth of some animals. They are articulated for grasping or biting.

jugal A bone on the side of the skull beneath the eye of some mammals, but not humans.

jugular vein A vein in the neck of vertebrates. It carries blood from the head and face to the anterior vena cava, and from there to the heart. There are four jugular veins, the external, posterior external, anterior, and anterior internal.

jugum A lobe of the forewing in some butterflies and moths. It couples the forewing and hindwing while the insect is flying.

karyotype The visual characteristics of the set of chromosomes found in a somatic cell of a given individual.

keel The sternum (breast bone) of a bird. This is enlarged into a shape resembling the keel of a boat to provide attachment for the large flight muscles.

kidney In vertebrates, the organ of nitrogenous waste excretion and osmoregulation.

kingdom The highest level in the taxonomic hierarchy.

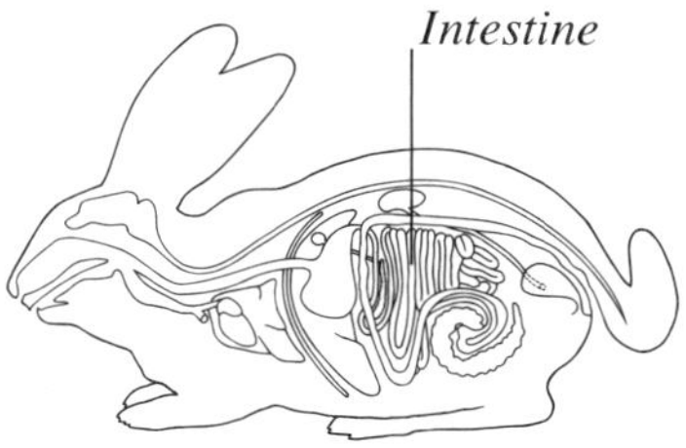

Intestine

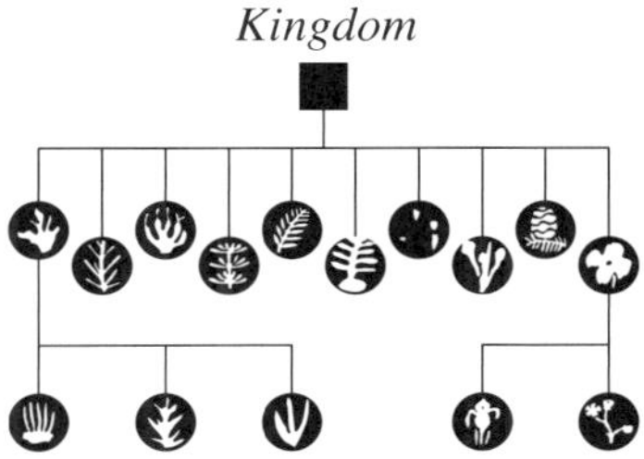

Kingdom

Klinefelter's syndrome In men, a congenital disorder resulting from the inheritance of the sex chromosome constitution XXY. Such individuals are sterile and have incompletely developed sex organs.

Krebs cycle (or citric acid cycle or tricarboxylic acid cycle). The major cyclic biochemical pathway in aerobic respiration. It is fed by glycolysis, and in it pyruvate is oxidized to carbon dioxide, and reduced NAD and NADP are formed. The cycle is named after Sir Hans Krebs. *See also* glycolysis, electron carrier chain.

labium The lower lip of an insect.

labor In humans, contractions of the uterus and associated biological events that lead to the baby and afterbirth (placenta) being expelled from the uterus.

labrum (1) In insects, the upper lip. It is hinged to the clypeus and in front of the mandibles.
(2) In some echinoderms, a projection from the peristome.

lachrymal A small, fragile bone located at the front of each orbit in mammalian skull.

lacteal In vertebrates, a lymph vessel draining a villus in the intestine. It receives fat absorbed across the intestinal wall.

lamina (pl. **laminae**) (leaf blade) The large flattened portion of the leaf.

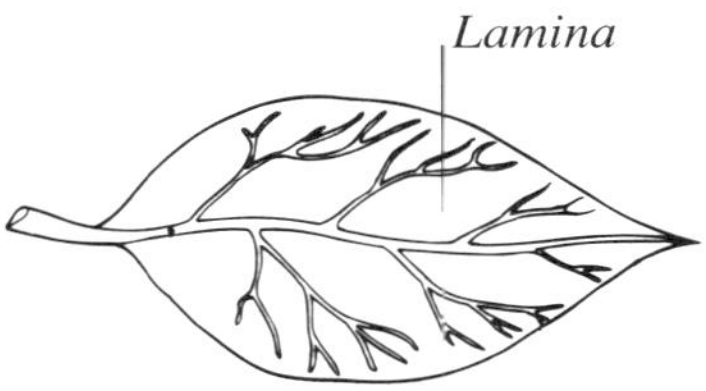

Lamina

lanugo Hair that covers the body of human embryos and is usually lost before birth.

large intestine In reptiles, birds, and mammals, the second major part of the intestine. Its primary function is to absorb water and prepare feces. *See* intestine.

larva (pl. **larvae**) An immature form that many animals develop from the zygote. The larva is quite different in structure and mode of life from the adult form into which it metamorphoses. *See* metamorphosis.

larynx The upper part of the trachea. It empties into the pharynx through the glottis, and in most mammals it contains vocal cords.

lateral Refers to a structure "at the side" of a plant or animal.

lateral line A pressure-sensitive sense organ running along the sides of a fish or larval amphibian. It detects vibrations in the water.

laterobronchus A tube from the bill to the abdominal air sac, forming part of the respiratory system of a bird.

latissimus dorsi A wide, flat muscle joined to the humerus and covering the lower part of the back of a mammal.

leech *See* Annelida.

legume (1) A member of the plant family Leguminosae. These plants have root nodules containing symbiotic, nitrogen-fixing bacteria.
(2) Fruit containing a seed pod, produced by plants of the family Leguminosae.

lens (1) In vertebrates, a transparent structure at the front of an eye. It focuses light onto the retina.
(2) In insects and crustacea, a transparent structure at the entrance of an ommatidium. It focuses light onto one or more light-sensitive cells.

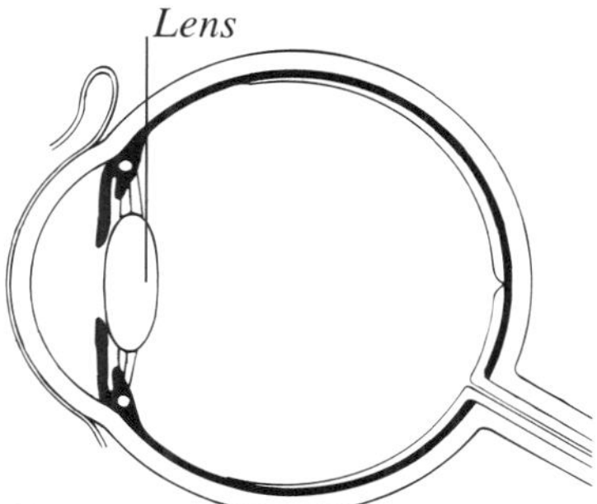

Lens

lenticel In plants, a small raised pore on the surface of the bark of woody plant stems. It permits gas exchange between the stem and its surroundings.

leucon The body of a sponge (Porifera), comprising many chambers.

leukocyte Another name for a white blood cell. It has a nucleus but no pigments. Leukocytes are important in defending the body against disease.

levator nasolabialis One of a pair of muscles, on either side of the muzzle of a mammal, that contract to raise the nose and upper lip.

Levator nasolabialis

Leydig cell (or interstitial cell). In male vertebrates, one of the testosterone-secreting cells of the testes.

LH *See* luteinizing hormone.

lienogastric artery An artery found in sharks. It branches from the dorsal aorta in the abdominal region.

ligament A band of connective tissue that joins bones to each other. It is made from tightly packed elastic fibers, allowing the joint to withstand shocks. *See* tendon.

light reactions The photosynthetic pathways that are directly dependent on light. They convert light energy to chemical energy, which, together with the reducing power they provide, fuel the dark reactions of photosynthesis.

limb One of the four main appendages of an animal used for locomotion or grasping.

lingual Relating to the tongue.

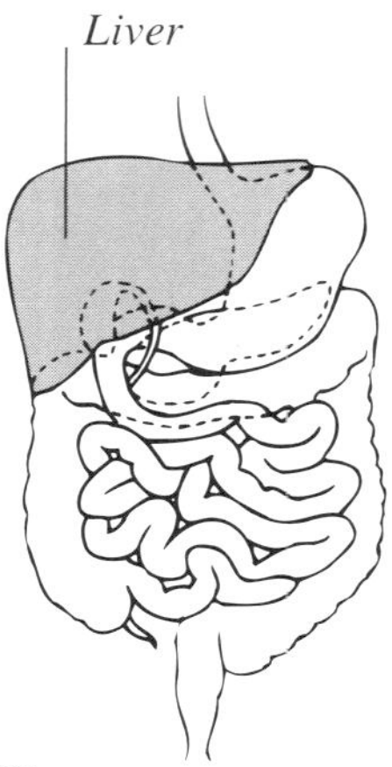

Liver

lipid A member of the class of organic molecules that are insoluble in water. Lipids include fats, oils, waxes, steroids, and phospholipids.

liver In animals, a large gland that opens into the gut. It usually plays a role in digestion. In vertebrates, its functions are numerous and include bile production and important roles in protein, fat, and carbohydrate metabolism.

lobe (1) In animals, one or two or more portions into which an organ or structure is divided by a fissure, e.g., as in the liver or a lung.
(2) In plants, one of many rounded projections or subdivisions of a leaf.

loin The posterior dorsal side of sheep and cattle, above the pelvis.

longitudinal Along the length of a body or structure.

loop of Henle In vertebrates, the large bend in a kidney tubule that extends through the kidney medulla. It is largely concerned with setting up a water potential gradient towards the inside of the medulla.

loph A ridge that connects the cusps of a tooth.

lophodont Describes teeth that have lophs.

lore The region of a bird's head immediately anterior to the eye.

lumbar plexus A group of nerves that arise from the lumbar region of the spinal column. In humans it comprises five main nerves, each of which branches into more nerves, some of the branches joining one another.

lumbar vertebra One of the vertebrae located between the thoracic and sacral vertebrae. In mammals the lumbar vertebrae are in the waist region.

lumen In organisms or cells, the space inside a sac- or tubelike structure.

lung (1) The respiratory organ of air-breathing vertebrates. It contains many sacs, called alveoli, with thin walls across which oxygen and carbon dioxide diffuse.
(2) Part of the mantle of terrestrial mollusks, involved in respiration.

luteinizing hormone (**LH**) (or interstitial cell-stimulating hormone [ISCH]). In vertebrates, a hormone secreted by the anterior pituitary gland. It stimulates the formation of the corpora lutea, ovulation, and estrogen secretion in females. In males it stimulates the interstitial cells of the testes to produce male sex hormones.

lymph In vertebrates, the colorless fluid found in the lymphatic system. It arises from absorbed tissue fluid.

lymphatic system In vertebrates, a system of thin-walled vessels that conduct lymph from tissues to the circulatory system. The system is primarily concerned with fluid drainage, fat transport, and with combating infection.

lymph node In mammals and birds, a structure associated with larger lymph vessels. It contains numerous lymphocytes and phagocytic white blood cells to counter invading pathogens.

lymphocyte In vertebrates, a form of white blood cell responsible for the production of specific antibodies in response to the presence of antigens. It is a major part of the body's immune system.

lysis The rupture of a plasma membrane, which liberates the cell contents.

lysosome In eukaryotic cells, a membrane-bound organelle that contains digestive enzymes.

macula A light-sensitive area found in the retina of many vertebrates that lack a fovea.

madreporite One of five genital plates on the aboral surface of an echinoderm. It is perforated and button-shaped. The madreporite connects the water-vascular system to the water outside the body.

malleus (or hammer). In mammals, the outer of three ossicles in the middle ear.

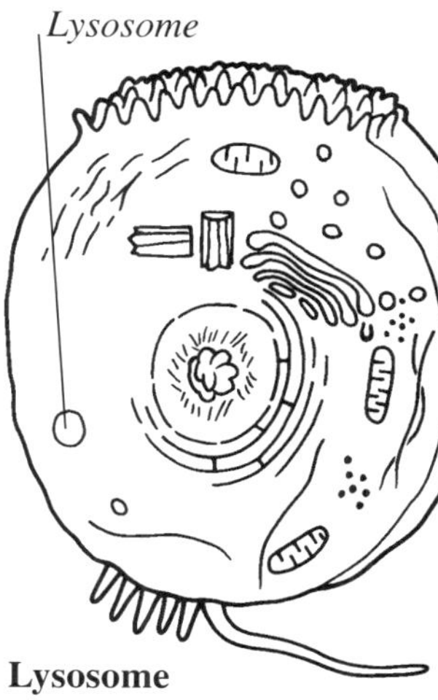

Lysosome

Lysosome

How a lysosome works
1 A particle (**a**) enters the cell (**b**) by a process such as phagocytosis (cell "eating").
2 The phagocytic vacuole or membranous vesicle (**c**) formed fuses with a lysosome (**d**).
3 The enzymes (**e**) in the lysosome digest the particle.
4 The resulting waste products (**f**) are secreted into the cell.
5 The wastes are expelled from the cell by exocytosis.

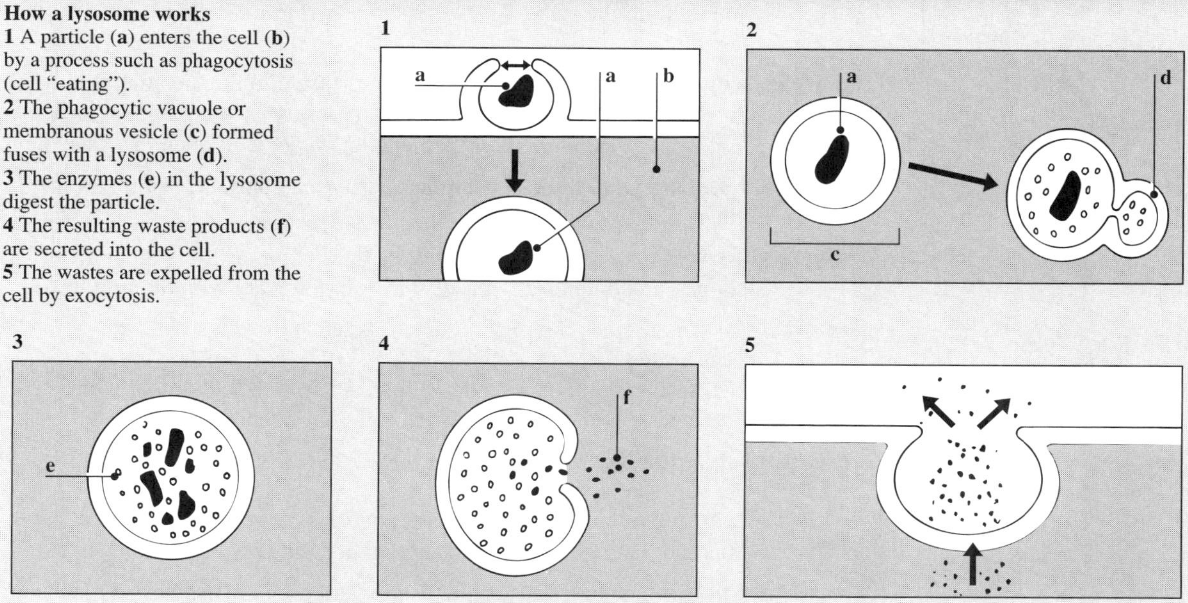

Malpighian tubules In insects and some arachnids, excretory tubular glands that empty into the hindgut.

maltose Disaccharide sugar formed from two glucose molecules. It is a product of starch digestion and is also found in some germinating seeds.

Mammalia A class of tetrapod vertebrates. Its members typically have hair, a diaphragm, a two-boned lower jaw, three ossicles in the middle ear, and females secrete milk from mammary glands.

mammary gland A gland on the ventral surface of a female mammal that secretes milk used to suckle the young. The number of mammary glands varies from one species to another, but there are always at least two.

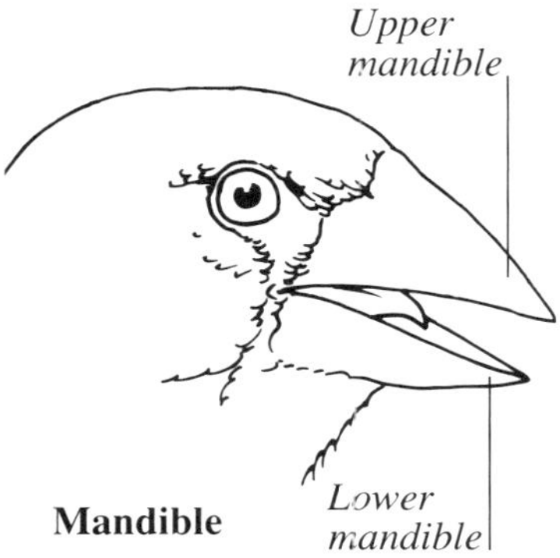

Mandible

mandible (1) In most vertebrates, the lower jaw.
(2) In birds, the lower jaw and bill, but the term is also applied to the two parts of the bill.
(3) In arthropods, one of a pair of mouthparts used to seize and cut food.

mane Long hair on the dorsal side of the neck of a mammal.

mantle A fold of skin on the dorsal surface of a mollusk. It encloses a cavity containing the gills. The shell is made from material secreted by the mantle.

marsupium (pl. **marsupia**) A pouch on the surface of a female animal in which her young are held. Some invertebrates possess marsupia and the marsupials are named for them, although not all marsupials have them.

masseter muscle One of the cheek muscles. When contracted, it raises the lower jaw.

mastoid process An outgrowth behind the ear in humans. It is made from bone and contains air spaces that communicate with the middle ear.

matrix (1) In animals, the intercellular substance in which cells are embedded.
(2) Generally, a background substance in which a structure or a process is found, e.g., the matrix of a mitochondrion.

maxilla (pl. **maxillae**) (1) The upper jaw of a vertebrate. It bears all the teeth except the incisors.
(2) One of a pair of mouthparts found in some arthropods. These are behind the mandibles and are used in eating.

maxillary gland One of a pair of glands possessed by crustaceans. They open into the maxillae, or second antennae, and are used to excrete waste.

maxillary palp One of a pair of jointed, sensory structures close to the maxillae of an insect.

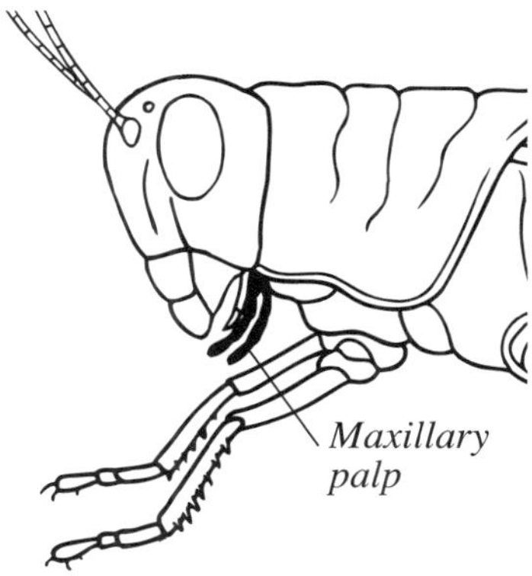

Maxillary palp

maxillary teeth Teeth that grow from the maxilla of a vertebrate. These comprise all the teeth of the upper jaw except for the incisors.

maxilliped In crustacea and centipedes, one of a pair of appendages just behind the maxillae that manipulate food prior to ingestion.

Meckel's cartilage One of a pair of cartilages that form the lower jaw of a cartilaginous fish. In bony fish, reptiles, and birds it forms the articular bone and in mammals the malleus.

median eye (or pineal eye). A structure resembling an eye found on the top of the head in lampreys, the tuatara, and some lizards. It has a lens and retina and a nerve links it to the brain.

median nerve A nerve that passes down the center of the forelimb of vertebrates.

median notch The notch at the center of the flukes of a whale or dolphin.

medulla In animals, the inner portion of an organ or structure. *See* cortex.

medulla oblongata In vertebrates, the posterior part of the hindbrain. In mammals, it coordinates involuntary activities, such as breathing, heartbeat, and dilation of blood vessels.

medusa (pl. **medusae**) A jellyfish. It is the free-swimming stage in the life cycle of a coelenterate.

meiosis (reduction division) The type of cell or nuclear division associated with a halving of chromosome number, from diploid to haploid. It also results in daughter cells that are genetically distinct from each other and from the parent cell. *See* mitosis.

melanism Darkly pigmented. A genetically determined trait.

melon The rounded protruberance on the head of some toothed whales, such as the beluga (white whale).

merocrine gland A gland that releases a secretion containing little or no material produced by the breakdown of its own cells. *See also* apocrine gland.

mesaxonic Describes a vertebrate limb in which the weight passes through the third digit.

mesenteric Refers to the artery that supplies blood to the intestines.

mesenteric artery One of the two arteries (superior and inferior mesenterics) that supply blood to the whole of the intestine, except the duodenum.

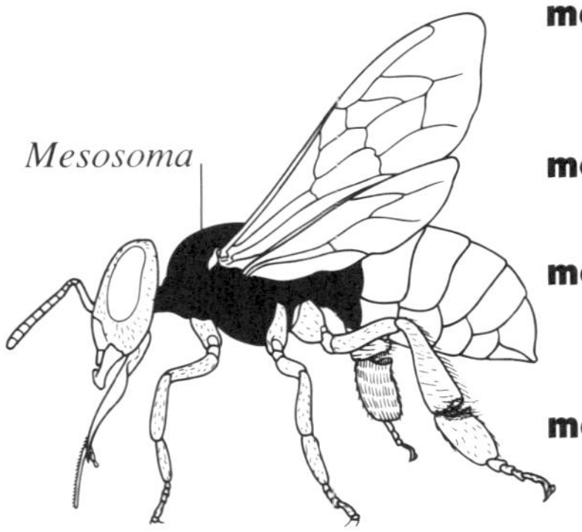

Mesosoma

mesentery A thin sheet of fibrous tissue that attaches organs to the body wall.

mesoderm The middle layer of cells in an embryo that develops from three layers of cells. The mesoderm gives rise to the axial skeleton, kidneys, skin, muscle, blood vessels, and connective tissue.

mesoglea In sponges (Porifera) and coelenterates, a layer of material between the outer and inner layers of the body wall.

mesophyll In plants, photosynthetic tissue and packing tissue (parenchyma) that is found between the upper and lower epidermis of the blade of a leaf.

mesosoma (1) In some arachnids, e.g., scorpions, the first set of segments behind the leg-bearing segments. *See* metasoma.
(2) The combined thorax and first abdominal segment of a bee, wasp, ant, or sawfly.

mesosome An infolding, often highly convoluted, of the plasma membrane of certain bacteria.

messenger ribonucleic acid or **messenger RNA** (**mRNA**) The form of RNA that conveys genetic information, in the form of a sequence of codons, from DNA to ribosomes, so directing the production of a specific polypeptide.

metacarpals In tetrapod vertebrates, the rod-shaped bones of the forefoot, one associated with each digit, that lie between the carpals and the phalanges. In humans, they support the palm of the hand.

metameric segmentation Having a body comprising a series of segments (metameres), all of which are similar.

metamorphosis In animals, the period of sharp transformation from the larval to the adult form. (*See also* illustration on page 73.)

metaphase In mitosis or meiosis, the stage following prophase when the chromosomes are aligned along the equator of the spindle.

metasoma In some arachnids, e.g., scorpions, the most posterior set of segments. The region lies behind the mesosoma.

metatarsals In humans, the five long bones that make up the instep of the foot.

metatarsus The middle part of the human foot that forms the instep and includes the metatarsals.

mica A naturally occurring, soft, translucent, and glasslike solid that cleaves into sheets. It is used as a thin barrier in experiments with plant hormones.

Metamorphosis (see entry on page 72)

- Many insects undergo complete metamorphosis, a process that entails four main stages: egg, larva, pupa, and imago (adult). Some of these stages have radically different body forms.
- Typically, the egg of an insect hatches into a wormlike larva (called a maggot in the case of flies, and a caterpillar in the case of butterflies). The larva passes through several stages or instars, shedding its skin and enlarging at each, before forming a "resting" pupa. The pupa finally turns into an adult (imago) with an entirely different body plan.

***Drosophila* life cycle**

- This radical change in form is illustrated by the life cycle of the fruit fly *Drosophila* (see right).
- There are three larval stages (instars), and the entire life cycle is completed within 9–10 days.

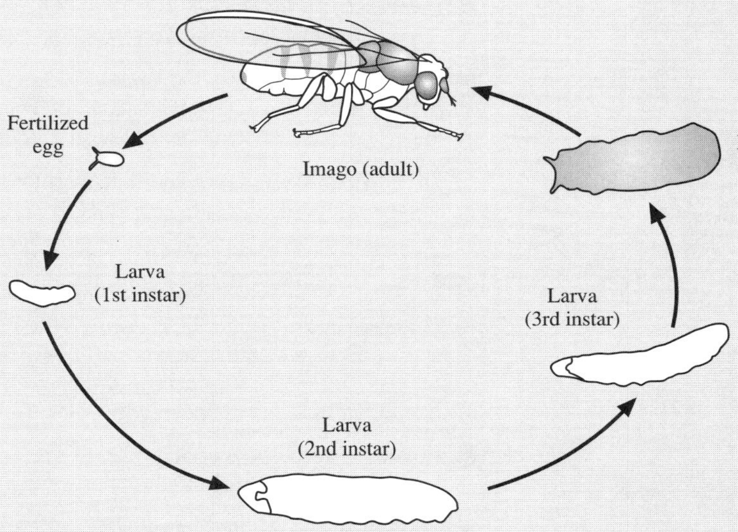

micropyle (1) In seed-bearing plants, the pore in an ovule through which the pollen tube enters prior to fertilization. It is later recognizable as a small opening in the seed coat through which water enters before germination.
(2) In insects, a small pore in the shell of an egg through which sperm passes.

microscope One of a variety of instruments for enlarging images of small objects. The magnifying glass, compound light microscope, and the transmission electron microscope are the most common forms.

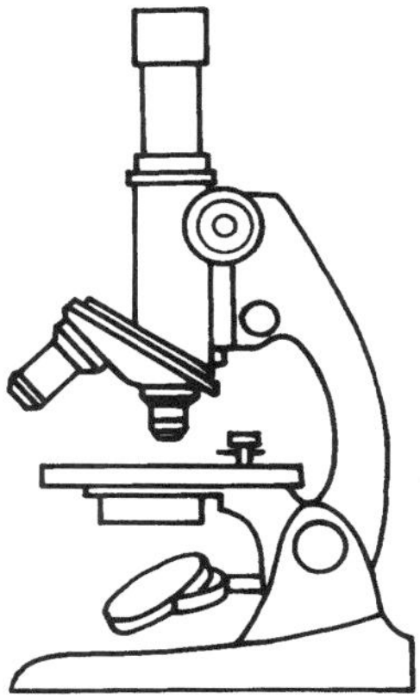

Microscope

microsporangium (pl. **microsporangia**) In plants, the structure that produces microspores (small spores). In cone-bearing and flowering plants, the microspores develop into pollen grains containing male gametes.

microsporophyll A modified leaf or leaf-like structure bearing microsporangia, as in the pinnae of pterophytes, the cones of cone-bearing plants, and the stamens of flowering plants.

microtubule A thick, tubular protein filament in the cytoplasm of eukaryotic cells. Microtubules are involved in spindle formation during cell division, form part of the skeletal framework of the cell, and comprise parts of cilia and flagella.

microvillus (pl. **microvilli**) In some cells, one of numerous ultramicroscopic finger-like projections that increase the cell's surface area.

midbrain In vertebrates, the region between the forebrain and hindbrain and extending from below the cerebrum to the pons. It is a relay center particularly concerned with hearing and sight.

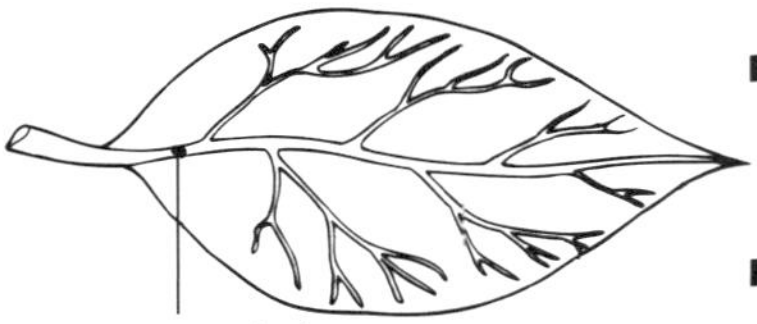

Midrib

middle lamella In plants, the narrow intercellular region between the cell walls of two adjacent cells. It is formed at cell division and before the new secondary cell walls of adjacent cells are laid down.

midrib In plants, the large central vein of a leaf blade.

millipede An arthropod, belonging to the class Diplopoda, in which the body is segmented. Each apparent segment is formed from two fused segments (somites), and therefore bears two pairs of legs. Most millipedes are herbivorous. Some curl into a ball if threatened.

Miocene A geological epoch, part of the Tertiary period, lasting from about 23.8–5.3 million years before the present.

miracidium The ciliated larval stage emerging from the egg of a fluke (class Trematoda, phylum Platyhelminthes).

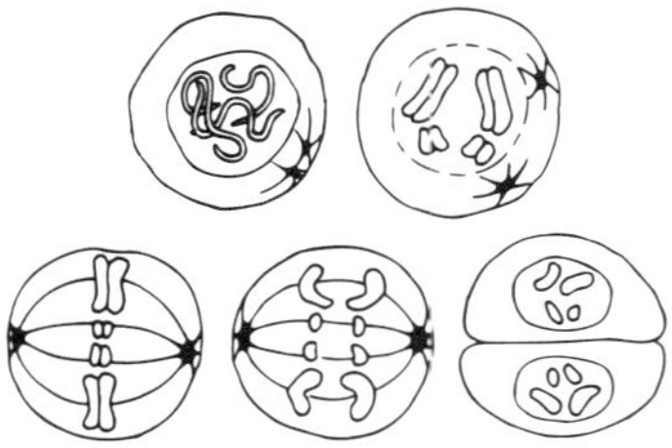
Mitosis

mitochondrion (pl. **mitochondria**) An organelle that is sometimes called the *power-house* of a cell. It is the major site of adenosine triphosphate (ATP) production. Most cells contain a large number of mitochondria. They are oval in shape, self-replicating, contain their own DNA, and synthesize some of their own proteins. (*See also* illustration on page 75.)

mitosis Cell (nuclear) division that gives rise to daughter cells that are genetically identical to each other and to the parent cell. *See* meiosis.

modulator A chemical that attaches to an allosteric enzyme, at a point other than the active site, and regulates the activity of the enzyme.

molar In mammals, one of several crushing teeth at either side of upper and lower jaws. They are situated behind the premolars and usually have three or more roots. Unlike premolars, they are not present as milk teeth.

mold (1) The general name for shallow fungal growth on a surface. (2) The fungi that cause such growth, such as the pin mold, *Mucor*.

molecule The smallest unit of an element or chemical compound that occurs naturally. It comprises at least two atoms.

Mitochrondria (see entry on page 74)

Mitochondria are involved in cellular respiration: the production of the cellular energy storage molecule ATP (adenosine triphosphate). Fatty acids and amino acids (building blocks of proteins) and glucose (simple sugar) can all be broken down to give energy. Glucose is the example given below.

Cellular respiration
1 Glucose (**a**) and oxygen (**b**) enter the mitochondrion.
2 Enzymes (**c**) break the glucose down, releasing energy (**d**).
3 This energy is used to bind a phosphate group to ADP (adenosine diphosphate) (**e**) to make ATP (**f**). Carbon dioxide and water are also formed.
4 When the cell needs energy, the bond that holds the phosphate to ATP is broken. This releases energy (**g**) and converts the ATP back into ADP.

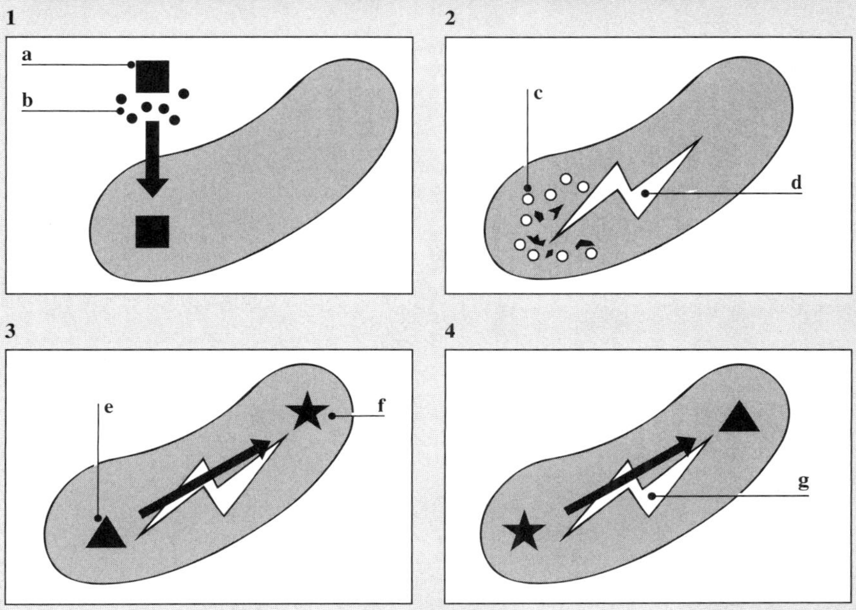

Mollusca The phylum of soft-bodied animals that includes clams, snails, slugs, and squids.

Monera The kingdom of prokaryotes. It includes bacteria and blue-green algae (cyanobacteria).

monocotyledon A member of the class Monocotyledonae within the division Anthophyta. Members are characterized by several features, including the presence of one seed leaf (cotyledon) in the embryo. *See also* dicotyledon.

monocyte A phagocytic white blood cell with a large nucleus. It engulfs pathogens.

monohybrid cross In genetics, breeding from parents that differ for one simply inherited characteristic.

monomyarian Possessing only one adductor muscle, a condition found in some bivalve mollusks.

monophyodont Possessing only one set of teeth, which are not replaced.

monosaccharide A single sugar unit. A member of the simplest group of sugars. Monosaccharides contain 3–7 carbon atoms, but biologically

Motor neuron

the most common are pentoses (5-C sugars) and hexoses (6-C sugars).

monosomy In eukaryotes, an unusual chromosome complement where one of the homologous pairs is missing a member.

monozygotic Refers to twins that have arisen from a single fertilized ovum. The twins are genetically identical.

motor neuron A nerve cell that conducts nerve impulses from the central nervous system to an effector.

mRNA *See* messenger ribonucleic acid.

mucosa or **mucous membrane** In vertebrates, a moist epithelium and its underlying connective tissue that lines many internal tubes and cavities that open to the exterior.

mucus (adj. **mucous**) (1) In vertebrates, the slippery secretion produced by a mucous membrane.
(2) In invertebrates, a general term for a sticky or slimy secretion.

multicellular Referring to organisms or their parts comprising many cells. *See also* unicellular.

multiple fission Mitosis resulting in many individuals being produced at the same time from one parent cell. Found in some protists, such as the malaria parasite *Plasmodium*.

musculocutaneous nerve A nerve that supplies some of the muscles of the forelimb of a vertebrate.

mutation An abrupt, stable, and inheritable change in the genetic DNA.

mycelium The system of hyphae that forms the vegetative body of a fungus. *See* hypha.

mycology The study of fungi.

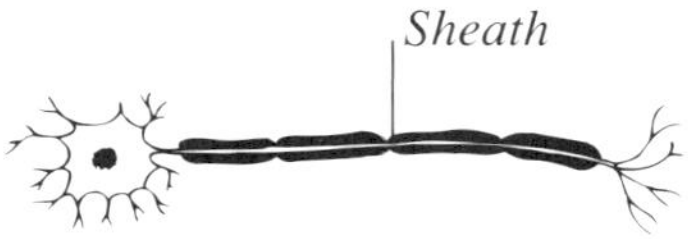

Myelin sheath

myelin sheath An insulating lipoprotein covering around the nerve fibers of many vertebrate and some invertebrate neurons.

myohyoid artery An artery that supplies blood to the lower jaw of vertebrates.

myosin A protein found in muscle cells that, together with actin, forms actomyosin, which provides the contractile mechanism of muscle tissue.

NADP *See* nicotinamide adenine dinucleotide.

nape The back of the neck of a mammal.

nares The passages connecting the nasal cavity to the mouth and nostrils.

nasal bone The bone of the nose.

nasal cavity An open space in the head of a tetrapod. It contains the olfactory organ and is connected by passages (nares) to the mouth and exterior of the animal.

nasute A termite soldier armed with a projection on its head, from which it squirts an adhesive or toxic fluid at enemies.

nectary A gland that produces nectar, a sugary solution, at the base of some flowers. Nectar is attractive to insects and helps facilitate insect pollination.

nematoblast *See* cnidoblast.

nematocyst A sac, the outer end of which is extended into a long, hollow thread, contained within the cnidoblast of coelenterates. The thread is kept coiled and immersed in liquid inside the sac. On stimulation of the cnidocil, it is expelled. There are various types of nematocyst. Some capture or hold prey, others are weapons; some are barbed, others inject venom.

nematode (or roundworm). An almost perfectly cylindrical worm belonging to the class Nematoda. Most are very small, the largest being about 2 inches (5 cm) long. There are a large number of species and many are parasites.

neopallium The main part of the cerebral cortex in humans. It is part of the roof of the cerebrum.

nephridiopore The opening (pore) by which a nephridium connects to the exterior.

nephridium A tube, opening to the exterior and lined with cilia, that is found in many invertebrates. It is concerned with excretion and the regulation of the water content of the body.

nephron The functional unit of a vertebrate kidney, comprising a kidney tubule, Bowman's capsule, and glomerulus.

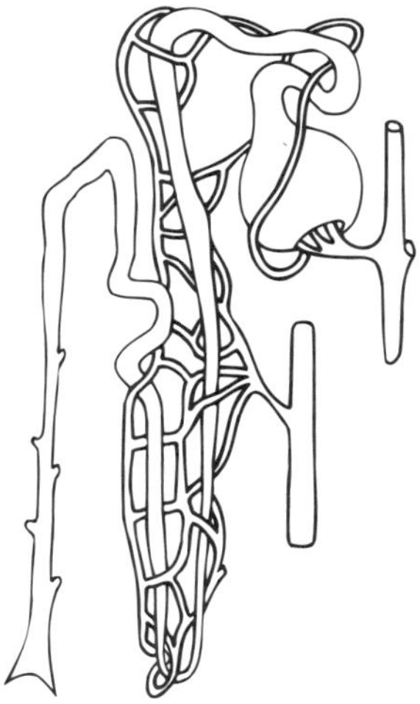

Nephron

nephrostome (1) In vertebrates, the opening of an excretory tubule into the cavity of the Bowman's capsule.
(2) In invertebrates, the opening of a nephridium into the coelom.

nerve A bundle of nerve fibers and their accompanying supportive tissue and blood vessels, enclosed in a common sheath of connective tissue.

nerve cord In invertebrates, a thick strand of nervous tissue running ventrally along the body and forming part of the central nervous system. It is analogous with the spinal cord of vertebrates.

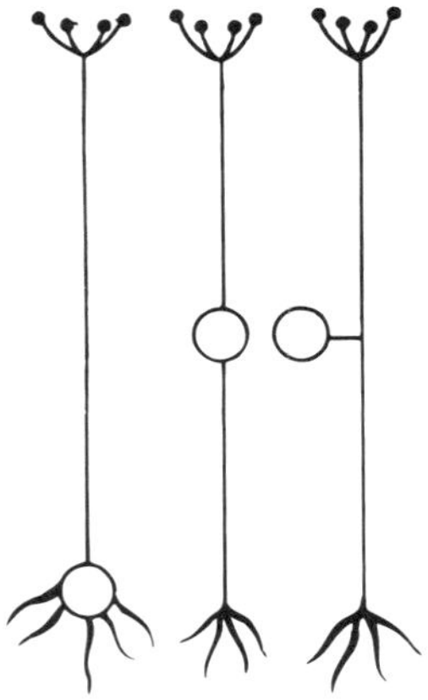
Neurons

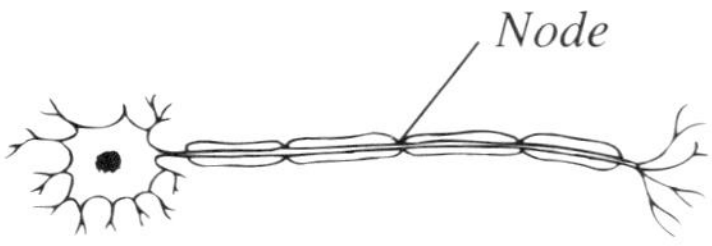

Node of Ranvier

nerve impulse The electrical signal or message conducted along a nerve fiber. It involves a rapid depolarization of the nerve cell membrane, traveling at high speed in one direction. *See* depolarization.

nervous system In multicellular animals, a network of cells that conducts electrical impulses that control the body.

neural arch An arch on the centrum of each vertebra through which the spinal cord runs.

neural spine A dorsal projection from the center of the neural arch.

neuron A nerve cell.

neuropodium The ventral part of the parapodium of a bristleworm (Polychaeta).

nicotinamide adenine dinucleotide (**NADP**) The most important hydrogen carrier (and hence electron carrier) in biological oxidation-reduction reactions, such as those associated with photosynthesis and respiration.

nictitating membrane A membrane resembling an eyelid that is found in some vertebrates. It is attached at the corner of the eye and is semitransparent. When drawn across the eye, like a third eyelid, it cleans and moistens the surface of the eye without excluding light.

nipple (or teat). A conical projection at the center of each mammary gland where milk ducts converge and open to the exterior.

nitrate The nitrate ion (NO_3^-). This inorganic ion is readily absorbed by plants and in soil and water is an important source of nitrogen.

nitrite bacteria Soil bacteria that, in the presence of oxygen, convert ammonium compounds into nitrites.

nitrogen-fixing bacteria Soil bacteria and symbiotic bacteria living in root nodules that convert atmospheric nitrogen into nitrogen compounds that can then be utilized by other organisms.

node A region on the plant stem from which one or more leaves arise.

node of Ranvier A gap, at regular intervals, in the myelin sheath surrounding the nerve fibers of sensory and motor neurons. Such nodes speed the conduction of nerve impulses along these fibers.

non-competitive inhibitor A substance that inhibits enzyme action by binding irreversibly with the active site of an enzyme.

non-disjunction Failure of a pair of homologous chromosomes to separate during meiosis. As a result, one daughter cell has an extra chromosome and the other has one too few.

non-polar An absence of charge separation on the surface of a molecule. Such molecules tend to dissolve in non-polar solvents.

norepinephrine (**noradrenaline**) *See* epinephrine.

nostril The external opening of the passages (nares) leading to the nasal cavity.

notochord A structure that extends almost the entire length of the body of chordates (and gives the phylum Chordata its name). It lies ventral to the nerve cord and provides flexible support to the body. In vertebrates it is wholly or partly replaced by the vertebral column in the course of embryonic development.

notopodium The dorsal part of the parapodium in bristleworms (Polychaeta).

nuchal Pertaining to the nape of the neck.

nuclear envelope *See* nuclear membrane.

nuclear membrane Two membranes separated by a space that enclose the nucleus of a eukaryotic cell, separating it from the cytoplasm.

nuclear pore A pore in the nuclear membrane through which substances can enter and leave the nucleus.

nucleolus An organelle found inside the nucleus of eukaryotic cells. It is where ribosomes are synthesized.

nucleoplasm The ground substance within the nucleus. *See* cytoplasm.

nucleotide A molecule or molecular subunit comprising a pentose sugar, a phosphate group (phosphoric acid derivative), and a purine or pyrimidine base. It is a key constituent of nucleic acids and other important biological molecules such as ATP and NADP.

nucleus (pl. **nuclei**) (1) In eukaryotic cells, the region surrounded by a nuclear membrane and containing the genetic material.
(2) In an atom, the central region containing one or more protons and (with the exception of hydrogen) neutrons.

nuptial pad A thick or horny pad on each thumb that helps a male frog to grasp the female during the sexual embrace.

nutrition The process by which an organism obtains the food supplies it needs to build and maintain its body.

nymph An immature stage in the life cycle of an insect that exhibits incomplete metamorphosis (via a series of gradual changes).

Obelia A genus of colonial cnidarians.

obliquus abdominis One of the muscles of the abdominal wall in vertebrates.

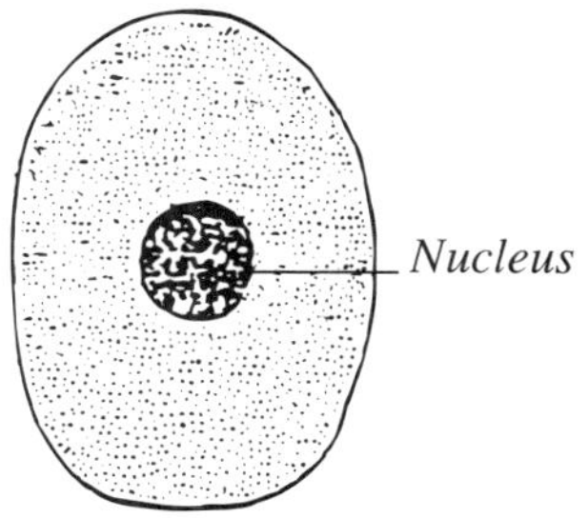

Nucleus

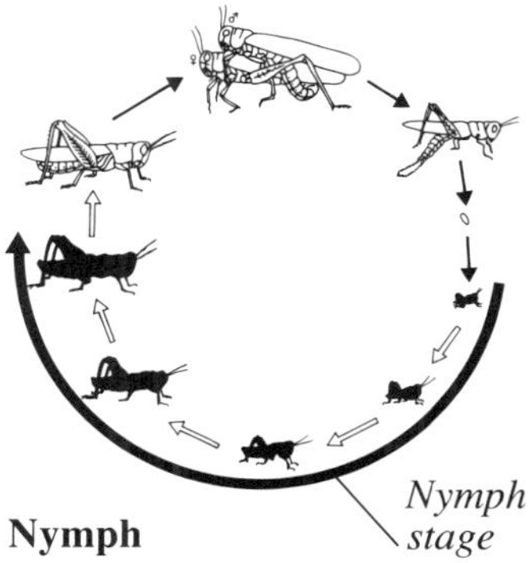

Nymph

obtect Describes insect pupae in which the body appendages adhere to the body.

obturator foramen The large opening in the pelvis of a mammal between the pubis and ischium.

obturator nerve The nerve that supplies the muscles of the upper hindlimb and knee of vertebrates.

occipital At the back.

occipital condyle A double projection of bone at the back of the skull in amphibians and mammals, but absent in most fish. It articulates with the first vertebra.

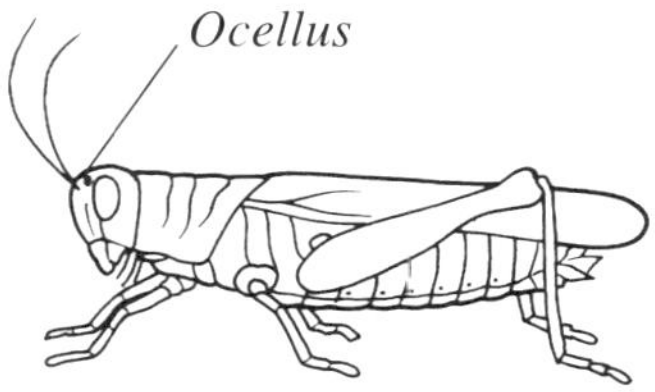

Ocellus

occiput (1) The back of the vertebrate cranium.
(2) The plates that cover the head of an insect.

occlusal Describes the biting or grinding surfaces of teeth.

ocellus (pl. **ocelli**) A simple eye, found in some invertebrates. It consists of a depression served by many light-sensitive nerves above which there is a single lens.

ocular plate One of the small plates, found in some echinoderms, that alternate with the genital plates.

oculomotor nerve The third cranial nerve in vertebrates. It serves the muscles that move the eyeball.

olfaction The sense of smell.

olfactory Pertaining to the sense of smell.

Oligocene A geological epoch, part of the Tertiary peiod, lasting from about 34–23.8 million years before the present.

omasum The third chamber of the three- or four-chambered stomach of a ruminant. It lies between the reticulum and the abomasum and is where water is absorbed.

ommatidium (pl. **ommatidia**) One of the light-sensitive units (facets) of a compound eye.

omotransversarius A muscle connecting the shoulder and upper forelimb in mammals.

onchosphere (or hexacanth). The six-hooked embryo that hatches from the egg and, if it enters a suitable host, develops into a larva.

oocyte In animals, a cell undergoing meiosis that will later give rise to an ovum.

oogenesis In animals, the formation of ova.

oogonium (1) A reproductive organ in some fungi and multicellular algae that produces female gametes (termed oospheres).
(2) In animals, a cell that undergoes repeated mitosis to form oocytes.

operculum (1) In bony fish, the flap covering the gills.
(2) A plate covering the entrance of the shell in some snails.
(3) The lid covering the tip of a moss capsule.

operon A cluster of closely linked genes comprising one or more structural genes, which produce enzymes for a given metabolic pathway, together with the regulatory genes that control their activity.

ophthalmic Relating to the eye.

opisthocoelous Describes a vertebra that has a concave posterior surface.

opisthosoma The posterior section of the body of a spider or mite.

optic nerve In vertebrates, the cranial nerve that supplies the eye.

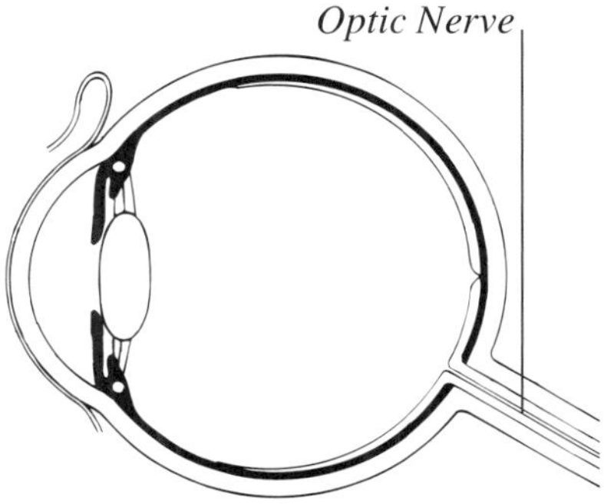

Optic Nerve

oral Referring to the mouth.

oral spine A moveable spine close to the mouth of an echinoderm.

orbicularis muscle A muscle that controls the face in the region around the eye (orbit) and eyelids or around the mouth.

orbit In vertebrates, a bony cavity in the skull that houses the eyeball.

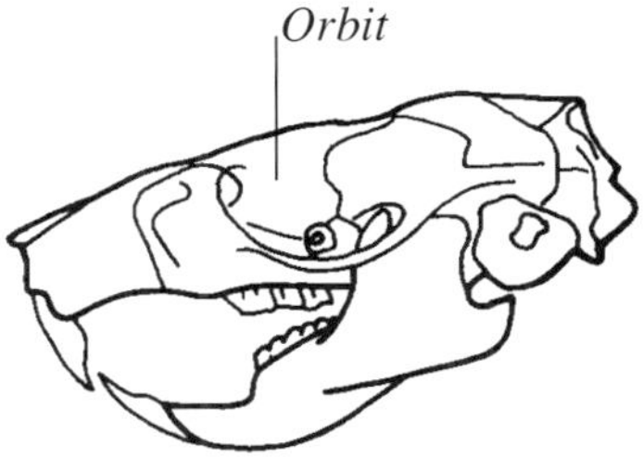

Orbit

orbitosphenoid A bone that forms part of the skull of rodents and lagomorphs (rabbits, hares, and pikas). It lies below the orbit and posterior to the lachrymal.

organ In plants and animals, a structure comprising several tissues that forms a functional unit, e.g., heart, lung, leaf, bulb. (*See also* illustration on page 82.)

organelle A specialized region of the cell that carries out particular functions, e.g., a mitochondrion. In eukaryotic cells, organelles are usually surrounded by a membrane.

organism An individual living thing. It comprises one or more cells.

organ system or **system** In plants and animals, several organs whose coordinated activity performs a given function or functions, e.g., the heart and blood vessels are parts of the circulatory system.

osculum (pl. **oscula**) In sponges, the opening through which water leaves.

osmoregulation Regulation of the body's salt and water balance.

osmosis Passage of water through a selectively permeable (semipermeable) membrane. Net movement is down a water potential gradient.

Organs (see entry on page 81)

Main organs of the human body
a Brain The brain receives information from the senses, and controls the rest of the body.
b Stomach The stomach stores food and begins to digest it.
c Heart The heart pumps blood around the body.
d Lungs Lungs take in oxygen from the the air, and get rid of carbon dioxide.
e Liver The liver performs hundreds of jobs, including releasing nutrients into the blood.
f Kidneys Kidneys filter water, salt, and poisonous waste out of the blood to make urine.

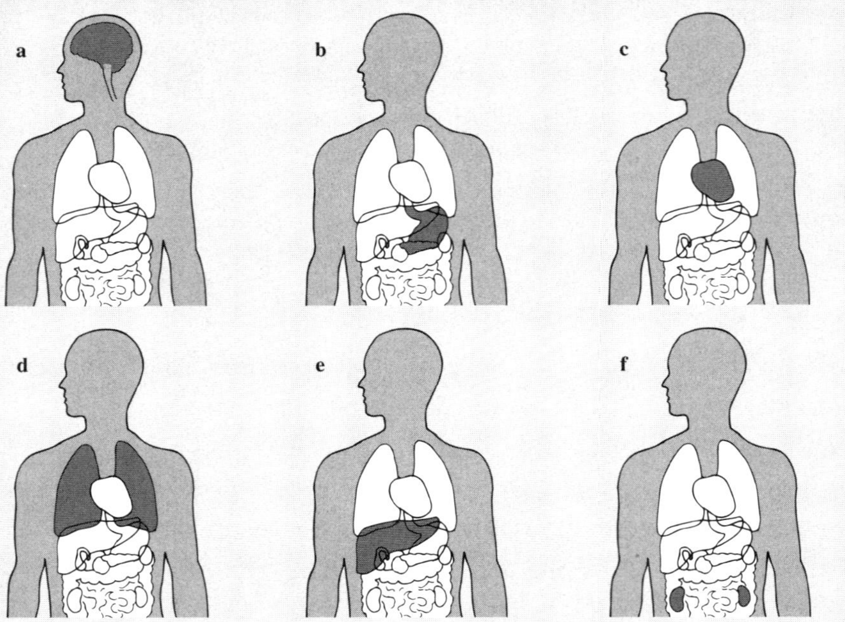

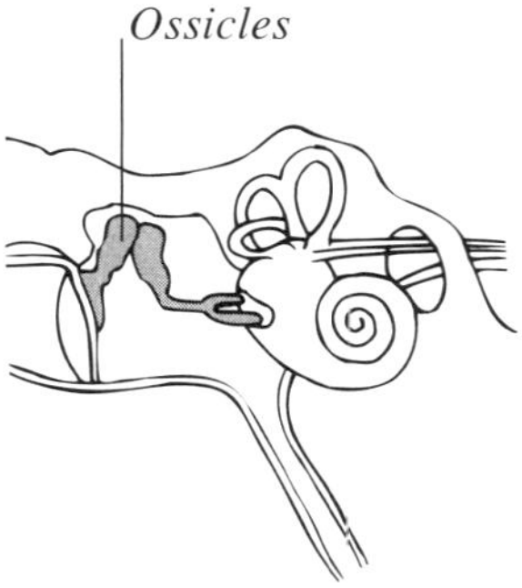

Ossicles *(of middle ear)*

ossicle (1) A small bone, especially one of the bones of the middle ear.
(2) One of the plates in an echinoderm that together form a lattice bound together with connective tissue. This comprises the skeleton of the animal.

osteichthyes The class that includes all the bony fish. They have skeletons made from bone, gill chambers covered by a gill cover, bony scales in the skin, and, in most species, a swim bladder.

ostium (pl. **ostia**) (1) In sponges (Porifera), one of many openings through which water is drawn into the body.
(2) In arthropods, an opening from the sinus (blood-filled space) surrounding the heart.

otolith In vertebrates, one of several chalky granules in the inner ear that, when displaced, signal position and movement of the head. Similar structures are found in sensory organs of some invertebrates.

ovarian artery and vein The blood vessels that supply the ovaries of a female mammal.

ovarian tubule A long, tubular extension from the ovary of an arthropod.

ovariole A small tube that with others makes up the ovary of an arthropod.

ovary (1) In flowering plants, the lower region of the carpel. It contains one or more ovules.
(2) In female animals, the organ that produces ova. In vertebrates, the ovary also produces a range of sex hormones.

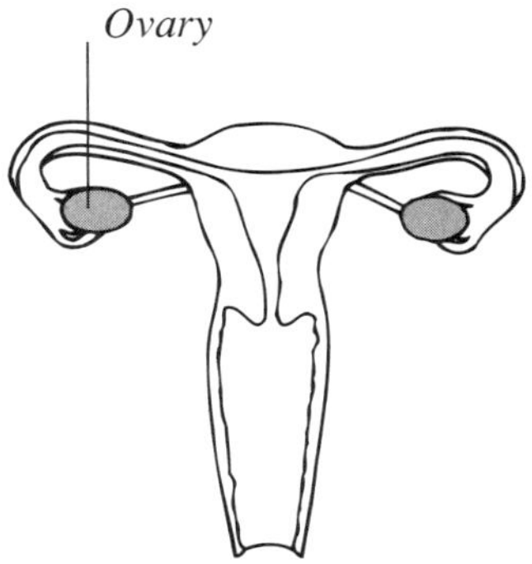

Ovary

oviducal funnel The common origin of the two oviducts in a female shark.

oviduct In female animals, the tube that carries ova from the ovary toward the exterior of the body.

ovipositor In female insects, a tubelike organ at the hind end of the abdomen through which eggs are laid.

ovisac A sac within the oviduct of many invertebrates where eggs are stored while they undergo certain stages in their development.

ovotestis The gland in a hermaphrodite animal, such as a snail, that produces both male and female gametes.

ovovitelline duct *See* oviduct.

ovulation In vertebrates, the release of a ripe ovum or oocyte from a follicle on the surface of an ovary.

ovule In seed-bearing plants, a structure within the ovary. When a female gamete inside it is fertilized, the ovule develops into a seed.

ovuliferous scale In cone-bearing plants, a surface structure that protects the developing seeds in a female cone. In a mature cone, the scales curl to release the seeds.

ovum (pl. **ova**) In animals, a mature female gamete or egg cell prior to fertilization. In many cases, the ovum is an oocyte.

oxidation A chemical reaction involving the addition of oxygen or the removal of electrons or hydrogen atoms. It always occurs in tandem with reduction, hence redox reactions. *See* redox, reduction.

oxidative phosphorylation The phosphorylation of ADP to ATP utilizing energy released during aerobic respiration.

oxytocin In birds and mammals, a polypeptide hormone produced by the posterior pituitary gland and secreted by the hypothalamus. In mammals, it triggers uterine contractions during labor and promotes milk release.

pacemaker *See* sino-atrial (SA) node.

pachydont A type of dentition found in some bivalve mollusks where there are few hinge teeth, but those present are big and heavy.

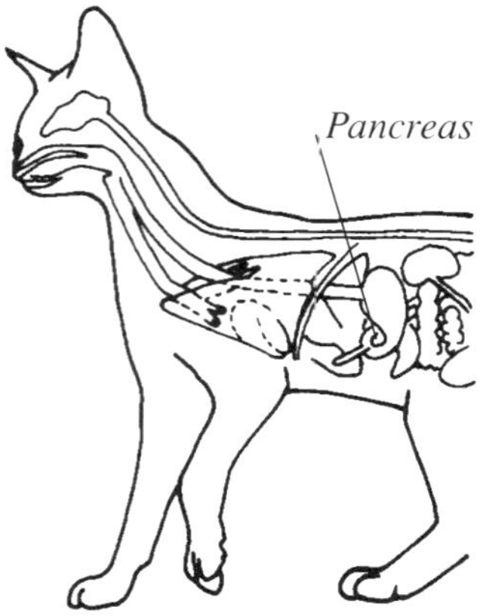

Pancreas

palate The roof of the mouth of a vertebrate. It separates the nasal and mouth cavities.

palatine Referring to the palate.

palatoquadrate A cartilage that forms part of the upper jaw of sharks.

palmaris longus A narrow muscle extending from the humerus to the carpus of a mammal. The palmaris brevis is a shorter muscle. In humans it is on the palms of the hand.

palmate Shaped like the palm of a hand, with spreading lobes that are united at one end.

palp A sensory structure possessed by many invertebrates and located near the mouth. Palps are usually associated with feeding.

pancreas A gland located between the duodenum and spleen in vertebrates. It secretes several digestive enzymes through a duct into the duodenum and contains groups of cells known as islets of Langerhans. The latter secrete glucagon and insulin.

papilla (pl. **papillae**) A small protuberance arising from the surface of an organ or organism. Papilla can be found on the tongue and in the kidneys as well as on the surface of many petals.

pappus (pl. **pappi**) A ring of fine hairs on the small dry fruits of flowering plants belonging to the family Compositae, e.g., dandelion. It acts as a parachute and aids in wind dispersal.

paragaster The internal cavity of a sponge.

parapodium A projection from part of the body of an invertebrate that is used either for locomotion or to fan water from which food particles are ingested.

parasite An organism that lives on or in another organism (its host) from which it gains food and often protection. A parasite causes some harm to its host but does not usually kill it.

parasitology The study of parasites and their interactions with hosts.

parasympathetic nervous system (**PNS**) In vertebrates, part of the autonomic nervous system. Its activity promotes digestion, the elimination of waste, the slowing of heart beat, and tends to bring physiological conditions to near normal, in contrast to the sympathetic nervous system.

parathyroid gland An endocrine gland that secretes a hormone that controls the concentration of calcium in the blood. The gland is located in the

Pappus

neck, near the thyroid gland. There are usually two pairs of parathyroids.

paratoid gland One of a pair of glands found in some toads. They lie near the eyes, neck, or shoulders. In some species the glands secrete toxins.

paraxonic Describes the condition in which the weight of an animal passes between the third and fourth digits.

parenchyma In plants, a packing tissue typically composed of large, thin-walled cells, sometimes with air spaces between. Mesophyll, pith, and cortex comprise mostly unspecialized parenchyma cells.

parietal One of a pair of bones that form most of the posterior part of the roof of the brain case in a vertebrate skull.

pastern The foreleg of a horse between the fetlock and the top of the hoof.

patagium A fold of skin that grows between the fore- and hindlimbs of a mammal. It is used like a wing in gliding or flying.

patella The kneecap, a bone located in front of the knee joint. It is present in most mammals and some reptiles and birds. The patella ligament passes over the bone, linking the muscles of the femur to those of the tibia.

Patella

pectinate Shaped like a comb.

pectinius muscle A flat muscle on the anterior side of the upper part of the hindlimb of a vertebrate.

pectoral In vertebrates, referring to the shoulder region or the region from which the anterior fins or limbs emerge.

pectoral girdle The shoulder girdle, comprising the bones that support the forelimbs or fins of a vertebrate.

pectoralis Two muscles, pectoralis major and, beneath it, pectoralis minor, on the ventral side of the pectoral girdle of a vertebrate.

pedal Pertaining to the foot.

pedicel (1) In insects, the second segment of the antenna.
(2) In spiders, the "stalk" connecting the prosoma and abdomen.
(3) In ants, bees, and wasps, the petiole.

pedipalp In arachnids, one member of the second pair of head appendages. In different species it serves as a mouthpart, sensory organ, or weapon.

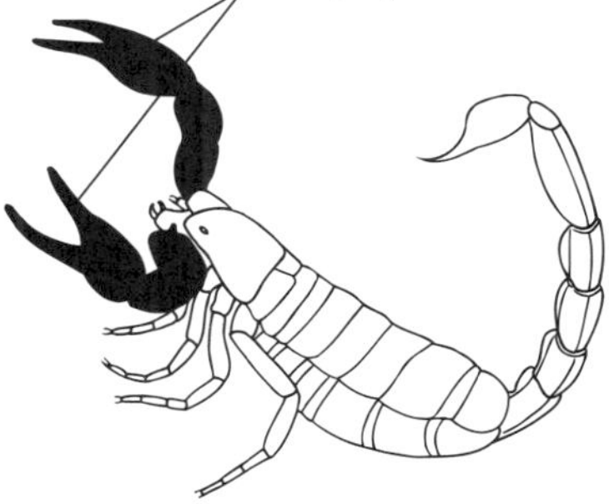

Pedipalp

peduncle (1) A synonym for pedicel.
(2) *See* caudal peduncle.

pelage The coat of a mammal, made from hair.

pelvic Pertaining to the pelvis.

pelvic girdle The hip girdle, comprising the bones that support the hindlimbs of a vertebrate.

pelvis The principal bone of the pelvic girdle.

pen The much reduced internal shell of a squid.

penis The organ with which a male animal transfers sperm to the female for internal fertilization or to eggs laid by the female for external fertilization.

pentadactyl Describes a limb that ends with five digits or that is evolutionarily modified from an ancestral form that possessed five digits. This is the characteristic limb in all tetrapods.

pepsin In vertebrates, a protease (protein-splitting enzyme) that hydrolyzes proteins to peptides. It is found in the gastric juice secreted by glands in the stomach walls.

peptide bond The bond that links two amino acids. It is formed by a condensation reaction between the carboxyl group of one amino acid and the amino group of the next.

pereiopod In crustacea, a thoracic appendage modifed for use as a walking leg.

pericardium (1) The sac that contains the heart.
(2) The cavity surrounding the heart.

perilymph The viscous fluid that surrounds the semicircular canals, utricule, and saccule of the inner ear. It protects these structures from mechanical injury and conducts vibrations from the middle ear.

periotic bone The single bone that surrounds the ear of a mammal.

peripheral nervous system (PNS) In animals, the part of the nervous system outside the central nervous system. In vertebrates, it largely comprises the nerves connecting the brain and spinal cord with sense organs and effectors.

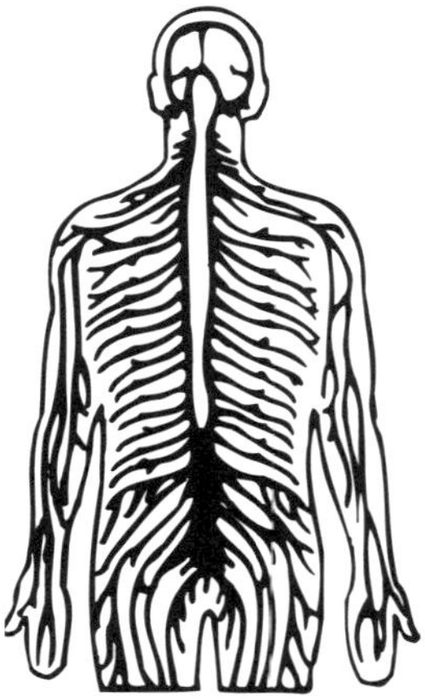

Peripheral nervous system

perisarc The cylindrical sheath that surrounds most colonial hydroids.

perissodactyl A mammal that belongs to the order Perissodactyla. It includes horses and rhinoceroses, animals with hoofs in which the weight is borne by the central digit. There are usually one or three functional toes. If a fourth is present, it is reduced in size. *See also* artiodactyl.

peristalsis Waves of contraction that pass along the muscular walls of tubular organs, such as parts of the alimentary canal. They mix and move the contents inside the tube.

peristome or **peristomium** The tissue surrounding the mouth of an invertebrate.

peroneal nerve A nerve in the lower hindlimb of vertebrates that is a branch from the internal popliteal nerve, behind the knee. It passes around the limb to the top of the fibula.

peroneus muscles Three muscles (peroneus longus, brevis, and tertius) on the upper part of the hindlimb of a vertebrate.

perradial canal A canal that branches from one of the radial canals of a medusa (jellyfish).

petal One of the leaf-like organs comprising the corolla of a flower. Petals are often brightly colored to attract insects. *See* flower.

petiole (1) The stalk that attaches the leaf blade to the stem. (2) The narrow stalk (the "wasp waist") that separates the thorax and gaster of bees, wasps, ants, and sawflies (Hymenoptera). *See* gaster.

phagocytosis The engulfing and subsequent ingestion of a pathogen or food item by a cell. It involves cytoplasm flowing around the item and then enclosing it in a vacuole.

phalange In tetrapod vertebrates, bones of the digits (fingers or toes).

pharynx In vertebrates, the part of the alimentary canal between the mouth and the esophagus. In tetrapods, the respiratory tract connects with it through the glottis. In fish, the gill slits arise from it.

phenotype The physical characteristic(s) of an individual produced by the expression of the organism's genotype. *See* genotype.

phloem In plants, specialized tissue that transports (translocates) food from regions where it is made or stored to other regions where it is stored or metabolized.

phosphate Like nitrate, it is an inorganic ion present in soil and is an important plant nutrient. Phosphate (PO_4^{3-}) is also a key component of ATP, nucleic acids, and other nucleotide-based molecules.

phosphoester bond The bond between a phosphate group and an ester, e.g., phosphate and a diglyceride bond to make a phospholipid.

phospholipid Any of a range of lipids in combination with one or more phosphate groups. Phospholipids are a major component of membranes.

phosphorylation The reaction in which a phosphate group is added to a molecule.

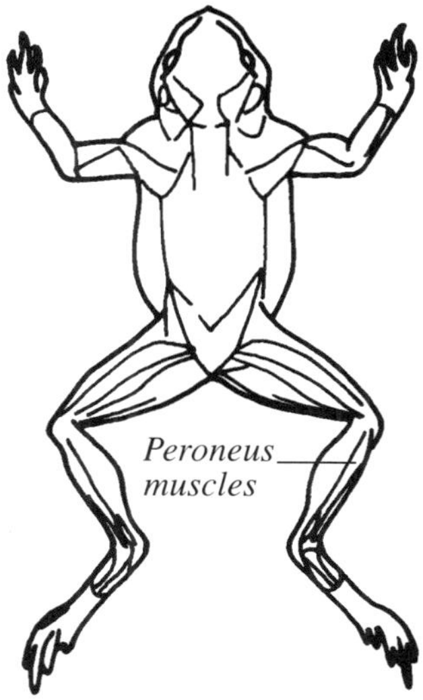

Peroneus muscles

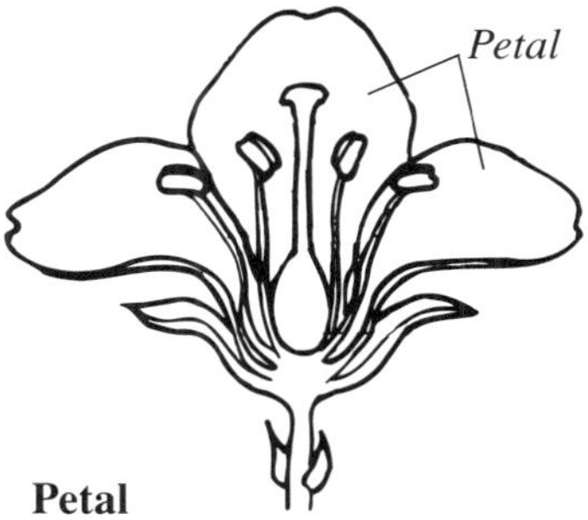

Petal

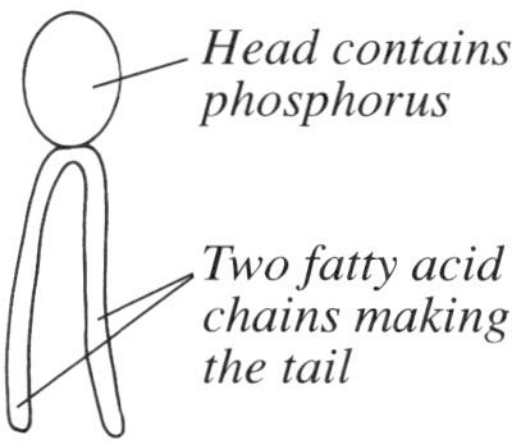

Phospholipid

photoautotrophic Referring to organisms that require light as a source of energy to manufacture their own organic nutrients from inorganic raw materials.

photophosphorylation The phosphorylation of ADP to ATP using light energy absorbed in photosynthesis. Cyclic photophosphorylation results in ATP production only, whereas noncyclic photophosphorylation also yields hydrogen atoms.

photosynthesis In green plants, blue-green algae (cyanobacteria), and certain bacteria and protists, the capturing of light energy and its storage as chemical energy in organic molecules synthesized from carbon dioxide and water. Oxygen is also produced.

photosystem A cluster of pigments associated with the light-dependent reactions of photosynthesis. Two kinds are recognized: photosystem I, which is involved in both cyclic and noncyclic photophosphylation, and photosystem II, which is involved in noncyclic photophosphorylation only.

phototropism In plants, a tropic response (tropism) to light.

physiology The study of how organisms work—the processes by which their bodies function.

pili (sing. **pilus**) Ultramicroscopic hair-like structures on the surface of a bacterium. They may be involved in agglutination or conjugation.

pilose Covered with down of fine hairs.

pin bone Part of the pelvis of cattle that forms a protrusion behind the rump.

pineal body *See* pineal gland.

pineal eye *See* median eye.

pineal gland or **pineal body** An outgrowth of the forebrain. The posterior part, called the epiphysis, secretes melatonin, a hormone affecting pigmentation in fish and amphibians, control of the circadian rhythm, and the development of the gonads. The anterior part resembles an eye in some species (*see* median eye). The pineal gland is absent in adult humans.

Pinna

pinna (pl. **pinnae**) (1) In ferns, the leaf-like structure that is part of a frond and itself comprises many pinnules.
(2) In mammals, the external flap of skin and cartilage forming part of the outer ear.

pinnate Carried on both sides of a central stem, like the barbs of a feather.

pinocytosis The engulfing and subsequent ingestion of liquid by a cell. It involves the cytoplasm infolding to surround a drop of liquid and then completely engulfing it to form a vesicle.

pistil In flowering plants: (1) Another name for the gynecium, the female reproductive organ comprising ovary, style, and stigma. (2) Each carpel of a gynecium that contains several.

pith In dicotyledonous plants, the central core of parenchyma in the stem and in some roots.

pituitary gland or **pituitary body** In vertebrates, an endocrine gland situated just below the hypothalamus, with which it is closely connected. The pituitary's anterior lobe secretes ACTH and growth hormone; its posterior lobe secretes vasopressin and oxytocin.

placenta (1) In plants, the part of the ovary wall that bears ovules. (2) In placental mammals (eutherians), a vascular organ in the pregnant female's uterus. It exchanges oxygen and nutrients between the blood of the mother and that of the fetus.

placoid scale (or dermal denticle). A fish scale of the type that covers the skin of cartilaginous fish, such as sharks. Made largely from dentine and projecting outward from the surface of the body, it consists of a hard base, which is embedded in the skin, and has a tip that appears to be like a spine.

plankton Buoyant, generally small organisms that drift on currents in the water column in sea or freshwater.

plant A member of the kingdom Plantae. Plants are autotrophic, have cellulose cell walls, react more slowly than animals to stimuli, and are unable to move freely (apart from certain motile microscopic plants).

plantigrade Describes a gait in which the entire base (sole) of the foot makes contact with the surface. Humans have a plantigrade gait.

planula The characteristic ciliated larva of cnidarians.

plasma (or blood plasma). In vertebrates, the clear, fluid part of blood in which blood cells and platelets are suspended.

plasmagel Another name for ectoplasm, the cytoplasm that is in a gel-like state. *See* ectoplasm.

plasma membrane The membrane surrounding a prokaryotic or eukaryotic cell composed of protein and fat (lipid) molecules.

plasmasol Another name for endoplasm, the cytoplasm that is in a near-liquid state. *See* endoplasm.

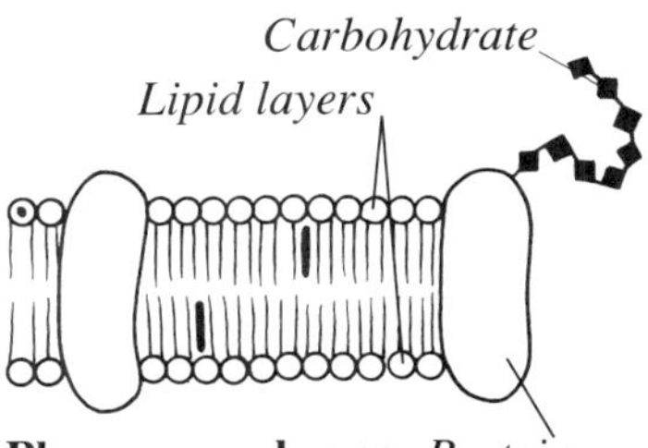

Plasma membrane

plasmid A small circular DNA molecule found in some bacteria and fungi. It is able to replicate independently of the organism's chromosomes. Plasmids are commonly used in genetic engineering as vehicles for transferring genes.

plasmodesma (pl. **plasmodesmata**) In plants, a fine cytoplasmic thread connecting the cytoplasm of one cell with that of its neighbor.

plastron The lower part of the shell of a turtle.

platelet In mammals, one of numerous cell fragments suspended in the blood. Platelets release thrombokinase, an enzyme involved in blood clotting.

Platelets

Structure and functions	Number per mm³ of blood	Life span	Cell type
Structure Platelets are not strictly cells. They are fragments of cells called megakaryocytes and do not have a nucleus. In vertebrates other than mammals, the equivalent cells are called thrombocytes; these do have a nucleus. **Functions** Platelets (and thrombocytes) assist in blood clotting.	250,000–500,000 Percentage of total blood composition: less than 1% Percentage of total blood cells: less than 2%	5–10 days	 2–4 µm diameter

Platyhelminthes Flatworms. An animal phylum that includes planarians, flukes, and tapeworms.

platyrrhine Describes the nostrils of a primate if these are widely separated and face to the sides. *See also* catarrhine.

Pleistocene A geological epoch, the first part of the Quaternary period, lasting from about 1.8 million–10,000 years before the present.

pleopod One of the appendages utilized by crustaceans for swimming, seizing food, carrying eggs, burrowing, making water currents, or for gas exchange in respiration. In males they are also used in copulation.

pleura (pl. **pleurae**) In birds and mammals, the membrane lining the lung (pulmonary) cavity and covering the lung surface.

pleural Referring to the lungs.

pleural cavity A space that surrounds the lungs of a mammal. It is filled with fluid and separated by the diaphragm from the abdominal cavity.

Pliocene A geological epoch, part of the Tertiary period, lasting from about 5.3–1.8 million years before the present.

plumule (1) In a seed plant, the terminal bud of the embryo from which the stem and first true leaves develop.
(2) In birds, a down feather.

pneumatophore In siphonophores, such as the Portuguese man o'war, a polyp that resembles a bladder and acts as a float.

pneumostome A small opening, like that into the respiratory cavity of a snail. The aperture allows air to enter.

PNS *See* parasympathetic nervous system, peripheral nervous system.

poikilotherm (or exotherm). An organism in which the body temperature fluctuates with the temperature of its surroundings. Invertebrates and fish are poikilotherms.

polar Referring to a molecule with charge separation on its surface. Such molecules tend to dissolve in polar solvents to form ions.

polar body In vertebrates, one of two cells formed in the meiotic divisions that lead to the formation of an oocyte. Polar bodies are redundant cells whereas the oocyte has the potential to become an ovum.

poll In some mammals, the top of the head between the ears.

pollen In seed-bearing plants, the microspores containing male gametophytes. They are usually carried by wind or insects to reach ovules, in cone-bearing plants, or stigmas, in flowering plants. *See* pollination.

pollen basket (or corbiculum). The modified tibia of the hind leg of a worker honeybee or female bumblebee. The outer surface of the tibia is bordered by strong hairs that form a flexible basket in which pollen is carried.

pollen brush or **pollen packer** The simplest structure for carrying pollen, found in some bees but not in honeybees or bumblebees. It consists of hairs on a hind leg or below the abdomen in some leaf-cutting bees. The bee combs pollen from its body with its front legs, moistens the pollen, and passes it to the back legs. With these it packs the pollen into its pollen basket.

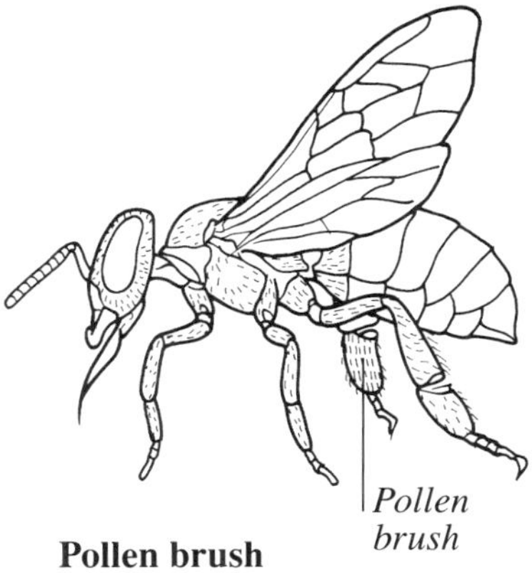

Pollen brush

pollex The digit on the side of the radius in the pentadactyl forelimb. In humans it is the thumb.

pollination The process in which pollen is carried from the male cone to female cone in cone-bearing plants, or from anther to the surface of the stigma, in flowering plants. This transport is usually facilitated by wind or insects.

polyp In cnidarians, the sessile stage of the life cycle. It has a tubular (hydroid) form.

polypeptide A molecule formed of a long chain of amino acids joined by peptide bonds. A protein is composed of one or more polypeptides.

polyploid Describing a nucleus, cell, or organism having three or more times the haploid number of chromosomes. *See also* haploid, diploid.

polysaccharide A long-chain carbohydrate formed by joining together many single sugar units (monosaccharides). Examples include starch and glycogen, used as energy stores, and cellulose, the dominant structural material in plant cell walls.

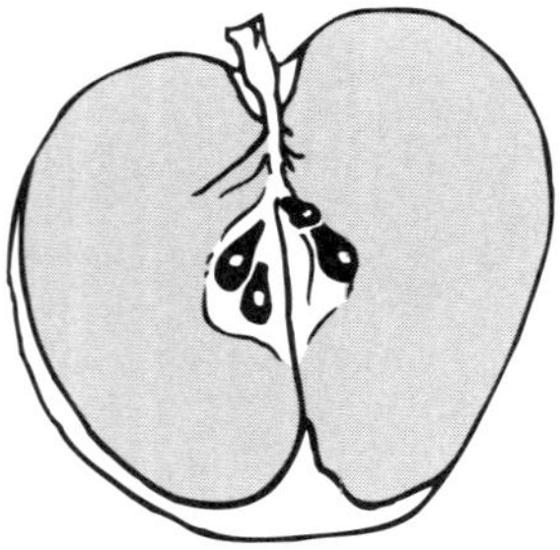

Pome (apple)

pome A "false" fruit (pseudocarp) that has developed from the receptacle, rather than from the ovary wall. For example, in an apple the flesh is the receptacle while the true fruit is the core.

pons or **pons Varolii** In mammals, a tract of nerve fibers that connects the medulla oblongata with the midbrain.

Porifera (sponges) A phylum of aquatic animals, mostly marine but some of them freshwater, that have no definite organs or tissues. They reproduce sexually. Pieces cut from a living sponge can grow into an entire animal.

porocyte A cell that guards the ostium of a sponge.

portal Referring to a vein that carries blood from one capillary system to another, rather than returning blood to the heart.

post- A prefix denoting "behind" or "after."

postcaval vein *See* vena cava.

posterior Furthest from the head. Situated at or toward the hind end of an animal. *See also* anterior.

postfrontal The posterior of three bones (prefrontal, frontal, postfrontal) in the skull of some vertebrates.

posttrematic A nerve at the back of the head of a shark, posterior to the pretrematic.

precaval vein *See* vena cava.

prefemur The segment of a centipede's leg between the trochanter and femur.

prefrontal The anterior of three bones (prefrontal, frontal, postfrontal) in the skull of some vertebrates.

premaxilla The bone that forms the anterior section of the upper jaw in vertebrates. In mammals it bears the incisors and in birds it comprises most of the upper bill.

premolar In mammals, one of several crushing teeth at either side of upper and lower jaws. They are situated in front of the molars and usually have two roots. Unlike molars, they are present in the milk teeth.

preopercular A bone in the head of fish located anterior to the opercular that covers and protects the gills.

pretrematic A nerve at the back of the head of a shark, anterior to the posttrematic.

primary feather One of the large, outer feathers of a bird that are used in flight. Birds have between 10 and 12 primaries.

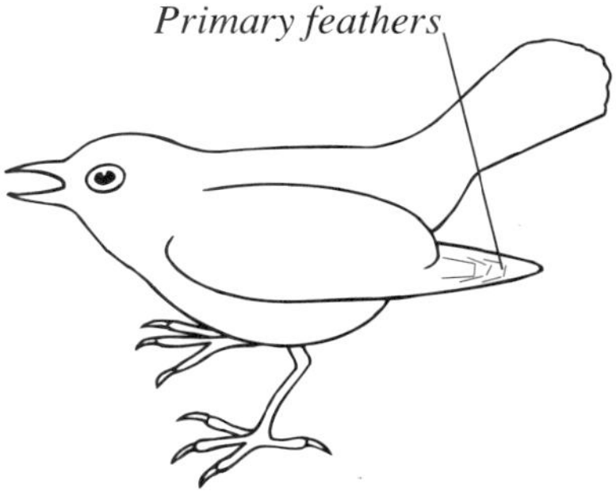

Primary feather

pro- A prefix denoting "before."

proboscis (1) A long flexible nose, as in an elephant.
(2) A tubular, sucking organ with a mouth at the end, as in planarians and certain leeches, or comprising mouthparts, as in certain insects.

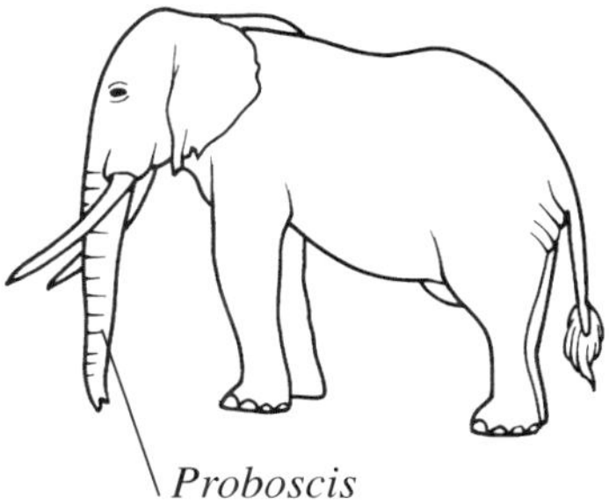

Proboscis

procelous Describes a vertebra that has a concave anterior surface.

procumbent Projecting forward almost horizontally.

producer In ecology, an organism such as a photosynthetic plant or bacterium able to manufacture its own food from inorganic substances, i.e., an autotroph. Ultimately, consumers depend on producers for their food. *See* autotrophic, consumer.

product A new substance formed as the result of a chemical reaction.

progesterone In mammals, a steroid hormone produced by the corpus luteum of the mammalian ovary and, during pregnancy, by the placenta. The hormone prepares the uterus for implantation of an ovum and for the subsequent nourishment and protection of the developing embryo and fetus.

proglottid or **proglottis** One of many segmentlike portions in a tapeworm. Each proglottid contains a set of reproductive organs.

prokaryotes Bacteria and blue-green algae (cyanobacteria): unicellular organisms that lack a true nucleus and membrane-bound organelles. The genetic material is suspended in the cytoplasm rather than surrounded by a nuclear membrane. (*See also* illustration on page 94.)

prolactin In mammals, a polypeptide hormone secreted by the anterior pituitary. In females, its effects include promoting breast development during pregnancy and milk production after childbirth.

Prokaryotes (see entry on page 93)

Prokaryotic cells These are the unicellular organisms called bacteria and cyanobacteria.

- Prokaryotic cells are small;
- simple in structure;
- lack a true nucleus;
- do not have membrane-enclosed organelles; and
- do not have an extensive cytoskeleton.
- Cilia and flagella (**a**) may be present.
- They usually have a rigid cell wall (**b**) outside the cell membrane (**c**).
- Prokaryotic cells are believed to have evolved before eukaryotic cells.

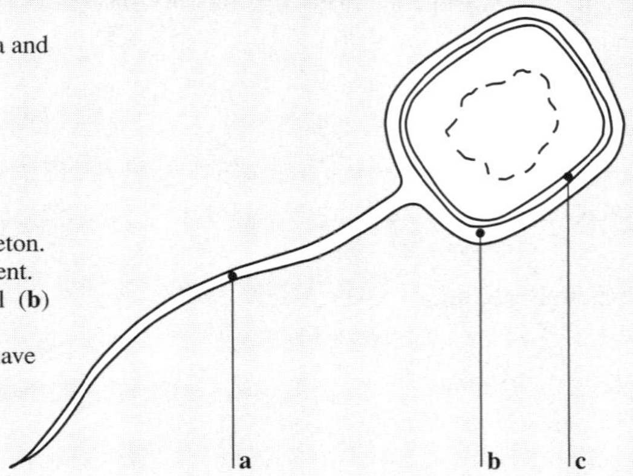

promoter A region of DNA to which RNA polymerase must bind before transcription of a nearby DNA sequence can take place.

pronator teres A muscle in humans that passes across the forearm and allows the hand to be turned so the palm faces upward or downward.

prootic One of the skull bones in many vertebrates, absent from mammals.

prop root In plants, a root that grows downward to the ground from a stem, trunk, or branch. It provides support.

prophase The first stage of mitosis or meiosis. Chromosomes appear in the nucleus and, in meiosis, homologous chromosomes pair.

prosoma In arachnids, the combined head and thorax.

prostate gland A gland, found in male animals, associated with reproductive systems. In mammals it secretes substances into the semen.

prostomium A segment that overhangs the mouth of an annelid. In the sandworm, it bears two pairs of eyes and a pair of tentacles.

protein An organic molecule composed of one or more polypeptide chains. Proteins have fundamental structural and metabolic roles in cells and tissues. For example, all enzymes are proteins.

protein synthesis The process by which cells manufacture proteins from constituent amino acids. It is based on the genetic information in the DNA of the chromosomes.

Protista The kingdom of unicellular eukaryotes. It includes animal-like forms, e.g., *Amoeba*; plantlike forms, e.g., *Euglena*; and colonial forms, e.g., *Volvox*.

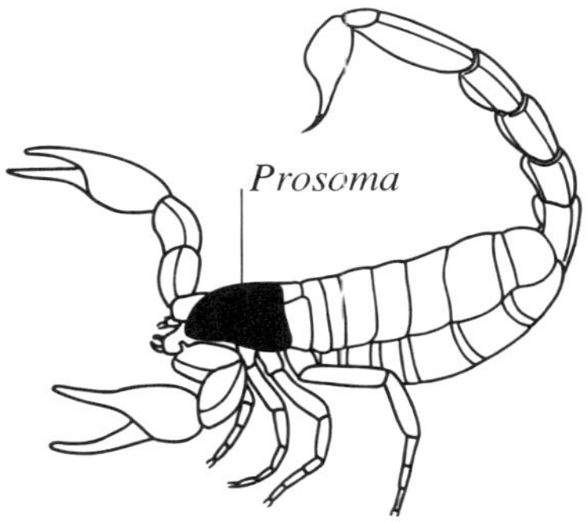

Prosoma

protonema In bryophytes (mosses and liverworts), the young gametophyte in its early stages—after germinating from a spore.

protractor A muscle that draws an appendage forward or away from the body. *See* retractor.

proventriculus The gizzard of some insects or stomach of some crustaceans. In some birds, such as the pigeon, it is the first part of the stomach, where food is mixed with gastric juice before being passed to the gizzard.

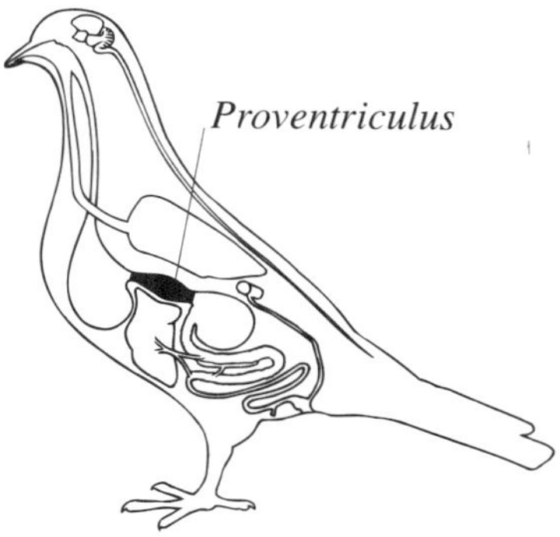

Proventriculus

pseudobranchial artery One of two arteries (afferent and efferent pseudobranchial arteries) that supply blood to the pseudobranch, a vestigial gill found in sharks.

pseudocoelom A body cavity, other than the gut, found in some invertebrate animals, including nematodes. The cavity lies between the body wall and the gut.

pseudopodium A temporary cytoplasmic extension characteristic of ameboid movement or phagocytosis.

Pteridophyta The plant division (phylum) containing ferns.

pterotic A bone on the top of the skull of fish.

pterygoid Part of the upper jaw in cartilaginous fish. In many bony fish, it is one of the bones of the upper jaw. In snakes and lizards, it bears teeth, but in birds and mammals it forms part of the roof of the mouth.

pubescent Covered with soft hair.

pubis or **pubic bone** In tetrapod vertebrates, one of two bones, sometimes fused together, in the ventral, forward-projecting part of the pelvic girdle.

pulmonary Referring to the lungs.

pulmonary artery and vein The blood vessels that carry blood to and from the lungs. In crocodiles, birds, and mammals, the pulmonary circulation is separate from the circulation to the remainder of the body. Unlike all other arteries and veins, the pulmonary artery (going from the heart) carries deoxygenated blood, and the pulmonary vein (going to the heart) carries oxygenated blood.

Punnett square In genetics, a grid used to show all the possible combinations of genotypes arising as the result of a specific genetic cross. It is named after the geneticist Reginald Crundall Punnett.

pupa (pl. **pupae**) or chrysalis. The sedentary phase between larva and adult in insects with complete metamorphosis, e.g., flies, butterflies, moths.

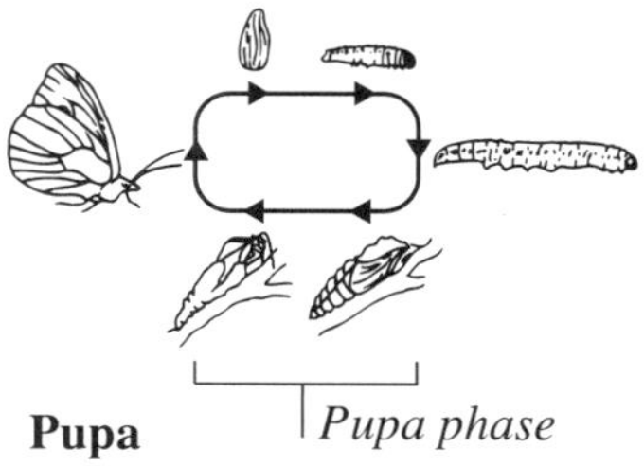

Pupa

During this phase the organism is undergoing dramatic tissue reorganization.

pupil In the vertebrate eye, the opening in the center of the iris. Altering the size of the pupil adjusts the amount of light entering the eye.

purine One of a group of nitrogen-containing bases, e.g., adenine and guanine, that are constituents of nucleotides found in nucleic acids, NADP and ATP. In nucleic acids, purines pair with pyrimidines. *See* base pairing, pyrimidine.

Purkinje fiber In vertebrates, modified heart muscle tissue that emerges as branches from the bundle of His and conducts excitation rapidly across the ventricles.

pygal shield The part of the carapace of a turtle that covers the tail.

pygidium The final segment of an insect.

pygostyle Fused vertebrae (six in many species, four in the pigeon) that support the tail of a bird.

pyloric cecum The end of the cecum that opens into the intestine of vertebrates.

pyloric sphincter A ring of muscle that surrounds the junction between the stomach and the intestine.

pyloric stomach (1) The end of the stomach closest to the intestine of a vertebrate.
(2) The smaller of the two stomachs of an echinoderm, located on the aboral side of the animal. *See also* cardiac stomach.

pyrenoid One of many small grains of protein found in the chloroplasts of photosynthetic protists, such as *Spirogyra*. It is associated with starch synthesis.

pyriformis A large muscle located partly inside the pelvis of vertebrates.

pyrimidine One of a group of nitrogen-containing bases, e.g., cytosine, thymine, and uracil, that are constituents of nucleotides found in nucleic acids. They pair with pyrimidines. *See* base pairing, purine.

quadrate In most vertebrates, a cartilage bone attached to the skull and articulating with the lower jaw. In mammals it is the incus of the ear.

quadratojugal A bone that forms part of the side of the skull in fish and amphibians.

quadriceps femoris A muscle on the front of the thigh.

quarter In cattle, the area on either side of the body that is posterior to the femurs.

queen The primary female reproductive in a colony of social insects.

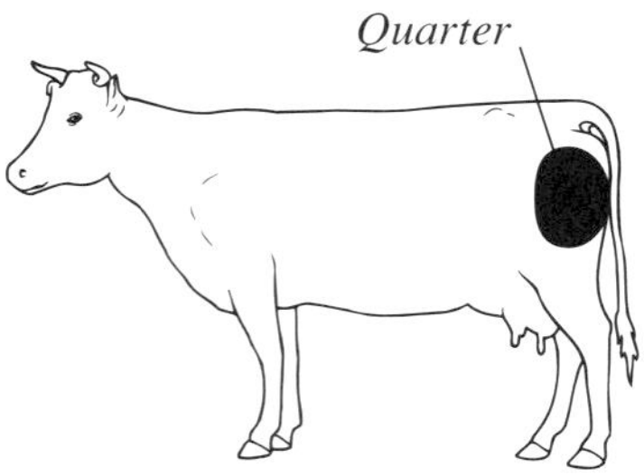

Quarter

rachis (1) In ferns, the main axis of a fern frond to which the pinnae are attached.
(2) In birds, the shaft of a feather.

radial canal (1) One of usually four canals in a medusa (jellyfish). They extend from the stomach in the center of the animal to the canal around the edge.
(2) One of the canals that form part of the water vascular system of echinoderms. The radial canals extend out from the ring canal into each of the arms.

radial nerve A nerve in vertebrates that passes along the lower forelimb on the side nearest the radius.

radial symmetry The arrangement of the parts of the body in which they are distributed symmetrically around the center. If the body is divided in two along any straight line through the central mouth, the resulting halves will be identical.

radicle In a seed plant, the root of the embryo below the cotyledon or cotyledons. It is normally the first organ to emerge from the seed case at germination.

radioulna The fused radius and ulna of a frog.

radius In tetrapod vertebrates, the anterior of two long bones in the lower forelimb. The bone on the thumb side of the human forearm.

radula (pl. **radulae**) In some mollusks, a tonguelike structure covered in small horny or chitinous teeth. It is used for rasping food.

ramus (pl. **rami**) (1) A branch, especially a projection from a bone.
(2) One of the branches of a crustacean limb.

Rathke's pouch *See* hypophysial sac.

rattle A warning device that gives rattlesnakes their common name. It consists of modified scales that are not shed with the rest of the skin. After each molt, one such scale remains, so the number of elements in the rattle indicates the number of times the snake has shed its skin.

receptacle In flowering plants, the upper end of a stalk that bears the flower parts.

receptor site The region of a cell or molecule that combines with a specific chemical to trigger a change in cellular or molecular activity.

recessive In genetics, an allele that is expressed only in the homozygous state. *See also* dominant.

recombinant DNA technology *See* genetic engineering.

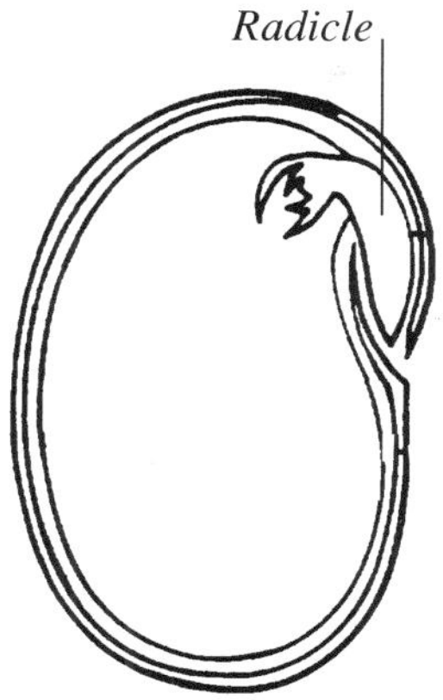

Radicle

rectum In vertebrates, the terminal part of the large intestine. It stores feces and expels them through the cloaca or anus.

rectus anticus muscle One of the muscles in the neck of vertebrates.

redia A larval form of flukes (phylum Platyhelminthes, class Trematoda). They develop from a sporocyst inside a snail host and give rise to cercaria larvae.

redox Abbreviation for reduction-oxidation, denoting the combined oxidation and reduction reactions in a chemical process. For example, the processing of hydrogen atoms in the electron transfer chain is a redox process: electron carriers are alternately oxidized and reduced as electrons from hydrogen atoms are passed along the series.

reduction A chemical reaction involving the removal of oxygen or the addition of electrons or hydrogen atoms. It always occurs in tandem with oxidation, hence redox reactions. *See* redox, oxidation.

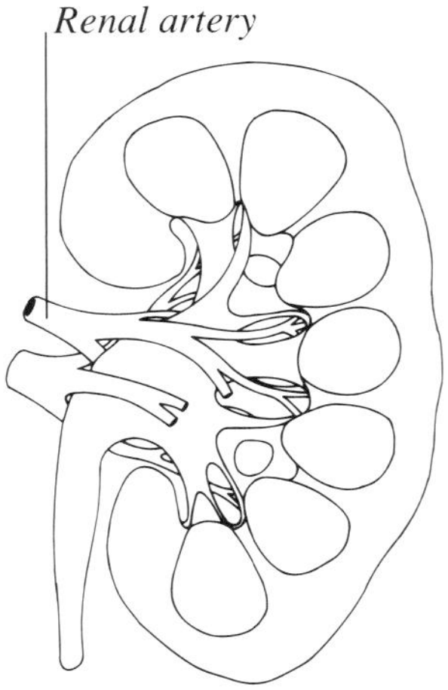

Renal artery

reflex In animals, a simple behavior where a particular stimulus invokes a rapid, specific, involuntary response.

reflex arc In animals, the nerve cells and their connections that coordinate reflex action. In vertebrates, the simplest reflex arcs comprise a sensory neuron, an association neuron, and a motor neuron.

remex (pl. **remiges**) One of the flight feathers (primaries and secondaries) of a bird.

renal Referring to the kidney.

renal artery and vein The blood vessels supplying the kidneys.

replication The duplication of genetic material. It involves one molecule of DNA acting as a template for the manufacture of an identical copy.

repressor A protein molecule that binds to an operator site on DNA and blocks transcription of a nearby DNA sequence.

reproduction The production of new individuals from existing individuals.

reproductive system In multicellular animals, the system of organs specialized for reproduction.

Reptilia The class of vertebrates that includes all the turtles, lizards, and snakes. They are poikilotherms, breathe air, and have a body covered with scales or, in turtles, by bony plates.

respiration (1) The chemical reactions by which an organism derives energy from food.
(2) Used more loosely to refer to breathing or gas exchange.

reticulum The second chamber of the ruminant stomach. In some ruminants, including camels, it is linked to the rumen, forming a single chamber.

retina In vertebrates, the light-sensitive layer at the back of the eye. It contains rods and cones.

retractor One of the muscles with which a mollusk pulls its shell down onto the surface on which it rests. Retractor muscles occur in pairs. In gastropods they are reduced in size.

retrix (pl. **retrices**) One of the tail feathers of a bird.

rhesus blood group A human blood grouping system based on the presence of a rhesus antigen on the surface of red blood cells. When entering the body of a rhesus negative person (without the antigen), rhesus positive blood (carrying the antigen) triggers the production of an antibody, so promoting possible incompatibility problems. The antigen system was first identified in rhesus monkeys.

rhinarium The patch of bare skin, without hair or fur, on the nose of most mammals.

rhizoids Small, root-like structures found at the base of a moss stem and on the under-surface of liverworts and fern prothalli. Like roots, they serve for anchorage and absorption.

rhizome A horizontal stem at or below ground level that bears a bud that can grow into shoots and establish new plants. It is an organ of vegetative propagation and perennation (overwintering form).

Rhizopus A member of the genus of bread molds.

rhomboideus One of two muscles (rhomboideus major and minor) in the dorsal side of the neck and shoulder of vertebrates.

rib One of the long, curved bones of a vertebrate that are attached to the vertebral column dorsally and enclose the thorax (the "rib cage").

rib cage *See* rib.

ribonucleic acid (**RNA**) Nucleic acid, similar in structure to DNA but predominantly or entirely single-stranded and with uracil in place of thymine as one of the component bases. In cells, RNA transfers encoded messages from DNA to the protein-manufacturing machinery in the cytoplasm. RNA is the genetic material of some viruses.

ribose The pentose (5-carbon) sugar found in RNA.

ribosomal ribonucleic acid (**rRNA**) The RNA that forms the structure of ribosomes. In eukaryotic cells, rRNA is manufactured in the nucleolus.

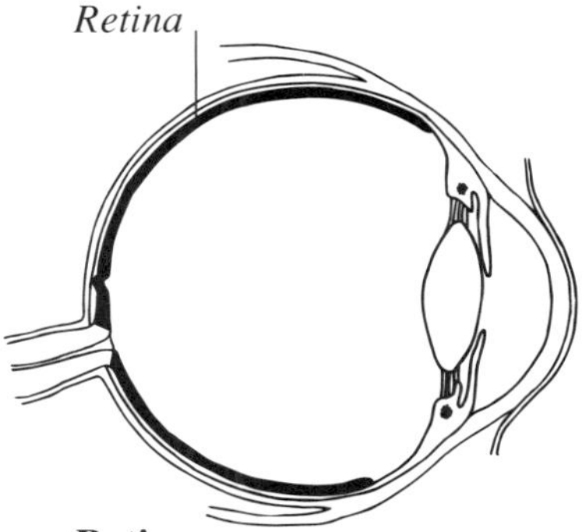

Retina

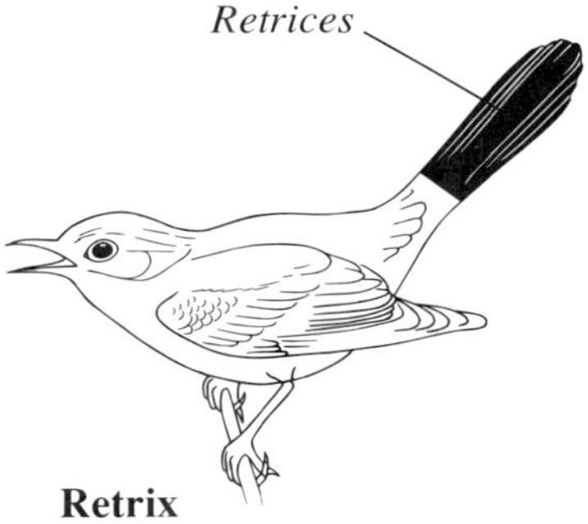

Retrix

ribosome The site of protein synthesis in the cytoplasm of a cell. At a ribosome, the nucleotide sequence of mRNA is translated into a polypeptide chain. A ribosome comprises two subunits of rRNA. *See* translation.

rictal bristle A modified, stiff feather found near the mouth of some birds. It has little or no vane. It may help the bird capture insects in flight.

ring canal (1) In coelenterate medusae, a canal that runs around the edge of the umbrella.
(2) In echinoderms, a circular canal surrounding the center of the animal and forming part of the water vascular system.

RNA *See* ribonucleic acid.

RNA polymerase The enzyme that catalyzes the transcription of an mRNA strand from a complementary strand of DNA. *See* transcription.

rod In vertebrates, one type of light-sensitive cell found in the retina of the eye. Rods are sensitive to low light levels but do not discriminate color or fine detail. *See* cone.

Root

root (1) In pteridophytes and anthophytes, the part of the plant that normally grows downward into the soil. Typically, it anchors the plant and absorbs water and minerals from the soil. Roots can be distinguished from stems on the basis of their internal structure and the absence of nodes and leaves.
(2) The part of a tooth that is embedded in the jaw bone beneath the gum.

rooter The upper part of the tip of the muzzle in the snout of a pig.

root hair The threadlike outgrowth from a root epidermal cell. In the root system, numerous root hairs increase the surface area for the absorption of water and minerals.

rostellum The projection from the scolex of a tapeworm that bears the two rows of hooks by which the animal attaches itself to its host.

rostrum An elongation of the snout. In a shark, the part of the head anterior to the mouth is a rostrum.

rough endoplasmic reticulum *See* endoplasmic reticulum.

roundworm *See* nematode.

rRNA *See* ribosomal ribonucleic acid.

rumen The first chamber of a ruminant's stomach. It contains bacteria and other microorganisms that partly digest cellulose in the food. Food is passed from the rumen to the reticulum.

ruminant A mammal belonging to a suborder of artiodactyls that includes cattle, sheep, goats, deer, antelopes, giraffes, and, in some classifications, camels. They all have a complex digestive system with three or four chambers to the stomach. The anterior teeth are usually highly modified, the upper incisors being absent and the canines reduced. Males and females of some species have horns or antlers.

rump The posterior region of a bird or mammal. It is the dorsal part of the back immediately forward of the tail.

runner A stolon (stem that grows along the ground), which, at its tip, grows roots and forms a new plant. The runner then decays.

Runner

saccule or **sacculus** In mammals, an organ of the inner ear that, together with the utricule, provides information on the position of the head relative to the pull of gravity. It contains chalky granules called otoliths. *See* otolith.

sacculus rotundus A swelling at the end of the small intestine of a rabbit, opening into the cecum.

sacral In vertebrates, referring to the lower vertebrae that articulate or are fused with the pelvic girdle.

sacral plexus A triangular mass of nerves in vertebrates in the sacrum.

sacrum In birds and mammals, sacral vertebrae that are fused together to form a single structure that is joined to the pelvis.

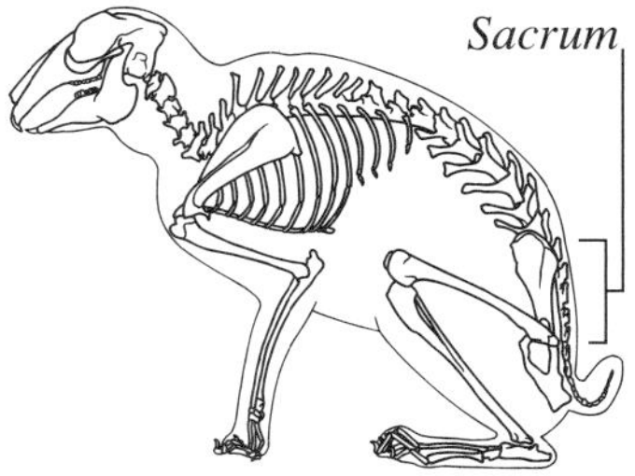

Sacrum

saddle (1) In some birds, including chickens, the posterior part of the dorsal side of the back.
(2) *See* clitellum.

saline (1) A general term referring to water that has a high or moderately high salt concentration.
(2) In laboratory usage, a salt solution of similar water potential to that of the biological material with which it is mixed.

saliva A watery fluid that is secreted into the mouth of many animals. It lubricates food; in some species it contains digestive enzymes; and it is released from salivary glands when food is present in the mouth or is anticipated.

salivary gland A gland that secretes saliva.

saltatorial Pertaining to limbs that are adapted for jumping.

salts A salt is the substance formed when an acid reacts with a base. In the body fluids of animals are a range of salts, of which sodium chloride or common salt (NaCl) is normally the most abundant.

saphenous nerve One of two nerves (the long and short saphenous) running most of the length of the hindlimb in mammals.

saprophytic Referring to organisms, notably many bacteria and fungi, that obtain organic nutrients in solution by feeding on decaying plant and animal material. They typically release digestive enzymes into their surroundings and then absorb the products of digestion.

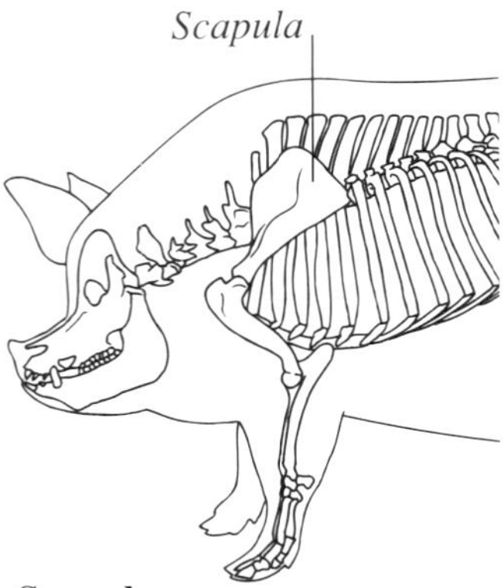

Scapula

sartorius A muscle in the upper part of the hindlimb of a mammal. It arises at the pelvis, crosses the upper leg to behind the knee, and ends at the tibia. It is the longest muscle in the human body.

scapula In vertebrates, the broad bone on the dorsal side of the shoulder girdle. In humans, the shoulder blade.

Schwann cell In vertebrates, one of many such cells that form a myelin sheath around the nerve fibers in the peripheral nervous system.

sciatic In vertebrates, referring to specific major nerves or blood vessels that pass through the hip region.

sciatic nerve One of two nerves (the small and great sciatic nerves) found on the posterior side of the hindlimb of a mammal. In humans, the great sciatic nerve is the thickest nerve in the body, measuring almost 20 mm in diameter.

sclera or **sclerotic coat** In vertebrates, the fibrous outer layer of the eyeball.

sclerite A hard plate of chitin, part of the exoskeleton of an arthropod.

sclerotic coat *See* sclera.

scolex The anterior end, or "head," of a tapeworm, bearing the hooks by which the animal attaches itself to its host.

scorpion An arachnid in which the abdomen is segmented and forms two parts, the mesosoma and metasoma. The metasoma (posterior) consists of ring-shaped segments terminating in a telson, modified as a sting that injects venom. Scorpions belong to the order Scorpiones and are considered to be the most primitive of arachnids.

scrotum In mammals, a muscular sac containing the testes. To promote sperm production, it maintains the testes at a temperature slightly lower than normal body temperature.

scute An enlarged bony plate or scale in the skin of an animal.

scutularis muscle A muscle on the top of a dog's head, immediately anterior to the ear.

sebaceous gland In mammals, a skin gland commonly associated with a hair follicle. It secretes an oily liquid, sebum, that helps lubricate the skin and hair and has antibacterial properties.

secondary feather One of the inner flight feathers in the wing of a bird. The secondaries are located along the trailing edge, between the body and the bend in the wing.

Secondary feather

secretion In plants and animals, the release of a useful substance or mixture of substances from a cell or gland in the body. The process is called secretion, and the substance or mixture itself is called a secretion.

sedentary Referring to an organism that stays in one place.

sediment The suspended particles that settle to the bottom of a liquid.

seed In anthophyte plants, the structure formed from a fertilized ovule. It comprises an embryo, often with a food store (endosperm), enclosed in a seed coat (testa). Seeds are commonly a resistant, dispersal stage in the life cycle.

seed-bearing plants Refers to those plant groups (e.g., Coniferophyta) whose members produce seeds

segment In higher animal phyla, refers to one of several or many similar body compartments, particularly obvious in annelids and arthropods. Segmentation in other phyla, such as chordates, is less obvious.

semen The ejaculate of male animals. A fluid comprising secretions (seminal fluid) mixed with sperm.

semicircular canals In vertebrates, three semicircular, fluid-filled tubes found in the inner ear. They are orientated in different planes and contain components that detect the orientation of the head.

semimembranosus One of the hamstring muscles of the inner, back thigh that flexes and rotates the leg.

seminal vesicle (1) In male mammals and some higher vertebrates, a paired gland that secretes fructose-rich fluid. This stimulates and provides an energy source for ejaculated sperm.
(2) In some invertebrates and lower vertebrates, the seminal vesicle is a sperm-storing structure.

seminiferous tubule In male vertebrates, it is one of numerous coiled tubes in which sperm are formed and develop prior to release and storage in the epididymis.

semitendinosus One of the inner, back thigh muscles that flexes and rotates the leg.

sensitivity An organism's ability to respond to a stimulus. In general, animals respond much more rapidly than plants.

sensory neuron A nerve cell that conducts impulses from a sensory receptor to the central nervous system.

sensory receptor (receptor) A structure—a cell or organ—that is specialized for detecting stimuli and responds by sending impulses through the nervous system via sensory neurons.

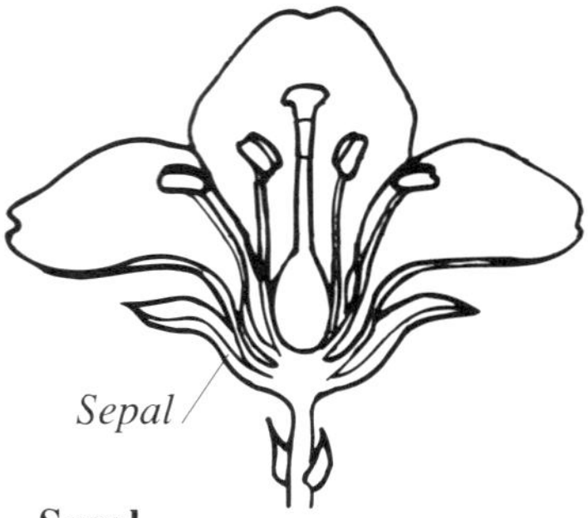

Sepal

sepal In a flower, one of several similar components in the outer whorl. Typically green and leaf-like, the sepals enclose the developing flower bud and then fold back when the flower opens. In some flowers, sepals are colored and have the appearance of petals.

septum (pl. **septa**) (1) In animals and plants, a partition separating two cavities.
(2) In fungi, a partition within a hypha.

serological Referring to studies involving antigen-antibody interactions.

serratus One of the muscles in the back of a vertebrate. The serratus magnus is located between the ribs and scapula. The serratus posticus superior is where the dorsal and lumbar regions join.

Sertoli cell In male vertebrates, a nutritive cell to which developing sperm (spermatids) attach.

serum (pl. **sera**) (1) The clear liquid that separates from clotted material after blood coagulates.
(2) The clear portion of blood or lymph after its cellular and other physical debris have been removed artificially.

sesamoid bone A small, round bone found in tendons that exert great pressure on the joints over which they move. There is one on the posterior side of the ankle of a chicken, and they also occur in the hands, feet, and knees of humans.

sessile (1) In botany, a fruit, flower, or leaf that lacks a stalk and sits directly on a stem.
(2) In zoology, an animal that normally stays in the same place, e.g. a barnacle.

seta (pl. **setae**) (1) In invertebrates, particularly crustaceans and insects, a structure resembling a bristle or stiff hair.
(2) In mosses and liverworts, the stalk supporting a sporogonium.

sex chromosomes The chromosomes that determine the sex of the individual. In humans, sex is determined by two chromosomes, which in females are homologous (XX) but in males are dissimilar (XY). (*See also* illustration on page 105.)

Sex chromosomes (see entry on page 104)

- In many animals and plants, sexual characters are determined by particular sex chromosomes.
- In such organisms, the other, nonsex chromosomes are called autosomes.

Human sex chromosomes

- Human body cells each contain 22 pairs of autosomes, and one pair of sex chromosomes.
- Females have an identical pair of sex chromosomes called X chromosomes.
- Males have one X chromosome and a much shorter Y chromosome.

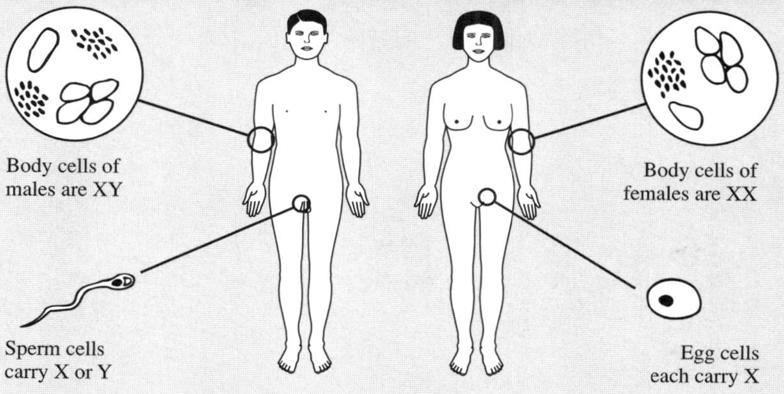

sex hormones In vertebrates, a range of hormones that control the development and functioning of primary and secondary sexual characteristics, and control the reproductive cycle. Such hormones include progesterone, estradiol-17ß, and testosterone.

sex linkage Refers to characteristics that are determined by genes carried on the sex chromosomes. Inheritance of these characteristics is thus linked to the sex of the individual.

sexual reproduction Reproduction in which the organism produces new individuals by the fusion of gametes or, in other ways, involves the mixing of genetic material from two different sources.

shell A hard, protective outer covering. The valves of a bivalve mollusk or brachiopod, plates of an echinoderm, exoskeleton of an arthropod, pen of a squid, and the carapace and plastron of a turtle can all be called shells.

shell beak The oldest part of a shell of a bivalve mollusk, located near the hinge.

shell gland In some flatworms, a gland that secretes a substance that causes the coating of its eggs to harden.

shoot or **shoot system** The above-ground part of the plant comprising stem, leaves, and any reproductive structures borne upon them.

sickle-cell anemia Anemia (a lack of oxygen-carrying pigment in the blood) as a result of red blood cells becoming deformed (sickling) and then being removed from circulation. The tendency is inherited and is determined by a gene at a single locus. (*See also* illustration on page 106.)

Sickle-cell anemia (see entry on page 105)

Red blood cells
Normal, healthy red blood cells (**a**) have a characteristic disk shape. They contain hemoglobin (**b**), which is the protein that transports the vital gas oxygen around the body.

Hemoglobin S
The gene for hemoglobin is slightly different in people with sickle-cell anemia. As a result, sufferers have a different type of hemoglobin, called hemoglobin S (**c**). When molecules of hemoglobin S are not carrying oxygen, they have a tendency to form long chains. These chains deform the red blood cells into a sickle shape (**d**).

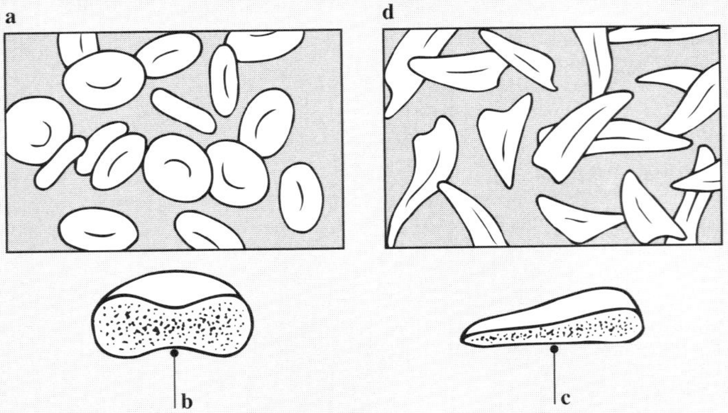

sickles Small feathers near the tail of some birds, such as chickens.

sieve plate In plants, part of the wall of a sieve tube element. It has large pores through which cytoplasmic strands extend from one sieve tube element to the next and play a role in intercellular transport. *See* sieve tube.

sieve tube In plants, a series of sieve tube elements connected end to end by sieve plates (abutting cell walls), providing connection from one element to the next. Sieve tubes form part of phloem tissue—the system that transports organic substances around the plant. *See* phloem.

siliceous Made from or containing silica (silicon dioxide).

silk gland A gland that secretes silk. Many arthropods produce silk, but the type and location of their silk glands vary widely. In spiders, the glands are in the abdomen; in mites, they are in the mouth; and in insects, such as the silk moth, silk is produced by the salivary glands.

simple eye An eye that consists of a single ocellus.

sino-atrial (**SA**) **node** (or pacemaker). Modified heart muscle tissue that is the source of the electrical excitation that stimulates the heart to contract rhythmically. This inherent rhythm is then modified by nervous or hormonal action.

sinus A space or cavity.

sinus venosus In lower vertebrates, a thin-walled additional chamber of the heart that receives blood from major veins and then empties it into the atria.

siphon A tube that directs water toward or away from the gills. Bivalve mollusks and gastropods have siphons.

siphonoglyph A groove with cilia found at one or both ends of the slit-shaped mouth of a sea anemone.

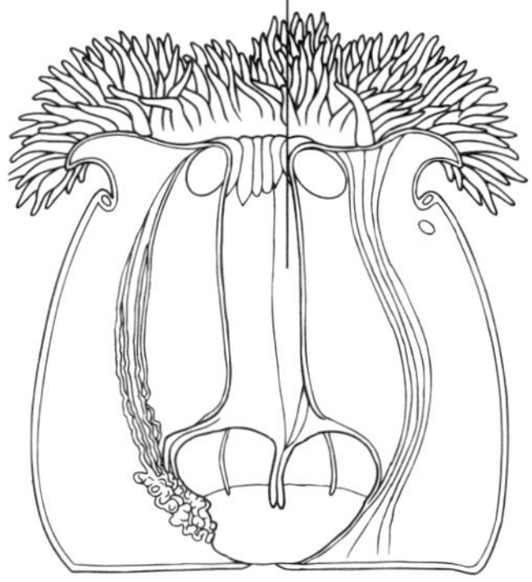

Siphonoglyph

skeleton Any structure that helps an organism retain a constant shape and supports its appendages and internal organs.

skin In animals, the external tissue layers, outside the musculature, that cover and protect the body. In vertebrates, it typically comprises two layers: an outer epidermis and an inner dermis. The skin covering varies in different vertebrate classes, e.g., feathers in birds, horny scales in reptiles, hair in mammals.

skull In vertebrates, the anterior part of the bony skeleton comprising the cranium (braincase), the sense capsules, and the mandible (lower jaw).

small intestine In reptiles, birds, and mammals, the first major part of the intestine. It comprises the duodenum, jejenum, and ileum and is adapted for digestion and absorption of food substances.

smooth endoplasmic reticulum *See* endoplasmic reticulum.

SNS *See* sympathetic nervous system.

solenocyte A tubular flame cell found in annelids, flatworms, and lancelets. The cell has a flagellum with which it wafts waste products along the tube.

soleus In humans, a large, flat muscle located immediately beneath the gastrocnemius. Its name refers to its shape, that of a sole fish.

solute The solid that is dissolved in a liquid (called the solvent).

solvent *See* solute.

somatotrophic hormone *See* growth hormone.

sorus (pl. **sori**) In ferns, a group of sporangia on a pinnule. It is usually covered in an indusium—a protective covering.

sperm (pl. **sperm**) or **spermatozoon** (pl. **spermatozoa**) A male gamete. It is small and, in most species, moves by means of a flagellum. (*See also* illustration on page 108.)

spermaceti Highly vascular tissue that is stored in the enlarged snout of sperm whales. A full-grown whale may carry one ton of spermaceti. Its function is unknown, but because it contains oils that solidify at about body temperature, it may help the animal maintain a constant body temperature. It may also help it achieve neutral buoyancy, because the density of spermaceti changes as it liquefies and solidifies.

Sperm (see entry on page 107)

Essential features

- A sperm is much smaller than the egg;
- it has three distinct regions: head, midpiece, and tail;
- and all of these are all covered by a plasma membrane.

a Nucleus
b Acrosome
c Neck
d Centriole
e Core
f Mitochondria
g Axial filament
h Fibrous sheath

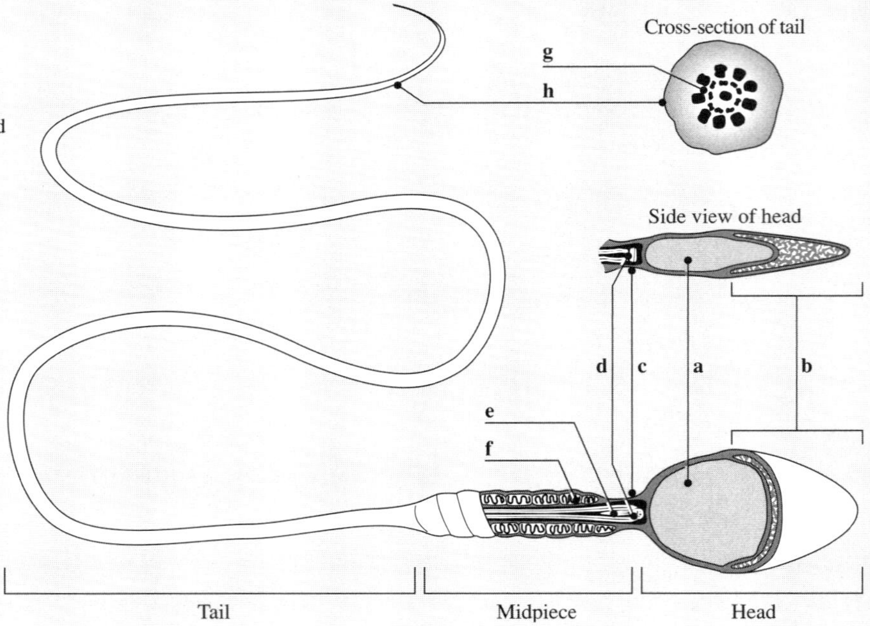

spermatheca A sac connected to the genital tract of a female insect and also found in annelids. It is used to store sperm and is lined with glandular cells that may provide nourishment for the sperm.

spermatid In animals, a cell resulting from the second meiotic division in spermatogenesis. The cell develops into a spermatazoon.

spermatocyte In animals, a cell undergoing meiosis that will later give rise to a spermatozoon.

spermatogenesis In animals, the formation of spermatozoa.

spermatogonium (pl. **spermatogonia**) In animals, a cell that undergoes repeated mitosis to give rise to spermatocytes.

spermatozoon *See* sperm.

spermoviduct The common duct along which both sperm and ova travel in a hermaphrodite animal, such as a snail.

sphenethmoid A small recess adjoining the nasal cavity in some vertebrates, including frogs and mammals.

sphenoid A bone on the side of the skull of a primate. It lies below the frontal, posterior to the zygomatic, and anterior to the temporal.

sphincter A ring of muscle that controls the diameter of a tube and therefore regulates the passage of material through it.

spicule A small spine or needle. In sponges (Porifera), spicules form a framework that provides support for the mass of the animal. Sponge spicules are made from calcium carbonate, silica, or a fibrous material called spongin. In some nematodes, such as ascaris, males have a copulatory spicule through which they release sperm.

spider An arachnid that belongs to one of about 30,000 species comprising the order Araneae. Spiders are predators, mostly on arthropods, but a few catch small vertebrates and some hunt fish. They produce silk, used to protect eggs as well as to capture prey.

spinal cord A tube enclosed in the spinal column that runs the length of the thorax and abdomen of vertebrates from the head. It consists of nerve cells and bundles of fibers connected to the brain at the anterior end. Pairs of nerves leave it at intervals, extending to all parts of the body.

spindle A spindle-shaped arrangement of microtubules in cells undergoing mitosis or meiosis. It provides a structural framework upon which chromosomes and chromatids move.

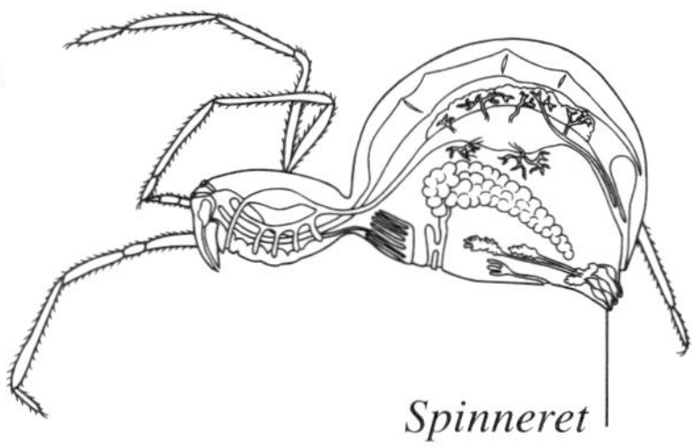

Spinneret

spinneret In spiders, one of usually four or six organs on the posterior end of the abdomen. They produce silk used to weave a spider's web.

spiracle (1) In insects and some arachnids, an external opening of the tracheal system.
(2) In cartilaginous fish and some bony fish, the modified first gill slit.
(3) In amphibian tadpole larvae, the exhalent opening of the gill chamber.

spiral valve A structure, spiral in shape, that controls the movement of material. There is a spiral valve between the ileum and rectum in sharks, and some species of frogs have one in the heart.

spire The tightly spiraling top of a snail shell.

Spirogyra A plantlike protist that forms chains of individual cells.

spleen An organ located to the posterior of the stomach in vertebrates. It stores red blood cells and breaks down old ones, storing the iron from them. It also destroys particles of foreign matter and produces lymphocytes.

splenius A muscle located on the dorsal side of the neck and upper thorax in vertebrates.

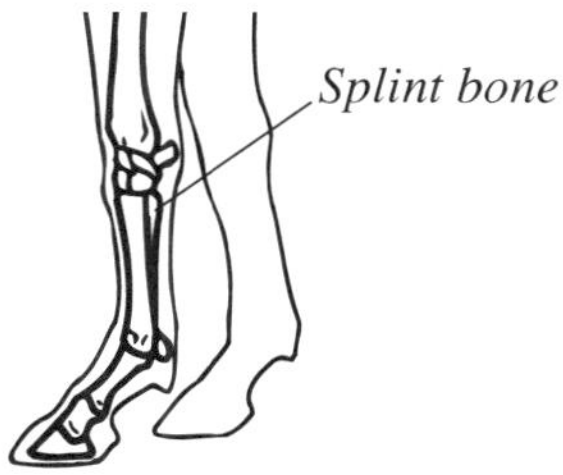

Splint bone

splint bone The fourth metacarpal of a horse.

sponge *See* Porifera.

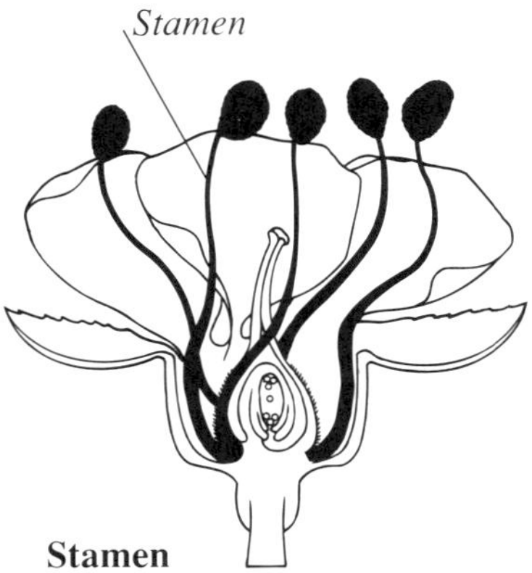

Stamen

spongin A structure made from interlinked collagen fibers that forms the skeleton of some sponges.

sporangium (pl. **sporangia**) In plants, fungi, and animals, a structure that produces spores.

sporophyte In plants that show alternation of generations, it is the diploid generation. It gives rise to spores. *See* gametophyte.

squamosal One of a pair of bones found on either side of the posterior part of the vertebrate skull. In mammals, it articulates with the lower jaw. In humans, the squamosal forms the squamous portion (from *squama*, meaning "scale") of the temporal bone.

stamen In flowering plants, the male reproductive organ of the flower. It comprises an anther and a stalk or filament, and produces pollen.

stapes or **stirrup** In mammals, the inner of three ossicles in the middle ear.

starch The storage polysaccharide of plants. It is insoluble or only partially soluble, formed from glucose molecules condensed together.

statocyst An organ that helps some aquatic invertebrates to remain horizontal while they are swimming. It consists of a small vesicle lined with sensory cells and containing mineral particles. As the animal moves the particles also move, stimulating the cells.

stele In plants, the cylindrical arrangement of vascular tissue at the center of a root or stem.

sterilization (1) The loss of an individual's ability to reproduce sexually. (2) The cleaning of an object to remove unwanted living microorganisms.

sternite The ventral part of a segment of an insect if this is not thickened. If it is, it is called a sternum.

sternocephalicus One of a pair of muscles that run along either side of the neck from the sternum to the head of a vertebrate.

sternocleidomastoid One of a pair of muscles found on either side of the neck of a human, running from the head to the sternum.

sternohyoideus One of a pair of muscles that is found on either side of the throat in some mammals. They run from the sternum to the region of the hyoid.

sternomandibularis A muscle on the ventral side of the neck of some vertebrates. It runs from the sternum to the jaw.

sternomastoideus One of a pair of muscles found on either side of the neck in some mammals. They run from just below the ears to the sternum.

sternum (pl. **sterna**) (1) In tetrapod vertebrates, the breast bone. (2) In arthropods, the cuticle on the ventral side of a segment.

steroid One of a group of lipids in which the molecule comprises several carbon rings. Though structurally similar, their functions are diverse. Cholesterol, estradiol-17ß, and testosterone are examples.

stifle The knee of a tetrapod.

stifle pad A patch of toughened skin on the knee of a camel.

stigma (pl. **stigmata**) In flowering plants, the terminal part of the carpel. It receives pollen.

stirrup *See* stapes.

stolon The "stalk" by which a member of an invertebrate colony is attached to the surface on which it rests.

stoma (pl. **stomata**) In plant leaves and stems, the opening between two guard cells that opens and closes to permit gas exchange.

stomach (1) In vertebrates, a saclike region of the alimentary canal between the esophagus and intestine. It temporarily stores and digests food. (2) In invertebrates, a general name for a saclike part of the alimentary canal behind the esophagus.

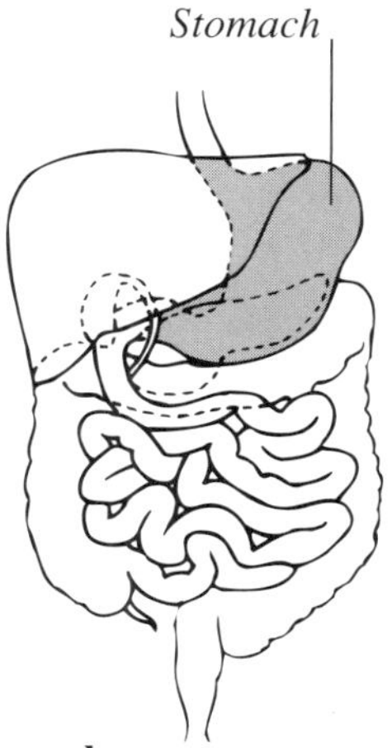

Stomach

stomium In ferns, the part of the sporangium wall that ruptures to release spores (dehiscence).

stone canal A strengthened canal in an echinoderm that links the madreporite to the water vascular system.

stopper pad The skin that covers the posterior side of the carpals of a dog.

strigil A brush on each foreleg of certain insects. It is made of hairs and used for grooming.

strobila The main part of the body of a tapeworm.

stroma (1) The matrix surrounding the grana of chloroplasts. (2) In animals, the intercellular material or supporting connective tissue of an organ.

style In flowering plants, where present, the elongated region of the carpel that supports the stigma.

stylets The piercing mouthparts of certain insects, e.g., the mosquito.

subclavian In vertebrates, passing under or located beneath, the clavicle.

subclavian artery and vein Blood vessels that cross the vertebrate body on the ventral side of the shoulder girdle and serve the forelimbs.

subcutaneous In vertebrates, situated immediately below the dermis of the skin.

sublingual gland One of a pair of salivary glands located beneath the tongue of vertebrates.

submucosa In vertebrates, a layer situated immediately below the mucosa.

substrate (1) A reactant in an enzyme-catalyzed reaction.
(2) or **substratum** The material on or in which an organism lives.

substrate-level phosphorylation The production of ATP from ADP using a phosphate derived from the hydrolysis of another high-energy compound. Such phosphorylations occur in glycolysis and the Krebs cycle.

sugar (1) A soluble carbohydrate comprising one or a few monosaccharide units.
(2) The common name for the disaccharide sucrose.

sulcus A groove.

sulfur bridge In a protein, a disulfide bond that connects two parts of the same polypeptide or two different polypeptides. Such bonds help determine the overall conformation of a protein molecule.

supernatent The liquid formed above sediment, e.g., a result of centrifugation.

supraoccipital A bone at the posterior base of the skull, forming the base of the occipital in humans.

suprascapular (1) The shoulder blade of a frog.
(2) An artery in the neck of vertebrates.

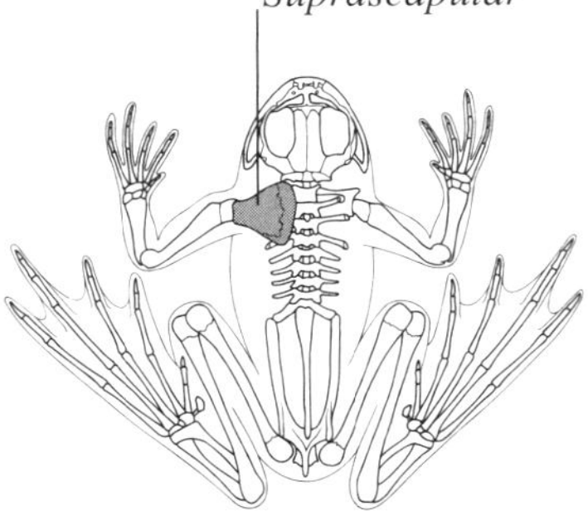

Suprascapular

sural nerve A nerve at the back of the knee of a vertebrate.

suspensory ligaments In the vertebrate eye, the ligaments that connect the lens to the ciliary body.

suture An immovable joint between bones, as in the skull.

sweat gland A gland in the skin of a mammal that secretes a dilute solution of blood salts. Evaporation of this solution absorbs latent heat from the body surface, thus cooling it.

swim bladder In bony fish, a gas-filled bladder that usually functions as a hydrostatic organ, allowing the fish to match its density to that of the surrounding water. In some species, it serves for gas exchange or sound production.

swimmeret One of the paired appendages to its body that a crustacean uses for swimming. In some crustaceans swimmerets are modified and used for burrowing or crawling.

switch The tip of the tail of cattle.

sympathetic nervous system (**SNS**) In vertebrates, part of the autonomic nervous system. Its activity tends to prepare the body for dealing with demanding or dangerous situations.

synapse The junction between two adjacent neurons. Chemical synapses relay impulses using chemical messengers. Electrical synapses relay impulses by the flow of electrons through channels created by the junctures.

synovial In vertebrates, refers to the fluid that lubricates joints and to the membrane that secretes that fluid.

synsacrum A bone in birds formed by the fusion of several vertebrae. The resulting long bone allows the standing body to be supported in an approximately horizontal position by a single pair of legs.

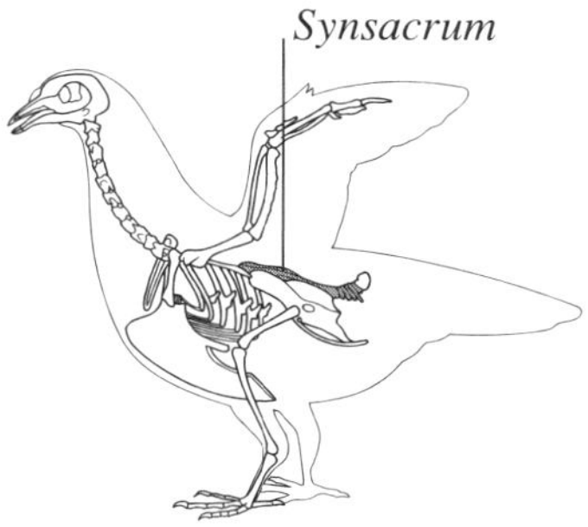

Synsacrum

synthesis In biology, refers to the formation of a substance following one or more chemical reactions.

syrinx The vocal organ of a bird.

systemic Applying to the body as a whole, not just part of it.

systemic arch The fourth aortic arch of vertebrates, which is the principal source of the blood supply to the body. In amphibians and reptiles, left and right aortic arches are both present. Adult birds have only the right arch and adult mammals only the left one.

systole The phase of the heart cycle in which the heart muscle is contracting. *See* diastole.

talon The foot of a bird of prey. It is adapted for seizing prey.

tapetum A layer of cells in or outside the retina of many nocturnal mammals. The cells contain crystals that reflect light back through the retina, increasing its sensitivity to low levels of illumination. When the pupil is fully dilated, reflection of a bright light from the tapetum is what causes the eyes of animals to shine at night.

tapeworm *See* Platyhelminthes.

tarsalis anticus and posticus Two muscles in the foot of a frog.

tarsals One of the bones of the ankle in terrestrial vertebrates.

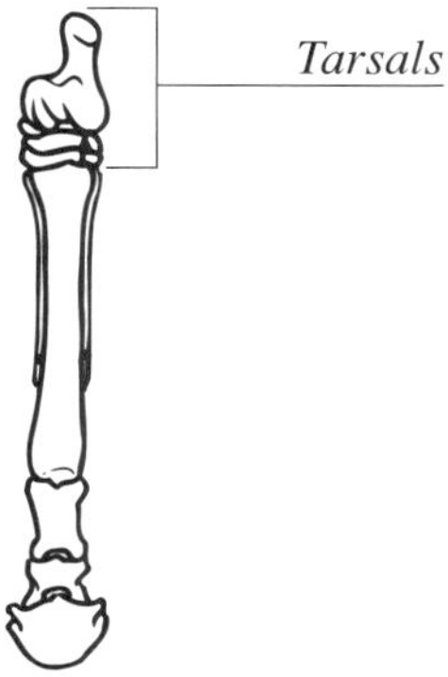

Tarsals (horse)

tarsometatarsus (pl. **tarsometatarsi**) The bone in the foot of a bird that is formed from the fusion of all but one of the distal tarsals with the metatarsals. The tarsometatarsus bears the second, third, and fourth digits.

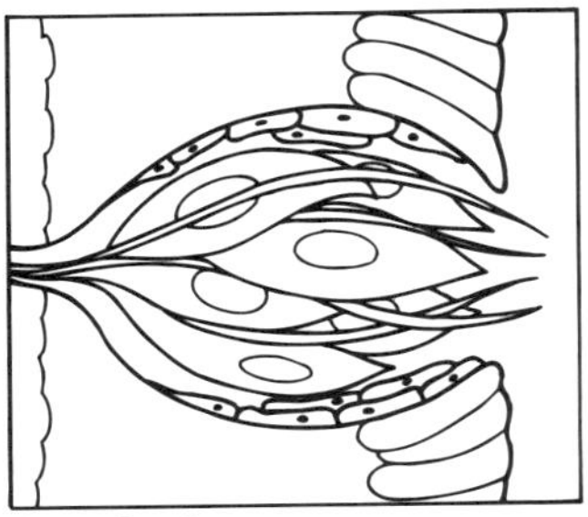

Taste bud

tarsus (1) The lower part of the leg of an insect. It consists of two to five segments.
(2) The bone of the lower part of the leg of a bird.
(3) The ankle bones of a mammal.
(4) Part of the eyelid of a vertebrate.

taste bud In vertebrates, the collections of cells that form sensory receptors sensitive to taste. They are found in the buccal cavity, particularly on the tongue.

taxonomy The scientific study of the identification and classification of living organisms.

teat *See* nipple.

tectorial membrane A membrane in the cochlea of the mammalian inner ear. It transmits vibrations to the sensory hair cells involved in sound detection.

telophase The final stage of mitosis or meiosis, occurring after anaphase. In mitosis and the second meiotic division, telophase encompasses the gradual disappearance of the visible chromosomes and the reappearance of nuclear membranes. In telophase of the first meiotic division, chromatids do not disperse and the second meiotic division immediately follows.

telson In crustaceans, the posterior projection of the last abdominal segment.

temporal A bone on the side of the skull in primates.

temporalis A muscle on each side of the head of a vertebrate.

tendon A cord or sheet of collagen-rich, inelastic connective tissue that attaches a muscle to a bone. *See* ligament.

tensor The name given to any muscle that tightens (tenses) the structure to which it is attached.

tentacle In invertebrates, a long, slender, flexible organ usually associated with the head region. The functions of tenctacles are diverse, and include grasping, feeling, and swimming.

teres Two muscles (teres major and minor) in each shoulder of a vertebrate. They link the scapula with the shoulder joint and upper part of the humerus.

tergum (pl. **terga**) In arthropods, the thickened cuticle on the dorsal side of a segment.

terminal Referring to a part at the end of a structure, e.g., a toe is the terminal part of a foot.

termite A social insect that can digest cellulose with the help of symbiotic bacteria in its gut. Some termites cultivate gardens of fungi.

terrestrial Concerned with the land, or more specifically, living on the ground.

test A shell that covers and protects some protozoa and invertebrates.

testa In anthophyte plants, the protective seed coat. It is derived from the integuments of the ovule.

test cross In genetics, a cross used to distinguish between an individual that is homozygous or heterozygous for a dominant trait. The partner used for crossing is homozygous recessive.

testis (pl. **testes**) The male sex organ that produces sperm.

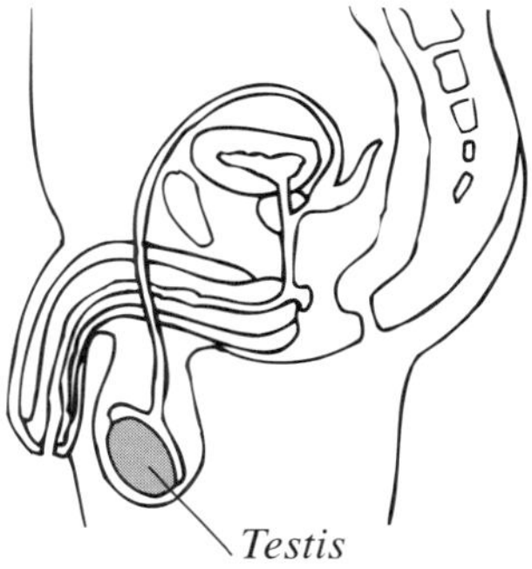

Testis

testosterone In vertebrates, the main steroid hormone produced by the testis. It is the chief male sex hormone and promotes the maturation and maintenance of the male reproductive system and the development of male secondary sexual characteristics.

tetraploid Describing a nucleus, cell, or organism having four times the haploid number of chromosomes. It is a form of polyploidy.

tetrapod Referring to four-footed vertebrates. This includes all the essentially terrestrial vertebrates: amphibia, reptiles, birds, and mammals. They have two pairs of pentadactyl limbs, although in some cases, e.g., snakes, these have been secondarily lost.

thalamus Part of the forebrain of a vertebrate. It coordinates sensory information and transmits it to the cerebrum.

thallus A simple plant or fungal body. It is not differentiated into stem, leaves, and roots. It may be unicellular or multicellular.

thoracic Referring to the thorax.

thoracolumbar vertebra One of the vertebrae of a lizard (there are 22 in *Lacerta agilis*) located between the cervical and sacral vertebrae.

thorax (1) In an insect, the three segments of the body that bear legs. They lie between the head and the abdomen.
(2) In a vertebrate, the anterior part of the body that contains the heart and lungs. In mammals, it is separated from the abdomen by the diaphragm.

thylakoid A flattened membrane-bounded sac in chloroplasts. The membranes contain photosynthetic pigments, and many thylakoids (in layers called lamellae) are stacked to form a granum. *See* granum.

thymus gland An endocrine gland in vertebrates. It is an important lymphocyte-producing organ in the juvenile and thus a major

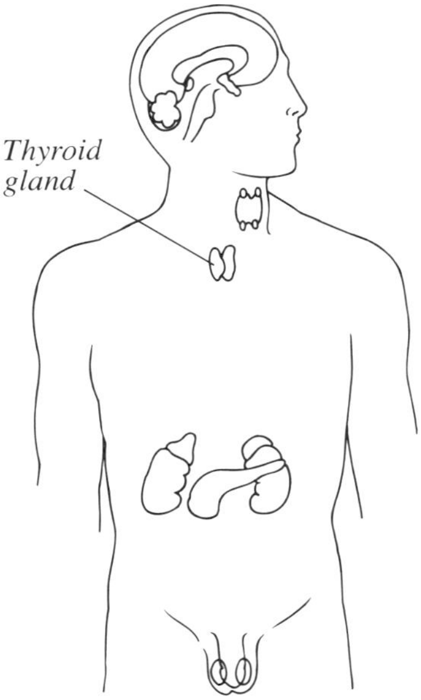

Thyroid gland

component of the immune system. Usually located in the lower neck region, its functional role declines in adulthood.

thyroid gland A vertebrate endocrine (hormone-producing) gland overlying the trachea that secretes thyroxine, a hormone that regulates metabolic rate.

thyroid-stimulating hormone (**TSH**) In vertebrates, a peptide hormone secreted by the anterior pituitary. It stimulates growth of the thyroid gland and thus thyroxine production.

tibia (1) The anterior long bone (the larger of two) of the lower hindlimb of a vertebrate (the shin bone).
(2) The shin bone. The large, thick, long bone in the lower leg.
(3) The long section of the leg of an insect, articulating proximally with the femur and distally with the tarsus.

tibial nerve Two nerves in the lower hindlimb of a vertebrate. The posterior tibial runs down the posterior side of the leg, the anterior tibial starts on the posterior side and crosses to the anterior side.

tibiale *See* astralagus.

tibialis Two muscles (tibialis anticus and posticus) in the lower hindlimb of a vertebrate.

tibiofibula The fused tibia and fibula of a frog.

tibiotarsal joint The joint between the tibiotarsus metatarsals of a bird. It is the equivalent of the ankle.

tibiotarsus The bone in the leg of a bird that is formed from the fusion of the tibia and the proximal tarsals. It is also fused with the fibula at several points. The tibiotarsus bears the first digit.

Tiedemann's body A pouch on the ring canal of an echinoderm that is believed to produce coelomocytes. Echinoderms have four or more, commonly five, such pouches.

tissue In an organism, an aggregation of cells, usually of the same kind, organized to carry out a particular function.

tissue fluid The fluid, usually derived from blood, that fills intercellular spaces in animals.

tongue A muscular organ attached to the floor of the mouth of most vertebrates. It bears taste buds and can manipulate food. In some animals it is prehensile and used to capture food; in other animals it acts as a sense organ.

tonoplast The membrane enclosing the sap vacuole in a plant cell.

tooth A hard structure in the mouth of a vertebrate that is used to seize, bite, tear, or crush food. The name is also given to structures resembling teeth in other animals. *See also* canine, incisor, molar, premolar.

topline The straight top to the back of a sheep.

torsion The twisting of the body of a gastropod through 180 degrees. This gives its nervous and digestive systems a U shape.

trachea (1) The windpipe of a vertebrate, leading from the throat to the point where the bronchi divide and enter the lungs.
(2) One of the tubes that perforates the exoskeleton of an insect and through which air enters the body.

tracheole One of many terminal branches of the insect's tracheal system. Tracheoles invade many of the insect's tissues and gas exchange occurs across their walls.

tragus A flap of cartilage that extends from the ear lobe of a mammal and lies in front of the external opening of the ear.

transcription The synthesis of RNA from a DNA template. The process is catalyzed by RNA polmerase.

transfer ribonucleic acid (**tRNA**) The form of RNA that ferries an amino acid to its place alongside a mRNA strand during protein synthesis.

transformation The alteration of the genotype of a cell or organism by the uptake of purified DNA.

translation The process by which ribosomes and tRNA decipher the genetic code in a mRNA in order to synthesize a specific polypeptide. The assembly of amino acids to form a polypeptide, in a sequence specified by the order of nucleotides in a molecule of mRNA.

transpiration The loss of water by evaporation from land plants. In anthophytes, the bulk of water loss occurs through stomata.

transverse section A cross section of an organism or structure.

trapezius A large, flat, triangular muscle that covers the top and back of each shoulder of a vertebrate, extending dorsally to the lumbar region.

tricarboxylic cycle *See* Krebs cycle.

triceps The muscle that lies along the full length of the posterior side of the upper forelimb of a vertebrate.

trichocysts In some ciliated protists, organelles that discharge a threadlike body used for defense or attachment.

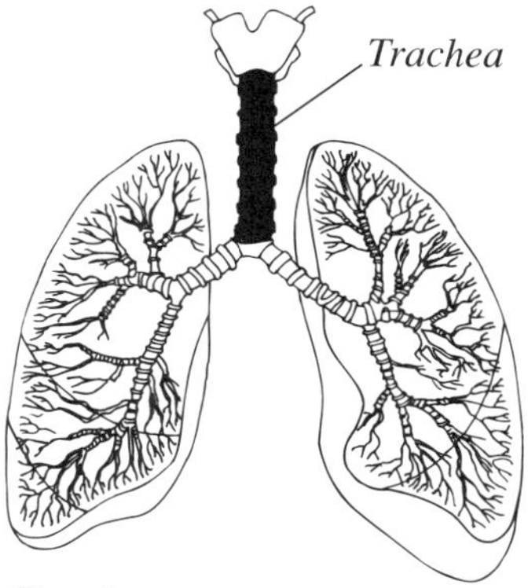

Trachea

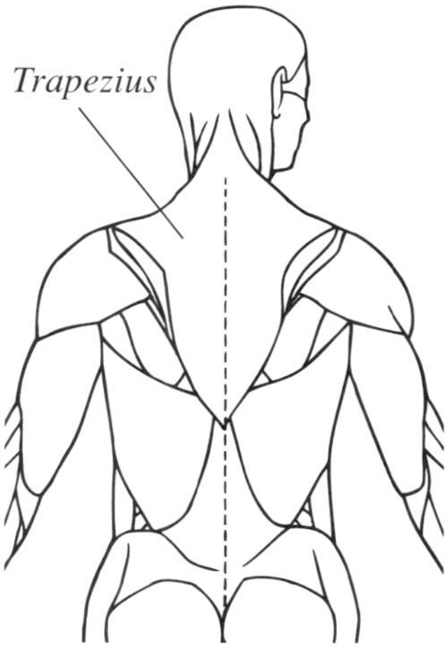

Trapezius

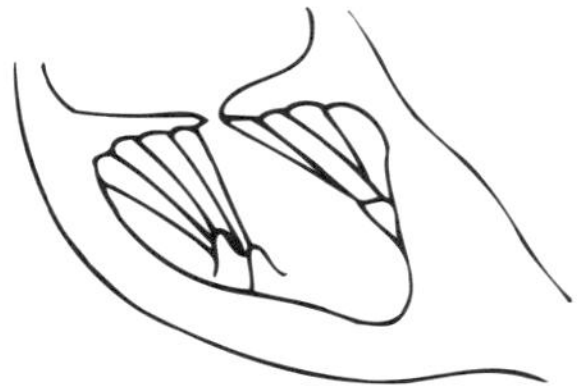

Tricuspid valve

tricuspid valve In birds and mammals, the heart valve between the right atrium and right ventricle.

trigeminal nerve The fifth cranial nerve in vertebrates, branching along each side of the head. Other branches serve the eye, maxilla, and mandible.

triglyceride A glycerol molecule condensed with three fatty acids. The basis of fats and oils commonly found in plants and animals.

triple X syndrome In humans, a congenital disorder caused by the presence of an additional X sex chromosome in a female. The individual has three X chromosomes (genotype XXX) and is female in appearance, though usually sterile.

triploblastic In all higher animal phyla, the condition in which the body is derived from three cell layers during development: the ectoderm, mesoderm, and endoderm.

trisomy The condition in which an otherwise normal diploid individual has one extra chromosome for one of the homologous pairs.

tRNA *See* transfer ribonucleic acid.

trochanter (1) The second segment of the leg of an insect. It articulates proximally with the coxa and distally with the femur.
(2) In vertebrates, one of several bony processes on the head of the femur, used for muscle attachment.

tropism In plants, a growth response in relation to a stimulus coming from a particular direction, e.g., geotropism (in response to gravity) or phototropism (in response to light).

truncus arteriosus In fish and amphibia, the major artery into which blood is pumped from the single ventricle.

TSH *See* thyroid-stimulating hormone.

tube foot In echinoderms, one of numerous small, fluid-filled projections from the body. They are connected to the water vascular system, and their shape and movements support a variety of functions, including locomotion, food handling, and gas exchange.

tuber A swollen underground stem (e.g., potato) or a swollen root (e.g., in a dahlia) for storage and perennation (overwintering form).

tubulin The globular protein in microtubules.

turbellarian A member of the Platyhelminth class Turbellaria. Typically a free-living flatworm with a protrusible pharynx, e.g., a planarian.

turbinal bones Delicate bones, covered with mucus membrane, found in the nasal cavity of mammals.

turgid (1) In plants, refers to a cell whose contents press out against the cell wall.
(2) A plant tissue that is stiff as a result of its component cells being turgid.

Turner's syndrome In humans, a congenital disorder caused by the absence of a sex chromosome. The individual has one X chromosome (genotype X0) and is female in appearance, though sterile.

tusk A modified canine tooth that projects forward from the mouth of a mammal as a conical, horn-like structure.

tympanic bone The bone that supports the tympanic membrane (eardrum) of a mammal. It is derived from the angular bone of the vertebrate skull.

tympanic membrane *See* eardrum, tympanum.

tympanum or **tympanic membrane** (1) In vertebrates, the vibratory membrane at the external opening of the middle ear. In mammals, called the eardrum.
(2) In insects, one of several vibratory membranes covering the components of the auditory organ.

typhlosole A ridge formed by an inward fold of the dorsal wall that runs longitudinally the full length of the intestine of an earthworm. It increases the surface area across which food can be digested. Some mollusks also have a typhlosole in the rectum.

udder The mammary gland of a domesticated mammal.

ulna In tetrapod vertebrates, the posterior of two long bones in the lower forelimb. The inner, larger of the two bones of the human forearm.

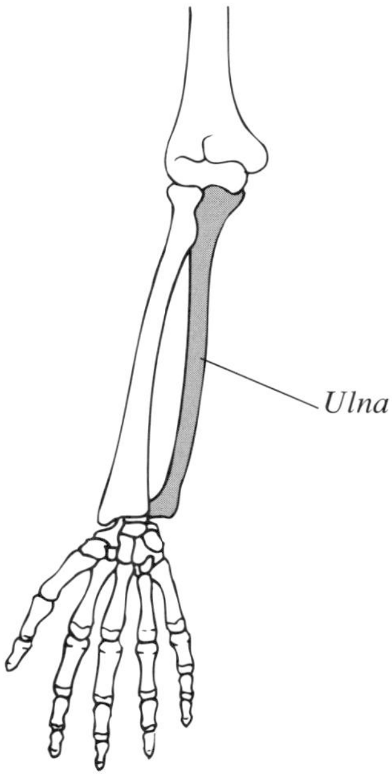

Ulna

ulnar nerve The nerve that lies along the lower forelimb of a vertebrate, on the same side as the ulna. Its branches serve the muscles of the lower forelimb, extending into the wrist.

umbilical arteries and veins The blood vessels associated with the umbilical cord that supply blood to the embryo of a placental mammal.

umbilical cord The cord that attaches the embryo of a placental mammal to the placenta. It consists of blood vessels supported by connective tissue and is severed after birth.

umbo A swelling at the top or center of the shell of a brachiopod or bivalve mollusk. It is the first part of the shell to form.

uncinate process A projection from a bird's rib. Ligaments from the uncinate process attach each rib to the one behind, strengthening the rib cage.

underline The ventral side of a sheep.

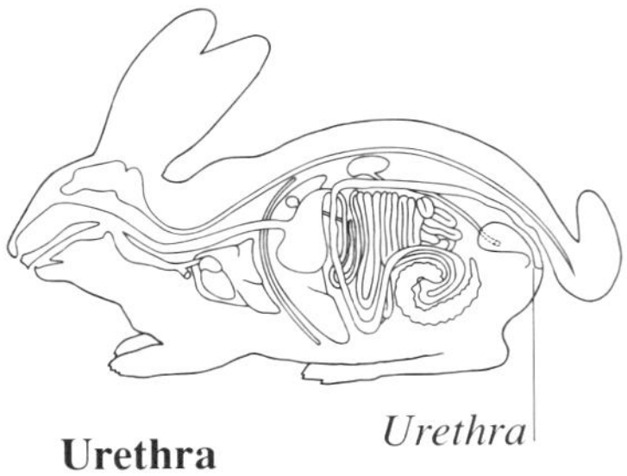

Urethra

ungulate A herbivorous mammal with hoofs.

unguligrade Describes a gait in which only the tips of the digits touch the ground, the digits ending in hoofs.

unicellular Referring to a single-celled organism. *See* multicellular.

uniramous Having no branches.

unques The claws at the tip of each leg of a fly.

urea In mammals and some other vertebrates, the main nitrogenous (nitrogen-containing) waste product. It is excreted via the kidneys.

ureter In mammals, the duct that carries urine from the kidney to the bladder for temporary storage.

urethra In mammals, the duct that carries urine from the bladder to the exterior. In males, it also receives ejaculated semen.

urinary In vertebrates, referring to the body system that produces and eliminates urine.

urine The final waste product of vertebrate metabolism. It is an aqueous solution of organic and inorganic compounds.

urinogenital In vertebrates, referring to the organs and structures of the urinary and reproductive systems, some of which are shared.

urohyal A bone on the ventral side of the head of some fish.

uroid The posterior region of an ameba, away from the region where pseudopodia are being extended.

uropod In many crustaceans, the most posterior appendage. If a telson is present, it is just in front of it.

urostyle A long bone, comprising several fused vertebrae, that is found in some fish and amphibians.

uterus The organ in a female mammal (other than the duck-billed platypus and monotremes) in which the embryo develops. In most species there are two uteri, but in primates only one.

utricle or **utriculus** In mammals, an organ of the inner ear that, together with the saccule, provides information on the position of the head relative to the pull of gravity. It contains chalky granules called otoliths.

vacuole A small sac enveloped in a membrane that is found in a cell.

vagina In most female mammals, the muscular, extensible tract that connects the uterus with the exterior. During copulation, it receives the penis and ejaculated sperm. It is also the birth canal through which the full-term fetus is born.

vagus nerve In vertebrates, the cranial nerve supplying the viscera, heart, and parts of the pharyngeal region.

valve (1) A flap of tissue that allows a fluid to flow in only one direction.
(2) One of the two shells of a bivalve mollusk.

vascular Referring to tissues that transport fluids and their dissolved substances around the body, e.g., blood vessels in animals; xylem and phloem in plants.

vascular bundle In pteridophyte and anthophyte plants, a longitudinal strand of vascular tissue composed mainly of xylem and phloem tissue.

vascular plants Refers to plant groups (e.g., Coniferophyta) whose members have a vascular system comprising xylem and phloem; previously called tracheophytes.

vas deferens A duct possessed by male animals. Sperm travels along it from the testis to the exterior, in the case of invertebrates, or to the urethra or cloaca and from there to the exterior, in the case of vertebrates.

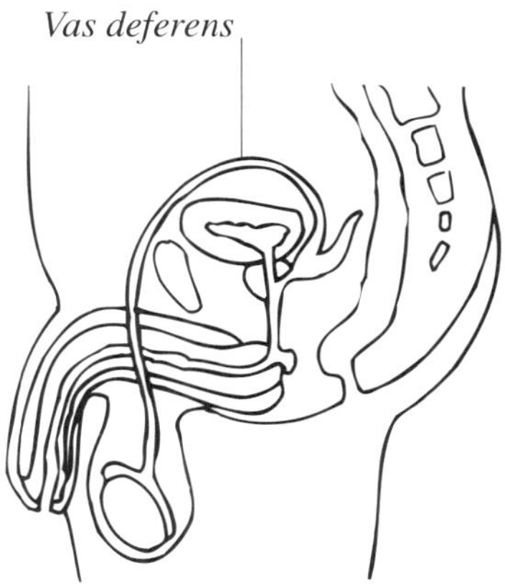

Vas deferens

vas efferens The tubes between the testis and vas deferens of a male animal.

vasopressin (or antidiuretic hormone [ADH]). In vertebrates, a peptide hormone secreted by the posterior pituitary gland. It promotes reabsorption of water by the kidney tubules.

vastus muscles Two muscles (vastus externus and internus) that lie one to either side of the upper hindlimb of a vertebrate.

vegetative propagation In plants, asexual reproduction by expansive growth and the subsequent detachment of large fragments of the plant body. Organs of vegetative propagation include tubers, stolons, and runners.

vein (1) In plants, the vascular bundle and supporting tissue in a flower part or leaf.
(2) In animals, a vessel carrying blood toward the heart.
(3) In insects, one of the chitinous tubes supporting the wing.

vena cava (pl. **venae cavae**) One of the principal veins conveying blood to the heart in a tetrapod. There are two venae cavae, the superior and inferior (also called the precaval and postcaval veins respectively). The superior serves the head, neck, chest, and arms, the inferior all of the body below the diaphragm.

vent The external opening of the cloaca in a bird.

ventral The side of an organism that is directed towards the surface on which it rests when the organism is in its usual stance. In vertebrates, the side of the body that is furthest from the spine. In humans and other bipedal species, it is the front of the body.

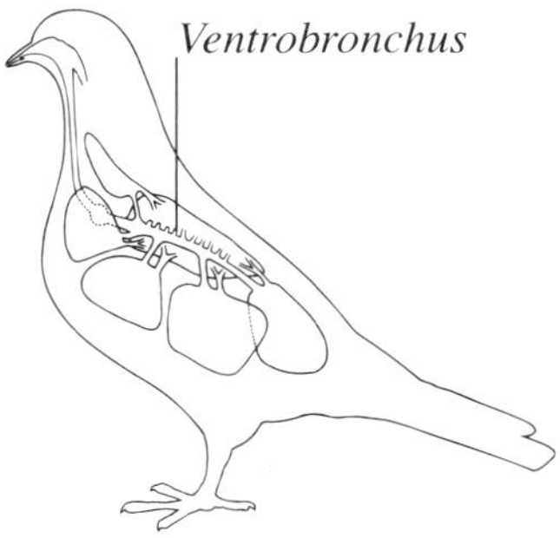

Ventrobronchus

ventricle (1) The chamber of the heart that receives blood from the atrium and pumps it into the arteries.
(2) One of a varying number of open cavities found in the brain of a vertebrate.
(3) A cavity in the pharynx of a mammal.
(4) A small pouch in the nasal cavity of a mammal.

ventriculus The middle part of the gut in arthropods.

ventrobronchus The middle part of each of the main bronchi in the respiratory system of a bird. It lies behind the syrinx and is connected to several of the air sacs.

venule A small vein that receives blood from a capillary network.

vermiform appendix *See* appendix.

vertebra (pl. **vertebrae**) One of the bones that are joined together to form the vertebral column.

vertebrate A fish, amphibian, reptile, bird, or mammal. These groups belong to the Vertebrata (or Craniata), a subphylum of the Chordata, comprising animals that have a bony or cartilaginous backbone (vertebral column), skeleton, and skull containing a brain.

vesicle In cells, a membrane-enclosed sac containing secretory products.

vestibule A passage that leads from one body cavity to another.

vestigial Referring to an organ or structure, now functionless or reduced, believed to be the remnant of a useful structure in an ancestor.

vibrissae (or whiskers). Stiff hairs or modified feathers that project from the skin of an animal. When vibrated, the hairs stimulate nerves in the skin. Vibrissae are found in many animals, but especially in mammals.

villus (pl. **villi**) (1) In vertebrates, one of numerous projections on the wall of the small intestine that increase the surface area for absorption.
(2) In mammals, one of many projections from the fetal side of the placenta. It increases the surface area for exchange of substances.

virology The study of viruses.

virus An infectious agent composed of nucleic acid (DNA or RNA) and protein. It requires a living host in order to reproduce and multiply. Viruses are responsible for many of the most debilitating diseases in animals and plants.

viscera In animals, the internal organs in the body cavity, especially those associated with the alimentary canal.

visceral nerve One of the nerves that serves the internal organs (viscera). In vertebrates, the visceral nerves also serve glands and the smooth muscles of the alimentary tract and jaws.

vitamins Complex organic substances in plants and animals that are essential in small amounts for various metabolic processes. Vitamins A, D, E, and K are fat-soluble; vitamins B and C are water-soluble. Lack of vitamins in the diet results in deficiency diseases.

viteline membrane In animals, the membrane surrounding the ovum, external to the plasma membrane.

vitellarium or **yolk gland** Part of the ovary of a flatworm that specializes in producing modified eggs called yolk cells.

vitreous humor In vertebrates, the jelly-like material filling the space between the lens and retina of the eye.

vomer A bone in the upper jaw of amphibians. In frogs, it is one of the bones that bear teeth (vomerine teeth).

vulva The external opening of the vagina in a female mammal.

water vascular system A system of interconnecting, water-filled canals and bladders found in echinoderms. The system connects with the water outside and is used to operate the tube feet.

wattle A bare patch of loose, fleshy skin that hangs from the jaw, eye, or throat of a bird. Wattles are often brightly colored. In some species they are molted each year.

whiskers *See* vibrissae.

white matter In vertebrates, tissue of the central nervous system composed mainly of myelinated nerve fibers that give the tissue a bright white appearance. *See* gray matter.

wing coverts Feathers based on the principal wing feathers of a bird.

withers The dorsal surface of some mammals, above the shoulders.

Wolffian duct A duct leading from the mesonephros, the middle part of the kidney of a vertebrate embryo, that becomes the kidney in fish and amphibians and the testis in other groups. In fish and amphibians, the Wolffian duct forms the urinary duct in females and the urinogenital duct in males. In other vertebrates, it degenerates in females and becomes the vas deferens in males.

worker A member of a colony of social insects that forages for food, tends the eggs and larvae, and maintains the nest structure.

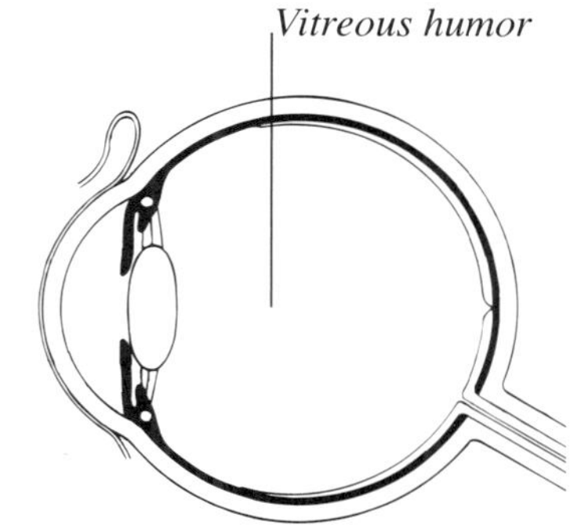

Vitreous humor

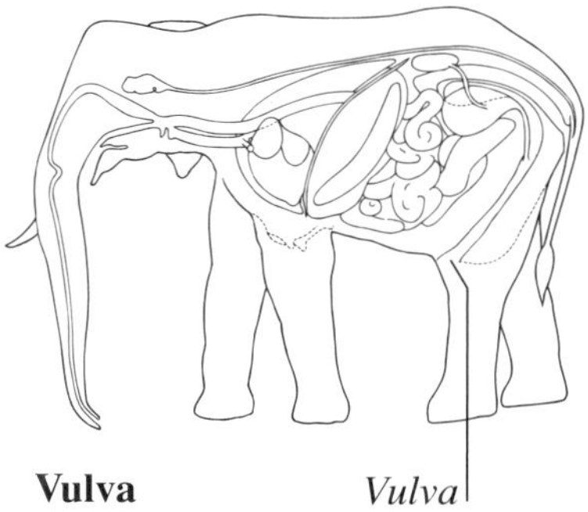

Vulva

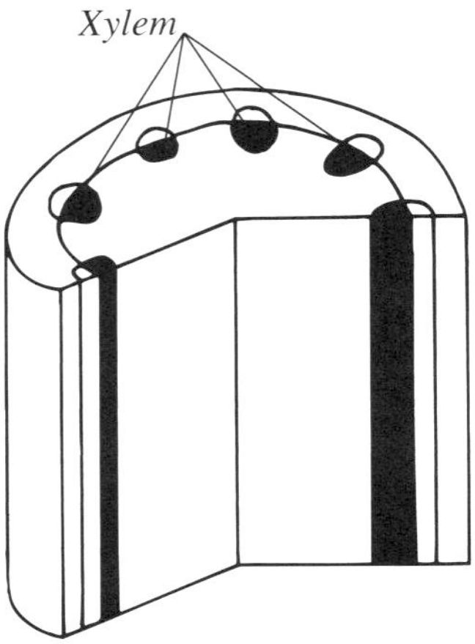

Xylem

worm *See* Annelida.

xylem Vascular; structually supportive plant tissue that conducts water and dissolved minerals from roots to stem and leaves. It is composed mainly of tracheids and xylem vessels with strengthened walls.

yeast Several genera of widely distributed unicellular fungi.

yolk In animals, the food store (largely protein and fat) found in the ovum.

yolk gland *See* vitellarium.

zalambdodont Describes molar teeth that are narrow at the front and back and have the two cusps completely or partly fused.

zona pellucida In mammals, a thick transparent membrane enclosing the mature ovum. It is secreted by the ovarian follicle.

zoology The scientific study of animals.

zygodactylous Describes the feet of a bird in which two toes point forward and two backward.

zygomatic arch An arch of bone found in the skull of a mammal. It lies between the lower edge of the orbit and the rear of the skull.

zygospore In certain proteins and fungi, a resistant, thick-walled spore formed after the fusion of gametes or gametangia.

zygote The fertilized ovum before it undergoes cell division and cleavage.

zymogen The inactive form of an enzyme that is activated by other chemicals at the required site of action.

SECTION TWO BIOGRAPHIES

Abū al-Qāsim Khalaf ibn Abbas az-Zahrawi (**Albucacis**) (ca. 936–ca. 1013) Arab surgeon who was Islam's most notable medical man of medieval times. His great 30-part medical treatise, *At-Tasrif* (*The Method*), was a detailed account of Arab medical knowledge of the time and was widely used by European doctors. The chapter on surgery was an improvement on the writings of Galen, 2nd-century Greek physician.

Addison, Thomas (1793–1860) English physician who, in 1849, was the first to describe the disease of underaction of the adrenal (suprarenal) glands, now known as Addison's disease. Addison also discovered a previously unrecognized form of anemia known as megaloblastic, "pernicious," or Addisonian anemia.

Adler, Alfred (1870–1937) Austrian psychologist who was initially a follower of Freud but who broke away from psychoanalysis to found his own school of psychology. He is best remembered for his concept of the "inferiority complex."

Adrian, Edgar Douglas, 1st Baron (1889–1977) British neurophysiologist who worked out the nature of the nerve impulse, showing it to be a frequency-modulated electrical signal. For this outstanding advance Adrian was awarded the 1932 Nobel Prize in physiology or medicine, which he shared with Charles Sherrington.

Albucasis *See* **Abū al-Qāsim**.

Alcmaeon (fl. 520 BCE) Greek philosopher, a pupil of Pythagoras, who taught that disease could be caused by faulty diet, lack of exercise, and various environmental causes.

Alder, Kurt (1902–58) German chemist who, in 1928, working with Otto Diels, discovered a relatively easy way to produce a ring (cyclic) compound, starting with a compound containing two double bonds, separated by a single bond. This is the Diels-Alder reaction, which became important in organic synthesis and earned Alder and Diels the 1950 Nobel Prize in chemistry.

Altman, Sidney (b. 1939) Canadian cellular biologist who worked on the formation of transfer RNA and showed that this involves an enzyme that contains both protein and RNA. He later made the remarkable finding that the RNA partly acted, by itself, as an enzyme. The implication was that early evolution could occur without protein enzymes. He shared the 1989 Nobel Prize in chemistry with Thomas Cech.

Anaximander (610–ca. 547 BCE) Greek philosopher credited with many imaginative scientific speculations, for example, that living creatures first emerged from slime and that humans must have developed from some other species that matured more quickly into self-sufficiency.

Anderson, Elizabeth Garrett (1836–1917) English nurse who became the first British woman to earn a medical degree and become a qualified and registered doctor. The profession repeatedly refused to admit her, but her father went to court and the doctors were forced to back down. In 1866, she opened St. Mary's Dispensary for Women and in 1877 she founded the London School of Medicine for Women.

Elizabeth Garrett Anderson

Anfinsen, Christian Boehmer (1916–95) U.S. biochemist who assisted in the sequencing of the enzyme ribonuclease, with its 128 amino acids, an achievement for which he shared the 1972 Nobel Prize in chemistry with Stanford Moore and William Stein. Anfinsen went on to study the three-dimensional (secondary and tertiary) structure of this important enzyme.

Arber, Werner (b. 1929) Swiss microbiologist who discovered the first of the range of enzymes capable of cutting DNA at certain sites so as to isolate lengths. These are called restriction enzymes and are the basis of genetic engineering.

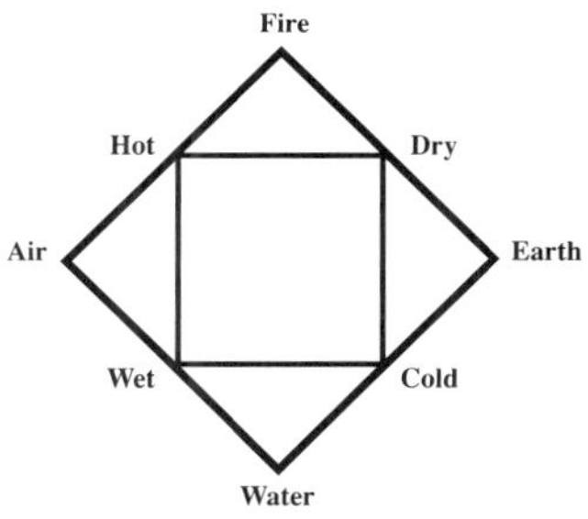

Diagram of the four elements (fire, earth, water, air) and four qualities (dry, cold, wet, hot) of Aristotelian physics

Aristotle (384–322 BCE) Greek philosopher who, through extensive writings, became historically the most influential figure of the ancient world. He covered every field of contemporary knowledge, but in science wrote on physics, biology, medicine, zoology, zoological taxonomy, and psychology. Much of what he wrote about fundamental science was pure imagination and was wrong. Unfortunately, he was accepted as an almost infallible authority, so for almost 2,000 years, scientific thought was misdirected and real progress hindered.

Aselli, Gasparo (1581–1625) Italian physician and anatomist who was the first to describe the lymph vessels, the fine tubes that, after a fatty meal, carry emulsified fat away from the intestine. He did not discover that these tubes end in a blood vessel in the chest but was aware that they were concerned with digestion.

Audubon, John James (1785–1851) U.S. ornithologist (bird specialist) and artist who attempted to include every species of bird in America in his major set of life-size color illustrations of 1,065 birds. The seven-volume book that resulted became a best-seller and Audubon has been famous ever since.

Avery, Oswald Theodore (1877–1955) Canadian-born U.S. bacteriologist who, in 1944, was the first to show that a change in the inheritable characteristics in organisms could result from deoxyribonucleic acid (DNA). Specifically, he showed that a nonvirulent, rough-coated bacterium could be made into the virulent, smooth-coated strain if it was accessed by DNA from a dead virulent strain. This observation triggered modern genetics and molecular biology.

Avicenna *See* **Ibn Sīnā**.

Axelrod, Julius (1912–2004) U.S. neuropharmacologist who was a member of the research team that discovered the neurotransmitter norepinephrine (noradrenaline). Axelrod was refused entry to several medical schools and decided to study pharmacology. In 1970, he along with Sir Bernard Katz and Ulf von Euler were awarded the Nobel Prize in physiology or medicine.

Babinski, Joseph-François-Felix (1857–1932) French neurologist who discovered a physical reflex, indicating damage in the nervous system above the level of the spinal nerves, that is still in use today.

Francis Bacon

Bacon, Francis (1561–1626) English philosopher and essayist whose book *The Advancement of Learning* (1605) drew serious attention for the first time to the fact that the real source of scientific knowledge was not the authority of pundits such as Aristotle but observation, experimentation, direct experience, and careful induction. This was the start of the scientific method that was to prove so fruitful.

Bacon, Roger (ca. 1220–92) English philosopher who tried to compile an encyclopedia containing all the knowledge of his day. The attempt failed but contained much valuable mathematical information and included some remarkable speculations about mechanical transport, heavier-than-air flying machines, and the possibility of circling the globe.

Baer, Karl Ernst von (1792–1876) Estonian biologist and researcher into animal prenatal development (embryology) who discovered the mammalian egg cell (ovum) and established the theory of the three developmental layers: the ectoderm, mesoderm, and endoderm. He showed how closely early embryos of different species resemble one another and how those of higher animals pass through stages similar to those in the development of simpler animals. Baer is considered the founder of modern embryology.

Baeyer, Johann Friedrich Wilhelm Adolf von (1835–1917) German chemist who devoted his life to the analysis and synthesis of organic molecules and published more than 300 important papers. He is especially noted for his studies of uric acid and organic dyes. His synthesis of indigo was of great commercial importance and for this achievement he was awarded the Nobel Prize in chemistry in 1905.

Baillie, Matthew (1761–1823) British physician who specialized in the study of disease in tissues (pathology) and, in 1793, published a book, *Morbid Anatomy of Some of the Most Important Parts of the Human Body*, that helped to establish pathology as a discipline in its own right.

Baird, Spencer Fullerton (1823–87) U.S. biologist whose published work on North American birds, mammals, and reptiles, and his administrative influence, did much to promote American field studies in ornithology and botany.

Bakewell, Robert (1725–95) British livestock breeder who, by selective breeding, was highly successful in improving the state of farm animals, especially sheep. His Leicester breed of sheep produced about twice the mutton of other breeds and quickly spread throughout the world.

Francis Balfour

Balfour, Francis Maitland (1851–82) Scottish embryologist who did much valuable research on the early development of fish with cartilage skeletons (elasmobranchii), a class whose eggs are fertilized internally. He wrote a notable text on embryology called *Treatise on Comparative Embryology* (1880) and originated the term *Chordata* for animals with backbones.

Baltimore, David (b. 1938) U.S. biochemist who shared the 1975 Nobel Prize in physiology or medicine with Howard Martin

Temin and Renato Dulbecco for discovering an enzyme, called reverse transcriptase, that could make DNA from RNA. This viral enzyme, which is present in retroviruses such as HIV, enables these viruses to insert their genome into the DNA of the host cell. Its discovery showed that Crick's fundamental genetic "dogma"—that the sequence is always from DNA to RNA to protein—was wrong.

Bamberger, Eugen (1857–1932) German chemist who first proposed the term *alicyclic* for unsaturated ring organic compounds. He worked on the synthesis of nitroso compounds and quinols, and investigated the structure of naphthalene.

Sir Joseph Banks

Banks, Sir Joseph (1743–1820) English botanist who accompanied Captain James Cook on his voyage around the world in the ship *Endeavour* and who persuaded King George III to make Kew Gardens in London into a center for botanical research. He caused many tropical fruits to be imported to the West and was a long-term president of the Royal Society of London.

Banting, Sir Frederick Grant (1891–1941) Canadian physiologist who, with Charles Herbert Best, showed that the "islets of Langerhans" in the pancreas produce a substance that could reverse the effects of diabetes. It was insulin. Banting and his laboratory chief, John James Macleod, were jointly awarded the Nobel Prize in physiology or medicine in 1923. Best, being a mere student, was ignored, but Banting immediately gave him half the prize money.

Barcroft, Sir Joseph (1872–1947) Irish physiologist who studied the oxygen-carrying property of hemoglobin, devised a way of measuring blood gases, and led three high-altitude expeditions to study the effects of lower atmospheric pressures on human respiratory function. He also studied acclimatization. His book *Respiratory Function of the Blood* (1914) was very influential.

Barger, George (1878–1939) Dutch-born British organic chemist who isolated ergotoxine from ergot and proceeded to study related amines with physiological properties. This eventually had two important effects: it drew attention to the role of neurotransmitters in the function of the nervous system, and it led to the development of a range of valuable drugs.

Barnard, Christiaan (1922–2001) South African surgeon who at Groote Schuur Hospital, Cape Town, in 1957 performed the world's first heart transplant. The patient died from a lung infection, partly as a result of the immunosuppressive drugs needed to prevent rejection of the transplanted heart. A second patient, Philip Blaiberg, lived for a year and seven months, thereby showing that the procedure was feasible.

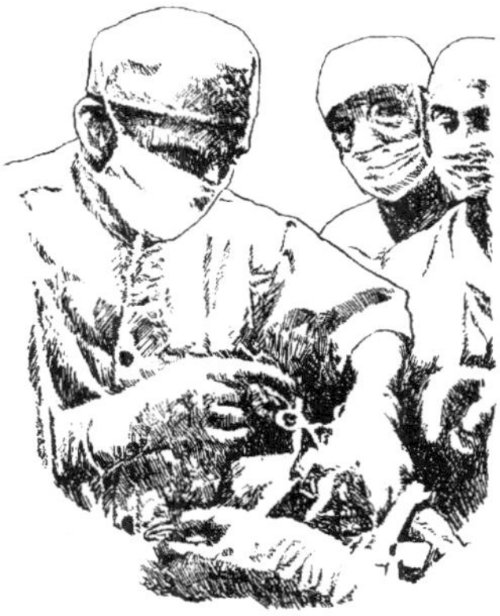

Christiaan Barnard operating

Barnard, Joseph Edwin (1870–1949) English physicist and microscopist who pioneered the application of photography to microscopic observations. He also improved the resolving power of the optical microscope by using ultraviolet light. This work was, however, overtaken by the development of the electron microscope.

Barr, Murray Llewellyn (1908–95) Canadian anatomist and histologist who showed that one of the X (sex) chromosomes, visible in nondividing female body cells, is a small, densely staining mass of chromatin, now known as the Barr body, which has become inactivated. The other X chromosome is of normal appearance and is genetically active. Barr also published an anatomical textbook on the human nervous system that went into many editions.

Caspar Bartholin

Bartholin, Caspar (1655–1738) Danish anatomist best remembered for his description of the pair of glands, one on each side of the vaginal opening, that secrete clear mucus under the influence of sexual excitement and facilitate sexual intercourse.

Bartholin, Thomas (1616–80) Danish mathematician and physiologist who discovered the thoracic duct (lymph duct) through which emulsified fats, carried from the intestine by the lymphatics, are returned to the circulation. He described the lymphatic system of the body and supported William Harvey against critics of his demonstration of the circulation of the blood.

Bates, Henry Walter (1825–92) British naturalist and explorer who collected enormous numbers of insect specimens. He studied the phenomena of insect protective mimicry, which provided persuasive evidence for the idea of natural selection and support for Charles Darwin's theory of evolution, which was then highly controversial.

Bateson, William (1861–1926) English geneticist and the first professor of genetics, Bateson translated Gregor Mendel's papers into English. His main achievement was to show that certain inheritable characteristics were nearly always passed on together. This principle of "linkage" was later shown to be due to the fact that the genes for linked characteristics were on the same chromosome. Bateson, however, did not believe that chromosomes had anything to do with inheritable physical characteristics.

Bauhin, Gaspard (1560–1624) Swiss botanist and anatomist who, in 1623, published a botanical catalog containing more than 6,000 species of plants. The general arrangement was somewhat haphazard and the taxonomy not based on any recognizable principle, but the species were grouped in a manner suggesting modern genera. The book provides a valuable historical account of the state of botany at the time.

Bayliss, Sir William Maddock (1860–1924) British physiologist who in 1902, working with Ernest Starling, first showed the existence of hormones. This was the start of the science of endocrinology. Bayliss also recognized the true nature of surgical shock and advocated the use of intravenous fluids. This advice saved many lives in World War I.

George W. Beadle

Beadle, George Wells (1903–89) U.S. biochemist who showed that particular genes code for particular enzymes. The technique used was to cause gene mutations that affected particular biochemical processes, thereby showing the immediate link between the gene and the enzyme. This was a major advance in genetics.

Beaumont, William (1785–1853) U.S. physician in Connecticut who added greatly to the knowledge of the functioning of the digestive system by making observations for 12 years on a live patient who had a permanent opening from his stomach to the exterior (a fistula), following an accidental gunshot wound. Beaumont made 238 observations of the stomach lining and the secretion of gastric juice. The patient lived to age 82; Beaumont died at age 68.

Beebe, Charles William (1887–1962) U.S. naturalist and underwater explorer best remembered for the Beebe bathysphere: a strong, sealed, spherical capsule, fitted with observation ports and light, that could be lowered to great ocean depths for scientific studies. Beebe reached a depth of 3,028 feet (923.5 m).

Emil von Behring

Behring, Emil Adolf von (1854–1917) German bacteriologist and assistant to Robert Koch, who discovered that animals who had been immunized against diphtheria and tetanus had substances in their blood capable of neutralizing the toxins produced by diphtheria and tetanus bacteria. This was the first proof of the existence of antibodies. Behring was awarded the 1901 Nobel Prize in physiology or medicine, the first to be awarded in this class.

Bell, Sir Charles (1774–1842) Scottish surgeon and anatomist best remembered for his description of the one-sided paralysis of the facial muscles known as "Bell's palsy"—the result of damage to the seventh cranial nerve on one side. Bell also made the fundamental distinction between motor and sensory nerves and showed that they were entirely distinct.

Pierre Belon

Belon, Pierre (1517–64) French naturalist who wrote works on the natural history of fish and of birds. He appears to have been the first to observe anatomical equivalents (homologs) in the vertebral bones of fish and mammals.

Benacerraf, Baruj (b. 1920) U.S. immunologist who showed that certain antigens of the surface of mouse cells, the H-2 system, play a critical role in the functioning of the immune system. Over 30 different genes are coded for the immune response (Ir) antigens in this system. Benacerraf then extended this work to the analogous human lymphocytic antigen (HLA) system in humans—greatly important in human pathology and physiology. For this work, he shared the 1980 Nobel Prize in physiology or medicine with George Snell and Jean Dausset.

Beneden, Edouard-Joseph-Louis-Marie van (1846–1910) Belgian embryologist who noticed that the number of chromosomes in the general body cells of an organism was constant, but that in the sperm and eggs the number was half of this constant. The full number was restored at the time of fertilization, indicating that half the chromosomes came from the father and half from the mother.

Bentham, George (1800–84) British botanist and classifier (taxonomist) who wrote one of the first books on British flora, *The Handbook of the British Flora* (1858). He also wrote extensively on Australian flora. His collection of many thousands of specimens of plants was presented to London's Kew Gardens in 1854.

Berger, Hans (1873–1941) German psychiatrist who was the first to produce a tracing of the electrical activity of the human brain. This was the electroencephalogram (EEG), which has become a useful clinical tool and a means of establishing brain death.

Berg, Paul (b. 1926) U.S. biochemist and molecular biologist who was one of the principal founders of genetic engineering. Berg developed techniques using specific DNA-cleaving enzymes capable of cutting out genes from the DNA of one mammalian species and inserting them into the DNA of another. For this work, he shared the 1980 Nobel Prize in chemistry with Walter Gilbert and Frederick Sanger. Berg also drew up strict rules to govern safe conduct in genetic engineering.

Claude Bernard

Bernard, Claude (1813–78) French physiologist, often described as the father of modern physiology. After receiving his medical degree, he devoted his life to research in physiology, eventually establishing it as a formal discipline in its own right. Among his many discoveries were the facts that complex food carbohydrates are broken down to simple sugars before absorption; that bile is necessary for the absorption of fats; that the body re-synthesizes the carbohydrate glycogen; and that the bore of arteries is controlled by nerve action.

Bert, Paul (1833–86) French physiologist who studied the effects of extremes of pressure on the human body. He investigated the way high pressures on divers cause nitrogen to dissolve in the blood, with attendant dangers when the pressure is suddenly released, and showed how to avoid these dangers.

Best, Charles Herbert (1899–1978) Canadian professional football and baseball player who gave up sports to work with Frederick Banting on the isolation of insulin. Best's contribution was considerable but, as a student, he was not nominated for the Nobel Prize. The head of the laboratory, John Macleod, who had done little to help, was. History, however, credits Banting and Best for the discovery of insulin. Best also showed how the effect of injected insulin could be prolonged by mixing it with zinc.

Bichat, Marie-François-Xavier (1771–1802) French surgeon and anatomist who founded the sciences of microscopic anatomy (histology) and microscopic pathology (histopathology). Bichat identified 21 different kinds of human tissue and demonstrated the changes that occurred in them in particular diseases. His book *Traité des membranes* (1800) was a milestone in the development of pathology.

Xavier Bichat

Bilharz, Theodor (1825–62) German physician, anatomist, and zoologist whose studies of the *Schistosoma* species of human worm parasites led to the disease resulting from it being named "bilharzia" and opened up a new era in tropical parasitology.

Billroth, Theodor Albert (1829–94) German surgeon who made contributions to military surgery, general surgery, microscopic anatomy (histology), and pathology. He was a pianist and friend of Johannes Brahms, who previewed many of his compositions in Billroth's house.

Bishop, John Michael (b. 1936) U.S. microbiologist and immunologist who was the first to prove that certain cancers could be caused by viruses. These became known as oncoviruses; they carry genes (oncogenes) that act on DNA to cause abnormal cell reproduction. This work earned Bishop and his colleague, Harold Varmus, the 1989 Nobel Prize in physiology or medicine.

Blackwell, Elizabeth (1821–1910) The first woman in the United States to be awarded a medical degree. In the face of strong prejudice and threats of mob violence, she set up the New York Dispensary for Poor Women and Children. Eventually her hospital gained acceptance.

Blane, Sir Gilbert (1749–1834) Scottish physician who, 50 years after James Lind had proved that scurvy in seamen could be prevented by a daily spoonful of citrus fruit juice, finally persuaded the Lords of the Admiralty to adopt this measure. In the meantime, thousands of British seamen had died of scurvy. Blane had a grave, cold manner, and was known privately as "Chilblane."

Blumberg, Baruch Samuel (b. 1925) U.S. immunologist who, in the course of the study of an immense number of samples from different populations, discovered an antigen in the blood of an Australian aborigine that reacted with an antibody in the blood of an American patient. The antigen proved to be a hepatitis B antigen and came to be known as the "Australian antigen." For this discovery Blumberg and his colleague, Carleton Gajdusek, shared the 1976 Nobel Prize in physiology or medicine.

Bonner, James Frederick (1910–96) U.S. molecular biologist who showed that the presence of a protein, histone, shuts down gene activity so that only those genes required in a particular situation are operative. Bonner also worked on the artificial synthesis of RNA.

Bordet, Jules-Jean-Baptiste-Vincent (1870–1961) Belgian bacteriologist who discovered a substance he called alexin, now known as complement, that is necessary to allow antibodies to enable phagocytes of the immune system to destroy invading bacteria. This made possible a range of tests for specific antibodies and antigens. Bordet was awarded the 1919 Nobel Prize in physiology or medicine.

Borlaug, Norman Ernest (b. 1914) U.S. agronomist and plant breeder who was one of the pioneers of the green revolution in agriculture. He was awarded the 1970 Nobel Peace Prize for his work on breeding improved wheat to be grown in India and Mexico.

Boveri, Theodor Heinrich (1862–1915) German biologist who confirmed Edouard Beneden's early work on chromosomes and showed that the number for the species had to be correct if a normal individual were to develop. He also showed that each chromosome determines a particular and fixed set of hereditable characteristics.

Bovet, Daniel (1907–92) Swiss pharmacologist and physiologist who isolated the sulfanilamide part of the red dye prontosil that was being used to treat bacterial infections in mice. This work led to the development of the sulfa drugs, which, until the development of penicillin and other antibiotics, were the most important class of medications.

Boyer, Herbert Wayne (b. 1936) U.S. biochemist and genetic engineering pioneer who showed that, by using an enzyme called an endonuclease, a DNA ring (a plasmid) from a bacterium could be inserted into the DNA of another bacterium or that of a toad. He was then able to clone the hybrid DNA by allowing bacteria containing it to reproduce. This achievement led to the commercial production of insulin and other valuable proteins.

Boyer, Paul Delos (b. 1918) U.S. chemist whose advances in the understanding of the mechanism by which the enzyme ATP synthase (ATPase) catalyzes the synthesis of ATP from ADP and phosphate earned him a share of the 1997 Nobel Prize in chemistry with Jens Skou and John Walker. Adenosine triphosphate (ATP) is a nucleotide of fundamental importance as the carrier of chemical energy in all living organisms.

Richard Bright

Bright, Richard (1789–1858) Scottish physician who described the inflammatory kidney disease nephritis, which for many years, was known as "Bright's disease" but which is now known to include a range of renal disorders.

Brown, Robert (1773–1858) Scottish botanist renowned for his investigation into the impregnation of plants. He was the first to note that, in general, living cells contain a central, dark-staining mass and to name it the nucleus. In 1827, he first observed the "Brownian movement" of fine particles in liquid caused by molecular movements.

Buffon commemorated on a postage stamp

Brunfels, Otto (ca. 1488–1534) German botanist who with two others, Hieronymus Bock and Leonhard Fuchs, are considered the pioneers of modern botany. Brunfels also produced accurate and detailed botanical illustrations of real scientific value.

Buchner, Eduard (1860–1917) German chemist who researched fermentation and showed that Louis Pasteur was wrong in insisting that fermentation required the exclusion of oxygen. For this finding Buchner was awarded the 1907 Nobel Prize in chemistry.

Buffon, Georges-Louis Leclerc, Comte de (1707–88) French naturalist who wrote a 44-volume work on natural history that, he hoped, would contain all that was known of the subject at the time. Buffon partly accepted the idea of evolution and realized that all species were, in some way or other, related to each other.

Burbank, Luther (1849–1926) U.S. horticulturist who pioneered the process of improving food plants through grafting, hybridization, and other means. He developed the Burbank potato and new varieties of plums and berries. He also developed new flowers, including the Burbank rose and the Shasta daisy.

Buridan, Jean (1300–58) Famous French philosopher of the 14th century who is said to have proved that a human could not act if affected by two equally powerful motives. This idea ("Buridan's ass") is the kind of proposition that, for many years during the Middle Ages, was widely, but pointlessly, argued by serious philosophers.

Sir Macfarlane Burnet

Burkitt, Dennis (1911–93) British physician noted for his discovery of the viral causation of a tumor now known as Burkitt's lymphoma. Burkitt was a pioneer in the development of geographic medicine and became influential for his conviction that high-fiber diets reduce the incidence of various bowel diseases, including cancer. This was based on observations of the colonic health of populations on high-fiber diets, but it has now been shown that in the Western world a high-fiber diet does not, apparently, confer this advantage.

Burnet, Sir Frank Macfarlane (1899–1985) Australian virologist who worked on immunological tolerance to antigens with Peter Brian Medawar and helped to found the modern discipline of immunology.

Albert Calmette

Butenandt, Adolf Friedrich Johann (1903–95) German biochemist who in 1931 isolated the male sex hormone androsterone. He also isolated a few milligrams of progesterone from the corpus luteum of the ovaries of female pigs. His methods must have been relatively inefficient, as no fewer than 50,000 pigs were required. For his work on hormones he was awarded the 1939 Nobel Prize in chemistry.

Calmette, Albert-Léon-Charles (1863–1933) French bacteriologist who studied under Louis Pasteur and who, with his colleague Camille Guérin, developed the BCG (Bacille Calmette-Guérin) vaccine against tuberculosis.

Calvin, Melvin (1911–97) U.S. biochemist who made notable advances in the understanding of photosynthesis, the processes by which sugars and complex carbohydrates such as starches are synthesized by plants from atmospheric carbon dioxide. Calvin used radioactive carbon tracers to follow the movement of carbon through the complex reactions. He also worked on theories of the chemical origin of life and on attempts to utilize carbon dioxide artificially. Calvin was awarded the Nobel Prize in chemistry in 1961 for his work on photosynthesis.

Camerarius, Rudolph Jakob (1665–1721) German botanist who first identified the male and female reproductive organs in plants.

Candolle, Augustin-Pyrame de (1778–1841) Swiss botanist and chemist who introduced the term *taxonomy* for the classification of plants by their morphology rather than physiology, as set out in his *Elementary Theory of Botany* (1813). His new edition of *Flore française* appeared in 1805. He accurately described the relationship between plants and soils, a factor that affects geographic plant distribution. He is remembered in the specific names of more than 300 plants, two genera, and one family.

Cannon, Walter Bradford (1871–1945) U.S. physiologist who introduced a contrast X-ray technique now known as the barium meal. Cannon used a bismuth preparation opaque to X-rays, but this has now been replaced by insoluble barium sulfate. Cannon also did important research on epinephrine (adrenaline) and other neurotransmitters.

Carlisle, Anthony (1768–1841) English physician who demonstrated that substances in solution could be decomposed by passing an electric current through them (electrolysis). This was the beginning of the study of electrochemistry.

Carnap, Rudolf (1891–1970) German philosopher of science who has had considerable influence on scientists. He taught that statements were meaningful only if they could be related to sensory experience and if they have logical consequences that are verifiable by observation or experience. This idea led to the philosophical school of logical positivism and to the dismissal, by some people, of most or all of the propositions of metaphysics and religion.

Carrel, Alexis (1873–1944) French-born U.S. surgeon who pioneered the surgery of blood vessels (vascular surgery), which led to the technical success of organ transplantation. This work was done mainly at the Rockefeller Institute for Medical Research in New York City. He also developed an artificial heart pump for short-term use. For his advances in surgery he was awarded the Nobel Prize in physiology or medicine for 1912.

Cech, Thomas Robert (b. 1947) U.S. biochemist who demonstrated the remarkable fact that a length of protein-free RNA could act as an enzyme for the cleaving and splicing of other RNA. This fact could explain much about the early evolution of organisms. Cech shared the 1989 Nobel Prize in chemistry with Sidney Altman.

Celsus, Aulus Cornelius (born ca. 10 BCE) Roman physician and encyclopedist who left a major text on medical history, medical and surgical practice, and diet and hygiene. This was later one of the first medical textbooks to be printed and became very influential.

Cesalpino, Andrea (1519–1603) Italian botanist who wrote a book outlining the principles of botany, including plant structure and an explanation of plant physiology, and proposed a scheme of plant classification—the first attempt at formal classification.

Chagas, Carlos Ribiero Justiniano (1879–1934) Brazilian physician who first described South American trypanosomiasis (Chagas' disease) and who was also the first to identify the organism *Pneumocystis carinii*, which became well known at the outset of the AIDS epidemic.

Chain, Sir Ernst Boris (1906–79) German-born British biochemist who isolated and purified penicillin and turned Alexander Fleming's discovery of the antibiotic into one of the greatest successes in the history of medicine. Chain, Howard Florey, and Fleming shared the 1945 Nobel Prize in physiology or medicine.

Chance, Britton (b. 1913) U.S. biophysicist who worked on proving that enzymes function by attaching themselves to the substance on which they act (the substrate). He achieved this with a spectroscopic technique using the enzyme peroxidase, which contains iron and absorbs certain light wavelengths strongly. Chance also helped to work out the way that cells get their energy from sugar by observing the fact that concentrations of adenosine diphosphate (ADP) are related to the oxidation-reduction states of the proteins in the respiratory chain.

Charcot, Jean-Martin (1825–93) French neurologist who studied nervous diseases and correlated these with specific brain changes, thereby greatly advancing the knowledge of the nervous system. His studies on hysteria had a major impact on the work of Sigmund Freud.

Jean-Martin Charcot

Chargaff, Erwin (1905–2002) Austrian-born U.S. biochemist who, in the mid-1940s, speculated that if DNA was the vehicle of inheritance, its molecule must vary greatly. Using the methods available at the time, however, he found that its composition was constant within a species but that it differed widely between species. In 1950, he established that the number of purine bases (adenine and guanine) was the same as the number of pyrimidine bases (cytosine and thymine). This was an important fact that James Watson and Francis Crick had to incorporate into their model of the structure of DNA.

Charnley, Sir John (1911–82) British orthopedic surgeon and pioneer of hip joint replacement surgery who, after overcoming many technological and surgical difficulties, succeeded in producing the design of a joint using a metal ball and fixation arm for the thigh bone part and a high-density polythene cup for the pelvic part. This was a major breakthrough in surgery from which millions have benefited.

Chittenden, Russell Henry (1856–1943) U.S. physiologist who discovered the glucose polymer, glycogen, in muscle and who determined the daily protein requirements of a human being, proving that the then estimate of 4.16 ounces (118 g) was an overestimate and that 1.76 ounces (50 g) a day was adequate to maintain health. Chittenden helped to establish biochemistry as a discipline in its own right.

Clarke, Sir Cyril Astley (1907–2000) English physician who developed a method of protecting the rhesus-positive fetuses of rhesus-negative mothers from blood cell damage by injecting the mothers with rhesus antibodies (anti-D immunoglobulin).

Claude, Albert (1898–1983) Belgian-born U.S. cell biologist who, using an electron microscope, revealed for the first time details of cell "little organs" (organelles), such as the endoplasmic reticulum and the folded structure of the mitochondria. Claude shared the 1974 Nobel Prize in physiology or medicine with Christian de Duve and George Palade.

Cohen, Seymour Stanley (b. 1917) U.S. biochemist who in 1946 began to investigate the viral infection of cells by tagging viral nucleic acid with radioactive phosphorus. The results of this work strongly suggested that DNA was the central substance in genetics.

Cohen, Stanley Harold (b. 1922) U.S. biochemist who worked on DNA-cutting enzymes. He helped to isolate nerve growth factor, and went on to isolate epidermal growth factor and to show how this substance interacted with cells to produce a range of effects. Cohen shared the 1986 Nobel Prize in physiology or medicine with Rita Levi-Montalcini.

Ferdinand Cohn

Cohn, Ferdinand Julius (1828–98) German botanist who instituted the science of bacteriology and proposed that bacteria should be classified as plants rather than as animals. He assisted Robert Koch in the study of anthrax and was an important contributor to the abandonment of the earlier idea of the "spontaneous generation" of living things. He also showed that cytoplasm in the cells of animals was virtually the same as that in the cells of plants.

Colles, Abraham (1773–1843) Irish anatomist and surgeon whose description of the physical signs of the fracture of the lower end of the radius bone ("dinner fork deformity") led to this being universally known as a Colles' fracture.

Matteo Colombo

Colombo, Matteo Realdo (1516?–59?) Italian anatomist who studied under Andreas Vesalius and based his statements on dissection rather than dogma. He was the first to show that blood circulated in a figure eight pattern: through the lungs, through the rest of the body, and back to the lungs. He also showed that arteries contain blood, not air (as the name suggests), and that blood from the lungs has a different appearance from blood going to them.

Correns, Karl Erich (1864–1933) German botanist who, independently of Gregor Mendel, described the laws of the inheritance of characteristics. He was also able to show that certain factors are inherited from a source other than material in the nucleus of the cell. This cytoplasmic inheritance was later shown to be from the mitochondrial DNA.

Cousteau, Jacques-Yves (1910–97) French oceanographer and inventor who produced a number of underwater devices, including the aqualung and the bathyscaph. He also pioneered underwater photography. As an author and filmmaker, he increased public interest in, and awareness of, the underwater world. He was also active in protecting the environment.

Crick, Francis Harry Compton (1916–2004) English molecular biologist who with James Watson in 1953 built a molecular model of the complex genetic material deoxyribonucleic acid (DNA). Crick was the principal solver of the riddle of the genetic code, showing that different triplets of bases defined different amino acids in the protein sequence. Later, he turned to neurophysiology and worked on brain function. With Watson and Maurice Wilkins, he won the Nobel Prize in physiology or medicine in 1962.

Cullen, William (1710–90) Scottish physician and medical teacher whose main contribution to science was the overthrow of the primitive but long-standing doctrine of the four humors. This had held back the progress of medicine for 1,500 years. Cullen taught the importance of the knowledge of body structure (anatomy) and function (physiology) and the scientific classification of diseases.

Culpeper, Nicholas (1616–54) English herbalist, apothecary, and astrologer whose book *The English Physician* ("Culpeper's Herbal") was widely used. It contains little of medical value, and some dangerous prescriptions, but showed that disease could be treated by drugs.

Illustration from "Culpeper's Herbal"

Cushing, Harvey Williams (1869–1939) U.S. pioneer of neurosurgery and professor of surgery at Johns Hopkins Hospital and later at Harvard. His pioneering work on the classification of brain tumors and on the function and disorders of the pituitary gland greatly advanced endocrinology.

Cuvier, Georges [Jean-Léopold-Nicolas-Frédéric], Baron (1769–1832) French anatomist, celebrated as the founder of comparative anatomy and paleontology. His studies of animals, fish, molusks, and fossils linked paleontology with comparative anatomy. He was a taxonomist who developed the first workable method of classifying mammals and was the first to propose that catastrophes were responsible for the extinctions of species.

Dale, Sir Henry Hallett (1875–1968) British pharmacologist who isolated acetylcholine from the ergot fungus. In 1921, after a hint from Dale, German pharmacologist Otto Loewi proved that acetylcholine was the neurotransmitter that was released at nerve endings in the autonomic nervous system. Dale and Loewi shared the 1936 Nobel Prize in physiology or medicine.

Carl Peter Dam

Dam, Carl Peter Henrik (1895–1976) Danish biochemist who discovered vitamin K by showing that a diet deficient in fatty content led to blood-clotting defects in chicks. He and U.S. biochemist Edward Adelbert Doisy were awarded the 1943 Nobel Prize in physiology or medicine for the discovery of the vitamin. Countless babies have been saved from dangerous bleeding by routine administration of vitamin K.

Darwin, Charles Robert (1809–82) English naturalist who revolutionized biology and was the originator, with Alfred Russel Wallace, of the theory of evolution through the process of natural selection. He wrote on his geological and zoological findings during his famous voyage from 1831 to 1836 on HMS *Beagle*. But it was the publication in 1859 of *On the Origin of Species* that put him in the front rank of scientists. This work, reinforced by geological and comparative anatomy studies, forced a paradigm shift on biology and was seen as overturning firmly held religious beliefs about the origins of life on Earth.

Darwin, Erasmus (1731–1802) English physician and grandfather of both Charles Darwin and Francis Galton. He wrote extensively on natural history, evolution, botany, and taxonomy. He held advanced early views on evolution and the impact of environment on life.

Davenport, Charles Benedict (1866–1944) U.S. zoologist and geneticist who originated the practice of applying statistics to evolutionary studies. He also tried to establish a genetic basis for skin pigmentation. He studied U.S. troops in World War I and, based on body measurements, worked on whether differences occurred between ethnic groups.

Davson, Hugh (1909–96) English physiologist who worked on cell membrane permeability with James Danielli and then became the outstanding authority of his day on the physiology of the eye. His work *The Physiology of the Eye* (1949) was a classic textbook that had an important influence on ophthalmic research and clinical practice and was required reading for all students of ophthalmology.

Deisenhofer, Johann (b. 1943) German molecular biologist who studied the Y-shaped antibody (immunoglobulin) molecule to discover which sites on the molecule served which particular function. He also researched the structure in the purple bacterium *Rhodopseudomonal viridis* in which photosynthesis occurs. This work earned him and his colleagues, Robert Huber and Hartmut Michel, the 1988 Nobel Prize in chemistry.

Delbrück, Max (1906–81) German-born U.S. biophysicist who did much to create bacterial and bacteriophage genetics, and, in 1946, showed that viruses can effect recombination of genetic material. He shared the 1969 Nobel Prize in physiology and medicine with Alfred D. Hershey and Salvador Luria.

Diels, Otto Paul Hermann (1876–1954) German chemist who, working with Kurt Alder, discovered a relatively easy method of synthesizing new cyclic, or ring, organic compounds by heating sterols with selenium to produce steroids, and thus drugs and medicines. Diels and Alder were awarded the Nobel Prize in chemistry in 1950.

Dobzhansky, Theodosius (1900–75) Russian-born U.S. geneticist whose studies of fruit flies showed that genetic variability in a species is large and that gene variations include many potentially lethal genes that nevertheless confer versatility when a population is exposed to environmental change. This work provided experimental evidence linking Darwinian theory with Mendelian laws of heredity. His writings include *Genetics and the Origin of Species* (1937).

Doherty, Peter (b. 1940) Australian immunologist who, working with Rolf Zinkernagel, was able to show how the T-cells of the human immune system can recognize when a cell has been infected with viruses. Killer T-cells look for two "flags" (antigenic chemical groups) displayed on the surface of the infected cell. One identifies the cell as "self," the other signals that viruses are inside. For this discovery, made between 1973 and 1975, the two men were awarded the 1996 Nobel Prize in physiology or medicine.

Doll, Sir William Richard (1912–2005) British physician, epidemiologist and medical statistician who, working with Austin Bradford Hill and others, had by 1957 proved the relationship between smoking and lung cancer. Later, Doll became regius professor of medicine at Oxford University.

Gerhard Domagk

Domagk, Gerhard (1895–1964) German physician who showed that the red dye prontosil could kill certain bacteria in animals. During his research his daughter became gravely ill with a streptococcal infection. In desperation, Domagk injected her with the dye and she made a full recovery. Domagk's work led to the development of the antibacterial sulfa drugs. In 1939, Domagk was awarded the Nobel Prize in physiology or medicine but refused it on instructions from his government.

Du Bois-Reymond, Emil (1818–96) German physiologist and pioneer of electrophysiology who investigated and demonstrated the role of the movement of electric charges in nerves and muscles. He showed that the charge on the inside of a nerve was opposite to that on the outside, and proposed, rightly, that the origin of the charges on nerves is chemical.

Dubos, René Jules (1901–82) French-born U.S. bacteriologist who worked at the Rockefeller Institute and whose interest in soil bacteria led him, in 1939, to isolate an antibiotic called tyrothricin. This work inspired others to discover other antibiotics, such as streptomycin and tetracycline.

Duggar, Benjamin Minge (1872–1956) U.S. plant pathologist who discovered the first antibiotic derived from soil. This was the first of the tetracycline class of drugs.

Dulbecco, Renato (b. 1914) Italian-born U.S. molecular biologist who showed how certain viruses can transform some cells into a cancerous state. He opened the way to advanced gene research and shared the 1975 Nobel Prize in physiology or medicine with David Baltimore and Howard Martin Temin.

Dupuytren, Guillaume Baron (1777–1835) French surgeon who first described the palmar deformity that leads to the slow and permanent bending of the ring and little finger into the palm.

Dutrochet, René-Joachim-Henri (1776–1847) French physiologist who was the first to study and name osmosis. He stated, in 1824, that "all tissues, all animal organs are actually only a cellular tissue variously modified."

Duve, Christian René de (b. 1917) English-born Belgian biochemist who used differential centrifugation to separate biochemical tissue fragments into layers and discovered the cell organelles (little organs), the lysosomes, and the peroxisomes. For this work, he shared the 1974 Nobel Prize in physiology or medicine with Albert Claude and George Palade.

Eccles, Sir John Carew (1903–97) Australian physiologist who discovered how impulses are transmitted from one nerve to another at synapses. Eccles showed that acetylcholine acts on channels in the nerve cell membrane to allow charged sodium and potassium atoms (ions) to pass through and reverse the local electrical charge. This leads to a movement of electrical charge along the nerve fiber. For this work, Eccles and his colleagues, Andrew Huxley and Alan Hodgkin, were awarded the 1963 Nobel Prize in physiology or medicine.

Sir John Eccles

Egas Moniz, António Caetano de Abreu Freire (1874–1955) Portuguese neurologist who was the first to use radio-opaque dyes in the bloodstream to produce X-ray pictures of the blood vessels of the brain and reveal abnormalities, such as brain tumors. This is called cerebral angiography. Moniz also pioneered prefrontal leukotomy for intractable psychotic disorders, now largely abandoned, but for which he shared the 1949 Nobel Prize in physiology or medicine with Walter Rudolf Hess.

Ehrlich, Paul (1854–1915) German medical researcher who used aniline dyes for the selective staining of disease organisms and realized that they might kill disease germs without killing the patient. He was right, and became the founder of chemotherapy.

For his studies on immunity he shared the Nobel Prize in physiology or medicine with Elie Metchnikoff in 1908.

Eichler, August Wilhelm (1839–87) German botanist who was one of the outstanding systematic and morphological botanists of his time. He studied flower symmetry and worked on the taxonomy of the higher plants.

Christiaan Eijkman

Eijkman, Christiaan (1858–1930) Dutch bacteriologist who inadvertently proved the existence of a dietary factor (a vitamin) necessary for health. Eijkman showed that beri-beri, caused by a diet of polished rice, could be cured by giving whole rice. Later, Frederick Hopkins showed that rice husks contain thiamine (B1), the vitamin necessary to prevent beri-beri. Eijkman and Hopkins shared the 1929 Nobel Prize in physiology or medicine.

Willem Einthoven

Einthoven, Willem (1860–1927) Dutch physiologist and professor of physiology at Leiden who invented the electrocardiograph (ECG) and first produced a record of the electrical activity of the heart. For this work, Einthoven was awarded the Nobel Prize in physiology or medicine in 1924.

Elton, Charles Sutherland (1900–91) English ecologist who was the author of classic books on animal ecology. His work on animal communities led to a recognition of the ability of many animals to counter environmental disadvantages by a change of habitats and to the general use of the concepts of "food chain" and "niche."

Elvehjem, Conrad Arnold (1901–62) U.S. biochemist who discovered the cure for the vitamin-deficiency disease pellagra. This is the B vitamin nicotinic acid (niacin).

Enders, John Franklin (1897–1985) U.S. bacteriologist who researched antibodies for the mumps virus. With Frederick Robbins and Thomas Huckle Weller, he achieved the cultivation of polio viruses in live human cells, thus greatly advancing virology, and in 1962 he developed an effective vaccine against measles.

Epstein, Sir Michael Anthony (b. 1921) English virologist who, working with his colleague Yvonne M. Barr, discovered a new virus, a member of the herpes family, that has been shown to cause glandular fever and Burkitt's lymphoma in children with a defective immune system from malaria. It can also cause naso-pharyngeal cancer. The virus is now called the Epstein-Barr virus.

Erasistratus of Ceos (b. third century BCE) Greek physician who rightly rejected the Hippocratic dogma of the four humors and recognized that every bodily organ has connected to it an artery, vein, and nerve. He studied the brains of humans and animals and concluded that the surface area is proportional to the intelligence of the species concerned. His views were largely ignored because of the status of Aristotle.

Erlanger, Joseph (1874–1965) U.S. physiologist who worked on surgical shock, the conducting systems of the heart, and the conduction of nerve impulses. Together with Herbert Gasser he was awarded the Nobel Prize in physiology or medicine in 1944 for his elucidation of the mechanism of nerve impulse transmission.

Euler-Chelpin, Hans von (1873–1964) Swedish chemist who carried out a great deal of the earliest work on enzymes. He showed their optimum conditions for function, interaction with vitamins, inhibition by metallic ions and other substances, and the distinction between yeast saccharases and those occurring in the intestine. For his work on enzymes he shared the 1929 Nobel Prize in chemistry with Arthur Harden.

Eustachio, Bartolommeo (1520–74) Italian anatomist who made a number of notable contributions to the subject but is best remembered for the Eustachian tube that connects the middle ear to the back of the nose.

Fabricius, Hieronymus (**Girolamo Fabrici**) (1537–1619) Italian anatomist and embryologist who, in his book *De Venarum ostiolis* (1603), gave the first accurate account of the veins of the body. Fabricius taught, and strongly influenced, William Harvey, who was later to prove that the blood circulated continuously rather than flowing and ebbing, as was previously believed.

Fallopius, Gabriel (**Gabriele Falloppio**) (1523–62) Italian anatomist and pupil of Andreas Vesalius, who, inspired by his master, labored to make anatomy an exact science. Fallopius is best known for his detailed account of the female reproductive system. The uterine (Fallopian) tubes are named after him. He also studied the bones of the human body. His best work was his *Observationes anatomicae* of 1561.

Carlos Finlay

Finlay, Carlos Juan (1833–1915) Cuban physician who in 1881 published a paper suggesting that yellow fever is transmitted by the mosquito now known as *Aedes aegypti*. He was laughed at. In 1900, however, Finlay put the idea to Walter Reed, whose research then showed that Finlay was right.

Finsen, Niels Ryberg (1860–1904) Danish physician and anatomist who showed that ultraviolet light could kill bacteria. He also used ultraviolet light to treat skin tuberculosis (lupus vulgaris). Finsen was awarded the 1903 Nobel Prize in physiology or medicine.

Fischer, Edmond Henri (b. 1920) U.S. biochemist who, working with Edwin Krebs, showed how glucose molecules—the body's main fuel—are released from the storage form, the glucose polymer glycogen. They showed that the enzyme glycogen phosphorylase, which catalyzes the release, is made operative by receiving a phosphate group from ATP and then made nonoperative by losing this group. Fischer and Krebs shared the 1992 Nobel Prize in physiology or medicine.

Emil Fischer

Fischer, Emil Hermann (1852–1919) German organic chemist who discovered the molecular structures of sugars, including glucose, found the structure of purines, isolated and identified amino acids, and worked on the structure of proteins. He received the Nobel Prize in chemistry in 1902 for his work on sugars and purines.

Fischer, Hans (1881–1945) German chemist who researched the molecular structure of chlorophyll, determined the structural formulae for biliverdin and bilirubin, synthesized both these bile products, and worked out and synthesized the structure of hemin. For the latter achievement, he was awarded the Nobel Prize in chemistry in 1930.

Fisher, Sir Ronald Aylmer (1890–1962) English statistician and geneticist who was one of the first to apply mathematical theory to biology. He studied the genetics of blood groups and explained the inheritance of the rhesus factor.

Fitzroy, Robert (1805–65) English naval captain, hydrographer, and meteorologist who was in command of the vessel *Beagle* when it carried Charles Darwin on the celebrated voyage (1831–36) that were to prompt his ideas of evolution by natural selection.

Fleming, Sir Alexander (1881–1955) Scottish bacteriologist who in 1928 discovered by chance the first antibiotic substance, penicillin, but without isolating it; Howard Florey and Ernst Chain perfected a method of producing the drug, which was mass-produced from 1942. Fleming also pioneered the use of salvarsan against syphilis, discovered the antiseptic powers of lysozyme (present in tears and mucus), and was the first to use antityphoid vaccines on humans. Fleming, Florey, and Chain won the Nobel Prize in 1945.

Sir Alexander Fleming
Medallic portrait.

Flemming, Walther (1843–1905) German biologist who, in 1882, gave the first modern account of cytology, including the process of cell division, which he named mitosis. He also did important work on the splitting of chromosomes and on microscopic technique.

Florey, Howard Walter (Baron Florey) (1898–1968) Australian pathologist who was the first to exploit the full potential of penicillin. In 1939, Florey and Ernst Chain began a research project on the mold extract that Alexander Fleming had discovered 11 years before. They isolated penicillin, and this led to large-scale production of the world's first antibiotic, saving millions of lives. Fleming, Florey, and Chain were awarded the 1945 Nobel Prize in physiology or medicine.

Howard Florey

Flourens, Marie-Jean-Pierre (1794–1867) French physiologist who proved that vision depends not only on the eyes but also on a region of the brain at the back of the cerebrum. He proved that the semicircular canals of the inner ear are necessary for balance, that the cerebellum, the smaller hindbrain, is concerned with coordination of movement, and that the nerve centers for respiration are in the medulla oblongata of the brain stem.

Foley, Frederick E. (1891–1966) U.S. surgeon who invented a self-retaining catheter for drainage of urine from the bladder, known as the Foley catheter.

Forbes, Edward (1815–54) British naturalist who was the first to suggest, correctly, that living organisms might exist deep in the oceans, below the level that can be reached by sunlight.

Forel, Auguste Henri (1848–1931) Swiss physician who used nerve degeneration methods to trace the course of long neurons and disprove the theory that grey matter was a network formed by the fusion of dendrites.

Forssmann, Werner Theodor Otto (1904–79) German surgeon who in 1929 showed, by demonstrating on himself, that a 26-inch fine tube could safely be passed up a vein and directed into the heart. This courageous doctor could take the matter no further because his colleagues pronounced the procedure to be too dangerous. Cardiac catheterization is now an indispensable procedure for investigation and treatment. Forssmann and two other doctors, André Cournand and Dickinson Richards, who later showed the practicality and value of the measure, were awarded the 1956 Nobel Prize in physiology or medicine.

Girolamo Fracastoro

Fracastoro, Girolamo (ca. 1483–1553) Italian physician, astronomer, and mathematician who, in a poem about a shepherd called Syphilis, described the recently recognized sexually transmitted disease. He was well ahead of his time in pointing out that many diseases were acquired by "contagion," which could be spread by contaminated clothes, bedding, and other material (fomites).

Sir Edward Frankland

Frankland, Sir Edward (1825–99) English organic chemist who became professor at the Royal Institution, London, in 1863. He propounded the theory of valency (1852–60), concerned with the number of chemical bonds that the atom may form. He was also an expert on sanitation.

Franklin, Rosalind Elsie (1920–58) English X-ray crystallographer whose work with Maurice Wilkins provided James Watson and Francis Crick with the vital structural data on which they were able to construct the model of the DNA molecule and achieve scientific immortality. She developed cancer and died in 1958, four years before she could have shared the 1962 Nobel Prize in physiology or medicine with Maurice Wilkins, James Watson, and Francis Crick.

Frisch, Karl von (1886–1982) Austrian ethologist and zoologist who was a key figure in developing ethology, using field observation of animals combined with ingenious experiments. He showed that forager honeybees communicate information on the location of food in part by the use of coded dances. He shared the 1973 Nobel Prize in physiology or medicine with Konrad Lorenz and Nikolaas Tinbergen.

Fuchs, Leonhard (1501–66) German botanist and physician who described hundreds of German and foreign plants, and is remembered by the generic name *Fuchsia*. Together with Otto Brunfels and Hieronymus Bock, he was one of the German pioneers of modern botany.

Leonhard Fuchs

Funk, Casimir (1884–1967) Polish-born U.S. biochemist who isolated the first vitamin and suggested, correctly, that others existed. He believed, wrongly, that they all contained an amine (–NH2) group, and suggested they be called "vital amines" or "vitamines." This was later amended to "vitamins."

Galen (129–ca. 199) Greek physician who demonstrated that arteries carry blood, not air. He is considered the founder of experimental physiology.

Gallo, Robert (b. 1937) U.S. medical scientist and head of the Tumor Cell Biology Laboratory at the American National Cancer Institute who shares with Luc Montagnier of the Pasteur Institute in Paris the credit for discovering the virus that causes AIDS (the HIV).

Galton, Sir Francis (1822–1911) English polymath and cousin of Charles Darwin who pioneered statistical analysis for studying mental and behavioral phenomena, invented ways of detecting color vision, promoted the use of fingerprints for criminal detection, coined the term *eugenics* and recommended its promotion.

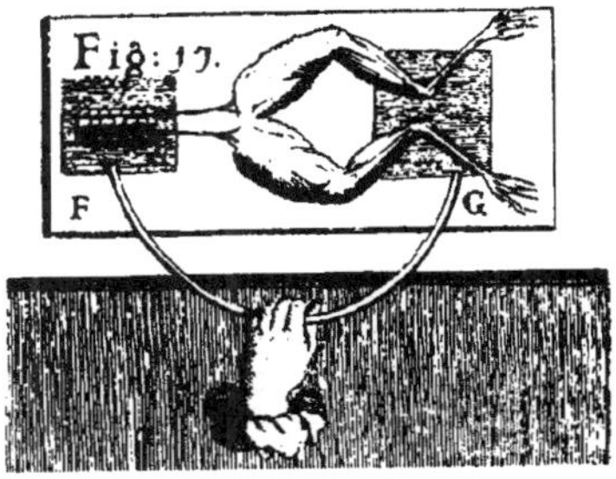

Diagram of Galvani's experiment on a frog's legs, demonstrating the role of electricity in nerves

Galvani, Luigi (1737–98) Italian physiologist who investigated the role of electrical impulses in animal tissue. In a famous experiment he connected a leg muscle of a frog to dissimilar metals and observed the twitching that took place (hence "to galvanize"). He gave his name to an elementary electric current meter, the galvanometer, and to the galvanic battery.

John Gerard

Garrod, Sir Archibald Edward (1857–1936) British physician who first recognized a new class of genetically induced diseases resulting from a mutation in a single gene that causes the absence or malfunctioning of a particular enzyme.

Gerard, John (1545–1612) British botanist and gardener who wrote a book entitled *Herball*, which contained most of the botanical knowledge of his day.

Gesner, Conrad (1516–65) Swiss naturalist who collected fossils and published a book, illustrated with woodcuts, to describe them. He devised an alphabetical scheme of classification of living things and published a compendious catalog of animals called *Historiae animalium* (1551–65).

Gibbon, John Heysham (1903–74). U.S. surgeon who invented the cardiopulmonary bypass (heart-lung machine), which allows the heart to be stopped for cardiac surgery or heart transplant.

Gilbert, Walter (b. 1932) U.S. physicist, biochemist, and molecular biologist who isolated the repressor molecule that causes genes to be operative or nonoperative and described the DNA nucleotide sequence to which it binds. For this work, he shared the 1980 Nobel Prize in chemistry with Paul Berg and Frederick Sanger.

Gill, Theodore Nicholas (1837–1914) U.S. fish specialist (ichthyologist) who was a leading taxonomist of his time. His writings greatly advanced the field of ichthyology.

Gilman, Alfred Goodman (b. 1941) U.S. biochemist who, working with Martin Rodbell, discovered the G protein, a class of chemical messengers that transfer incoming information from receptors in cell membranes to the producers of the second messenger, the hormone that then moves to the effector sites within the cell. G proteins remain inactive until a signal reaches the cell. They then activate. Disease processes can interfere with G proteins. For this work, Gilman and Rodbell were awarded the 1994 Nobel Prize in physiology or medicine.

Glisson, Francis (ca. 1597–1677) English physician who suggested, wrongly, that the lymphatics carried fluid for lubricating the body cavities back to the blood vessels. He produced an excellent description of the gross anatomy of the liver and introduced the term *irritability* for tissues that contract when stimulated.

Goebel, Karl Immanuel Eberhard von (1855–1932) German botanist and distinguished plant morphologist who wrote *Organographie der Pflanzen* (1898–1901) and founded the botanical institute and gardens in Munich.

Goethe, Johann Wolfgang von (1749–1832) German poet, novelist, lawyer, philosopher, prime minister, physicist, botanist, geologist, and comparative anatomist. Because of his status as an acknowledged genius, Goethe's views on scientific matters commanded much respect in his time, but his real contribution to the advancement of science was negligible, and some of his assertions were seriously misleading. He tried to refute Sir Isaac Newton's theory of light and proposed a theory of color vision. Even so, Goethe inspired many people to study science.

Goldschmidt, Richard Benedikt (1878–1958) German biologist who conducted experiments on X (sex) chromosomes and theorized that it is not the qualities of individual genes but the serial pattern in the chromosomes and the chemical configuration of their molecules that are decisive hereditary factors. He was right on the latter point.

Golgi, Camillo (1843–1926) Italian microscopic anatomist who developed a method of selective silver-staining of nerve tissue that enabled him to trace nerve connections throughout the nervous system. This led to remarkable advances in the understanding of the organization of the system. Golgi also described some of the cell internal structures (organelles). He shared the 1906 Nobel Prize in physiology or medicine with Santiago Ramón y Cajal.

Goode, George Brown (1851–96) U.S. fish expert (ichthyologist) and fish commissioner 1887–88 who wrote *American Fish* (1888) and *Oceanic Ichthyology* (1895).

Graaf, Reinier de (1641–73) Dutch physician and anatomist who published an important account of the function of the pancreatic digestive juice and of the ovaries, which he so entitled. He described the ovarian follicle that is now called the Graafian follicle, but was unable to determine its function.

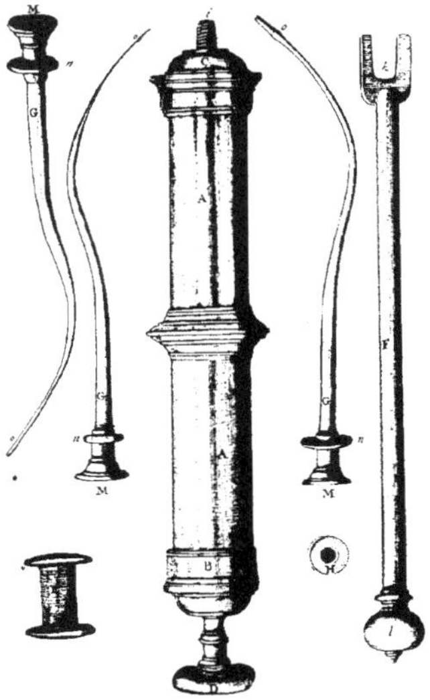
De Graaf's surgical syringe

Asa Gray

Grassi, Giovanni Battista (1854–1925) Italian insect specialist (entomologist) who proved that the *Anopheles* mosquito carried the malarial parasite in its digestive tract. This was an important early step in the understanding of the transmission of the disease.

Gray, Asa (1810–88) U.S. botanist who between 1838 and 1842 published the book *Flora of North America*. He also produced *Genera Florae Americae Boreali-Orientalis Illustrata* (1845–50), *A Free Examination of Darwin's Treatise* (1861), and *Manual of the Botany of the Northern United States* (1848), known as *Gray's Manual*.

Gray, Henry (1827–61) English anatomist who in 1858 published the first edition of a textbook of anatomy, based on his own dissections, that was to become the most celebrated and long-surviving text on the subject in modern times. *Gray's Anatomy*, which became the world's most famous anatomy text, consists of 1,600 closely packed pages and bears as its endpapers an enlarged photograph of the great anatomist himself in the dissecting room surrounded by his students.

Grew, Nehemiah (1641–1712) British botanist who carried out some of the earliest research into plant anatomy.

Guérin, Camille (1872–1961). French bacteriologist who developed with Albert Calmette the Bacille Calmette-Guérin (BCG) vaccine against tuberculosis.

Gullstrand, Allvar (1862–1930) Swedish ophthalmologist who studied and explained the optics of the eye. He showed how it focused for near vision, he explained corneal astigmatism and its optical correction, and he invented an ophthalmoscope for illuminating and examining the inside of the eye. Gullstrand was awarded the 1911 Nobel Prize in physiology or medicine.

Gurdon, John Bertrand (b. 1933) English geneticist and cell biologist who demonstrated that fully differentiated animal cells retain their totipotentiality—their potential ability to form cells of any other tissue. This indicates that each cell contains all the necessary information to become any kind of cell, and that cells develop as a result of local environmental stimuli.

Ernst Haeckel

Haeckel, Ernst Heinrich Philipp August (1834–1919) German naturalist, and one of the first to sketch the genealogical tree of animals, explaining that the life history of individuals is a recapitulation of its historic evolution. This seductive and plausible idea ("ontogeny recapitulates phylogeny") commanded wide support, especially after Haeckel had published popular books on the subject, but was based on dishonest drawings and was wrong.

Hahnemann, Samuel Christian Friedrich (1755–1843). German physician who invented the system of medicine known as homeopathy, for which there is no rational scientific basis. As a tribute to the human desire for miracles, however, homeopathy, in spite of its absurdities, persists to this day.

Haldane, John Burdon Sanderson (1892–1964) British-born Indian biochemist and geneticist. He researched enzymes, population genetics, and a mathematical analysis of natural selection, but is best remembered for his writings on popular science, which were highly successful in his day.

Hales, Stephen (1677–1761) English botanist and chemist and founder of plant physiology whose book *Vegetable Staticks* (1727) was the basis of vegetable physiology. He was one of the first to use instruments to measure the nutrition and movement of liquids within plants. He also invented machines for ventilating, distilling sea water, and preserving meat.

Haller, Albrecht von (1708–77) Swiss biologist and physiologist who explained the function of nerve and muscle tissue. He correctly described the function of bile in the emulsification and absorption of dietary fats and the mechanism of breathing. He produced an eight-volume physiology textbook, *Elementa physiologiae corporis humani* (1757–66), as well as several major bibliographies of medical subjects.

Halstead, William Stewart (1852–1922) U.S. surgeon who introduced the use of sterile rubber gloves for surgeons and made many other important advances in surgery.

Harden, Sir Arthur (1865–1940) British chemist who shared the 1929 Nobel Prize in chemistry with Hans Euler-Chelpin for their classic work on fermentation enzymes. Harden proved that living organisms are not necessary for fermentation and that the process can be inhibited if a factor is removed by dialysis. This was the enzyme. He also showed that fermentation of sugars begins by phosphorylation to form an ester.

Title page of Harvey's *On the Motion of the Heart* (1628)

Harrison, Ross Granville (1870–1959) U.S. biologist who introduced the hanging-drop culture method (1907) for the study of living tissues. Using this method, he showed that nerve fibers are outgrowths of nerve cells.

Harvey, William (1578–1657) English physician who, in his book *On the Motion of the Heart* (1628) was the first to demonstrate that the blood circulates. His emphasis on observation and experiment eventually did much to relieve medicine of the deadening influence of Galen and transform it into a scientific discipline. However, Harvey's claims were scorned. He was vilified, his work was ignored, and he was forced out of his hospital appointment into poverty and loneliness. He died of a stroke, unaware that, in due course, he would become one of the most important figures in the history of medicine.

Hashimoto, Hakaru (1881–1934) Japanese physician and specialist in thyroid gland diseases who first described the form of thyroid inflammation (thyroiditis) associated with his name.

Hayem, Georges (1841–1920) French physician and hematologist who first described blood platelets (cell fragments necessary for clotting) and researched the formation of red and white blood cells in the bone marrow. His principal importance is in the way he encouraged the clinical application of the results of scientific work in physiology and pathology.

Hermann von Helmholtz
Commemorated on a postage stamp.

Helmholtz, Hermann Ludwig Ferdinand von (1821–94) German physicist, physiologist, mathematician, and polymath who invented the ophthalmoscope, investigated the physics of music and optics, worked out the basis of color vision, and showed the equivalence of energy in food intake, muscular action, and heat production. The three-color (trichromatic) theory of color vision is known as the Young-Helmholtz theory.

Helmont, Jan Baptista van (1579–1644) Flemish physician, physiologist, and chemist who invented the word *gas*, deriving it from a Greek word for "chaos." He distinguished gases other than air, regarded water as a prime element, believed that digestion was due to "ferments" that converted dead food into living flesh, proposed the medical use of alkalis for excess acidity, and believed in alchemy. His works were published by his son.

Herophilus (ca. 335–ca. 280 BCE) Greek anatomist who is generally taken to be one of the founders of the subject. Herophilus helped to found the school of anatomy and medicine in Alexandria, where he undertook human dissection during a short period when this was authorized to advance medical knowledge. He recognized the functions of the brain, distinguishing sensory and motor modalities, and described most of the organs of the body. He originated the term *duodenum* from his observation that it was 12 finger-breadths long. The work of Herophilus was later acknowledged by Galen, Celsus, and others.

Hershey, Alfred Day (1908–97) U.S. biologist who became an expert on bacteriophage ("phage") and early in the 1950s, with U.S. geneticist Martha Chase, proved that the DNA of this organism is its genetic information-carrying component. Later, with others, they showed that the DNA of other organisms fulfills the same key genetic role. Hershey shared the 1969 Nobel Prize in physiology and medicine with Max Delbrück and Salvador Luria.

Hertwig, Oskar Wilhelm August (1849–1922) German zoologist who proved that sperm and egg nuclei must fuse for fertilization to occur. He also showed that, although thousands of sperm are in contact with the egg, only one is necessary for fertilization.

Walter Hess

Hess, Walter Rudolf (1881–1973) Swiss neurophysiologist whose lifelong studies of the basal ganglia of the brain and the hypothalamus revealed considerable detail of the function and connections of this part of the brain and its role in regulating the activities of internal organs. He shared the Nobel Prize in physiology or medicine in 1949 with Antonio Egas Moniz.

Hevesy, Georg Karl von (**George de Hevesy**) (1885–1966) Hungarian-born Swedish radiochemist who was the first to suggest the use of radioactive tracers in chemical and biological work. This was to become a technique of great power and value. On Niels Bohr's recommendation, Hevesy also searched for and found a new element, number 72, which he named hafnium. He was awarded the Nobel Prize in chemistry in 1943.

Archibald Hill

Hill, Archibald Vivian (1886–1977) British physiologist, noted for his work on the series of biochemical reactions that provide the energy for muscle contraction, for which he shared the 1922 Nobel Prize in physiology or medicine with Otta Meyerhof. Hill was a professor at the Royal Society and president of the British Association for the Advancement of Science.

Hill, Sir Austin Bradford (1897–1991) English epidemiologist and statistician who worked closely with Richard Doll and others to demonstrate the causal link between cigarette smoking and lung cancer.

Hippocrates (ca. 460–ca. 377 BCE) Greek physician, commonly described as the father of medicine, whose teachings are known by more than 70 books of medical writing produced by his students and their successors. These writings are attributed to him and contain much that is sound in medical diagnosis, prognosis, and observation, ethics, and hygiene. Unfortunately, they promote the sterile and misleading doctrine of the four humors as being the primary seats of diseases. This led medicine astray for 1,600 years and encouraged blood-letting treatment that killed millions of patients. Hippocrates is also remembered for the Hippocratic oath for doctors, which provides a basis for ethical medical practice.

Sir Alan Hodgkin

Hodgkin, Sir Alan Lloyd (1914–98) English neurophysiologist who, working with Andrew Huxley and using microelectrodes on nerve fibers, showed that the nerve impulse is actually a zone of depolarization (reversal of electric charge) that moves along the fiber. For this he shared the Nobel Prize in physiology or medicine or in 1963 with Andrew Huxley and John Eccles.

Hodgkin, Dorothy Mary (née Dorothy Mary Crowfoot) (1910–94) Cairo-born British chemist who used X-ray diffraction techniques to determine the three-dimensional molecular structure of penicillin, in 1949; vitamin B12, in 1957; and, finally, insulin, in 1969. In 1964, Hodgkin became the third woman to receive the Nobel Prize in chemistry.

Hodgkin, Thomas (1798–1866) English physician and pathologist who was the first to describe the disease of lymph nodes now named after him. In 1832, Hodgkin published his findings in six cases of widespread enlargement of the lymph nodes, then wrongly thought to be glands. Later microscopic studies showed that only some of Hodgkin's cases were of the malignant type we now call Hodgkin's disease.

Hooker, Sir Joseph Dalton (1817–1911) English botanist and traveler who went on several expeditions that resulted in works on the flora of New Zealand, Antarctica, and India, as well as *Himalayan Journals* and the monumental work *Genera Plantarum*. From one trip to the Himalayas, he introduced the rhododendron to Europe. With Thomas Henry Huxley, he was a strong supporter and friend of Charles Darwin.

Sir Joseph Hooker

Hooker, Sir William Jackson (1785–1865) British botanist and father of Joseph Hooker, who helped to found and was a director of the Royal Botanical Gardens at Kew, London. His private collection was once one of the finest herbariums in Europe.

Hopkins, Sir Frederick Gowland (1861–1947) English biochemist who was the first to make a general scientific study of vitamins and show their importance in the maintenance of health. In 1929 he shared the Nobel Prize in medicine or physiology with Christiaan Eijkmann.

Houssay, Bernardo Alberto (1887–1971) Argentinian physiologist who investigated internal secretions. His work on the pituitary gland greatly advanced the discipline of endocrinology. He found a pituitary hormone that acted in the opposite way to insulin and demonstrated that the control of endocrine hormonal production involves complex feedback mechanisms. For this work, he shared the Nobel Prize in physiology or medicine in 1947 with Carl Cori and Gerty Cori

Huber, Robert (b. 1937) German biochemist who helped to determine antibody structure and binding sites, showed that there was a very small structural difference between the active and the inactive form of the enzyme phosphorylase, and, with Harmut Michel and Johann Deisenhofer, worked out the detailed structure of the membrane-bound region in which photosynthesis occurs in the purple bacterium

Rhodopseudomonal viridans. For this work, which threw much light on the processes of photosynthesis, he and his colleagues were awarded the 1988 Nobel Prize in chemistry.

Humboldt, Friedrich Heinrich Alexander von (1769–1859) German naturalist, explorer, and scientific observer who made many contributions to the Earth sciences and botany. His work on geomagnetism led to the discovery of the magnetic pole. With Aimé Bonpland he went to South America and gathered an enormous amount of data and about 60,000 specimens of flora. Humboldt is best remembered for his great work of scientific popularization, *Kosmos* (1845–62), which was widely influential on the lay scientific thought of his time.

Hunter, John (1728–93) Scottish anatomist and surgeon who taught Edward Jenner; built up a magnificent museum of anatomical and pathological specimens; investigated and described many anatomical details, including the placental circulation in the fetus, the olfactory nerves, and the descent of the testis; and investigated the clotting of blood, the function of the lymphatics, the transmission of infection, including sexually transmitted diseases, and the formation of pus. He also made many contributions to surgical technique and dentistry.

Hutchinson, Sir Jonathan (1828–1913) English surgeon who specialized in ophthalmology, dermatology, and syphilis, and amassed a museum of specimens and drawings. He was the first to describe the characteristic notched teeth of congenital syphilis.

Huxley, Sir Andrew Fielding (b. 1917) English physiologist and grandson of Thomas Henry Huxley who, using a giant squid nerve fiber (axon), provided the physicochemical explanation of the nerve impulse and its propagation as a zone of depolarization that shifts along the axon. Huxley, like his namesake Hugh Huxley, also did important work on muscle contraction. He shared the 1963 Nobel Prize in physiology or medicine with Alan Hodgkin and John Eccles, and was president of the Royal Society, 1980–85.

Huxley, Hugh Esmor (b. 1924) English molecular biologist who proposed the "sliding filament" theory of muscle contraction, which has never been seriously challenged. Huxley is unrelated to the family that came to prominence with Charles Darwin's close friend and supporter Thomas Henry Huxley.

Huxley, Sir Julian Sorell (1887–1975) English biologist and prolific popular science writer, grandson of Thomas Huxley, who did much to spread biological knowledge among the lay public of his day. He was also a regular radio broadcaster. He studied the development of many organisms and had a great interest in biological classification. He promoted eugenics and researched animal behavior, coining the term *ethology* for this new science. He urged that physiology, ethnology, and other factors be included in the determination of species.

Huxley, Thomas Henry (1825–95) English biologist, physiologist, physician, polemicist, and witty writer whose ardent and vocal support of Charles Darwin's theory of evolution by natural selection compensated for the latter's meekness and retiring nature. During the HMS *Rattlesnake* expedition to the South Seas (1846–50), he collected and studied specimens of marine animals, particularly plankton. His book *Man's Place in Nature* (1863) was controversial because he suggested that the closest relatives of human beings are the anthropoid apes.

Ibn Sīnā (Avicenna) (980–1037) Arab physician and the most celebrated philosopher of medieval Islam whose book *Canon medicinae* was the most influential medical text for centuries.

Jackson, John Hughlings (1835–1911) English neurologist who made many important contributions to the science of neurology but who is best remembered for his studies of epilepsy. By careful post-mortem examination of patients' brains, he was able to show the cause of many neurological diseases and explain much about brain function.

Jacob, François (b. 1920) French biologist who, with Jacques Monod, demonstrated that the function of some genes is to regulate the action of others; also with Monod, he correctly proposed the existence of messenger RNA, which carries the genetic information to the site of protein synthesis. Jacob and Monod jointly shared the Nobel Prize in physiology or medicine in 1965 with André Lwoff.

Jeffreys, Alec John (b. 1950) English molecular biologist who developed DNA fingerprinting. This method produces a

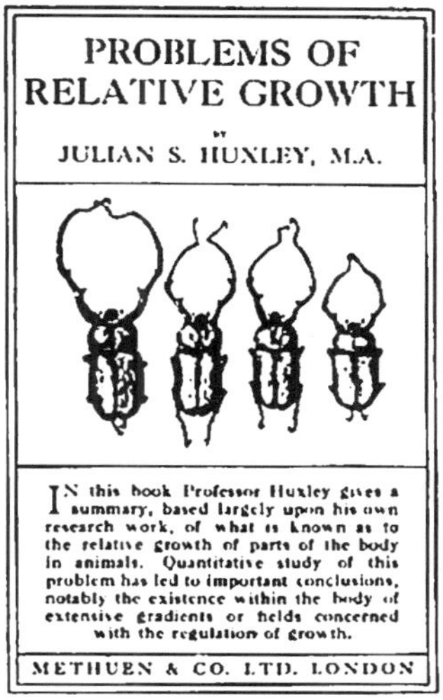

PROBLEMS OF RELATIVE GROWTH

BY

JULIAN S. HUXLEY, M.A.

IN this book Professor Huxley gives a summary, based largely upon his own research work, of what is known as to the relative growth of parts of the body in animals. Quantitative study of this problem has led to important conclusions, notably the existence within the body of extensive gradients or fields concerned with the regulation of growth.

METHUEN & CO. LTD. LONDON

Title page of one of Julian Huxley's many books, *Problems of Relative Growth* (1932)

Illustration of Ibn Sīnā's treatment for a dislocated spine

pattern that is unique to each individual, by breaking up DNA with restriction endonuclease enzymes, separating the different length fragments by electrophoresis, tagging them with radioactive tracers, and producing a contact print on photographic film.

Jenner, Edward (1749–1823) English country doctor who, having heard a milkmaid say that she was immune to smallpox because she had had cowpox, scratched some cowpox fluid into the arm of a small boy and then, in 1796, with incredible rashness, innoculated the boy with virulent smallpox fluid. Fortunately the boy escaped infection. Jenner published his results and the government awarded him an enormous *ex gratia* payment. The World Health Assembly declared smallpox eradicated in 1980.

Johannsen, Wilhelm Ludvig (1857–1927) Danish botanist who introduced the term *gene* and the terms *genotype* for the whole genome and *phenotype* for the resulting characteristics of the organism. He pioneered experimental genetics and showed that differences between genetically identical plants are solely of environmental origin.

James Joule

Joule, James Prescott (1818–89) English physicist who laid foundations for the theory of the conservation of energy. He is famous for experiments in heat, which he showed to be a form of energy. He also showed that if a gas expands without performing work, its temperature falls. The joule, a unit of work or energy, is named after him. With William Thomson, Lord Kelvin, he devised an absolute scale of temperature.

Jussieu, Antoine-Laurent de (1748–1836) French taxonomist who demonstrated that the organizational elements in a plant are the best way to classify it. Most of his classifications are still used today. Jussieu believed that the most important difference between living and nonliving things is organization, which is possessed by the former but not the latter. He lived long before the dawn of digital computers.

Kaposi, Moricz (1837–1902) Viennese dermatologist who first described the multiple skin tumors, known as Kaposi's sarcoma, that became well known with the onset of the AIDS epidemic.

Kendall, Edward Calvin (1886–1972) U.S. biochemist who studied the hormones produced by the outer zone (cortex) of the adrenal gland and from his findings synthesized cortisone. This led to the valuable range of corticosteroid drugs. In 1950, Kendall and his colleague, Philip Hench, shared the Nobel Prize in physiology or medicine with Tadeus Reichstein.

Edward C. Kendall

Kendrew, Sir John Cowdery (1917–97) English molecular biologist who established the three-dimensional structure of muscle hemoglobin (myoglobin) by X-ray crystallography in 1959. He was awarded the 1962 Nobel Prize in chemistry together with Max Perutz.

Kettlewell, Henry Bernard David (1907–79) English geneticist and entomologist who demonstrated the survival value—in their separate ways—of both the dark coloration found on peppered moths in industrial regions and the original light coloration in rural areas, thus showing the effectiveness of natural selection as an evolutionary process.

Kitasato, Shibasaburo (1852–1931) Japanese physician and bacteriologist who was the first to culture the tetanus bacillus, which made it possible to create a vaccine against the disease. He also found how to make tetanus antitoxin, a valuable means of treating the disease. Kitasato also isolated the bubonic plague bacillus.

Klug, Sir Aaron (b. 1926) South African chemist whose work on determining the structure of viruses, including the polio virus, earned him the 1982 Nobel Prize in chemistry. Klug used a variety of techniques, including X-ray diffractions, electron microscopy, and structural modeling.

Knight, Andrew (1758–1838) English botanist who studied the patterns of growth of plant ra phenomenon known as tropism, later rigorously studied by Charles Darwin and his son Francis.

Koch, Heinrich Hermann Robert (1843–1910) German bacteriologist who developed culture media for incubating organisms, studied the transmission of infectious disease, isolated the tuberculosis germ, and laid down strict rules for deciding whether a particular disease was caused by a particular bacterium (Koch's postulates). Koch was awarded the Nobel Prize in physiology or medicine in 1905.

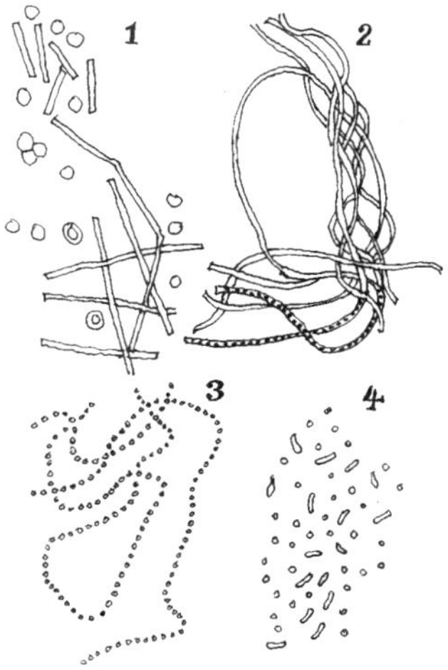

Drawings by Koch of four stages in the development of anthrax bacilli

Kocher, Emil Theodor (1841–1917) Swiss surgeon noted for his pioneer work on the function and disorders of the thyroid gland and for his surgical advances in the management of dislocated shoulder, hernia, and bone marrow inflammation (osteomyelitis). Kocher was awarded the 1909 Nobel Prize in physiology or medicine for his work on the thyroid.

Köhler, Georges Jean Franz (1946–95) German immunologist who discovered how to produce monoclonal antibodies, one of the most significant advances in medical technology of the 20th century. Köhler fused B cells (antibody-producers) with a cancer cell, thereby starting an immortal clone of hybrid cells capable of producing a large quantity of a particular antibody. He shared the 1984 Nobel Prize in physiology or medicine with César Milstein and Niels Jerne.

Albert von Kölliker

Kölliker, Rudolf Albert von (1817–1905) Swiss embryologist and microscopic anatomist who researched the sperm of invertebrates and asserted, correctly, that the embryo and fetus result from continuous repeated cell division, starting with the egg (ovum). He stressed the importance of the cell nucleus, so pioneering the study of the cell itself (cytology).

Kosterlitz, Hans Walter (1903–96) German-born Scottish pharmacologist and physiologist who, working with John Hughes, discovered the natural morphinelike body opiates, the enkephalins (endorphins), and showed that they are blocked by the drug naloxone, which antagonizes morphine.

Kovalevsky, Aleksandr Onufriyevich (1840–1901) Russian embryologist who showed the remarkable similarities in the early embryonic stages of animals of widely differing species. This observation was taken up, and carried too far, by Ernst Haeckel.

Krebs, Sir Hans Adolf (1900–81) German-born English biochemist who elucidated the cyclical series of biochemical reactions by means of which energy is provided for cell function and for the synthesis of biomolecules. This important process is known as the Krebs cycle and is fundamental to cell physiology. Krebs shared the Nobel Prize in medicine or physiology with Fritz Lipmann in 1953.

Lamarck, Jean-Baptiste-Pierre-Antoine de Monet, Chevalier de (1744–1829) French naturalist who made the basic distinction between vertebrates and invertebrates. In his famous *Philosophie Zoologique* (1809), he postulated, mistakenly, that acquired characteristics can be inherited by later generations. Once Darwin's theory of evolution was widely understood, Lamarck was made the unjustified butt of generations of students' humor. His contributions to zoology were, however, solid and important.

Jean Lamarck

Landsteiner, Karl (1868–1943) Austrian physician, chemist, and immunologist who discovered blood groups and showed how to identify a person's group, so making blood transfusion safe. For this work, he was awarded the 1930 Nobel Prize in physiology or medicine. In 1940, Landsteiner also discovered the rhesus factor.

Laveran, Charles-Louis-Alphonse (1845–1922) French physician and parasitologist who in 1878, while studying red blood cells under a microscope, saw for the first time the parasite that causes malaria. In 1907, he was awarded the Nobel Prize in physiology or medicine.

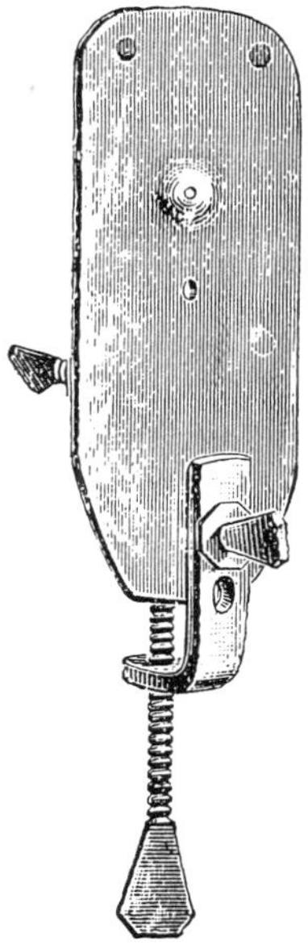

Van Leeuwenhoek's single-lens microscope

Leeuwenhoek, Antoni van (1632–1723) Dutch amateur microscopist who, using home-made single-lens microscopes, observed motile single-celled animals (protozoa), spermatozoa, bacteria, blood capillaries, and many other previously invisible biological entities. His reports and drawings were sent to the Royal Society in London, where they were seen to be of the first importance and were widely publicized from 1683.

Lehn, Jean-Marie (b. 1939) French chemist who showed that sodium and potassium ions can pass across biological membranes in a nonpolar environment by being enclosed within a cavity or channel in a large organic molecule. This discovery opened up a new branch of organic chemistry called supramolecular chemistry and won Lehn a share of the 1987 Nobel Prize in chemistry, with Charles Pedersen and Donald Cram.

Leloir, Luis Frederico (1906–87) Argentinian biochemist who made a number of biochemical advances important to medicine. He discovered the hormone angiotensin, which raises blood pressure; he showed how the energy-storage polysaccharide

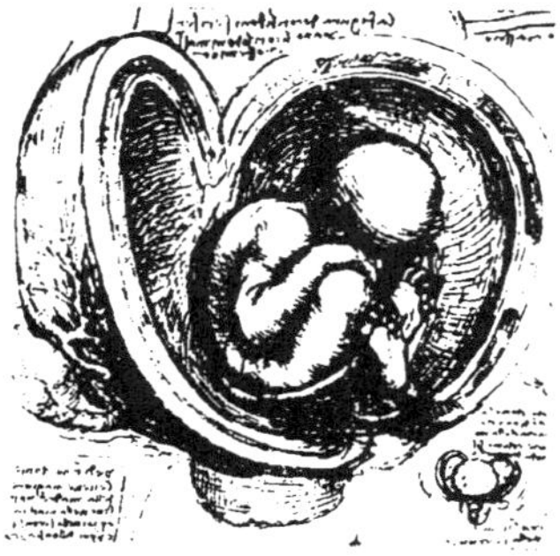

Drawing of a fetus in the womb by Leonardo da Vinci

glycogen is a polymer built up from units of glucose; and he showed how galactose is converted to glucose. For these findings, he was awarded the 1970 Nobel Prize in chemistry.

Leonardo da Vinci (1452–1519) Italian painter, sculptor, engineer, and scientist who studied and made contributions to biology, physiology, anatomy, mechanics, hydrodynamics, and aerodynamics. His notebooks contain numerous sketches illustrating ideas for machines and devices, many of which were well ahead of their time and must have inspired later engineers and scientists.

Leuckart, Karl Georg Friedrich Rudolf (1822–98) German zoologist who pioneered human parasitology and investigated and described the life cycles of many of the parasites of human beings, including roundworms, tapeworms, and liver flukes.

Levi-Montalcini, Rita (b. 1909) Italian physician and biological researcher who discovered the protein substance that prompts embryonic nerve cells to put out fibers (axons) and grow toward and make contact with their target cells. The substance is called nerve growth factor. For this work, she shared the 1986 Nobel Prize in physiology or medicine with Stanley Cohen.

Lewis, Edward Bok (1918–2004) U.S. developmental biologist who, in collaboration with Eric Wieschaus and Christiane Nüsslein-Volhard, identified homeobox genes, which determine that the correct organs form in the correct places early in the development of the embryo. This provided a solution to the question of how genetics could organize the body's architecture, and it won the three scientists the 1995 Nobel Prize in physiology or medicine.

Li, Choh Hao (1913–89) Chinese-born U.S. biochemist who isolated several pituitary hormones and worked out the amino acid sequence of growth hormone and then synthesized it. He also established the sequence in ACTH, the pituitary hormone that prompts the adrenals to produce cortisone.

Liebig, Justus, Freiherr von (1803–73) German chemist, one of the most illustrious of his time, equally skilled in method and in practical applications. He made his name both in organic and animal chemistry and in the study of alcohols. He founded the science of agricultural chemistry and discovered chloroform.

Lind, James (1716–94) Scottish naval surgeon who discovered that the serious and often fatal bleeding disease scurvy, common in sailors, could be cured with lemon juice. It took 50 years for the Admiralty to accept his advice, but eventually British sailors came to be known as "limeys." Later, vitamin C was identified as the substance whose deficiency causes the disease.

Linnaeus, Carolus *See* **Linné, Carl von**.

Linné, Carl von (**Carolus Linnaeus**) (1707–78) Swedish naturalist and physician who introduced the binomial nomenclature of generic and specific names for animals and plants, which permitted the hierarchical organization later known as systematics. The generic name is always written with a capital letter; the specific name with a lowercase initial letter.

Carl von Linné

Lipmann, Fritz Albert (1899–1986) German-born U.S. biochemist who showed how citric acid is formed from oxaloacetate and acetate, and that an unrecognized cofactor, coenzyme A, is required. Lipmann isolated this factor. The formation of citric acid is the first step in the important energy-producing Krebs cycle. Lipmann shared the 1953 Nobel Prize in physiology or medicine with Hans Krebs.

Lister, Joseph, 1st Baron Lister (1827–1912) English surgeon who was one of the first to try during surgery to prevent sepsis, which was claiming the lives of many patients. Lister used an aerosol of carbolic acid and is said to have started his operations by intoning, "Let us spray!" His method was rapidly succeeded by aseptic surgery with sterilization of all instruments, but it drew attention to the vital importance of avoiding infection. He also initiated the practice of draining abscesses with a tube.

Lister's carbolic acid disinfectant spray

Loewi, Otto (1873–1961) German pharmacologist who proved that nerve impulse transmission is transferred from nerve to muscle by a chemical mediator. He distinguished acetylcholine from adrenaline for this function, and the former was later identified by Henry Dale. He shared the Nobel Prize in physiology or medicine with Dale in 1936.

Löffler, Friedrich August Johannes (1852–1915) German bacteriologist who was the first to culture the diphtheria bacterium. He established the cause of glanders and swine erysipelas and proved that there were disease-causing entities smaller than bacteria that would pass through filters that easily retained bacteria. These were called "filterable viruses," but they were not then known to be organisms.

Carl Ludwig

Lorenz, Konrad Zacharias (1903–89) Austrian zoologist and student of animal behavior whose accounts of early imprinting, bonding, and aggression became common coinage as a result of his highly successful popular books, such as *King Solomon's Ring* (1949) and *On Aggression* (1963). Considered one of the founders of ethology, he shared the 1973 Nobel Prize in physiology or medicine with Karl von Frisch and Nicholaas Tinbergen.

Lower, Richard (1631–91) British physician, anatomist, and physiologist who proved that arterial blood is changed by air and concluded that the function of breathing is to add something essential to the blood. This finding helped to oppose the widespread and dangerous practice of bloodletting.

Ludwig, Carl Friedrich Wilhelm (1816–95) German physiologist and inspiring teacher whose study of the body as a machine led to the abandonment of the scientifically meaningless concept of "vital force" (*vis vitalis*). Ludwig is regarded by many as the greatest teacher of physiology of the 19th century.

Luria, Salvador Edward (1912–91) Italian-born U.S. biologist who worked with Max Delbrück and Alfred Hershey on the role of DNA in viruses that infect bacteria. During the 1940s, he made some basic discoveries in the mutation of bacteria and viruses. He shared the 1969 Nobel Prize in physiology or medicine with Delbrück and Hershey.

Magendie, François (1783–1855) French physiologist and pharmacologist who showed that the nerves emerging near the front of the spinal cord activate the muscles, while those emerging near the back of the cord carry sensation up to the brain. He also investigated the medical uses of alkaloid drugs, such as morphine, curare, strychnine, and quinine.

Magnus, Heinrich Gustav (1802–70) German physicist and chemist who studied tellurium and selenium and the gases in the blood. He is best remembered for his discovery of the fact that a flow of air over a rotating cylinder produces a sideways force. This effect, the Magnus effect, has been used to propel sailing boats and is well known to high-handicap golfers.

Maillet, Benoit de (1656–1738) French naturalist who, while accepting that the biblical account of the Creation was true, insisted, nevertheless, that new animal and plant forms had come into existence during the history of the Earth.

Malpighi, Marcello (1628–94) Italian physician and anatomist who discovered and described the blood capillaries and demonstrated the importance of the microscope in anatomical studies. Malpighi's findings finally showed how blood from the arteries could reach the veins via the lungs and so continue to circulate. He was also the first to observe many of the physiological processes of plant and insect life.

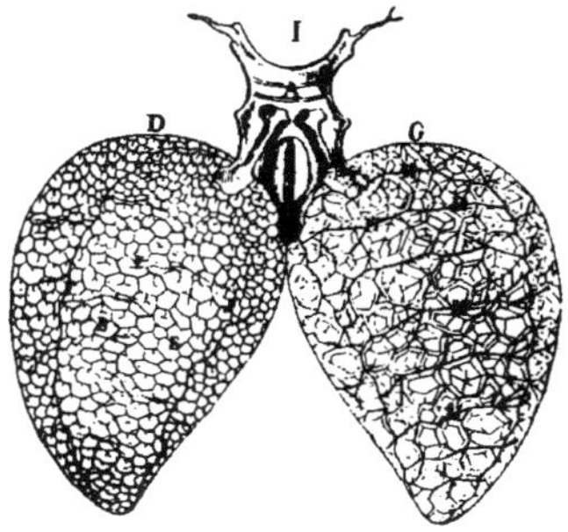

Sketch by Malpighi of capillaries in a frog's lungs

Manson, Sir Patrick (1844–1922) Scottish physician and tropical medicine specialist who proved that many tropical diseases, such as elephantiasis, sleeping sickness (trypanosomiasis), and bilharzia (schistosomiasis), are transmitted by insects. His suggestion to Ronald Ross led the latter to prove that malaria is transmitted by mosquitoes.

Martin, Archer John Porter (1910–2002) English biochemist who developed methods of partition chromatography, using columns of silica gel, for the separation of amino acids from the mixture produced by the hydrolysis of proteins. This method greatly facilitated the work of determining the structure of proteins. He shared the 1952 Nobel Prize in chemistry.

Masters, William (1915–2001) U.S. gynecologist noted for his scientific studies of human sexual behavior and responses in the laboratory. With his colleague, Virginia Johnson (b. 1925), whom he married, he continued to investigate the physiology of human sexual intercourse using volunteer subjects, and also advocated therapy. Their book *Human Sexual Response* (1966) became a best-seller.

Mayr, Ernst Walter (1904–2004) German-born U.S. zoologist whose early work was on the ornithology of the Pacific. Later, he was best known for neo-Darwinian views on evolution, as developed in his books *Animal Species and Evolution* (1963) and *Evolution and the Diversity of Life* (1976). He also worked on the classification of organisms, and on population genetics.

McClintock, Barbara (1902–92) U.S. geneticist who, working on maize DNA, demonstrated how genes are turned on and off (activated and deactivated) by other genes. These genes could be copied from one chromosome to another and were later named "transposons," but are more popularly known a "jumping genes." She won the Nobel Prize for physiology or medicine in 1983.

McIndoe, Sir Archibald Hector (1900–60) New Zealand-born pioneer of plastic and reconstructive surgery who, during World War II, organized a burn unit in England for the treatment of hundreds of airmen burned in the course of duty. After the war, McIndoe remained in England to train plastic surgeons from all over the world.

Medawar, Sir Peter Brian (1915–87) British immunologist—and a leading pioneer of immunology—whose work in preventing rejection of foreign tissue led to the success of transplant operations. In 1960, he shared the Nobel Prize in physiology or medicine with Frank Burnet, for research on immunological tolerance in relation to skin and organ grafting. Medawar was a talented writer on popular scientific and philosophical topics and a staunch and eloquent opponent of pseudoscience.

Austrian postage stamp commemorating Mendel

Mendel, Gregor Johann (1822–84) Austrian priest, biologist, and botanist whose careful research into the inheritance of characteristics in some 30,000 pure bred and hybrid pea plants laid the foundations of the science of genetics. He coined the terms *dominant* and *recessive* and evolved laws of inheritance. His work was published in 1865 in an obscure journal and, in spite of his efforts to have it recognized, was ignored for many years, until he himself lost interest in it.

Merrifield, Robert Bruce (b. 1921) U.S. chemist who developed an ingenious and rapid way of synthesizing proteins by lining up the constituent amino acids in the right order on a polystyrene bead, a process that has now been automated. This work earned him the 1984 Nobel Prize in chemistry.

Metchnikoff, Elie (1845–1916) Russian biologist working in France who discovered cells, which he named *phagocytes* (literally, "eating cells"), that existed in the blood and tissues and which could engulf and digest foreign material. With this and other findings, he originated the science of immunology, which is now a large and highly complex discipline. In 1908, Metchnikoff shared the Nobel Prize in physiology or medicine with Paul Ehrlich for his discovery of phagocytes.

Meyerhof, Otto Fritz (1884–1951) German-born U.S. biochemist whose work on muscle physiology showed that lactic acid is produced from muscle glycogen during muscle contraction in anaerobic conditions. He also showed that the utilization of glucose as a fuel in living cells involved a cyclic biochemical pathway. For these discoveries, he shared the Nobel Prize in physiology or medicine with Archibald Hill in 1922.

Otto Meyerhof

Michel, Hartmut (b. 1948) German biochemist who, working with Robert Huber and Johann Deisenhofer, established the structure of an area of a bacterium in which photosynthesis takes place. He and his colleagues were awarded the 1988 Nobel Prize in chemistry for this work.

Miescher, Johann Friedrich (1844–95) Swiss physiologist who was one of the first to suggest that the information for inheritable characteristics might be present in the form of a code, represented by spaced-out elements of some kind.

Miller, Stanley Lloyd (b. 1930) U.S. chemist who studied the possible origins of life on Earth by using laboratory equipment to simulate supposed early atmospheric gaseous content and electric sparks to simulate lightning. He succeeded in forming amino acids, the units of proteins. Later work on the enzymatic function of RNA added credibility to Miller's ideas.

Mitchell, Peter Dennis (1920–92) English biochemist who revolutionized thought on the process of oxidative phosphorylation, in which adenosine triphosphate (ATP) is regenerated from adenosine diphosphate (ADP) and phosphate. Breakdown of ATP to ADP releases large amounts of energy for cell functions from the phosphate bonds. Mitchell proposed that electron transport formed a proton gradient across the mitochondrial membrane and that this gradient directly brought about the synthesis of ATP from ADP. He was awarded the Nobel Prize in chemistry in 1978.

Hugo von Mohl

Mohl, Hugo von (1805–72) German botanist and pioneer of the microscopic study of plant structure and of research into plant physiology. He was the first to recognize protoplasm, now called cytoplasm, as the principal substance of cells. He was also one of the earliest workers fully to understand and explain osmosis.

Molina, Mario (b. 1943) U.S. chemist who, working with F. Sherwood Rowland and Paul Crutzen, alerted the world to the danger of damage being caused to the ozone layer of the atmosphere, about 9–30 miles up, from artificially produced nitrogen oxides and chlorofluorocarbon (CFC) gases. The ozone layer protects us against dangerous concentrations of ultraviolet frequencies in sunlight. For this work, the three men were awarded the 1995 Nobel Prize in chemistry.

Moniz, Antonio Egas *See* **Egas Moniz, António Caetano de Abreu Freire**.

Monod, Jacques-Lucien (1910–76) French biochemist who worked with François Jacob on messenger RNA. In *Chance and Necessity* (1970), he proposed that humans are the product of chance in the universe.

Montagnier, Luc (b. 1932) French molecular biologist who, as head of the viral oncology unit at the Pasteur Institute in Paris, led the team that discovered the human immunodeficiency virus (HIV), the cause of AIDS. At the time, the virus was called HLTV-III, and it was actually isolated by the virologist Françoise Barré-Sinoussi, who, although little recognized by the scientific establishment, has been recognized by some as one of the 100 most powerful women in the world.

Moore, Stanford (1913–82) U.S. biochemist who, working with William Stein, invented a chromatography process that could separate from a mass of enzyme-digested protein all the constituent amino acids so that they could be identified and quantified. Moore and Stein also invented an automated method of determining the base sequence in a length of RNA. Moore, Stein, and Christian Anfinsen were awarded the 1972 Nobel Prize in chemistry.

Morgagni, Giovanni Battista (1682–1771) Italian anatomist and pathologist who was a pioneer of post-mortem examination to detect the presence of disease and the causes of death. In his book *De sedibus et causis morborum per anatomen indagatis* (1761) he described the findings in hundreds of autopsies.

Thomas H. Morgan

Morgan, Thomas Hunt (1866–1945) U.S. geneticist and biologist. He carried out experiments with the *Drosophila* fruit fly, from which he established a chromosome theory of heredity involving genes for specific characteristics aligned on chromosomes. This major breakthrough in genetics earned him the 1933 Nobel Prize in physiology or medicine.

Muller, Hermann Joseph (1890–1967) U.S. geneticist who proved that gene mutations could be induced in the fruit fly *Drosophila* by X-rays. Muller identified the gene as the real unit of inheritance and concluded, correctly, that a mutation is simply a change in the chemical structure of the gene. This work earned him the Nobel Prize in physiology or medicine in 1946.

Mullis, Kary Banks (b. 1944) U.S. biochemist who, while driving one evening, conceived the idea of the polymerase chain reaction (PCR) that was to become one of the most important advances in genetic research, engineering, and medicine since Francis Crick and James Watson. PCR provides millions of copies of any DNA fragment. He shared the Nobel Prize in chemistry in 1993 with Michael Smith.

Naudin, Charles (1815–99) French botanist and horticulturist who experimented with plant hybridization and found that certain characteristics were inherited on a regular basis.

Needham, John Turberville (1713–81) British naturalist who tried to prove the existence of the spontaneous generation of living organisms by boiling mutton broth and then sealing it in glass containers. Organisms resulted, but this was because some spores had survived the rather too brief boiling.

Newton, Alfred (1829–1907) English zoologist who in 1866 was appointed the first professor of zoology and comparative anatomy at Cambridge University and wrote valuable works on ornithology, notably *A Dictionary of Birds* (1893–96).

Noguchi, Hideyo (1876–1928) Japanese bacteriologist who was the first to culture the spirochaete organism *Treponema pallidum*, which causes syphilis. He also isolated the germ responsible for kala azar (leishmaniasis). Noguchi went to West Africa to do research into yellow fever but contracted the disease and died from it.

Nüsslein-Volhard, Christiane (b. 1942) German developmental biologist who, in collaboration with Edward Lewis and Eric F. Wieschaus, identified the homeobox genes, those that determine that the correct organs form in the correct places, early in the development of the embryo. This provided a solution to the question of how genetics could organize the body's architecture, and it won the three scientists the 1995 Nobel Prize in physiology or medicine.

Ochoa, Severo (1905–93) Spanish-born U.S. biochemist who became a professor of biochemistry at New York University in 1954. A year later, he showed how cells use an enzyme to join DNA fragments. This work led to genetic engineering. For this discovery, Ochoa and Arthur Kornberg, a fellow worker on DNA, shared the 1959 Nobel Prize in physiology or medicine.

Sir Richard Owen

Owen, Sir Richard (1804–92) English zoologist and comparative anatomist who maintained a hostile attitude to Darwin's evolution theory. His essay on parthenogenesis (virgin birth) was a pioneer work.

Paget, Sir James (1814–99) English surgeon who described three diseases, of bone, nipple, and penis, that are all known as Paget's disease.

Palade, George Emil (b. 1912) Romanian-born U.S. physiologist who improved techniques for preparing cells for electron microscopy and also studied the fine structure of the cell organs (organelles), especially the mitochondria, the endoplasmic reticulum, the Golgi apparatus, and the ribosomes. He showed that protein synthesis occurs in the ribosomes. For this work, Palade shared the 1974 Nobel Prize in physiology or medicine with Albert Claude and Christian de Duve.

Pander, Christian Heinrich (1794–1865) Russian-born German anatomist and embryologist who made notable advances in the understanding of early embryonic development but then seemed to lose interest and left the advancement of the work to others. He originated the term *blastoderm*.

Parkinson, James (1755–1824) British physician, geologist, and paleontologist who was the first to describe appendicitis and, in the book *An Essay on the Shaking Palsy* (1817), the disease that now bears his name.

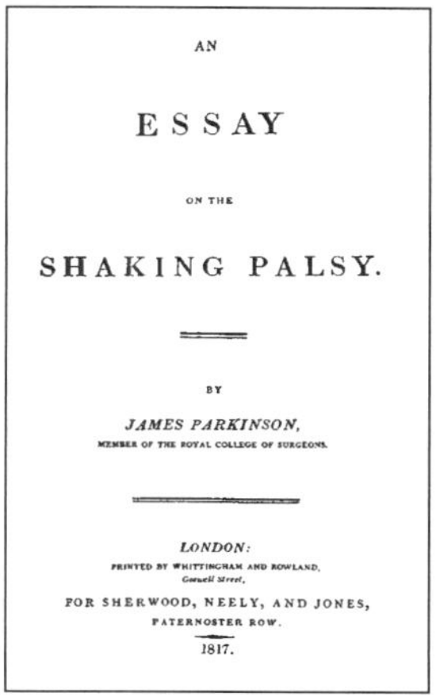

AN
ESSAY
ON THE
SHAKING PALSY.
BY
JAMES PARKINSON,
MEMBER OF THE ROYAL COLLEGE OF SURGEONS.
LONDON:
PRINTED BY WHITTINGHAM AND ROWLAND,
Goswell Street,
FOR SHERWOOD, NEELY, AND JONES,
PATERNOSTER ROW.
1817.

Title page of Parkinson's *An Essay on the Shaking Palsy* (1817)

Pasteur, Louis (1822–95) French chemist and founder of modern bacteriology who proposed the *germ* theory of disease in the late 1860s. This was, perhaps, the greatest single advance in the history of medicine. He also developed "pasteurization:" rapid, short-term heating to kill harmful bacteria in wine and milk.

Pauling, Linus Carl (1901–94) U.S. chemist noted for his germinal work *The Nature of the Chemical Bond* (1939), which applied quantum theory. He made major advances in the understanding of protein structures and was awarded the Nobel Prize in chemistry in 1954. His work also covered inorganic complexes, protein structure, antibodies, DNA structure, and the molecular basis of some genetic diseases. Pauling's stubborn belief in the efficacy of vitamin C has now been vindicated with recent understanding of the biological effect of free radicals and the value of vitamin C as a biological antioxidant.

Pavlov, Ivan Petrovich (1849–1936) Russian physiologist who worked on the physiology of the circulation and digestion but is most famous for his study of "conditioned" reflexes, in which a stimulus that would not by itself produce a particular effect will do so if repeatedly offered in conjunction with the normal stimulus for that effect. This finding so impressed Pavlov that he came to see brain function as largely a matter of conditioned reflexes. The term *conditioned* was a mistake in translation; Pavlov actually wrote *conditional.*

Ivan Pavlov

Pecquet, Jean (1622–74) French anatomist who discovered the thoracic duct.

Pedersen, Charles John (1904–89) U.S. chemist who produced a crown-shaped cyclic polyether that was given the name *crown ether* and discovered that compounds of this kind would bind sodium and potassium ions strongly, making alkali metal salts that are soluble in organic solvents. This work helped to explain how these metallic ions are transported across biological membranes, a matter of great importance in physiology and pharmacology. For this work, he was awarded a share in the 1987 Nobel Prize in chemistry.

Wilhelm Pfeffer

Perutz, Max Ferdinand (1914–2002) Austrian-born British biochemist who, using X-ray diffraction and other methods, achieved the extraordinarily complex task of determining the molecular three-dimensional structure of hemoglobin. For this work, he shared the 1962 Nobel Prize in chemistry.

Pfeffer, Wilhelm Friedrich Philipp (1845–1920) German botanist who researched osmosis and the permeability of protoplasts (the contents of the plant cell, including the cell membrane, within the cell wall) and concluded that the latter could be actively modified. He wrote the standard work on plant physiology (1881).

Porter, Rodney Robert (1917–85) British biochemist who first suggested that antibodies are Y-shaped. In 1962, Porter showed that the gamma globulin antibody could be split by an enzyme into three large fragments. Two of these could bind antigens and were known as "Fab" (fragment antigen binding); the third, a crystalline fragment, could not. Porter showed that this third fragment is common to all antibodies and that it is the Fab fragments, which exist in thousands of different forms, that give antibodies their specificity. This important discovery led to his being awarded the 1972 Nobel Prize in physiology or medicine with Gerard Edelman.

Praxagoras (fl. 400 BCE) Greek physician who promoted the misleading doctrine of the four humors (blood, phlegm, yellow bile, and black bile) but is believed to have been the first to distinguish between arteries and veins.

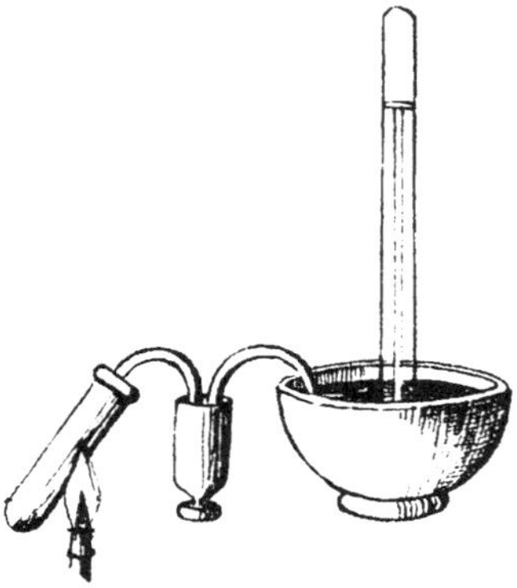

Priestley's apparatus for collecting the oxygen given off when saltpetre is heated

Priestley, Joseph (1733–1804) English chemist and Presbyterian minister who pioneered the study of the chemistry of gases and, in 1774, was one of the discoverers of oxygen. He was not the first to identify oxygen, as is often stated, but he achieved priority in publication. The Swedish apothecary Carl Scheele isolated oxygen in 1772.

Pringsheim, Nathanael (1823–94) German botanist who pioneered the scientific study of algae.

Prusiner, Stanley Ben (b. 1942) U.S. neurologist and biochemist who was the first scientist since the discovery of viruses to detect an entirely new infective agent. As a young neurology resident, Prusiner was in charge of a patient who died of Creutzfeldt-Jakob disease (CJD), and he decided to research the cause. Ten years later, he isolated small protein bodies, which he called prions, and he showed that these were the cause of CJD and of the similar bovine spongiform encephalopathy. He was awarded the Nobel Prize in physiology or medicine in 1997.

Purkinje, Jan Evangelista, *See* **Purkyně, Jan Evangelista**.

Purkyně, Jan Evangelista (**Jan Evangelista Purkinje**) (1787–1869) Czech physiologist and microscopic anatomist (histologist) who studied nerve cells and their fibers, describing their different characteristics in different parts of the nervous system. He used a mechanical cutter (microtome) to make very thin slices of tissue for staining and microscopy and showed how to perceive the shadows of one's own retinal blood vessels.

Jan Purkyně

Ramón y Cajal, Santiago (1852–1934) Spanish neuroanatomist who developed a method of staining nerve tissue that revealed the detailed connections of the central nervous system. He traced many long nerve axons to their destinations. His work revolutionized neurology and earned him, with Camillo Golgi, the 1906 Nobel Prize in physiology or medicine.

Ray, John (1627–1705) English naturalist who originated basic principles of plant classification into cryptogams, monocotyledons, and dicotyledons. His major work was *Historia generalis plantarum* (1686–1704), but he also wrote on birds, fish, and insects. He was the first to propose the concept of species.

Raynaud, Maurice (1834–81) French surgeon who first described the disorder of the fingers in cold weather, characterized by successive color change from white to blue to red.

Rāzi, Abū Bakr Muhammad ibn Zakarīyā ar- (**Rhazes or Al-Razi**) (854–925) Persian physician and alchemist who based his practice on rational grounds, observation, and experience; taught high ethical standards in medical care; and also treated poor patients without fees. He recorded all the medical knowledge of his time and wrote 10 medical treatises of his own.

René Réaumur

Réaumur, René-Antoine Ferchault de (1683–1757) French entomologist, physicist, and metallurgist who invented an opaque white glass known as Réaumur porcelain, improved the thermometer and proposed a new scale, showed that digestion was a chemical process, and described hereditary transmission of abnormality in a family. His six-volume *History of Insects* (1734–42) laid the basis for the study of entomology.

Redi, Francesco (1626–97) Italian physician and poet who wrote a book on animal parasites and proved that maggots cannot form on meat that has been covered to exclude flies.

Walter Reed

Reed, Walter (1851–1902) U.S. Army Medical Corps officer who discovered the cause of yellow fever. Following up a suggestion by Carlos Finlay, Reed arranged for six volunteers to be bitten by *Aedes aegypti* mosquitoes that had fed on yellow fever patients. Five of them contracted the disease. Reed and the bacteriologist James Carroll then proved that the mosquito was carrying a virus. Reed is remembered by the hospital in Washington, D.C., that is named after him.

Reichstein, Tadeus (1897–1996) Polish-born Swiss biochemist whose work led to the synthesis of vitamin C and who elucidated the chemistry of the natural corticosteroid hormones of the adrenal gland. He was able to isolate 29 natural steroids. This work led to the production of a range of steroid drugs of great medical value that have saved many lives. In 1950, he shared the Nobel Prize in physiology or medicine with Edward Kendall and Philip Hench.

Remak, Robert (1815–65) German physician who demonstrated the myelin sheath of nerves and who showed that the main fiber (axon) of spinal nerves runs all the way from the spinal cord to the muscles of other tissues.

Rhazes *See* **Rāzi, Abū Bakr Muhammad ibn Zakarīyā ar**.

Richet, Charles-Robert (1850–1935) French physiologist who worked on immunization and discovered and researched the phenomenon of anaphylaxis, the abnormal and often dangerous immune response to a repeat dose of an antigen. In 1913, he received the Nobel Prize in physiology or medicine.

Robbins, Frederick Chapman (b. 1916) U.S. virologist who worked with John Enders and Thomas Huckle Weller to develop methods of growing disease viruses.

Rodbell, Martin (1925–98) U.S. biochemist who, working with Alfred Gilman, discovered the G protein, a previously unknown class of chemical messengers that, activated by an external hormone (the "first messenger") binding to a cell membrane receptor, effectively turn on the producers of the "second messenger," the hormone that then moves to the effector sites within the cell and initiates the effect of the external hormone. Disease processes can interfere with the G proteins. For this work, Rodbell and Gilman were awarded the 1994 Nobel Prize in physiology or medicine.

Rokitansky, Karl, Freiherr von (1804–78) Bohemian pathologist who described and enlarged the knowledge of the bodily changes in hundreds of different diseases, mainly by keeping careful records of the thousands of post-mortem examinations carried out by him and his assistants.

Rose, William Cumming (1887–1984) U.S. biochemist who investigated the individual role of the 20 amino acids in dietary protein and discovered that 10 of them are indispensable to rats but only eight are indispensable to humans. These are known as the "essential" amino acids. The others can be synthesized in the body.

Ross, Sir Ronald (1857–1932) Indian-born British physician and bacteriologist who in 1898, using a microscope, found malarial parasites in a mosquito, proving that malaria was transmitted by female *Anopheles* mosquitoes, and followed its life history. Ross was awarded the 1902 Nobel Prize in physiology or medicine.

Rous, Francis Peyton (1879–1970) U.S. pathologist who, working with chicken sarcomas, was the first to prove that some cancers are induced by viruses. These viruses are now called oncoviruses. Rous was awarded a share in the 1966 Nobel Prize in physiology or medicine.

Pierre Roux

Roux, Pierre-Paul-Émile (1853–1933) French bacteriologist who discovered diphtheria antitoxin by promoting antibody production in horses. Serum from these animals has saved thousands of lives. Roux worked with Louis Pasteur and Elie Metchnikoff at the Pasteur Institute in Paris, and from 1905 to the time of his death, was its director.

Ruska, Ernst August Friedrich (1906–88) German electrical engineer who developed the world's first electron microscope. This used an electron beam of an energy that produced a wavelength, and hence optical resolution, of a few angstrom units and allowed a magnification of a million times. This instrument revolutionized biological research and earned him a share in the 1986 Nobel Prize in physics.

Sabin, Albert Bruce (1906–93) U.S. microbiologist and immunologist who in the 1950s developed a live vaccine against poliomyelitis that can be taken by mouth and came into widespread use in the early 1960s. The Sabin vaccine allows the protection to be spread in the same way as the disease is spread (fecal-oral route) and provides longer-lasting immunity than the Salk vaccine.

Julius von Sachs

Sachs, Julius von (1832–97) German botanist who proved that chlorophyll is centrally involved in the natural synthesis of sugars from carbon dioxide and water, with the release of oxygen. He was also the first to find chlorophyll in plant chloroplasts.

Salk, Jonas Edward (1914–95) U.S. physician and virologist who developed the first effective vaccine against poliomyelitis, using polio viruses killed with formalin. The vaccine was first used in 1954, with excellent results. By 1958, half the U.S. population under 40 had been vaccinated, and the incidence of the disease had dropped to a very low level.

Sanger, Frederick (b. 1918) English biochemist who after 12 years of work was able to establish the molecular structure of the protein insulin, with its 51 amino acids. He was also able to show the small differences between the insulin of different mammals. Sanger later turned to DNA sequencing and, by laborious methods, was able to determine the base sequence of mitochondrial DNA and of the whole genome of a virus. For his work on insulin, he was awarded the Nobel Prize in chemistry in 1958; for his achievements in DNA sequencing, he shared in the 1980 Nobel Prize in chemistry with Paul Berg and Walter Gilbert.

Schleiden, Matthias Jakob (1804–81) German botanist who did much to establish cell theory. He showed that cells are the units of structure in plants and animals, and that organisms are aggregates of cells arranged according to definite laws.

Schwann, Theodor Ambrose Hubert (1810–82) German physiologist who finally established the fact that animals as well as plants are composed of cells. He discovered pepsin, the first digestive enzyme found in animal tissue, discovered the Schwann cells in the myelin sheath of nerves, and showed the role of yeast cells in the fermentation of sugars. He also demonstrated the role of microorganisms in putrefaction, and effectively abolished the idea of the "spontaneous generation" of living things in putrefying meat.

Serveto, Miguel (Michael Servetus) (1511–53) Spanish physician and theologian who was the first to claim, correctly, that blood passes from the right ventricle through the lungs and returns to the left ventricle. His book was pronounced heretical and burned, and Servetus was imprisoned. He escaped, and three copies of his book survived.

Miguel Serveto

Sherrington, Sir Charles Scott (1857–1952) British physiologist whose extensive research and writings on the functioning of the nervous system placed neurophysiology on a sound scientific footing. Sherrington received his country's Order of Merit in 1924 and, for his work on neurophysiology, shared the Nobel Prize in physiology or medicine in 1932 with Edgar Adrian.

Siebold, Karl Theodor Ernst von (1804–85) German zoologist and parasitologist who pointed out that protozoa are single-celled creatures and that a wide range of animal behavior could be shown by a single-celled creature. He was also the first to study cilia and to show how these are used for locomotion. He also studied the freshwater fish of central Europe.

Simpson, Sir James Young (1811–70) Scottish professor of midwifery who, in the face of much theological opposition, pioneered general anesthesia, first with ether and then with chloroform, for childbirth and surgery. In 1853, Queen Victoria effectively silenced those who continued to assert that it was God's will that women should suffer in childbirth by accepting chloroform for her eighth confinement.

Skou, Jens Christian (b. 1918) Danish chemist who established that the enzyme sodium potassium-ATPase was the first enzyme known to promote the transport of ions across a cell membrane. Ionic transport across membranes is fundamental to the transmission of nerve impulses. For this work, Skou was shared the Nobel Prize in chemistry in 1997 with Paul Boyer and John Walker.

Smith, Michael (1932–2000) British-born Canadian chemist who discovered how to produce deliberate mutations in DNA at precise locations (site-directed mutagenesis), a technique that enabled him to code for new proteins with new properties. He shared the 1993 Nobel Prize in chemistry with Kary Mullis.

Soranus of Ephesus (ca. 98–138) Greek physician and surgeon who, by careful observation, established most of the principles for the correct management of childbirth. His book *On Midwifery and the Diseases of Women* had a strong influence on obstetrics and gynecology until the 17th century.

Sørensen, Søren Peter Lauritz (1868–1939) Danish chemist who, in 1909, while describing the effect of hydrogen ion concentration on enzyme activity, proposed the use of a negative logarithm of this concentration as a measure of acidity and alkalinity. This became the standard pH scale now in universal use. He also studied amino acids, enzymes, and proteins. He and his wife Magrete were the first to crystallize the egg protein albumin.

Spallanzani, Lazzaro (1729–99) Italian biologist and naturalist who, between 1767 and 1778, carried out basic experiments to disprove ideas of the spontaneous generation of life. He also demonstrated the true nature of digestion and the functions of spermatozoa and ova and, in 1785, was the first, so far as is known, to try artificial insemination and succeed.

Spemann, Hans (1869–1941) German zoologist who showed that early embryonic cells are totipotential, that is, able to develop into any tissue, depending on their location in the developing body. For this work, he was awarded the Nobel Prize in physiology or medicine in 1935.

Stanley, Wendell Meredith (1904–71) U.S. virologist and biochemist who isolated the tobacco mosaic virus and showed that it consists only of nucleic acid and protein and that samples can be purified by chemical methods. This raised the still-unresolved question of whether or not viruses are living organisms. In 1946, Stanley shared the Nobel Prize in chemistry with James Sumner and John Howard Northrop.

Wendell Stanley

Starling, Ernest Henry (1886–1927) English physiologist who, with William Bayliss, showed that when food enters the stomach, a substance is released into the bloodstream that causes the pancreas to secrete digestive juices (enzymes) into the bowel. This was the first demonstration of a hormone and the foundation of the science of endocrinology.

Stein, William Howard (1911–80) U.S. biochemist who worked with Stanford Moore to produce a new method of column chromatography by which they were able to separate and identify amino acids from a mix of material produced by the hydrolysis of proteins. He, Moore, and Christian Anfinsen shared the 1972 Nobel Prize in chemistry.

Steller, Georg Wilhelm (1709–46) German naturalist and explorer who studied numerous species, including the sea lion, the eider duck, and the jay that is named after him, the Steller jay.

Steno, Nicolaus (Niels Stensen) (1638–86) Danish physician, naturalist, and theologian who did fundamental work in anatomy, geology, crystallography, paleontology, and mineralogy. He was the first to point out the true origin of fossil animals (1669), explain the structure of the Earth's crust, and distinguish between sedimentary and volcanic rocks.

Steptoe, Patrick Christopher (1913–88) British gynecologist and infertility specialist who pioneered in vitro fertilization. In the late 1960s, he developed a method of "harvesting" eggs from the ovaries and fertilizing them with the partner's sperm in a glass dish ("in vitro"). The first "test-tube" baby, Louise Joy, was born in 1978. Steptoe was also a pioneer of the now standard "keyhole" (laparoscopic) gynecological surgery.

Patrick Steptoe

Eduard Strasburger

James B. Sumner

Thomas Sydenham

Strasburger, Eduard Adolf (1844–1912) German botanist who was one of the first to describe the features of cell division, including the realignment and movement of chromosomes during mitosis. He also suggested the terms *cytoplasm* and *nucleoplasm*.

Sturtevant, Alfred Henry (1891–1970) U.S. geneticist who produced a genetic map of the four chromosomes of the fruit fly *Drosophila*, relying on the probability that genes separated at the crossing over of chromosome segments during cell division are more likely to be situated remote from each other on the chromosome. Work of this kind led to the acceptance of the fact that chromosomes are the vehicles of heredity.

Sumner, James Batcheller (1887–1955) U.S. biochemist who crystallized the enzyme urease and proved that it is a protein. He then partly determined its mode of function and produced antibodies to it. He proceeded to investigate and purify a considerable range of enzymes active in human biochemistry. He shared the 1946 Nobel Prize in chemistry with Wendell Stanley and John Howard Northrop.

Susruta (fl. 500) Indian surgeon whose teaching and methods uncannily anticipated modern surgical practice. He advocated a detailed knowledge of anatomy, great surgical cleanliness, effective methods of making incisions, and good surgical techniques with practice on models. He developed a wide range of instruments, including scalpels, scissors, cauteries, forceps, catheters, syringes, sounds, sutures, and sewing needles. Regrettably, his teachings did not catch on in the West and had to be rediscovered well over 1,000 years later.

Swammerdam, Jan (1637–80) Dutch zoologist and entomologist who in a period of 10 years, carried out much research on insect morphology and classification, wing expansion from the pupa stage, muscle contraction, lymph vessels, and ovarian follicles. He was the first to observe red blood corpuscles and to demonstrate that a contracting muscle does not change its volume, only its shape.

Sydenham, Thomas (1624–89) English physician, known as the English Hippocrates, who based his medical practice on close observation rather than dogma. His first principle was to avoid harming the patient, and his books were widely influential. He wrote accurately about gout, measles, and hysteria.

Diagram of Tagliacozzi's skin grafts, showing sources and destinations of healthy skin

Tagliacozzi, Gaspare (1546–99) Italian surgeon who pioneered plastic surgery, using principles that are still applied today. His speciality was the reconstruction of lost noses, using a flap of skin from the arm. He understood that a good blood supply was necessary for a graft to take, and always left one end of the flap in its original position until the other end had healed in its new place and established its blood supply.

Takamine, Jokichi (1854–1922) Japanese-born U.S. chemist who in 1901 isolated a substance for adrenal glands that was shown to be epinephrine (adrenaline). This was the first isolation of a pure hormone.

Tansley, Sir Arthur George (1871–1955) English botanist who pioneered the science of plant ecology. He was also active in promoting various organizations devoted to wildlife preservation and ecology, such as the British Ecological Society and Nature Conservancy.

Taussig, Helen Brooke (1898–1986) U.S. surgeon and pediatric cardiologist who pioneered surgery in babies for congenital heart defects, proving that this could be safe and successful. In 1962, Taussig went to Europe to investigate the epidemic of fetal abnormalities and deduced that thalidomide was the cause. As a result, the drug was never approved for use in the United States.

Theiler, Max (1899–1972) South African-born U.S. virologist who showed in 1926 that yellow fever is caused by a virus, not by a bacterium, as was then thought. He developed a serum test for yellow fever immunity and in 1929 produced an effective vaccine against yellow fever. In 1951 he was awarded the Nobel Prize in physiology or medicine.

Theophrastus (ca. 372–ca. 287 BCE) Greek philosopher and botanist, most of whose writings have been lost, but who, in his books *Historia Plantarum* and *Plantarum Causae*, briefly described about 450 species of plants. He described features of plant organization, distinguishing these from those of animals, and went into the medical uses and diseases of plants. A great deal of later botany was founded on these works.

Theorell, Axel Hugo Theodor (1903–82) Swedish biochemist who crystallized muscle hemoglobin, investigated enzymes such as peroxidases and dehydrogenases, invented an electrophoresis (electrical attraction) arrangement for separating proteins of different molecular weight, and introduced fluorescence spectrometry. His work earned him the Nobel Prize in physiology or medicine in 1955.

Thompson, Sir D'Arcy Wentworth (1860–1948) Scottish zoologist who applied mathematics and physics to biological development and forms and showed that the shape of an animal, especially a fish, could be converted from that of one species to that of another by superimposing it on a graph and then changing the coordinates.

Thomson, Sir Charles Wyville (1830–82) Scottish zoologist and marine biologist who showed that living creatures exist at great depths in the oceans.

Thunberg, Carl Peter (1743–1828) Swedish botanist who amassed one of the largest collections of botanical specimens of his time. He was also the first Western botanist to interest himself in Japanese flora and wrote extensively on them in *Flora Japonica* (1784). He also dealt with the flora of South Africa.

Tinbergen, Nikolaas (1907–88) Dutch-born British zoologist and ethologist who made a major study of animal behavior under normal conditions in the wild. He and Lorenz are considered to be the founders of ethology. Tinbergen shared the 1973 Nobel Prize in physiology or medicine with Konrad Lorenz and Karl von Frisch.

Todd, Sir Alexander Robertus (**Baron Todd of Trumpington**) (1907–97) Scottish biochemist who worked on the chemistry of a range of vitamins and other natural products and who showed how the four bases (adenine, guanine, cytosine, and thymine) are attached to sugar and phosphate groups. This is how DNA is formed, and various combinations of these bases, taken three at a time, form the genetic code. For this work, Todd was awarded the 1957 Nobel Prize in chemistry.

Tradescant, John (1570–1638) British naturalist, botanist, traveler, and head gardener to King Charles I, who was a notable pioneer in the collection and cultivation of plants, some from as far away as Russia, and who introduced many new species of plants into English gardens. He was the first to open a museum to the public, in Lambeth, London.

Tradescant, John (1608–62) British botanist and plant collector, son of John Tradescant, who continued his father's work as a collector and cultivator of plants. He collected in Virginia, and took over his father's job as head gardener to King Charles I. In his will, he left the museum he had inherited to Elias Ashmole, and this became the celebrated Ashmolean Museum in Oxford, England.

Trembley, Abraham (1710–84) Swiss naturalist who studied the grafting and regeneration of animal tissue, but with only limited success.

Tschermak von Seysenegg, Erich (**or Tschermak-Seysenegg, Erich**) (1871–1962) Austrian botanist who drew attention to the long-neglected work of Gregor Mendel, thereby arousing new interest in genetics.

Tswett, Mikhail Semenovich (1872–1919) Russian botanist who in 1906 devised a percolation method of separating plant pigments, thus making the first chromatographic analysis.

Tull, Jethro (1674–1741) English lawyer, farmer, writer, and inventor who devised a machine for planting seeds in rows. He had a major influence on plant cultivation, suggesting the use of manure and the importance of hoeing around plants to remove weeds so as to reduce competition for nutrients.

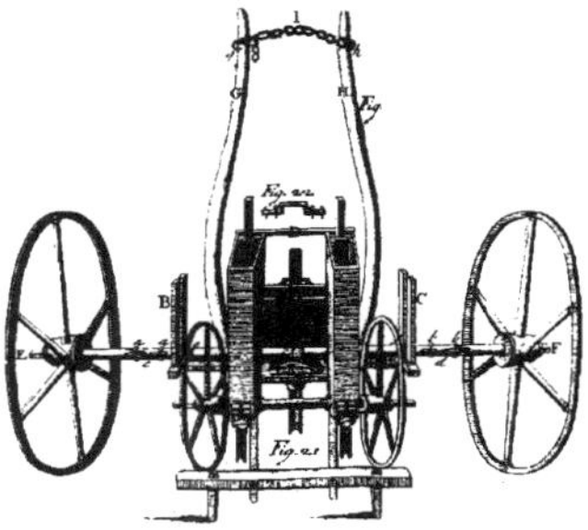

Illustration of a seed drill from Tull's *Horse Hoeing Husbandry* (1733)

Vesalius, Andreas (1514–64) Belgian anatomist and artist, whose wonderfully illustrated book on anatomy, *De Humani Corporis Fabrica* (1543), provided the first reliable source for anatomical knowledge. This work, based on dissection and observation, corrected many of the errors that had been based on undue respect for Galen's accuracy. Vesalius also challenged Aristotle's doctrine that the heart was the seat of personality.

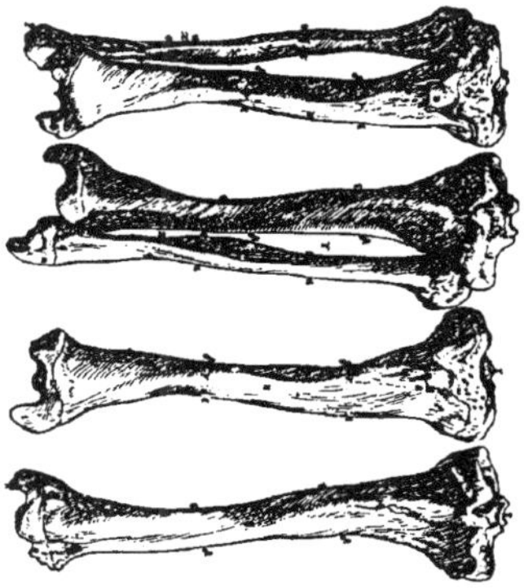

Drawings of leg bones from Vesalius' 1743 anatomy book

Vigneaud, Vincent du (1901–78) U.S. biochemist whose principal contribution to science was in the field of amino acids. He showed how a series of these important protein constituents are synthesized in the body. He also achieved the laboratory synthesis of thiamine and penicillin and the hormones oxytocin and vasopressin. He was awarded the 1955 Nobel Prize in chemistry.

Vinci, Leonardo da *See* **Leonardo da Vinci**.

Virchow, Rudolf Ludwig Carl (1821–1902) German pathologist, epidemiologist, and cellular biologist who proved that cells derive only from other cells. He also showed that all diseases arise from cell disorder. Virchow has been described as the founder of cellular pathology.

Virtanen, Artturi Ilmari (1895–1973) Finnish biochemist who discovered the chemical pathways by which bacteria in certain plant root nodules can achieve the fixation of nitrogen into compounds usable by plants. This work earned him the 1945 Nobel Prize in chemistry.

Hugo de Vries

Vries, Hugo Marie de (1848–1935) Dutch botanist and geneticist who from 1890 devoted himself to the study of heredity and variation in plants, significantly developing Mendelian genetics and evolutionary theory. *Die Mutationstheorie* (The mutation theory), in which he showed that mutations occur in organisms, was published 1901–3.

Wagner von Jauregg, Julius (**or Wagner-Jauregg, Julius**) (1857–1940) Austrian psychiatrist who treated general paralysis of the insane (GPI) by inducing malaria in his patients. Wagner von Jauregg was awarded the 1927 Nobel Prize in physiology or medicine but this was an inappropriate award. Fever therapy was of little benefit, was highly dangerous, and was soon condemned by the whole profession.

Selman A. Waksman

Waksman, Selman Abraham (1888–1973) Russian-born U.S. microbiologist and biochemist who developed streptomycin, the first important antibiotic after penicillin, from the mold *Streptomyces griseus*. This drug was effective against tuberculosis, against which penicillin was useless. For his discovery of streptomycin, Waksman was awarded the 1953 Nobel Prize in physiology or medicine.

Waldeyer-Hartz, Heinrich Wilhelm Gottfried von (1839–1921) German microscopic anatomist (histologist) who classified cancers on the basis of their cellular structure and of the tissue from which they arose. This work led to a much more precise diagnosis of cancers and to greater accuracy in assessing the probable outcome (prognosis).

Walker, Sir John Ernest (b. 1941) British chemist whose studies on the detailed structure of the enzyme ATP synthase (ATPase) confirmed Paul D. Boyer's account of the function of this important enzyme and earned him a share of the 1997 Nobel Prize in chemistry with Paul Boyer and Jens Skou.

Wallace, Alfred Russel (1823–1913) Welsh naturalist whose memoir, sent to Charles Darwin in 1858 from the Moluccas in the East Indies, was read at a meeting of the Linnaean Society in London at which Darwin's paper was also read. Wallace's paper virtually duplicated Darwin's theory of evolution by means of natural selection and hastened Darwin's publication of his book *On the Origin of Species*. This paradigm-shifting work was extended by Wallace's book *Contributions to the Theory of Natural Selection* (1870). Wallace was a man of great generosity and apparently quite free from jealousy. He called his own later book on evolution *Darwinism* (1889).

Alfred Wallace

Wassermann, August von (1866–1925) German bacteriologist who developed the Wassermann reaction blood test for syphilis in 1906. Wassermann became director of the Kaiser Wilhelm Institute in 1913 and remained there until his death. The Wassermann test has now been replaced by more specific and rapid tests.

Watson, James Dewey (1928–2004) U.S. bird expert (ornithologist) who worked at the Cavendish Laboratory, Cambridge, England, with Francis Crick and, in 1953, made the greatest biological discovery of the 20th century: the structure of DNA. Their joint paper in *Nature* is one of the most important scientific communications ever made, and it revolutionized genetics and molecular biology. Watson shared with Maurice Wilkins and Crick the Nobel Prize in physiology or medicine in 1962, and in 1988 became head of the Human Genome Project to sequence the whole of human DNA.

Weismann, August Freidrich Leopold (1834–1914) German biologist who suggested that sperm and ova contained a "germ plasm" by means of which inheritable characteristics were passed on. He located the germ plasm in what we now call the chromosomes. He also described the halving of the full number of the chromosomes in sperm and eggs. He was thus one of the pioneers of the modern science of genetics. To prove that acquired characteristics are not passed on, he cut off the tails of 22 generations of mice and showed that the offspring continued to have tails.

Went, Friedrich August Ferdinand Christian (1863–1935) Dutch botanist and specialist in tropical agriculture whose Utrecht School was renowned for its research into plant physiology.

Wharton, Thomas (1614–73) English physician who, with others, speculated on the purpose or function of what were later to be called the endocrine glands. He also described the duct of the submandibular salivary gland, which is known as Wharton's duct.

Whewell, William (1794–1866) English naturalist and philosopher of science who wrote about catastrophism, a term he invented for the now abandoned belief that during the history of the Earth, major convulsions must have occurred to account for the irregular shape of mountains, coastlines, gorges, and so on.

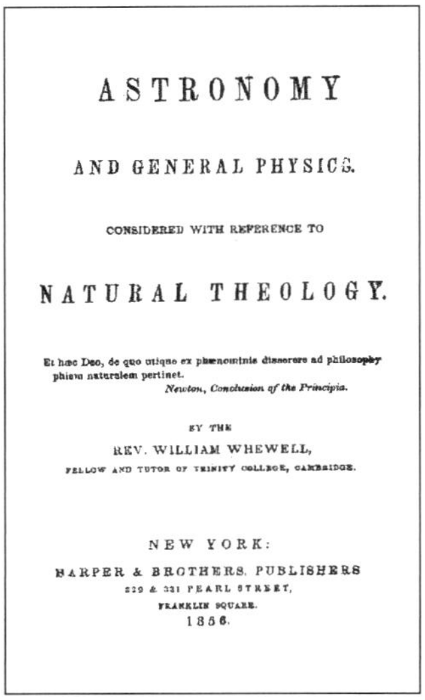

ASTRONOMY

AND GENERAL PHYSICS

CONSIDERED WITH REFERENCE TO

NATURAL THEOLOGY.

Et hæc Deo, de quo utique ex phænominis disserere ad philosophy phiam naturalem pertinet.

Newton, Conclusion of the Principia.

BY THE

REV. WILLIAM WHEWELL,

FELLOW AND TUTOR OF TRINITY COLLEGE, CAMBRIDGE.

NEW YORK:

HARPER & BROTHERS, PUBLISHERS

329 & 331 PEARL STREET,

FRANKLIN SQUARE.

1856.

Title page of Whewell's *Astronomy and General Physics* (1856)

White, Gilbert (1720–93) British naturalist and clergyman, remembered for his best-selling book *The Natural History of Selborne* (1789), on the animal and plant life of Selborne in Hampshire, England, which has remained in print for more than 200 years.

Wieschaus, Eric Francis (b. 1947) U.S. developmental biologist who in collaboration with Edward Lewis and Christiane Nüsslein-Volhard identified the homeobox genes, those that determine that the correct organs form in the correct places early in the development of the embryo. This provided a solution to the question of how genetics could organize the body's architecture, and it won the three scientists the 1995 Nobel Prize in physiology or medicine.

Wilkins, Maurice Hugh Frederick (1916–2004) New Zealand-born British biophysicist who with Francis Crick, James Watson and Rosalind Franklin worked to determine the molecular structure of DNA by X-ray crystallography. Wilkins shared the Nobel Prize in 1962 with Crick and Watson.

Wilson, Edmund Beecher (1856–1939) U.S. zoologist and embryologist who demonstrated the central importance of the chromosomes in genetics.

Edmund Wilson

Windaus, Adolf Otto Reinhard (1876–1959) German biochemist who studied the drug digitalis, was an authority on cardiac poisons, established the structure of cholesterol, and researched vitamin D and some of the B vitamins. He was awarded the 1928 Nobel Prize in chemistry.

Wöhler, Friedrich (1800–82) German chemist whose synthesis of urea from ammonium cyanate in 1828 was the first time a compound of organic origin had been prepared from inorganic material. This achievement revolutionized organic chemistry and showed that living organisms were not fundamentally different in structure from nonliving matter. Wöhler also isolated aluminum in 1827 and beryllium in 1828, discovered calcium carbide, from which he obtained acetylene, and published many analyses of minerals.

Wright, Sewell (1889–1988) U.S. geneticist best known for his work on genetic drift and for proposing a theory of evolution that does not require natural selection.

Sewell Wright

Yalow, Rosalyn Sussman (b. 1921) U.S. nuclear physicist who developed the technique of radioimmunoassay—a means of detecting and precisely measuring extremely small amounts of almost any substance to which antibodies are formed. Yalow's method is used for a great variety of purposes and earned her a share in the 1977 Nobel Prize in physiology or medicine.

Yersin, Alexandre-Emile-Jean (1863–1943) Swiss bacteriologist who discovered the bacillus that causes bubonic plague. Yersin, a student of Pasteur, isolated and cultured the germ, initially known as *Pasteurella pestis*, and then prepared an effective serum against the disease. The organism is now called *Yersinia pestis* in honor of Yersin.

Yonge, Charles Maurice (1899–1986) English marine biologist who studied coral physiology, oyster physiology, and the ecology of the Great Barrier Reef off the east coast of Australia. He wrote a number of popular books on marine biology.

Young, Thomas (1773–1829) English polymath, many of whose achievements in physics were so far ahead of his time that they were ignored in his lifetime. He studied medicine; explained eye focusing, astigmatism, and color vision; explained the physics of elasticity; established the wave theory of light; and translated the Rosetta stone and elucidated Egyptian hieroglyphics. He proposed a restriction of the term *energy* to something like its current scientific meaning. His notes remained unknown and neglected in the archives of the Royal Institution until after many of his discoveries had been made again by others. He had been forced to resign his professorship at the Royal Institution because his lectures were much too difficult for a general audience to understand.

Zinkernagel, Rolf (b. 1944) Swiss immunologist who, working with Peter Doherty, was able to show how certain T-cells of the human immune system can detect when a cell has been infected with viruses. Killer T-cells look for two "flags" (antigenic chemical groups), displayed on the surface of the infected cell. One identifies the cell as "self," the other signals that viruses are inside. For this discovery, made between 1973 and 1975, the two men were awarded the 1996 Nobel Prize in physiology or medicine.

Zsigmondy, Richard Adolf (1865–1929) German chemist who invented the dark ground illumination method of microscopy and showed that color changes in colloidal solutions are due to particle aggregation. He made many advances in colloidal chemistry, for which he was awarded the 1925 Nobel Prize in chemistry.

SECTION THREE CHRONOLOGY

1550–1501 BCE
Surgical instruments on an Egyptian relief at Kom Ombo.

1600 BCE • Ebers and Smith papyruses describe Egyptian medicine, including case histories and medicines.

1550–1501 BCE • An Egyptian text on surgery written.

ca. 1100 BCE • Zoological collections of exotic animals established in China.

520–511 BCE • Greek philosopher Anaximander introduces the idea of evolution.

500–491 BCE • Greek physician Alcmaeon of Croton dissects human cadavers, noting the optic nerve and Eustachian tubes. Indian physician Susrata performs cataract operations in India.

ca. 491 BCE • First recorded dissection of human corpse for scientific purposes carried out by Greek physician Alcmaeon.

460 BCE • Birth of Hippocrates, whose work as a physican is known from about 70 extant books written by him, his students, or followers.

450–441 BCE • Greek philosopher Empedocles recognizes the heart is center of the system of blood vessels.

350–341 BCE • Greek philosopher Aristotle classifies 500 species of animals into eight classes, and dissects many species.

340–331 BCE • Greek physician Praxagoras distinguishes between arteries and veins.

320 BCE • First systematic book on botany written by Greek philosopher Theophrastus.

3rd century BCE • Chinese *Book of Medicine of the Yellow Emperor* describes human anatomy and the circulation of the blood.

300–291 BCE • Greek physician Diocles writes the first book on anatomy. Greek physicians Herophilus and Erasistratus perform public dissections in Alexandria, describing the prostate gland, Fallopian tubes, duodenum, ovaries, spleen, liver, and retina.

295 BCE • Nerves divided into *sensory* and *motor* by Greek physician

Herophilus, who later names a section of the small bowel, the duodenum, and the prostate gland.

293 BCE • Greek anatomist Herophilus indentifies the role of veins and arteries as being connected with blood.

280–271 BCE • Greek physician Erasistratus notes the relationship between the circulatory system and the lungs.

ca. 50 BCE • Existing knowledge of natural history summarized in 37-volume work by Roman scholar Pliny the Elder.

304 CE • First record of biological control of pests made by Chinese writer Hsi Han.

ca. 1000 • Arab physician Avicenna (Ibn Sīnā) writes *Canon of Medicine*, a work that becomes a standard reference in Europe until the 17th century.

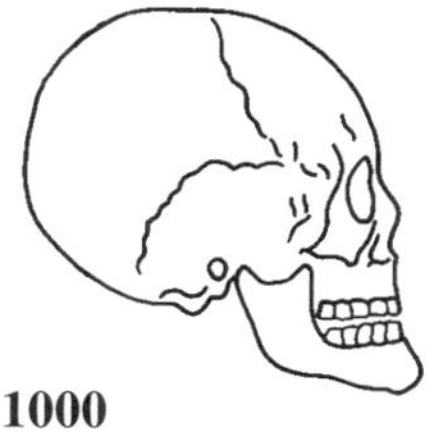

ca. 1000
Skull of Avicenna (Ibn Sīnā).

ca. 1220 • Translation of Greek philosopher Aristotle's classifications of animals into Latin by Scottish naturalist Michael Scot.

ca. 1250 • Greek philosopher Aristotle's ideas on botany and biology introduced to Europe by German scientist Albertus Magnus.

1250–59 • In *On Animals* Albertus Magnus, the German scholar, describes his dissections of various animals.

1252 • Englishman Richard of Wendover writes his treatise on anatomy.

ca. 1276 • Italian scholar Giles of Rome writes *De Formatione Corporis in Utero*, a treatise on the development of the human fetus.

1316 • *Anatomia*, the first book on human anatomy and dissection, appears in the West. It is based on the dissection of cadavers, and written by Italian anatomist Mondino dei Liucci.

1476 • Publication in Venice of Greek philosopher Aristotle's 4th-century BCE work on animal structure, function, reproduction, physiology, and development.

1483 • Publication of treatise on plants by Greek botanist and philosopher Theophrastus.

1490
Padua theater holds anatomy lectures.

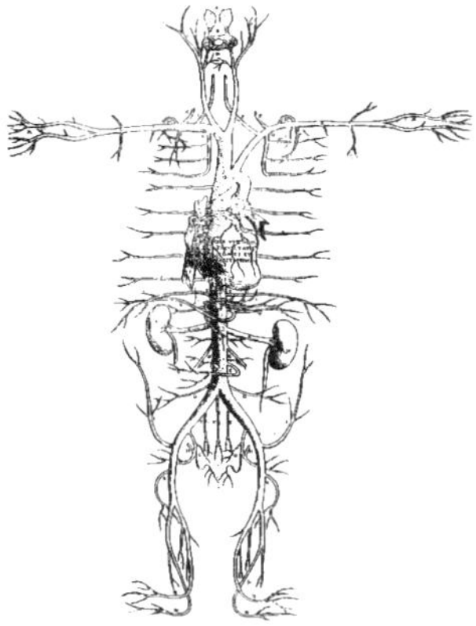

1543
Vesalius' drawing of the human arterial system.

1551
Konrad Gesner publishes volumes on zoology.

1490 • A theater opens in Padua, Italy, for the purpose of demonstrating the dissection of human corpses.

ca. 1500 • Detailed anatomical drawings of dissected human bodies made by Italian artist and scientist Leonardo da Vinci.

1517 • Fossils explained as organic remains by Italian scholar Girolamo Fracastoro.

1537 • Spanish physician Michael Servetus (Miguel Serveto) discovers circulation of blood in lungs. Later he publishes anonymously a book maintaining that blood circulates between the heart and lungs.

1540–42 • Englishman John Falconer develops first herbarium.

1542 • French physician Jean-François Fernel describes peristalsis and appendicitis for the first time. Observation of plant habits, locales, and characteristics described by German botanist Leonhard Fuchs. Botanical garden established in Leipzig, Germany.

1543 • Flemish anatomist Andreas Vesalius writes his great work *De Humani Corporis Fabrica*, the first accurate description of human anatomy.

1550 • Book on natural history implying belief in evolutionary change published by Italian scientist Geronimo Cardano.

1551 • Swiss naturalist Conrad Gesner writes the first of four volumes of *Historia Animalium*, marking the beginning of the scientific discipline of zoology. French naturalist Pierre Belon observes homologs (similarities) in vertebrate bones from fish to mammals.

1552 • Italian anatomist Bartolommeo Eustachio writes his book on anatomy that will not be published until 1714.

1554 • Systematic study of plant classification published by Italian naturalist Ulisse Aldrovandi.

1555 • French naturalist Pierre Belon writes *L'Histoire de la Nature des Oyseaux* in which he classifies 200 species of birds and compares their bones with those of humans.

1559 ● Circulation of blood from right chamber of heart, through lungs, and back to left chamber of heart (pulmonary circulation) described by Italian anatomist Realdo Colombo.

1561 ● Anatomical study of the inner ear and the female reproductive system carried out by Italian anatomist Gabriel Fallopius (Gabriele Falloppio), after whom the Fallopian tubes are named.

1565 ● Book containing first illustrations of fossils published by Swiss scientist Conrad Gesner.

1567 ● Botanical garden founded in Bologna, Italy.

1580 ● Italian scientist Prospero Alpini is first to discover plants have two sexes.

1583 ● Plant classification system proposed by Italian botanist Andrea Cesalpino.

ca. 1590 ● Simple, single lens microscope invented by Dutch lens maker Zacharias Janssen.

1597 ● Greatest survey of botanical knowledge to date, *Herball*, published by English botanist John Gerard.

1598 ● Italian lawyer Carlo Ruini publishes *Vraye Cognoissance du Cheval*, a monograph on the dissection of a horse, illustrated by himself with great accuracy.

1599 ● *Natural History*, a three-volume work by Italian naturalist Ulisse Aldrovandi, is published; it is the most important contribution to zoology so far.

1601 ● In *De Vocis Auditusque Organis Historia Anatomica*, Italian anatomist Julius Casserius (Guilio Casserio) describes the anatomy of the larynx and the ear.

1603 ● Italian anatomist Hieronymus Fabricius (Girolamo Fabrici) describes in detail the valves in veins in his book *De Venarum Ostiolis*.

1604 ● Italian anatomist Hieronymus Fabricius (Girolamo Fabrici) writes *De Formata Foetu*, a study of embryology that includes the circulation of blood in the umbilical cord. German astronomer Johannes Kepler describes the function of the eye.

1609 • Completion of five books on human sensory organs by Italian anatomist Julius Casserius (Giulio Casserio).

ca. 1610 • Italian astronomer and physicist Galileo Galilei studies insect anatomy with the aid of a microscope he has designed and built himself.

1614 • First scientific study of metabolism by Italian scientist Sanctorius Sanctorius (Santorio Santorio).

1616 • English physician William Harvey lectures to the Royal College of Physicians about the circulation of the blood.

1621 • Italian anatomist Hieronymus Fabricius's *De Formatione Ovi et Pulli* is published posthumously (he died in 1619). It describes the embryological development of chickens and elevates embryology to the status of a scientific discipline.

1622 • Lacteal vessels discovered by Italian anatomist Gasparo Aselli.

1623 • Swiss anatomist and herbalist Gaspard Bauhin writes *Pinax Theatri Botanici*, in which he attempts a botanical classification and introduces the practice of binomial nomenclature, in which one name refers to the genus of an organism and the second to the species.

1628 • English physician William Harvey publishes *Exercitatio Anatomica de Motu Cordis et Sanguinis*, in which he describes the circulation of the blood.

1644 • Reflex action explained by French philosopher and scientist René Descartes.

1647 • Italian physician Georg Wirsung discovers the pancreatic duct named for him (the duct of Wirsung). French anatomist Jean Pecquet discovers the thoracic duct.

1650 • English anatomist and physiologist Francis Glisson lays foundations for knowledge of the anatomy of the liver.

1644
Descartes' diagram to illustrate reflex action.

1651 • English physician William Harvey publishes *Exercitationes de Generatione Animalium*, in which he describes the way organs differentiate in the developing embryo. English physician Nathaniel Highmore discovers the maxillary sinus.

1652 • Danish anatomist Thomas Bartholin writes *De Lacteis Thoracicis*, in which he describes the lymphatic system and shows it is to be found in humans. In the same year, Swedish anatomist Olof Rudbeck demonstrates the lymphatic system of a dog to Queen Christiana of Sweden.

1654 • English anatomist and physician Francis Glisson writes *Anatomia Hepatis*, in which he describes the anatomy of the liver.

1656 • English anatomist Thomas Wharton provides the first description of the submaxillary gland in his *Adenographia, or a Description of the Glands of the Whole of the Body*.

1658 • Dutch anatomist Jan Swammerdam describes red blood cells. In his *Biblia Naturae,* he describes his dissection of insects under a microscope (published 1737–38).

1660 • Italian physiologist Marcello Malpighi shows that the lungs consist of small pockets containing air and a complex system of small blood vessels.

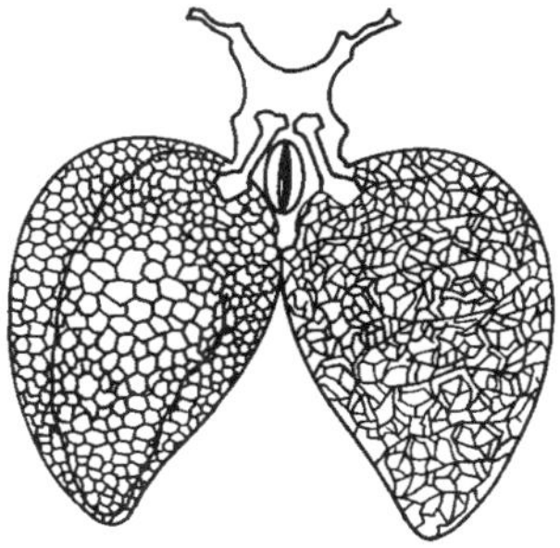

1660
The structure of the lung according to Marcello Malpighi.

ca. 1660 • Single-lens microscope developed by Dutch biologist Antoni van Leeuwenhoek.

1665 • Italian physiologist Marcello Malpighi publishes *De Cerebro*, in which he proposes that the nervous system consists of bundles of fibers that are connected to the spinal cord and from there to the brain. Dutch anatomist Frederick Ruyson demonstrates the existence of valves in the lymphatic system. In *Micrographia*, English microscopist Robert Hooke provides the first description of cells (which he observed in cork).

1667 • Lung function demonstrated by English biologist Robert Hooke. Plants classified by number of their seed leaves by English naturalist John Ray, establishing categories of monocots and dicots.

1668 • Italian naturalist and physician Francesco Redi refutes theory of spontaneous generation. Microscopic findings on anatomy of silkworms published by Italian physician Marcello Malpighi.

1669 • English physician Richard Lower describes, in *Tractatus de Corde*, the structure of the heart and observes that blood changes color in the lungs. Italian physiologist Marcello Malpighi publishes *Silkworms*, the first detailed anatomical description of an invertebrate. Dutch anatomist Jan Swammerdam describes the reproductive structures of insects in detail.

1671 • Italian physiologist Francesco Redi dissects the torpedo fish and examines its electric organ. First treatise on plant anatomy published by Italian physician Marcello Malpighi.

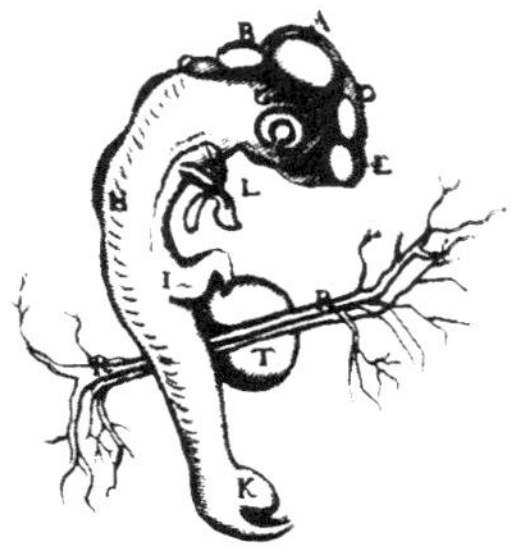

1673
Marcello Malpighi describes the embryo's development.

1672 • Dutch anatomist Reinier de Graaf describes his discovery of the ovarian follicle later named after him.

1673 • Chick embryo's development described by Italian physician Marcello Malpighi.

1675 • Danish naturalist and physician Nicolaus Steno (Niels Stensen) shows that the young of dogfish develop in eggs inside the body of their mother before being born live. He concludes that mammals also develop from eggs.

1677 • Dutch microscopist Anton van Leeuwenhoek reports his observation of human sperm, the first time they have been observed, and supposes them to be human larvae.

1679 • English naturalist Nehemiah Grew provides detailed descriptions of sexual reproduction of plant cells. Italian physiologist and mathematician Giovann Borelli publishes *De Motu Animalium*, in which he explains the mechanical action of muscles in moving bones.

ca. 1680 • American entomologist John Banister classifies 52 species of North American insects.

1683 • Protozoa observed for first time by Dutch biologist Anton van Leeuwenhoek using a microscope.

1691 ● English naturalist John Ray publishes *The Wisdom of God Manifested in the Works of Creation*, in which he proposes that fossils are the remains of animals that lived in the distant past.

1693 ● In *Synopsis Animalium Quadrupedum et Serpenti* English naturalist John Ray classifies animals, on the basis of their hooves, toes, and teeth, and makes the revolutionary suggestion that whales are mammals.

1694 ● More than 8,000 species of plant described by French botanist Joseph Pitton de Tournefort, who also devises an artificial classification system.

1700s ● Term *evolution* used by Swiss naturalist and entomologist Charles Bonnet to describe concept that periodic catastrophes result in increasingly higher life-forms.

1711 ● Italian anatomist Luigi Marsili shows that corals are animals, not plants.

1714 ● A work written in 1552 by Italian anatomist Bartolommeo Eustachio is published, describing the adrenal glands, the structure of the teeth, and the Eustachian tubes, which were named after him.

1727 ● Plant physiology established by English botanist Stephen Hales in his work *Vegetable Staticks*.

1727
Hales measures the rate at which sap flows upward through a plant.

1729 ● Distinction between organic and inorganic growth made by French scientist Louis Bourget.

1733 ● English chemist and botanist Stephen Hales publishes *Haemastaticks*, in which he describes his studies of blood pressure and blood flow in animals.

1734 ● French physicist René-Antoine Ferchault de Réaumur publishes his six-volume *Mémoires pour Servir à l'Histoire des Insectes*, an early work on entomology.

1735 ● *Systema Naturae* is published by Swedish botanist Carolus Linnaeus (Carl von Linné), in which he introduces the system of biological classification that remains in use to the present day.

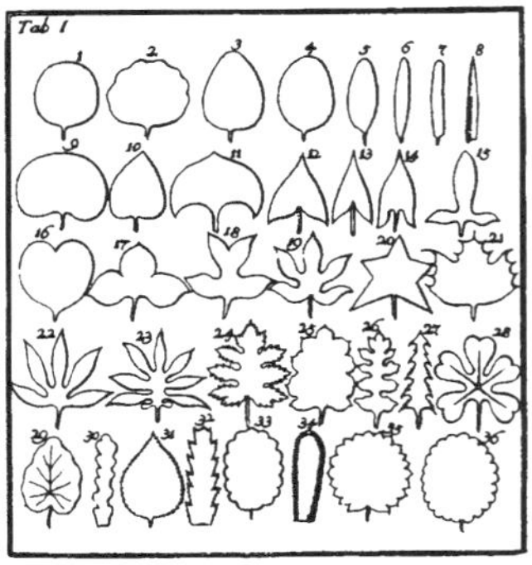

1737
Drawings of plants classified and numbered by Carolus Linnaeus.

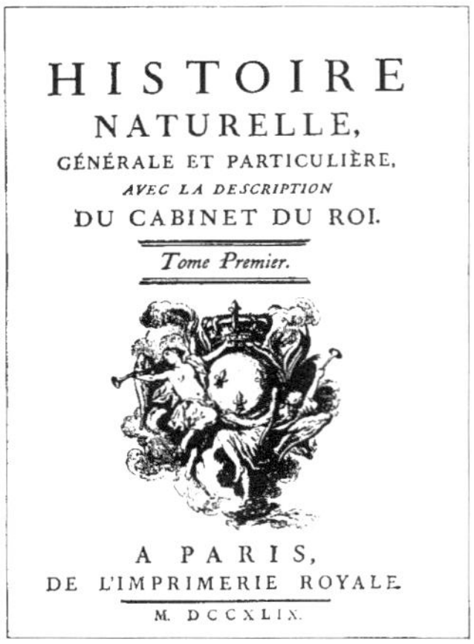

HISTOIRE
NATURELLE,
GÉNÉRALE ET PARTICULIÈRE,
AVEC LA DESCRIPTION
DU CABINET DU ROI.
Tome Premier.
A PARIS,
DE L'IMPRIMERIE ROYALE.
M. DCCXLIX.

1749
Title page of Buffon's first volume of Histoire naturelle.

1737 • Around 18,000 plant species classified by Swedish botanist Carolus Linnaeus (Carl von Linné). Dutch anatomist Jan Swammerdam describes his dissection of insects under a microscope in *Biblia Naturae*.

1738 • *Petri Artedi Seuci, Medici, Ichthyologia Sive Opera Omnia de Piscibus* by Swedish zoologist Peter Artedi, edited by Linnaeus (Carl von Linné), is published posthumously. It contains taxonomical descriptions of fish.

1739 • Hydra discovered by Swiss naturalist Abraham Trembley.

1740 • Swiss naturalist and entomologist Charles Bonnet makes the discovery that female aphids can reproduce without fertilization.

1744 • In his *Mémoires*, Swiss naturalist Abraham Trembley describes his work on hydra and his observation of the regeneration of polyps.

1747 • Swiss physiologist Albrecht von Haller publishes *Primae Lineae Physiologiae*, the first textbook on physiology.

1749 • French naturalist Georges-Louis Leclerc, Comte de Buffon, defines a species as a group of organisms that can interbreed to produce fertile offspring. His work *Histoire naturelle, générale et particulière*, published in the same year, is the first of 44 volumes in which Buffon seeks to provide a popular account of all that is known about minerals and animals.

1749–89 • Interest in evolution is aroused by publication of the multivolume series *Histoire naturelle*, written by French naturalist Georges-Louis Leclerc, Comte de Buffon.

1751 • French mathematician Pierre-Louis Moreau de Maupertuis publishes *Système de la Nature*, in which he speculates about the origin of species by chance and the heritability of traits. In *Essay on the Vital and Other Involuntary Motions of Animals*, Scottish physiologist Robert Whytt argues that involuntary motion is caused by the stimulation of irritable tissue.

1752 • French physicist René-Antoine Ferchault de Réaumur discovers the way gastric juices function, showing that digestion is chemical and not mechanical.

1756 • English naturalist John Turberville Needham and French naturalist Georges-Louis Leclerc, Comte de Buffon, perform an experiment that seems to show that tiny animals appear spontaneously when a sealed flask of broth is boiled.

1758 • Tree structure and physiology described by French botanist Henri du Monceau.

1759 • In *Theoria Generationes*, German physiologist Kaspar Friedrich Wolff describes the differentiation of tissues in a developing embryo, refuting the earlier notion of sperm containing tiny animals or people, called homunculi. Wolff also claims there is a "vital force" (*vis essentialis*) at the center of all living matter, an idea that comes to dominate much of 18th-century thought about biology.

1760 • Kew Botanical Gardens opens in London, England. It contains examples of plants gathered from all over the world.

1761 • In his five-volume work *De la Nature*, French naturalist Jean-Baptiste Robinet maintains that species form a linear chain of progression with no gaps.

1763 • Results of experiments on plants using animals carrying pollen published by German botanist Josef Kölreuter.

1764 • Swiss naturalist Charles Bonnet publishes *Contemplation de la Nature*, in which he proposes a theory of "preformation," according to which every egg contains a miniature version of the organism that will develop from it, and that this miniature organism bears eggs containing its descendants, and so *ad infinitum*.

1766 • Swiss physiologist Albrecht von Haller shows that nerves stimulate muscle contraction and that all the nerves are connected to the spinal column.

1767–68 • Italian naturalist Lazzaro Spallanzini conducts experiments that fail to support the theory of spontaneous generation, proposed in 1748 by John Turberville Needham and Georges-Louis Leclerc, Comte de Buffon. He publishes *Prodromo d' un Ouvrage sur les Réproductions Animales*, in which he describes how he boiled bottles of broth for periods of one-half to three-quarters of an hour, then sealed them tightly, and found no living organisms appeared when the contents cooled. German physiologist Kaspar Friedrich Wolff publishes *De Formatione Intestinarum*, describing how organs form in embryos.

1768–71 • Thousands of plant species collected by English botanist Joseph Banks during an around-the-world voyage.

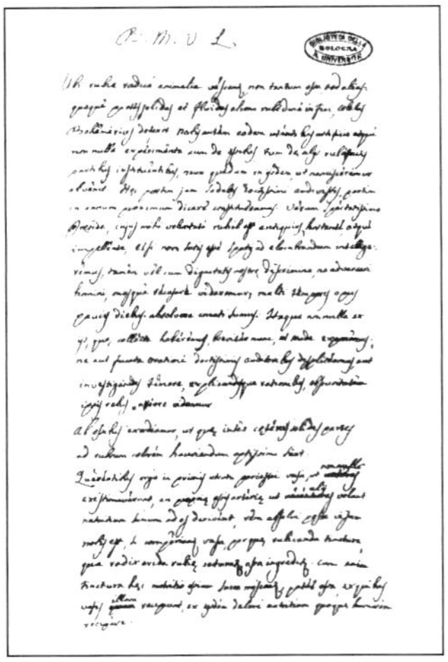

1771
Page from Galvani's work on "animal electricity."

1771 • Electrical action on muscles discovered by Italian anatomist Luigi Galvani, who thinks he has found "animal electricity."

1775 • Danish entomologist Johann Christian Fabricius publishes *Systema Entomologiae*, in which he classifies insects according to the structure of their mouth parts rather than by their wings.

1778 • Function of sperm and egg in fertilization studied by Italian anatomist Lazzaro Spallanzani. Modern classification of teeth (molars, bicuspids, cuspids, incisors) established by Scottish surgeon John Hunter.

1780 • Calorimeter developed by French chemists Pierre-Simon de Laplace and Antoine Lavoisier.

1782 • Hookworm identified by German zoologist Johann Goeze.

1784 • Cerebrospinal fluid discovered by Italian physician Domenico Cotugno.

1794
Signature of Erasmus Darwin.

1789 • French botanist Antoine-Laurent de Jussieu classifies plants into natural families.

1793 • Plant pollination process described by German botanist Christian Sprengel.

1794–96 • English physician Erasmus Darwin publishes *Zoonomia*, containing his ideas about the evolution of species.

1797 • French biologist Marie-François-Xavier Bichat classifies tissues into 21 types, including bone, blood, and muscle. Term *phylum* adopted by French biologist Georges (Baron) Cuvier for a taxonomic category more general than class, but more specific than kingdom.

1799 • George Shaw, English naturalist, provides the first scientific description of the duck-billed platypus in *The Naturalist's Miscellany*. A complete mammoth is discovered frozen in Siberia.

1800 • Word *biology* introduced by German scientist Karl Friedrich Burdach for study of morphology, physiology, and psychology of humans.

1801 • French naturalist Jean-Baptiste-Pierre-Antoine de Monet, Chevalier de Lamarck, publishes *Système des Animaux sans Vertèbres*, in which he proposes a method for classifying invertebrates and gives an outline of his views on evolution.

1805 • In his *Leçons d'Anatomie Comparée*, French anatomist Georges (Baron) Cuvier, initiates the scientific discipline of comparative anatomy.

1806 • Importance of intercellular space for gas conduction in plants determined by Italian botanist Giovanni Amici.

1809 • French naturalist Jean-Baptiste Lamarck publishes *Philosophie Zoologique*, in which he proposes that animals have evolved from simpler forms as a consequence of the amount of use members of each generation make of their various limbs and organs. Use or disuse leads to enlargement and development or reduction in size and atrophy, respectively. This idea comes to be known as the inheritance of acquired characteristics.

1810s • German naturalist and poet Johann Wolfgang von Goethe is among the first to popularize the term *morphology* to describe the study of organic form.

1811 • Spinal nerve functions discovered by Scottish physician Charles Bell.

J. W. von Goethe

Herzoglich Sachſen-Weimariſchen Geheimenraths

Verſuch

die Metamorphoſe

der Pflanzen

zu erklären.

Gotha,

bey Carl Wilhelm Ettinger.

1790.

1810s
Title page of Goethe's book on the morphology of plants.

1812 • Word *taxonomy* first used by French botanist Augustin-Pyrame de Candolle for classification of species.

1814 • Starch-iodine reaction discovered by French scientists J.J. Colin and H.G. de Claubry.

1815 • French naturalist Jean-Baptiste Lamarck founds modern invertebrate biology and is first to use the words *vertebrate* (an animal with a bony skeleton and well-developed brain) and *invertebrate* (an animal that lacks these features).

1817 • Chlorophyll isolated and named by French chemists Pierre-Joseph Pelletier and Joseph-Bienaimé Caventou. German zoologist Christian Pander discovers in chick embryos the three embryonic layers that form early in the development of vertebrate embryos.

1820s • Animals arranged into four groups (vertebrates, articulates, mollusks, and radiates) by French biologist Georges (Baron) Cuvier.

1822
Mary Mantell discovers the first fossil dinosaur.

1822 • First fossil dinosaur, an iguanodon, discovered by Mary Mantell. French naturalist Jean-Baptiste Lamarck publishes *Histoire des Animaux sans Vertèbres*, in which he distinguishes between vertebrate and invertebrate animals.

1826 • Eggs of mammals observed and identified by Estonian embryologist Karl Ernst von Baer.

1827 • U.S. ornithologist and naturalist John James Audubon starts publishing his ornithology collection, containing more than 1,000 paintings of bird life. In *De Ovi Mammalium et Hominis Genesi*, Estonian biologist Karl Ernst von Baer reports his observation of eggs in mammals, including humans, and proposes that mammals develop from eggs.

1828 • Plant kingdom sorted into six classes by French botanist Adolphe Théodore Brongniart. Estonian biologist Karl Ernst von Baer develops his theory of embryonic layers in *Über Entwicklungsgeschichte der Tiere*. He proposes that eggs develop into four layers of tissue.

1830 • Invention of achromatic microscope by English optician Joseph Lister.

1831 • Discovery of cell nucleus in plants by British botanist Robert Brown.

1831–36 • English naturalist Charles Darwin voyages aboard HMS *Beagle*; he gathers much of the evidence he will later use to establish his theory of evolution by natural selection.

1834 • German-Swiss physiologist Gabriel Gustav Valentin and Czech physiologist Jan Purkyně discover that ova are moved through the oviducts by cilia.

1835 • Czech physiologist Jan Purkyně finds that animal tissues are made from cells.

1836 • Yeast found to be a living organism.

1837 • Lower portion of the brain stem (the medulla oblongata) found to be the body's respiratory center by French surgeon Marie-Jean-Pierre Flourens.

1838 • Cellular structure of plants discovered by German botanist Matthias Schleiden. German chemist Justus von Liebig founds biochemistry.

1839 • Cellular structure of animals discovered by German botanist and zoologist Theodor Schwann. Czech physiologist Jan Purkyně coins the term *protoplasm* to describe the contents of the cell.

1841 • Swiss physiologist Rudolf Albert von Kölliker describes spermatozoa.

1842 • Name *dinosaur*, meaning "terrible lizard," coined by English zoologist Richard Owen.

1843 • Nervous system found to use electricity to send impulses.

1844 • Scottish author and publisher Robert Chambers publishes anonymously his *Vestiges of the Natural History of Creation*, in which he promotes the idea of the evolution of species, helping remove prejudice and prepare the way for the work of Charles Darwin and Alfred Wallace. German-Swiss physicist Gabriel Gustav Valentin discovers that food is broken down during digestion by pancreatic juices.

1845 • German physician Robert Remak corrects Karl Ernst von Baer's idea that there are four embryonic layers. He shows there are only three, and calls them the *ectoderm*, *mesoderm*, and *endoderm*.

1847 • Basis for modern cell theory put forward by German botanist Matthias Schleiden and German zoologist and botanist Theodor Schwann.

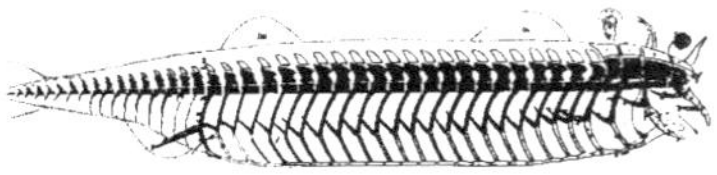

1848
Sir Richard Owen's vertebrate archetype.

1848 • English zoologist Sir Richard Owen publishes *On the Archetype and Homologies of the Vertebrate Skeleton*, in which he proposes that skulls and other body parts are modified vertebrae. This is similar to an earlier idea proposed by German philosopher Johann Wolfgang von Goethe and developed by German naturalist Lorenz Oken from 1807.

1849 • Swiss physiologist Rudolf Albert von Kölliker discovers that nerve fibers are extensions of nerve cells.

1851 • French physiologist Claude Bernard discovers that some nerves control the dilation of blood vessels and other nerves control their contraction. German botanist Hugo von Mohl describes protoplasm and advances cell theory for plants.

1852 • German physician and physiologist Robert Remak shows that tissue growth is due to cell division. Swiss physiologist Rudolf Albert von Kölliker discovers how sperm originate.

1856 • Remains of early human ancestor who inhabited much of Europe and areas of bordering Mediterranean Sea found in Neander Valley, Germany, and named Neanderthal Man.

1858 • The secretary reads to a meeting of the Linnean Society and subsequently publishes in the *Journal of the Linnean Society* correspondence between English naturalists Charles Robert Darwin and Alfred Russel Wallace, and between Darwin and U.S. botanist Asa Gray, outlining the theory of the evolution of species by means of natural selection, which Darwin and Wallace have developed. English surgeon Henry Gray publishes *Anatomy, Descriptive and Surgical*, which quickly becomes a standard textbook and is still in print, now more usually known as *Gray's Anatomy*. French physiologist Claude Bernard discovers vasodilator and vasoconstrictor nerves.

1859 • English naturalist Charles Darwin publishes *On the Origin of Species by Means of Natural Selection, or the Preservation of Favoured Races in the Struggle for Life*.

1860 • Laws of inheritance formulated by Austrian biologist and abbot Gregor Mendel. French physician Georges Hayem is the first accurately to count platelets in blood. Evolutionary theory put forward by English naturalist Charles Darwin is criticized by many notable scientists.

1861 • Swiss physiologist Rudolf Albert von Kölliker explains embryological development in terms of cell theory. Theory of protoplasm developed by German cytologist Max Schultze.

1865 • French physiologist Claude Bernard publishes *Introduction à l'Étude de la Médicine Expérimentale*, in which he maintains that biological phenomena obey physical and chemical laws and there is no "vital force."

1866 • Word *ecology* first used to refer to organism-environment relationship by German biologist Ernst Haeckel.

1867 • Rules for botanical nomenclature established by the International Botanical Congress.

1868 • Scottish zoologist Charles Wyville Thomson discovers different forms of life at bottom of the ocean.

1869 • Swiss physician Johann Friedrich Miescher discovers nucleic acids and names them *nuclein*.

1870 • English biologist Alfred Russel Wallace and American biologist Edward Cope both publish books that support the theory of evolution by natural selection.

1871–81 • Russian embryologist Aleksandr Onufriyevich Kovalevsky discovers that invertebrate embryos develop from three layers of cells, as do vertebrate embryos, and he identifies the notochord.

1872 • Science of bacteriology founded by German botanist Ferdinand J. Cohn.

1873 • Discovery of Golgi apparatus within cells by Italian histologist Camillo Golgi. Mitosis recognized for the first time. German botanist Nathanael Pringsheim makes first scientific studies of algae.

1874 • German surgeon Christian Albert Billroth studies bacteria.

1875 • German zoologist Oscar Hertwig demonstrates that fertilization takes place when one sperm enters the ovum.

1876 • Anaerobic organisms discovered by French chemist Louis Pasteur.

1876
Louis Pasteur discovers anaerobic organisms.

1877 • Term *biochemistry* coined by German biochemist F. Hoppe-Seyler. Process of osmosis explained by German botanist Wilhelm Pfeffer.

1880 • Scottish physiologist Francis Maitland Balfour classifies animals possessing notochords (skeletal rods) as the phylum Chordata.

1882 • Chromosomes and cell division discovered by German biologist Friedrich Löffler. Observing changes in plant cells during division, German botanist Eduard Adolf Strasburger divides protoplasm into nucleoplasm and cytoplasm.

1884 • Russian biologist Elie Mechnikoff discovers phagocytes, which exhibit ameboid movement.

1887 • Belgian cytologist Edouard-Joseph-Louis-Marie van Beneden discovers each species has fixed number of chromosomes.

1888 • German biologist Theodor Boveri observes and names the self-duplicating centrosome. Name *chromosomes* suggested by German anatomist Heinrich Wilhelm Gottfried von Waldeyer-Hartz for the chromatin threads that appear during cell division.

1890 • Discovery of bioblasts (later named mitochondria) within cells by Swiss cytologist Richard Altmann.

1892 • Germ-plasm theory of heredity introduced by German biologist August Weismann. Field of bioelectromagnetics founded when French physician and physicist Jacques-Arsène d'Arsonval begins studying the effect of electricity on biological systems. Francis Galton, English anthroplogist, publishes *Finger Prints*, in which he shows the differences in types of fingerprints and their possible use in identification.

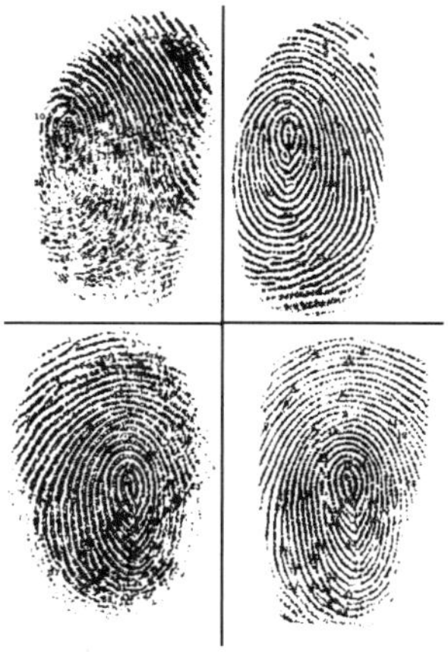

1892
Fingerprints showing persistence of pattern through childhood, from Galton's Finger Prints.

1896 • American biologist Edmund Beecher Wilson claims that animals and plants consist of structural units, which he describes as *cells*.

1898 • Guidelines for naming animals developed by International Commission on Zoological Nomenclature, set up by the International Congress of Zoology. Italian histologist Camillo Golgi describes the reticular formation in cell cytoplasm, which becomes known as the Golgi apparatus or body.

1899 • Swiss cytologist Richard Altmann renames *nuclein* as *nucleic acid*, which is later found to consist of deoxyribonucleic acid (DNA) and ribonucleic acid (RNA).

1900 • Existence of ABO blood group system demonstrated by Austrian-born American physician Karl Landsteiner. Gregor Mendel's work on heredity is rediscovered independently by three botanists—Dutchman Hugo de Vries, German Karl Erich Correns, and Austrian Erich Tschermak von Seysenegg; the science of genetics is born.

1900
Mendel's work on peas rediscovered. Drawing shows the second-generation results of crossing green and yellow (shown in black) peas.

1901 • Concept of mutation in organisms formulated by Dutch biologist Hugo de Vries.

1902 • AB blood group discovered by American physician Karl Landsteiner. Conditioned (or acquired) reflexes discovered by Russian biologist Ivan Petrovich Pavlov. Chromosome theory formulated independently by American geneticist Walter Sutton and German biologist Theodore Boveri; they show that the behavior of chromosomes during cell division mirrors Mendelian inheritance. Chromosomes are, therefore, assumed to carry hereditary traits.

1904 • Discovery of Rhesus factor in blood by Rockefeller Institute scientists. Russian physiologist Ivan Petrovich Pavlov receives the Nobel Prize in physiology or medicine for his explanation of the physiology of digestion. Spanish histologist Santiago Ramón y Cajal shows that the nervous system is composed of nerve cells and processes leading from them.

1905 • Swiss-born British zoologist Edmund Wilson observes X and Y chromosomes in mammals.

1906 • Italian histologist Camillo Golgi and Spanish histologist Santiago Ramón y Cajal receive the Nobel Prize in physiology or medicine for their explanation of the structure of the nervous system. Term *genetics* coined by English biologist William Bateson.

1909 • 570-million-year-old fossils of invertebrates found in Burgess Shales, Canada, by American scientist Charles Walcott. English biologist William Bateson produces first application of Mendel's laws to animals. Terms *gene*, *genotype*, and *phenotype* coined by Danish biologist Wilhelm Johannsen to describe carrier of hereditary factors. Swiss physiologist Emil Theodor Kocher receives the Nobel Prize in physiology or medicine for his studies of the thyroid gland.

1910 • Austrian zoologist Karl von Frisch shows that fish are not colorblind. Evidence of the chromosome theory of heredity is provided by American geneticist and embryologist Thomas Hunt Morgan.

1911 • First chromosome map devised by American geneticists Thomas Hunt Morgan and Alfred Henry Sturtevant. Swedish physiologist Allvar Gullstrand receives the Nobel Prize in physiology or medicine for his studies of light refraction in the eye.

1913 • English physiologist Archibald Vivian Hill discovers that muscle cells use oxygen after contracting, rather than during contraction.

1914 • English physiologist Henry Hallett Dale isolates acetylcholine and suggests it is involved in the transmission of nerve impulses. American biologist Edward Calvin Kendall identifies thyroxin, secreted by the thyroid gland. American biologist Fritz Albert Lipmann explains the action of adenosine triphosphate (ATP).

1915 • Americans Thomas Hunt Morgan, Calvin Bridges, Alfred Henry Sturtevant, and Hermann Joseph Muller assert that chromosomes contain invisible genes that determine hereditary traits, in their influential book *The Mechanism of Mendelian Heredity*.

1917 • Scottish biologist D'Arcy Wentworth Thompson publishes *On Growth and Form*, in which he shows the importance of differential growth rates in the development of different animal forms from a common basic plan.

1925 • American teacher John Thomas Scopes is found guilty of teaching the theory of evolution in a public school.

1926 • Term *homeostasis* coined by American physiologist Walter Bradford Cannon.

1927 • American physician Karl Landsteiner discovers M and N blood groups.

1930 • Austrian-American physician Karl Landsteiner receives the Nobel Prize in physiology or medicine for defining the four human blood groups.

1930s • The study of population genetics is established by British scholars John Burdon Sanderson Haldane and Ronald Fisher, and American scholar Sewell Wright.

1931 • Evidence of genetic recombination in corn is provided by Harriet Creighton and American geneticist Barbara McClintock.

1932 • Urea cycle discovered by British biochemist Hans Krebs. Some of the first pictures of cell division taken by British biologist R.G. Canti.

1933 • Nobel Prize in physiology or medicine awarded to American geneticist Thomas Hunt Morgan for proving that chromosomes transmit hereditary traits between generations.

ON
GROWTH AND FORM
BY
D'ARCY WENTWORTH THOMPSON
Cambridge:
at the University Press
1917

1917
Title page of Thompson's On Growth and Form.

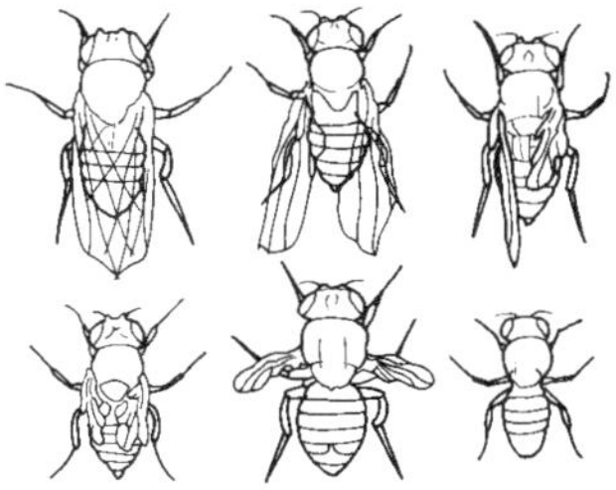

1933
Hereditary traits proven to be carried by chromosomes.

1935 • British plant ecologist Sir Arthur George Tansley introduces concept of the ecosystem. Nobel Prize awarded to German biologist Hans Spemann for his discovery of organizer effect in embryo development.

1937 • Citric acid cycle (later called the Krebs cycle) discovered by British biochemist Hans Krebs. Neo-Darwinism is born with the publication of *Genetics and the Origin of Species*, written by American geneticist Theodosius Dobzhansky.

1938
Early fish, coelacanth, discovered.

1938 • Discovery of a live coelacanth off South Africa; the species of fish was thought to have been extinct for 60 million years.

1944 • DNA shown to be fundamental in determining heredity, by Canadian bacteriologist Oswald T. Avery.

1949 • In the United States, the first photograph of genes is taken by Daniel Chapin Pease and Richard Baker.

1950 • Belgian cytologist Albert Claude discovers endoplasmic reticulum in cells' cytoplasm. Protein-building role of essential amino acids established by American biochemist William Cumming Rose.

1950s • Cellular mechanism used to control a variety of metabolic processes discovered by American biochemists Edmond H. Fischer and Edwin G. Krebs.

1951 • American biologist James Frederick Bonner shows that mitochondria perform oxidative phosphorylation.

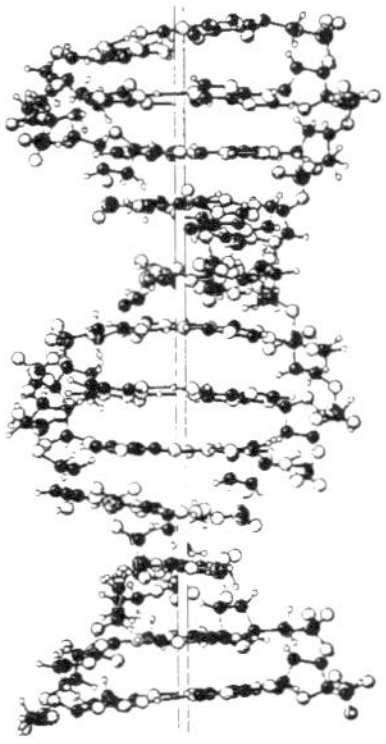

1953
DNA structure discovered.

1953 • Structure of DNA discovered by English molecular biologist Francis Crick and American geneticist James Watson, using X-ray studies by English crystallographer Rosalind Franklin and British physicist Maurice Wilkins.

1955 • Lysosomes discovered and named by Belgian cytologist Christian René de Duve.

1956 • Romanian-American physiologist George Emil Palade discovers that ribosomes consist mainly of RNA.

1957 • All details of plant photosynthesis discovered and isolated by American biochemist Melvin Calvin.

1958 • Russian Ilya Darevsky discovers species of lizard that reproduces without fertilization by males.

1960 • John Prescott and Kenneth Norris prove that the bottle-nosed dolphin (*Tursiops truncatus*) uses echolocation in much the same way bats use it in the air.

1960s • For the first time, ecology becomes identified with environmental concerns such as preservation, pesticides, and pollutants.

1962 • Francis Crick, James Watson, and Maurice Wilkins receive the Nobel Prize in physiology or medicine for their discovery of the molecular structure of DNA.

1964 • Discovery of first cell receptors by American microbiologists Keith Porter and Thomas F. Roth.

1967 • British biologist John B. Gurden first to successfully clone an animal.

1968 • Evidence of existence of life found in rocks dating back three billion years. The U.S. Supreme Court declares laws banning the teaching of the theory of evolution on the grounds that it is unchristian to be unconstitutional.

1969 • Single gene isolated for first time by American biologist Jonathan Beckwith.

1970 • Theory of endosymbiosis produced by American biologist Lynn Margulis.

1971 • Fundamental work on insect societies published by sociobiologist Edward O. Wilson.

1972 • Punctuated equilibrium theory of evolution proposed by American scientists Stephen Jay Gould and Niles Eldredge.

1973 • Americans Stanley Cohen and Herbert Boyer construct recombinant DNA molecules. Work begins on isolation of neurotransmitters.

1974 • Cytoskeleton of a cell revealed for the first time. Remains of 3-million-year-old human ancestor ("Lucy") discovered by American anthropologist Donald Johanson.

1960
John Prescott and Kenneth Norris explain dolphin navigation.

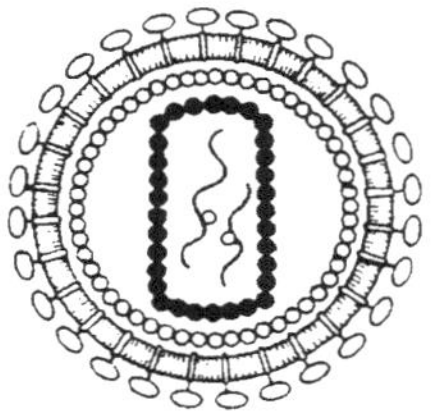

1981
U.S. medical authorities recognize AIDS.

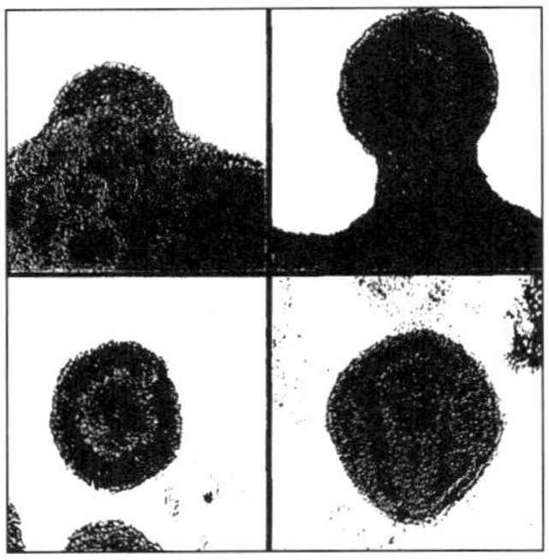

1984
Sequence of transmission electron micrographs shows formation of HIV.

1975 • Plant and animal cells fused by British researchers J.A. Lucy and E.C. Cocking.

1978 • First "test-tube" baby (conceived outside the body) born in United Kingdom. 3.6-million-year-old footprints are found in Tanzania by Anglo-Kenyan paleontologist Mary Leakey.

1980 • The U.S. Supreme Court rules that "a live human-made microorganism is patentable subject matter." This means bacteria and other single-celled organisms that have been altered genetically can be patented.

1981 • Acquired Immune Deficiency Syndrome (AIDS) first recognized by U.S. medical authorities.

1983 • World's first artificially made chromosome created at Harvard College. American geneticist Barbara McClintock is awarded Nobel Prize in physiology or medicine for her discovery of "jumping genes."

1984 • Allan Wilson and Russel Higuchi of University of California, Berkeley, clone genes from cells taken from the skin of quagga, a type of zebra that had been extinct for a century. Discovery of human immunodeficiency virus (HIV), the cause of AIDS, by French scientist Luc Montagnier and American physician Robert Gallo.

1985 • Technique of genetic fingerprinting introduced by British biologist Alec Jeffreys.

1986 • American scientists discover first gene known to inhibit cell growth while researching cancer growth patterns. In the United States, first license granted for the marketing of a genetically engineered living organism.

1988 • Genetically engineered mouse patented by researchers at Harvard Medical School. Fossil remains discovered by Israeli and French archaeologists prove that true *Homo sapiens* has been on Earth for more than 90,000 years, twice as long as previously thought. Proteinlike substances, which form cell-like units in water and which are very similar to ancient protocells, made by American biochemist Sidney Fox.

1989 • American biologist Stephen Jay Gould puts forward controversial argument that 570 million years ago there was an explosion of life-forms that produced many more basic body plans than exist today.

1991 • Contrary to theories of Gregor Mendel, geneticists discover that behavior of genes may depend on which parent they were inherited from. Total number of fungi types worldwide estimated to be 1.6 million by British mycologist David Hawksworth.

1992 • DNA fragments are extracted from a termite that has been embedded in amber for 30 million years. First comprehensive maps of two human chromosomes completed as part of the Human Genome Project. Discovery of what may be the oldest and largest living organism on Earth, a giant mold growing in Michigan.

1993 • DNA extracted from a weevil that has been fossilized in amber for 120 to 135 million years. Human embryos cloned for the first time. Remains of a 4-million-year-old human ancestor uncovered by an international team working in Ethiopia.

1994 • Discovery of earliest known land life, dating from 1.2 billion years ago. Hsu Chin-Yuan and Li Chia-Wei of the National Tsing Hua University, Taiwan, discover granules containing iron in abdominal cells of honeybees. These are believed to be receptors allowing the bees to use the Earth's magnetic field in navigation and comb-building.

1997 • Carles Vilà and Robert K. Wayne of the University of California, Los Angeles, use molecular genetics to prove that the wolf (*Canis lupus*) is the sole wild ancestor of the domestic dog (*Canis familiaris*). In Febuary, Ian Wilmut and his colleagues at the Roslin Institute, Scotland, announce the birth of Dolly, a lamb cloned from a body cell of an adult ewe.

1997
First cloned mammal, Dolly, the sheep.

1998 • American scientists Robert Furchgott, Louis Ignarro, and Ferid Murad awarded the Nobel Prize in physiology or medicine for their discoveries concerning nitric oxide as a signaling molecule in the cardiovascular system.

1999 • German-born American scientist Günter Blobel awarded the Nobel Prize in physiology or medicine for his discovery that proteins have intrinsic signals that govern their transport and localization in the cell. The National Human Genome Research Institute (NHGRI) and other Human Genome Project (HGP)-funded scientists unravel for the first time the genetic code of an entire human chromosome.

2000 • Birth of the first successfully cloned piglets takes place in Blacksburg, Virginia, created by the same company that produced Dolly, bringing closer the prospect of genetically modified animal organs being used for human transplant. The international Human Genome Project consortium and representatives from the private company Celera Genomics jointly announce that they each have created a working draft of the entire human genome sequence. The draft issued with known gaps and errors, but provides the basis for further research.

2001 • Scientists report that human fat is a source of stem cells that could be changed into muscle, cartilage or bone cells under laboratory conditions. Previously, scientists believed that embryos were the only source of stem cells.

2002 • A Chinese research team and a Swiss company, Syngenta AG, publish two separate versions of the full genetic map of the rice plant.

2003 • Scientists complete the sequencing of all three billion base pairs in the human genome.

2004 • South Korean scientists report replicating a human embryo.

2005 • Photograph by two Japanese scientists marks the first-ever record of a live giant squid in the wild. Scientists devise ways to isolate embryonic stem cells from mice without destroying viable embryos.

SECTION FOUR
KEY ADVANCES

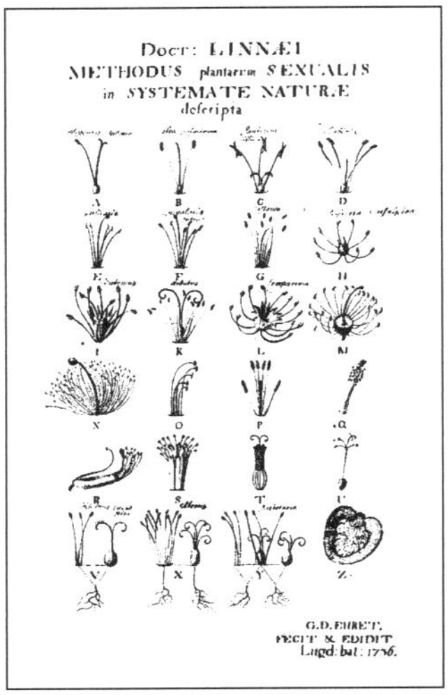

Animal and plant classification
Illustrations of plants under Linnaeus's (von Linné's) system.

amino acid (1) Louis-Nicolas Vauquelin (France) isolates asparagine, the first of 80 amino acids discovered. [1806]
(2) William Cumming Rose (U.S.) establishes the protein-building role of essential amino acids. [1950]

anatomy (1) Diocles (Greece) writes the first anatomy book. [ca. 350]
(2) Andreas Vesalius (Belgium) publishes the first accurate illustrated book on human anatomy. [1543]

animal and plant classification Carolus Linnaeus (Carl von Linné) (Sweden) develops the system of binomial nomenclature used today. [1735]

bacteria Anton van Leeuwenhoek (the Netherlands) discovers bacteria in the human mouth. [1683]

bacteriology (1) Ferdinand Julius Cohn (Germany) founds the science of bacteriology. [1872]
(2) Robert Koch (Germany) founds modern medical bacteriology. [1880s]

biochemistry Justus von Liebig (Germany) founds the science of biochemistry. [1838]

biology Gottfried Treviranus (Germany) and Jean-Baptiste Lamarck [France] independently define the meaning of biology as the study of all life. [1802]

biotin Vincent du Vigneaud (U.S.) isolates biotin—also known as vitamin B_7 or vitamin H. [1942]

blood cells Jan Swammerdam (the Netherlands) describes red blood cells. [1658]

blood circulation (1) Michael Servetus (Miguel Serveto) (Spain) discovers the circulation of blood in the lungs. [1537]
(2) Realdo Colombo (Italy) describes the circulation of blood from the heart through the lungs and back. [1559]
(3) William Harvey (England) publishes *Exercitatio De Motu Gordis et Sanguinis*, in which he describes the flow of blood. [1628]

blood groups (1) Karl Landsteiner (U.S.) demonstrates the existence of ABO groups. [1900]
(2) Landsteiner discovers the AB blood group. [1902]
(3) Landsteiner discovers the M and N blood groups. [1927]

blood vessels Praxagoras (Greece) realizes that both veins and arteries carry blood. [ca. 340 BCE]

botany Theophrastus (Greece) founds the science of botany. [ca. 300 BCE]

calorimeter Carl von Voit (Germany) and Max Josef von Pettenkofer (Germany), devise the first calorimeter capable of holding human beings. [ca. 1860]

capillary (1) Marcello Malpighi (Italy) observes capillaries in frogs' lungs. [1660]
(2) Robert Boyle (Ireland) traces blood passing through capillaries from arteries to veins. [1663]
(3) Schack August Steenbert Krogh (Denmark) demonstrates capillary control. [1900–10]

cell (1) Robert Hooke (England) first describes cells in *Micrographia*¸ an account of his study of cork structure. [1665]
(2) Jan Purkyně (Czechoslovakia) finds that animal tissues are made from cells. [1835]
(3) Matthias Jakob Schleiden (Germany) discovers the cellular structure of plants. [1838]
(4) Theodor Schwann (Germany) discovers the cellular structure of animals. [1839]

Cell
Robert Hooke observes cells under a microscope and describes them in his book Micrographia *[1665].*

cell division Friedrich Löffler (Germany) discovers cell division. [1882]

cell nucleus Robert Brown (Scotland) discovers nuclei in plant cells. [1831]

cell receptors Keith Porter (U.S.) and Thomas F. Roth (U.S.) discover cell receptors. [1964]

cell theory Matthias Jakob Schleiden (Germany) and Theodor Schwann (Germany) independently formulate cell theory. [1838 & 1839 respectively]

chlorophyll Pierre-Joseph Pelletier (France) and Joseph-Bienaimé Caventou (France) isolate chlorophyll. [1817]

chromosome (1) Friedrich Löffler (Germany) discovers chromosomes. [1882]
(2) Edouard-Joseph-Louis-Marie van Beneden (Belgium) discovers that each species has a fixed number of chromosomes. [1887]
(3) Heinrich Wilhelm Gottfried von Waldeyer-Hartz (Germany) first uses the word *chromosome*. [1888]
(4) Walter Stanborough Sutton (U.S.) and Theodore Boveri

(Germany) independently formulate chromosome theory. [1902]
(5) Edmund Wilson (U.S.) discovers that X and Y chromosomes are tied to sex determination. [1905]
(6) Thomas Hunt Morgan (U.S.), Calvin Bridges (U.S.), Alfred Henry Sturtevant (U.S.) and Hermann Joseph Muller (U.S.) assert that chromosomes contain invisible genes that determine hereditary traits. [1915]

citric acid cycle Hans Krebs (U.K.) discovers the citric acid cycle, later called the Krebs cycle. [1937]

clone (1) Robert Briggs (U.S.) and Thomas J. King (U.S.) transplant living nuclei into frogs' eggs. [1952]
(2) T.T. Puck (U.S.), S.J. Cieciura (U.S.), and P.I. Marcus (U.S.) successfully grow clones of human cells in vitro. [1956]
(3) John B. Gurdon (U.K.) successfully clones an animal (a leopard frog). [1967]
(4) Ian Wilmut (U.K.) clones a lamb. [1997]

cytoplasm Eduard Adolf Strasburger (Germany) uses the term *cytoplasm* to describe the protoplasm found outside the cell nucleus. [1882]

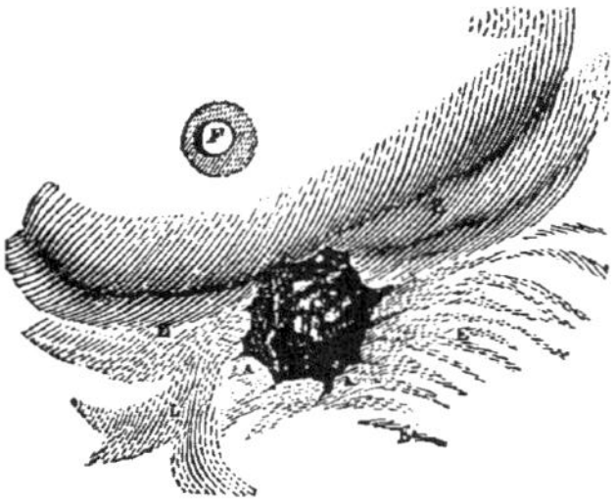

Digestion
Sketch by Beaumont of his surgical opening into a patient's stomach.

digestion (1) William Beaumont (U.S.) shows that gastric juice is the active substance involved in digestion. [1833]
(2) Gabriel Gustav Valentin discovers that pancreatic juices break down food during digestion. [1844]

DNA (1) Johann Friedrich Miescher (Switzerland) discovers DNA while studying the composition of white blood cells. [1869]
(2) Oswald T. Avery (Canada) shows that DNA is fundamental in determining heredity. [1944]
(3) James Watson (U.S.) and Francis Crick (U.K.) discover that the DNA molecule is a double helix. [1953]

ecology Ernst Haeckel (Germany) first uses the word *ecology* to refer to organism-environment relationship. [1861]

ecosystem Sir Arthur George Tansley (U.K.) introduces the concept of ecosystem. [1935]

embryology Publication of *De Formatione Ovi et Pulli* by Hieronymus Fabricius (Girolamo Fabrici) (Italy) elevates embryology to a science. [1621]

endocrinology Nicole Pende (Italy) identifies and names endocrinology as a new branch of medicine. [1909]

endorphins Choh Hao Li (U.S.) and David Chung (U.S.) discover beta-endorphin. [1976]

enzyme (1) Wilhelm Friedrich Kulme (Germany) introduces the term *enzyme* to describe substances that bring about chemical reactions in living organisms. [1878]
(2) James Batcheller Sumner (U.S.) crystallizes the first pure enzyme. [1926]

evolution (1) Erasmus Darwin (U.K.) publishes *Zoonomia* containing his ideas about the evolution of species. [1794–96]
(2) In *Philosophie Zoologique*, Jean-Baptiste Lamarck (France) advances the concept of the inheritance of acquired characteristics. [1809]
(3) Robert Chambers (U.K.) publishes *Vestiges of the Natural History of Creation* in which he promotes the idea of the evolution of the species. [1844]
(4) Charles Darwin (U.K.) publishes *On the Origin of Species*. [1859]

eye Johannes Kepler (Germany) describes the function of the eye. [1604]

fertilization Oskar Hertwig (Germany) and Hermann Foil (Switzerland), working independently, determine that the nucleus of the sperm fuses with the egg nucleus. [1875]

food chain Gottfried Semper (Germany) introduces the concept of food chain in a work entitled *Animal Life as Affected by the Natural Conditions of Existence* [1891]

gene (1) Wilhelm Ludvig Johannsen (Denmark) introduces the term *gene*. [1909]
(2) Thomas Hunt Morgan (U.S.), Calvin Bridges (U.S.), Alfred Henry Sturtevant (U.S.), and Hermann Joseph Muller (U.S.) assert that chromosomes contain invisible genes that determine heredity. [1915]
(3) Daniel Chapin Pease (U.S.) and Richard Baker (U.S.) first photograph genes. [1949]

genetic code (1) George Gamow (U.S.) suggests that nucleic acids act as a "genetic code." [1954]
(2) Marshall Warren Nirenberg (U.S.) works out the first item of the genetic code. [1961]
(3) Human Genome Project scientists unravel the genetic code of an entire human chromosome. [1999]

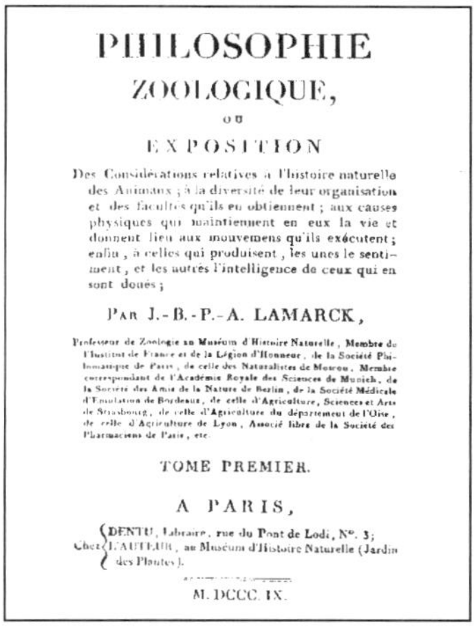

PHILOSOPHIE
ZOOLOGIQUE,
OU
EXPOSITION

Des Considérations relatives à l'histoire naturelle des Animaux ; à la diversité de leur organisation et des facultés qu'ils en obtiennent ; aux causes physiques qui maintiennent en eux la vie et donnent lieu aux mouvemens qu'ils exécutent ; enfin, à celles qui produisent, les unes le sentiment, et les autres l'intelligence de ceux qui en sont doués ;

PAR J.-B.-P.-A. LAMARCK,

Professeur de Zoologie au Muséum d'Histoire Naturelle, Membre de l'Institut de France et de la Légion d'Honneur, de la Société Philomatique de Paris, de celle des Naturalistes de Moscou, Membre correspondant de l'Académie Royale des Sciences de Munich, de la Société des Amis de la Nature de Berlin, de la Société Médicale d'Emulation de Bordeaux, de celle d'Agriculture, Sciences et Arts de Strasbourg, de celle d'Agriculture du département de l'Oise, de celle d'Agriculture de Lyon, Associé libre de la Société des Pharmaciens de Paris, etc.

TOME PREMIER.

A PARIS,

Chez DENTU, Libraire, rue du Pont de Lodi, N°. 3;
L'AUTEUR, au Muséum d'Histoire Naturelle (Jardin des Plantes).

M. DCCC. IX.

Evolution
Lamarck's Philosophie Zoologique *[1809]*.

Evolution
Charles Darwin.

genetic engineering Stanley Cohen (U.S.) and Herbert Boyer (U.S.) inaugurate the science of genetic engineering when they successfully construct DNA molecules by combining genetic materials from two different sources. [1973]

genetic fingerprinting Alec Jeffreys (U.K.) develops a method of analyzing DNA from blood, hair, etc. to determine whether a given person is tied to a given crime. [1985]

genetic map Thomas Hunt Morgan (U.S.) and Alfred Henry Sturtevant (U.S.) draw the first chromosome maps for fruit flies. [1911]

genetic recombination (1) Barbara McClintock (U.S.) finds evidence of genetic recombination in corn. [1931]
(2) Joshua Lederberg (U.S.) and Edward Lawrie Tatum (U.S.) demonstrate genetic recombination in bacteria. Working independently of each other, Max Delbrück (U.S.) and Alfred Day Hershey (U.S.) demonstrate genetic recombination of bacteriophage. [1946]

Genetics
Gregor Mendel crossbreeds garden peas [1865].

genetics (1) Gregor Mendel (Austria) formulates the laws of genetics. [1860]
(2) William Bateson (England) suggests that the study of inheritance be called *genetics*. [1906]

genotype Wilhelm Ludwig Johannsen (Denmark) coins the term *genotype* to refer to the genetic constitution of an organism. [1909]

germ theory (1) Friedrich Gustav Jacob Henle (Germany) suggests that disease is caused by microorganisms. [1840]
(2) Louis Pasteur (France) develops the germ theory of disease. [1865]

heart (1) William Harvey (England) presents the idea that the heart acts as a pump, sending blood to the arteries. [1628]
(2) Richard Lower (England) describes the structure of the heart in *Tractatus de Corde*. [1669]

hemoglobin Ernst Felix Hoppe-Selyer (Germany) crystallizes hemoglobin. [1862]

histology Marie-François-Xavier Bichat (France) founds the study of histology when he publishes *General Anatomy*, in which he identifies various types of tissues. [1800]

hormone Ernest Henry Starling (U.K.) uses the term *hormone* to describe circulating chemical messengers. [1905]

immunization In *An Inquiry into the Causes of Effects of the Variolae Vaccine*, Edward Jenner (England) describes his successful experiments with vaccinations. [1798]

insulin (1) Nicolas Paulesco (Romania) discovers insulin in the human pancreas. [1921]
(2) Sir Frederick Grant Banting (Canada), Charles H. Best (Canada), John J. Macleod (U.K.), and James Collip (Canada) discover a method of extracting insulin for use by diabetics. [1921]

invertebrate biology Jean-Baptiste Lamarck (France) begins modern invertebrate biology with the publication of his seven-volume *Natural History of Invertebrates*. [1815–22]

leukocyte Elie Metchnikoff (Russia) observes white blood corpuscles (leukocytes) moving to damaged areas where they ingest small particles. [1883]

lungs (1) Marcello Malpighi (Italy) shows that the lungs consist of small pockets containing air and a complex system of blood vessels. [1660]
(2) Robert Hooke (England) demonstrates lung function. [1667]

lymphatic system Thomas Bartholin (Denmark) describes the lymphatic system. [1652]

lysosome Christian René de Duve (Belgium) discovers and names lysosomes. [1955]

meiosis E. van Beneden (Belgium) discovers the process of meiosis. [1883]

mitochondria Richard Altmann (Switzerland) discovers what he terms *bioblasts* (later named mitochondria). [1890]

mitosis (1) A. Schneider (Germany) observes visible changes in the cell nucleus during cell division. [1873]
(2) Walther Flemming (Germany) assigns the term *mitosis* to this process. [1882]

morphology Johann Wolfgang Goethe (Germany) coins the term *morphology* in the course of his botanical studies. [1790–1810]

Immunization
Sketch of the milkmaid's cowpox sores from which Jenner made smallpox vaccine.

mutation (1) Hugo de Vries (the Netherlands) uses the term *mutation* to describe sudden changes in hereditary material in plants. [1901]
(2) Thomas Hunt Morgan (U.S.) extends de Vries's work to animals. [1907]

nerves (1) Albrecht von Haller (Switzerland) shows that nerves stimulate muscle contraction and that all nerves are connected to the spinal column. [1766]
(2) Sir Charles Bell (U.K.) discovers spinal nerve functions. [1811]
(3) Rudolf Albert von Kölliker (Switzerland) discovers that nerve fibers are extensions of nerve cells. [1849]

neuron (1) Santiago Ramón y Cajal (Spain) identifies neurons as the functional cells of the brain. [1889]
(2) Heinrich Wilhelm Gottfried von Waldeyer-Hartz (Germany) first calls these nerve cells neurons.

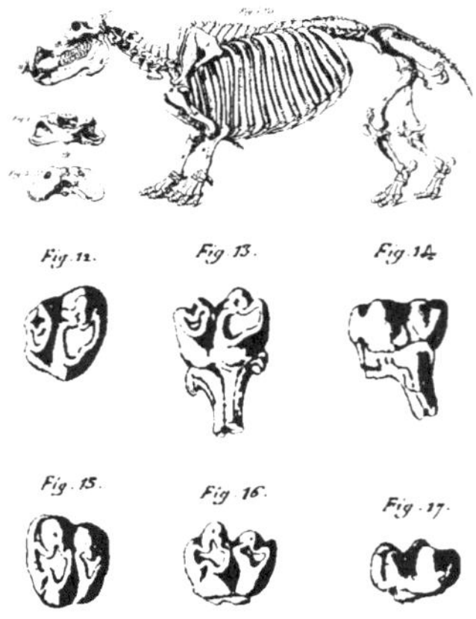

Paleontology
Studies of a hippopotamus skeleton by Georges Cuvier.

niacin Joseph Goldberger (U.S.) and George Wheeler (U.S.) discover niacin. [1928]

nucleic acids Johann Friedrich Miescher (Switzerland) discovers nucleic acids. [1869]

osmosis Wilhelm Pfeffer (Germany) explains the process of osmosis. [1877]

paleontology The publication of Georges (Baron) Cuvier's (France) *Recherches sur les Ossemens Fossiles* establishes the science of paleontology. [1812]

parthenogenesis Charles Bonnet (Switzerland) discovers that female aphids can reproduce without fertilization. [1740]

pasteurization Louis Pasteur (France) first pasteurizes milk. [1856]

penicillin Alexander Fleming (U.K.) discovers penicillin, ushering in the modern age of antibiotics. [1928]

pepsin (1) Theodor Schwann (Germany) discovers and isolates pepsin. [1836]
(2) John Howard Northrop (U.S.) crystallizes pepsin. [1930]

peptide Emil Hermann Fischer (Germany) develops a method for combining amino acids to make segments of proteins he calls peptides. [1907]

peristalsis Jean-François Fernel (France) describes peristalsis. [1542]

phenotype Wilhelm Ludvig Johannsen (Denmark) coins the term *phenotype*. [1909]

photosynthesis (1) Jan Ingenhousz (the Netherlands) demonstrates that green portions of plants give off oxygen in the presence of sunlight. [1779]
(2) Melvin Calvin (U.S.) discovers and isolates all details of plant photosynthesis. [1957]

pollination Christian Sprengel (Germany) describes plant pollination. [1793]

protein (1) Gerardus Johannes Mulder (the Netherlands) introduces the term *protein* to describe what he thinks are the basic building blocks of albuminous substances. [1838]
(2) Emil Hermann Fischer (Germany) builds a protein molecule. [1907]

protoplasm (1) Jan Evangelista Purkyně (Czechslovakia) uses the term *protoplasm* for colloidal fluid found in certain cells. [1839]
(2) Max Schultze (Germany) develops the theory of protoplasm. [1861]
(3) Eduard Adolf Strasburger (Germany) divides protoplasm into nucleoplasm and cytoplasm. [1882]

pulmonary circulation Realdo Colombo (Italy) describes pulmonary circulation. [1559]

recombinant DNA Stanley Cohen (U.S.) and Herbert Boyer (U.S.) construct recombinant DNA molecules. [1973]

recombinant RNA Eleanor A. Miele (U.S.), Donald R. Mills (U.S.), and Fred Russell Kramer (U.S.) successfully construct the first recombinant RNA molecule. [1983]

red blood cells Jan Swammerdam (the Netherlands) describes red blood cells. [1658]

reflex action René Descartes (France) explains reflex action. [1644]

Rh factor Karl Landsteiner (U.S.) and Alexander Wiener (U.S.) discover the Rh factor. [1904]

ribosome George Emil Palade (U.S.) discovers tiny particles rich in RNA, which he named *ribosomes*. [1956]

RNA (1) Phoebus Aaron Theodore Levene (U.S.) shows that there are two varieties of sugar in nucleic acid, namely RNA and

DNA. [1911]
(2) Severo Ochoa (U.S.) successfully synthesizes RNA. [1955]

sperm Anton van Leeuwenhoek (the Netherlands) observes sperm. [1677]

succession F.E. Clements (U.S.) introduces the concept of succession in *Research Methods in Ecology*. [1905]

synapse (1) Heinrich Wilhelm Gottfried von Waldeyer-Hartz (Germany) becomes the first person to observe that cells in the nervous system never actually meet. [1891]
(2) Charles Scott Sherrington (U.K.) coins the term *synapse* to describe the gap between nerve cells. [1897]

teeth John Hunter (U.K.) classifies teeth into molars, cuspids, and incisors. [1778]

tissue culture Ross G. Harrison (U.S.) invents tissue culture. [1907]

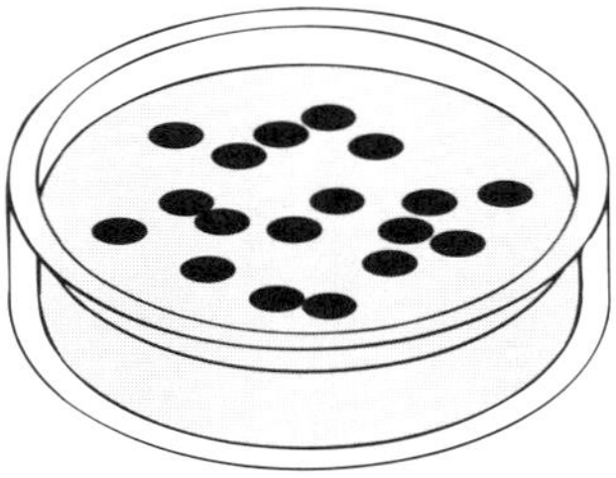

Tissue culture
Cell culture in a petri dish.

tryptophan Sir Frederick Hopkins (U.K.) discovers tryptophan. [1900]

urea cycle Hans Krebs (U.K.) discovers the urea cycle. [1932]

valves Hieronymus Fabricius (Girolamo Fabrici) (Italy) describes in detail the valves in veins. [1603]

virus (1) Dmitri Iosifovich Ivanovsky (Russia) proves the existence of a pathogenic agent smaller than bacteria. [1892]
(2) Wendell Meredith Stanley (U.S.) isolates and crystallizes a virus for the first time. [1935]

vitamin A Elmer Vernon McCollum (U.S.) and Marguerite Davis (U.S.) find vitamin A in butter and egg yolk. [1913]

vitamin B Edward Vedeer (U.S.) and Robert Williams (U.S.) detect vitamin B. [1912]

vitamin C Albert Szent-Györgyi Nagyrapolt (U.S.) isolates vitamin C. [1932]

vitamin D Elmer Vernon McCollum (U.S.) discovers vitamin D. [1922]

vitamin E Herbert McLean Evans (U.S.) and K.J. Scott (U.S.) discover vitamin E. [1922]

vitamin K Carl Peter Henrik Dam (Denmark) discovers vitamin K. [1930s]

yeast Anton van Leeuwenhoek (the Netherlands) observes yeast. [1690]

SECTION FIVE
NOBEL PRIZE WINNERS

NOBEL PRIZE WINNERS IN PHYSIOLOGY OR MEDICINE

1901 • **Emil Adolf von Behring** (1854–1917), Germany, "for his work on serum therapy, especially its application against diphtheria, by which he has opened a new road in the domain of medical science and thereby placed in the hands of the physician a victorious weapon against illnesses and deaths."

1902 • **Ronald Ross** (1857–1932), United Kingdom, "for his work on malaria, by which he has shown how it enters the organism and thereby has laid the foundation for successful research on this disease and methods of combating it."

1903 • **Niels Ryberg Finsen** (1860–1904), Denmark, "in recognition of his contribution to the treatment of diseases, especially lupus vulgaris, with concentrated light radiation, whereby he has opened a new avenue for medical science."

1904 • **Ivan Petrovich Pavlov** (1849–1936), Russia, "in recognition of his work on the physiology of digestion, through which knowledge on vital aspects of the subject has been transformed and enlarged."

1905 • **Robert Koch** (1843–1910), Germany, "for his investigations and discoveries in relation to tuberculosis."

1906 • **Camillo Golgi** (1843–1926), Italy; **Santiago Ramón y Cajal** (1852–1934), Spain, "in recognition of their work on the structure of the nervous system."

1907 • **Charles-Louis-Alphonse Laveran** (1845–1922), France, "in recognition of his work on the role played by protozoa in causing diseases."

1908 • **Elie Metchnikoff** (1845–1916), Russia; **Paul Ehrlich** (1854–1915), Germany, "in recognition of their work on immunity."

1909 • **Emil Theodor Kocher** (1841–1917), Switzerland, "for his work on the physiology, pathology, and surgery of the thyroid gland."

1906
Santiago Ramón y Cajal

1908
Elie Metchnikoff

1910 • **Albrecht Kossel** (1853–1927), Germany, "in recognition of the contributions to our knowledge of cell chemistry made through his work on proteins, including the nucleic substance."

1911 • **Allvar Gullstrand** (1862–1930), Sweden, "for his work on the dioptrics of the eye."

1912 • **Alexis Carrel** (1873–1944), France, "in recognition of his work on vascular suture and the transplantation of blood vessels and organs."

1913 • **Charles Robert Richet** (1850–1935), France, "in recognition of his work on anaphylaxis."

1914 • **Robert Bárány** (1876–1936), Austria, "for his work on the physiology and pathology of the vestibular apparatus."

1915–1918 • No prize given.

1919 • **Jules Bordet** (1870–1961), Belgium, "for his discoveries relating to immunity."

1920 • **Schack August Steenberg Krogh** (1874–1949), Denmark, "for his discovery of the capillary motor regulating mechanism."

1921 • No prize given.

1922 • **Archibald Vivian Hill** (1886–1977), United Kingdom, "for his discovery relating to the production of heat in the muscle;" **Otto Fritz Meyerhof** (1884–1951), Germany, "for his discovery of the fixed relationship between the consumption of oxygen and the metabolism of lactic acid in the muscle."

1923 • **Frederick Grant Banting** (1891–1941), Canada; **John James Richard Macleod** (1876–1935), Canada, "for the discovery of insulin."

1924 • **Willem Einthoven** (1860–1927), the Netherlands, "for his discovery of the mechanism of the electrocardiogram."

1925 • No prize given.

1913
Charles Richet

1920
August Krogh

1930
Karl Landsteiner

1926 • **Johannes Andreas Grib Fibiger** (1867–1928), Denmark, "for his discovery of the Spiroptera carcinoma."

1927 • **Julius Wagner von Jauregg** (1857–1940), Austria, "for his discovery of the therapeutic value of malaria inoculation in the treatment of dementia paralytica."

1928 • **Charles Jules Henri Nicolle** (1866–1936), France, "for his work on typhus."

1929 • **Christiaan Eijkman** (1858–1930), the Netherlands, "for his discovery of the antineuritic vitamin;" **Sir Frederick Gowland Hopkins** (1861–1947), United Kingdom, "for his discovery of the growth-stimulating vitamins."

1930 • **Karl Landsteiner** (1868–1943), Austria, "for his discovery of human blood groups."

1931 • **Otto Heinrich Warburg** (1883–1970), Germany, "for his discovery of the nature and mode of action of the respiratory enzyme."

1932 • **Sir Charles Scott Sherrington** (1857–1952), United Kingdom; **Edgar Douglas Adrian** (1889–1977), United Kingdom, "for their discoveries regarding the functions of neurons."

1933 • **Thomas Hunt Morgan** (1866–1945), U.S., "for his discoveries concerning the role played by the chromosome in heredity."

1934 • **George Hoyt Whipple** (1878–1976), U.S.; **George Richards Minot** (1885–1950), U.S.; **William Parry Murphy** (1892–1987), U.S., "for their discoveries concerning liver therapy in cases of anemia."

1935 • **Hans Spemann** (1869–1941), Germany, "for his discovery of the organizer effect in embryonic development."

1936 • **Sir Henry Hallett Dale** (1875–1968), United Kingdom; **Otto Loewi** (1873–1961), Austria, "for their discoveries relating to chemical transmission of nerve impulses."

1936
Otto Loewi

1937 • **Albert von Szent-Györgyi Nagyrapolt** (1893–1986), Hungary, "for his discoveries in connection with the biological combustion processes, with special reference to vitamin C and the catalysis of fumaric acid."

1938 • **Corneille-Jean-François Heymans** (1892–1968), Belgium, "for the discovery of the role played by the sinus and aortic mechanisms in the regulation of respiration."

1939 • **Gerhard Domagk** (1895–1964), Germany, "for the discovery of the antibacterial effects of prontosil."

1940–1942 • No prize given

1943 • **Henrik Carl Peter Dam** (1895–1976), Denmark, "for his discovery of vitamin K;" **Edward Adelbert Doisy** (1893–1986), U.S., "for his discovery of the chemical nature of vitamin K."

1944 • **Joseph Erlanger** (1874–1965), U.S.; **Herbert Spencer Gasser** (1888–1963), U.S., "for their discoveries relating to the highly differentiated function of single nerve fibers."

1945 • **Sir Alexander Fleming** (1881–1955), United Kingdom; **Sir Ernst Boris Chain** (1906–79), United Kingdom; **Sir Howard Walter Florey** (1898–1968), United Kingdom, "for the discovery of penicillin and its curative effect on various infectious diseases."

1946 • **Hermann Joseph Muller** (1890–1967), U.S., "for the discovery of the production of mutations by means of X-ray irradiation."

1947 • **Carl Ferdinand Cori** (1896–1984), U.S.; **Gerty Therese Cori** (1896–1957), U.S., "for their discovery of the course of the catalytic conversion of glycogen;" **Bernardo Alberto Houssay** (1887–1971), Argentina, "for his discovery of the part played by the hormone of the anterior pituitary lobe in the metabolism of sugar."

1948 • **Paul Hermann Müller** (1899–1965), Switzerland, "for his discovery of the high efficiency of DDT as a contact poison against several arthropods."

1947
Bernardo Houssay

1948
Paul Müller

1949 • **Walter Rudolf Hess** (1881–1973), Switzerland, "for his discovery of the functional organization of the interbrain as a coordinator of the activities of the internal organs;" **Antonio Egas Moniz** (1874–1955), Portugal, "for his discovery of the therapeutic value of leucotomy in certain psychoses."

1950 • **Edward Calvin Kendall** (1886–1972), U.S.; **Tadeus Reichstein** (1897–1996), Switzerland; **Philip Showalter Hench** (1896–1965), U.S., "for their discoveries relating to the hormones of the adrenal cortex, their structure and biological effects."

1951 • **Max Theiler** (1899–1972), South Africa, "for his discoveries concerning yellow fever and how to combat it."

1952 • **Selman Abraham Waksman** (1888–1973), U.S., "for his discovery of streptomycin, the first antibiotic effective against tuberculosis."

1953 • **Hans Adolf Krebs** (1900–81), United Kingdom, "for his discovery of the critic acid cycle;" **Fritz Albert Lipmann** (1899–1986), U.S., "for his discovery of co-enzyme A and its importance for intermediary metabolism."

1954 • **John Franklin Enders** (1897–1985), U.S.; **Thomas Huckle Weller** (b. 1915), U.S.; **Frederick Chapman Robbins** (1916–2003), U.S., "for their discovery of the ability of poliomyelitis viruses to grow in cultures of various types of tissue."

1955
Hugo Theorell

1955 • **Axel Hugo Theodor Theorell** (1903–82), Sweden, "for his discoveries concerning the nature and mode of action of oxidation enzymes."

1956 • **André Frédéric Cournand** (1895–1988), U.S.; **Werner Forssmann** (1904–79), Federal Republic of Germany; **Dickinson Woodruff Richards** (1895–1973), U.S., "for their discoveries concerning heart cauterization and pathological changes in the circulatory system."

1957 • **Daniel Bovet** (1907–92), Italy, "for his discoveries relating to synthetic compounds that inhibit the action of certain body substances, and especially their action on the vascular system and the skeletal muscles."

1958 • **George Wells Beadle** (1903–89), U.S.; **Edward Lawrie Tatum** (1909–75), U.S., "for their discovery that genes act by regulating definite chemical events;" **Joshua Lederberg** (b. 1925), U.S., "for his discoveries concerning genetic recombination and the organization of the genetic material of bacteria."

1959 • **Severo Ochoa** (1905–93), U.S.; **Arthur Kornberg** (b. 1918), U.S., "for their discovery of the mechanisms in the biological synthesis of ribonucleic acid and deoxyribonucleic acid."

1959
Severo Ochoa

1960 • **Sir Frank Macfarlane Burnet** (1899–1985), Australia; **Peter Brian Medawar** (1915–87), United Kingdom, "for discovery of acquired immunological tolerance."

1961 • **Georg von Békésy** (1899–1972), U.S., "for his discoveries of the physical mechanism of stimulation within the cochlea."

1962 • **Francis Harry Compton Crick** (1916–2004), United Kingdom; **James Dewey Watson** (1928–2004), U.S.; **Maurice Hugh Frederick Wilkins** (b. 1916), United Kingdom and New Zealand, "for their discoveries concerning the molecular structure of nucleic acids and its significance for information transfer in living material."

1963 • **Sir John Carew Eccles** (1903–97), Australia; **Alan Lloyd Hodgkin** (1914–98), United Kingdom; **Andrew Fielding Huxley** (b. 1917), United Kingdom, "for their discoveries concerning the ionic mechanisms involved in excitation and inhibition in the peripheral and central portions of the nerve cell membrane."

1964 • **Konrad Bloch** (1912–2000), U.S.; **Feodor Lynen** (1911–79), Federal Republic of Germany, "for their discoveries concerning the mechanism and regulation of the cholesterol and fatty acid metabolism."

1967
Ragnar Granit

1972
Rodney Porter

1965 • **François Jacob** (b. 1920), France; **André Lwoff** (1902–94), France; **Jacques Monod** (1910–76), France; "for their discoveries concerning genetic control of enzyme and virus synthesis."

1966 • **Payton Rous** (1879–1970), U.S., "for his discovery of tumor-inducing viruses;" **Charles Brenton Huggins** (1901–97), U.S., "for his discoveries concerning hormonal treatment of prostatic cancer."

1967 • **Ragnar Granit** (1900–91), Sweden; **Haldan Keffer Hartline** (1903–83), U.S.; **George Wald** (1906–97), U.S., "for their discoveries concerning the primary physiological and chemical visual processes in the eye."

1968 • **Robert W. Holley** (1922–93), U.S.; **Har Gobind Khorana** (b. 1922), U.S.; **Marshall W. Nirenberg** (b. 1927), U.S., "for their interpretation of the genetic code and its function in protein synthesis."

1969 • **Max Delbrück** (1906–81), U.S.; **Alfred D. Hershey** (1908–97), U.S., **Salvador E. Luria** (1912–91), U.S., "for their discoveries concerning the replication mechanism and the genetic structure of viruses."

1970 • **Sir Bernard Katz** (1911–2003), United Kingdom; **Ulf von Euler** (1905–83), Sweden; **Julius Axelrod** (1912–2004), U.S., "for their discoveries concerning the humoral transmitters in the nerve terminals and the mechanisms for their storage, release and inactivation."

1971 • **Earl W. Sutherland, Jr.**, (1915–74), U.S., "for his discoveries concerning the mechanisms of the action of hormones."

1972 • **Gerald Maurice Edelman** (b. 1929), U.S.; **Rodney Robert Porter** (1917–85), United Kingdom, "for their discoveries concerning the chemical structure of antibodies."

1973 • **Karl von Frisch** (1886–1982), Federal Republic of Germany; **Konrad Lorenz** (1903–89), Austria; **Nikolaas Tinbergen** (1907–88), United Kingdom, "for their discoveries concerning organization and elicitation of individual and social behavior patterns."

1974 • **Albert Claude** (1899–1983), Belgium; **Christian de Duve** (b. 1917), Belgium; **George E. Palade** (b. 1912), U.S., "for their discoveries concerning the structural and functional organization of the cell."

1975 • **David Baltimore** (b. 1938), U.S.; **Renato Dulbecco** (b. 1914), U.S.; **Howard Martin Temin** (1934–94), U.S., "for their discoveries concerning the interaction between tumor viruses and the genetic material of the cell."

1976 • **Baruch S. Blumberg** (b. 1925), U.S.; **D. Carleton Gajdusek** (b. 1923), U.S., "for their discoveries concerning new mechanisms for the origin and dissemination of infectious diseases."

1977 • **Roger Guillemin** (b. 1924), U.S.; **Andrew V. Schally** (b. 1926), U.S., "for their discoveries concerning the peptide hormone production of the brain;" **Rosalyn S. Yalow** (b. 1921), U.S., "for the development of radioimmunoassays of peptide hormones."

1978
Daniel Nathans

1978 • **Werner Arber** (b. 1929), Switzerland; **Daniel Nathans** (1928–99), U.S.; **Hamilton O. Smith** (b. 1931), U.S., "for the discovery of restriction enzymes and their application to problems of molecular genetics."

1979 • **Allan M. Cormack** (1924–98), U.S.; **Godfrey N. Hounsfield** (1919–2004), United Kingdom, "for the development of computer-assisted tomography."

1980 • **Baruj Benacerraf** (b. 1920), U.S.; **Jean Dausset** (b. 1916), France; **George D. Snell** (1903–96), U.S., "for their discoveries concerning genetically determined structures on the cell surface that regulate immunological reactions."

1981 • **Roger W. Sperry** (1913–94), U.S., "for his discoveries concerning the functional specialization of the cerebral hemispheres;" **David H. Hubel** (b. 1926), U.S.;

1982
Sune Bergström

1982
Bengt Samuelsson

Torsten N. Wiesel (b. 1924), Sweden, "for their discoveries concerning information processing in the visual system."

1982 • **Sune K. Bergström** (1916–2004), Sweden; **Bengt I. Samuelsson** (b. 1934), Sweden; **John R. Vane** (1927–2004), United Kingdom; "for their discoveries concerning prostaglandins and related biologically active substances."

1983 • **Barbara McClintock** (1902–92), U.S., "for her discovery of mobile genetic elements."

1984 • **Niels K. Jerne** (1911–94), Denmark; **Georges J. F. Köhler** (1946–95), Federal Republic of Germany; **César Milstein** (1927–2002), Argentina and United Kingdom, "for theories concerning the specificity in development and control of the immune system and the discovery of the principle for production of monoclonal antibodies."

1985 • **Michael S. Brown** (b. 1941), U.S.; **Joseph L. Goldstein** (b. 1940), U.S., "for their discoveries concerning the regulation of cholesterol metabolism."

1986 • **Stanley Cohen** (b. 1922), U.S.; **Rita Levi-Montalcini** (b. 1909), Italy and U.S., "for their discoveries of growth factors."

1987 • **Susumu Tonegawa** (b. 1939), Japan, "for his discovery of the genetic principle for generation of antibody diversity."

1988 • **Sir James W. Black** (b. 1924), United Kingdom; **Gertrude B. Elion** (1918–99), U.S.; **George H. Hitchings** (1905–98), U.S., "for their discoveries of important principles for drug treatment."

1989 • **J. Michael Bishop** (b. 1936), U.S.; **Harold E. Varmus** (b. 1939), U.S., "for their discovery of the cellular origin of retroviral oncogenes."

1990 • **Joseph E. Murray** (b. 1919), U.S.; **E. Donnall Thomas** (b. 1920), U.S., "for their discoveries concerning organ and cell transplantation in the treatment of human disease."

1991 • **Erwin Neher** (b. 1944), Federal Republic of Germany; **Bert Sakmann** (b. 1942), Federal Republic of Germany, "for their discoveries concerning the function of single ion channels in cells."

1992 • **Edmond H. Fischer** (b. 1920), U.S.; **Edwin G. Krebs** (b. 1918), U.S., "for their discoveries concerning reversible protein phosphorylation as a biological regulatory mechanism."

1993 • **Richard J. Roberts** (b. 1943), United Kingdom; **Phillip A. Sharp** (b. 1944), U.S., "for their discovery of split genes."

1994 • **Alfred G. Gilman** (b. 1941), U.S.; **Martin Rodbell** (1925–98), U.S., "for their discovery of G-proteins and the role of these proteins in signal transduction in cells."

1995 • **Edward B. Lewis** (1918–2004), U.S.; **Christiane Nüsslein-Volhard** (b. 1942), Federal Republic of Germany; **Eric F. Wieschaus** (b. 1947), U.S., "for their discoveries concerning genetic control of early embryonic development."

1996 • **Peter C. Doherty** (b. 1940), Australia; **Rolf M. Zinkernagel** (b. 1944), Switzerland, "for their discoveries concerning the specificity of the cell mediated immune defense."

1997 • **Stanley B. Prusiner** (b. 1942), U.S., "for his discovery of Prions—a new biological principle of infection."

1998 • **Robert F. Furchgott** (b. 1916), U.S.; **Louis J. Ignarro** (b. 1941), U.S.; **Ferid Murad** (b. 1936), U.S., "for their discoveries concerning nitric oxide as a signaling molecule in the cardiovascular system."

1999 • **Günter Blobel** (b. 1936), U.S., "for the discovery that proteins have intrinsic signals that govern their transport and localization in the cell."

2000 • **Arvid Carlsson** (b. 1923), Sweden; **Paul Greengard** (b. 1925), U.S.; **Eric R. Kandel** (b. 1929), U.S., "for their discoveries concerning signal transduction in the nervous system."

2001 • **Leland H. Hartwell** (b. 1939), U.S.; **R. Timothy Hunt** (b. 1943), United Kingdom; **Sir Paul Maxime Nurse** (b. 1949), United Kingdom, "for their discoveries of key regulators of the cell cycle."

2002 • **Sydney Brenner** (b. 1927), United Kingdom; **Howard Robert Horvitz** (b. 1947), U.S.; **John E. Sulston** (b. 1942), United Kingdom, "for their discoveries concerning 'genetic regulation of organ development and programmed cell death'."

2003 • **Paul C. Lauterbur** (b. 1929), U.S.; **Sir Peter Mansfield** (b. 1933), United Kingdom, "for their discoveries concerning magnetic resonance imaging."

2004 • **Richard Axel** (b. 1946), U.S.; **Linda B. Buck** (b. 1947), U.S., for their "research in odorant receptors and the organization of the olfactory system."

2005 • **Barry J. Marshall** (b. 1951), Australia; and **J. Robin Warren** (b. 1937), Australia, for their discovery of "the bacterium Helicobacter pylori and its role in gastritis and peptic ulcer disease."

SECTION SIX
CHARTS & TABLES

Elements

In the following table elements are listed by letter symbol. The list includes the atomic number, element name, and the atomic weight of each element.

* indicates the atomic weight of the isotope with the lowest known half-life.

Periodic table of the elements

1 H																	2 He
3 Li	4 Be											5 B	6 C	7 N	8 O	9 F	10 Ne
1 Na	12 Mg											13 Al	14 Si	15 P	16 S	17 Cl	18 Ar
19 K	20 Ca	21 Sc	22 Ti	23 V	24 Cr	25 Mn	26 Fe	27 Co	28 Ni	29 Cu	30 Zn	31 Ga	32 Ge	33 As	34 Se	35 Br	36 Kr
37 Rb	38 Sr	39 Y	40 Zr	41 Nb	42 Mo	43 Tc	44 Ru	45 Rh	46 Pd	47 Ag	48 Cd	49 In	50 Sn	51 Sb	52 Te	53 I	54 Xe
55 Cs	56 Ba	57-71 -	72 Hf	73 Ta	74 W	75 Re	76 Os	77 Ir	78 Pt	79 Au	80 Hg	81 Tl	82 Pb	83 Bi	84 Po	85 At	86 Rn
87 Fr	88 Ra	89-103 -	104 Rf	105 Db	106 Sg	107 Bh	108 Hs	109 Mt	110 Ds	11 Rg	112 Uub	113 Uut	114 Uuq	115 Uup	116 Uuh		

57 La	58 Ce	59 Pr	60 Nd	61 Pm	62 Sm	63 Eu	64 Gd	65 Tb	66 Dy	67 Ho	68 Er	69 Tm	70 Yb	71 Lu
89 Ac	90 Th	91 Pa	92 U	93 Np	94 Pu	95 Am	96 Cm	97 Bk	98 Cf	99 Es	100 Fm	101 Md	102 No	103 Lr

Letter symbol	Atomic number	Name	Atomic weight
Ac	89	actinium	227.0278*
Ag	47	silver	107.868
Al	13	aluminum	26.98154
Am	95	americium	243.0614*
Ar	18	argon	39.948
As	33	arsenic	74.9216
At	85	astatine	209.987*
Au	79	gold	196.9665
B	5	boron	10.81
Ba	56	barium	137.33
Be	4	beryllium	9.0128
Bh	107	bohrium	264
Bk	97	berkelium	247.0703*
Bi	83	bismuth	208.9804
Br	35	bromine	79.904
C	6	carbon	12.011
Ca	20	calcium	40.08
Cd	48	cadmium	112.41
Ce	58	cerium	140.12
Cf	98	californium	251.0796*
Cl	17	chlorine	35.453
Cm	96	curium	247.0703*
Co	27	cobalt	58.9332
Cr	24	chromium	51.996
Cs	55	cesium	132.9054
Cu	29	copper	63.546
Db	105	dubnium	262
Ds	110	darmstadtium	271
Dy	66	dysprosium	162.5
Er	68	erbium	167.26
Es	99	einsteinium	254.088*
Eu	63	europium	151.96
F	9	fluorine	18.9984
Fe	26	iron	55.847
Fm	100	fermium	257.0951*
Fr	87	francium	223.0197*
Ga	31	gallium	69.72
Gd	64	gadolinium	157.25
Ge	32	germanium	72.59
H	1	hydrogen	1.0079
He	2	helium	4.0026
Hf	72	hafnium	178.49
Hg	80	mercury	200.59
Ho	67	holmium	164.9304
Hs	108	hassium	269
I	53	iodine	126.9045
In	49	indium	114.82
Ir	77	iridium	192.22
K	19	potassium	39.0983
Kr	36	krypton	83.8
La	57	lanthanum	138.9055
Li	3	lithium	6.941
Lr	103	lawrencium	260.105*
Lu	71	lutetium	174.967
Md	101	mendelevium	258.099*
Mg	12	magnesium	24.305
Mn	25	manganese	54.938
Mo	42	molybdenum	95.94
Mt	109	meitnerium	268
N	7	nitrogen	14.0067
Na	11	sodium	22.98977
Nb	41	niobium	92.9064
Nd	60	neodymium	144.24
Ne	10	neon	20.179
Ni	28	nickel	58.69
No	102	nobelium	259.101*
Np	93	neptunium	237.0482*
O	8	oxygen	15.9994
Os	76	osmium	190.2
P	15	phosphorus	30.97376
Pa	91	protoactinium	231.0359
Pb	82	lead	207.19
Pd	46	palladium	106.42
Pm	61	promethium	144.9128*
Po	84	polonium	208.9824*
Pr	59	praseodymium	140.9077
Pt	78	platinum	195.08
Pu	94	plutonium	244.0642*
Ra	88	radium	226.0254*
Rb	37	rubidium	85.4678
Re	75	rhenium	186.207
Rf	104	rutherfordium	261
Rg	111	roentgenium	272
Rh	45	rhodium	102.9055
Rn	86	radon	222.0176*
Ru	44	ruthenium	101.07
S	16	sulfur	32.064
Sb	51	antimony	121.75
Sc	21	scandium	44.9559
Se	34	selenium	78.96
Sg	106	seaborgium	266
Si	14	silicon	28.0855
Sm	62	samarium	150.36
Sn	50	tin	118.69
Sr	38	strontium	87.62
Ta	73	tantalum	180.9479
Tb	65	terbium	158.9254
Tc	43	technetium	96.9064*
Te	52	tellurium	127.6
Th	90	thorium	232.0381
Ti	22	titanium	47.88
Tl	81	thallium	204.383
Tm	69	thulium	168.9342
U	92	uranium	238.029*
Uub	112	ununbium	285
Uuh	116	ununhexium	292
Uup	115	ununpentium	288
Uuq	114	ununquadium	289
Uut	113	ununtrium	284
V	23	vanadium	50.9415
W	74	tungsten	183.85
Xe	54	xenon	131.29
Y	39	yttrium	88.9059
Yb	70	ytterbium	173.04
Zn	30	zinc	65.381
Zr	40	zirconium	91.224

Elements by groups

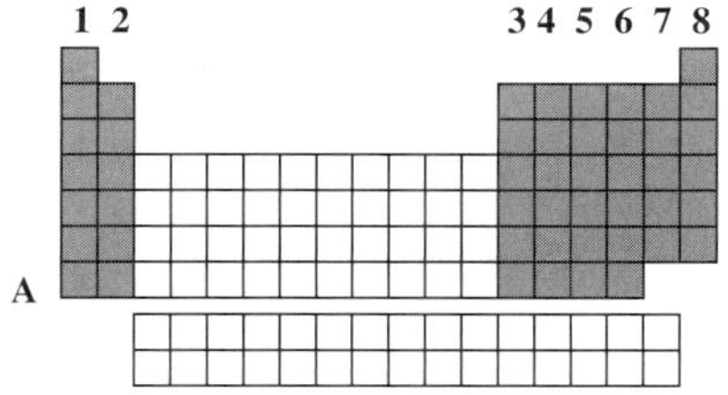

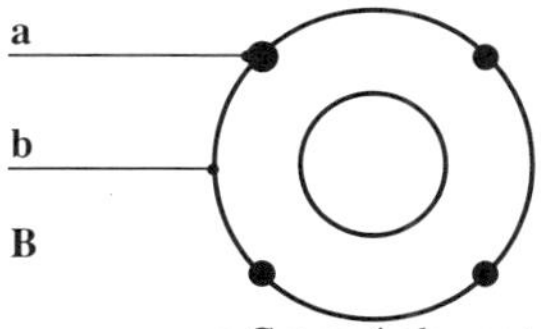

a Group 4 element

A The eight groups read downward.
B The groups rank elements by number of electrons (**a**) in an atom's outer shell (**b**): Group 1, one electron; Group 2, two electrons, and so on through Group 8. Elements with the same number of outer shell electrons share similar properties. (Note: hydrogen fits no group, and helium, although in Group 8, has only two electrons.)

Group 1 Alkali metals, the sodium family, with one electron in the outer shell. These are similar, very active metals.
Group 2 Alkaline-earth metals, the calcium family, with two electrons in the outer shell.
Group 3 Nonmetallic through metallic elements, with increasingly complex atoms. All have three electrons in the outer shell, and stable inner shells.
Group 4 Nonmetallic through metallic elements, also with increasingly complex atoms. All have four electrons in the outer shell, and stable inner shells.
Group 5 The nitrogen family—from nonmetallic nitrogen and phosphorus to metallic bismuth. All have five electrons in the outer shell, and stable inner shells.
Group 6 The oxygen family—from oxygen to metallic polonium. All have six electrons in the outer shell, and stable inner shells.
Group 7 The halogen family of active nonmetals. All have seven electrons in the outer shell, and stable inner shells.
Group 8 The inert gases. None chemically combines with any element. All (except helium) have eight electrons in the outer shell.

Electron arrangement of atoms

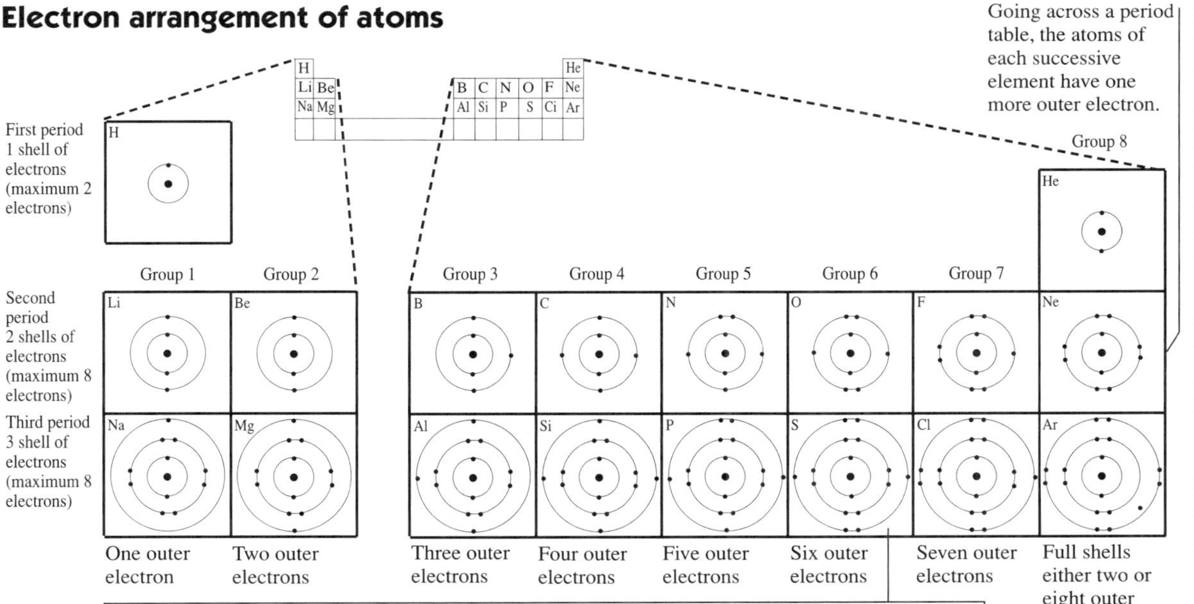

The electronic structure of the atom of any element determines its position in the periodic table. For example, sulfur a) is the third period because it has three shells of electrons and b) it is in group six because it has six outer electrons. So the electronic structure of sulfur is 2.8.6 ← Group 6 ← three shells

Living organisms

Kingdoms
1 Monera
2 Protista
3 Fungi
4 Plantae
5 Animalia

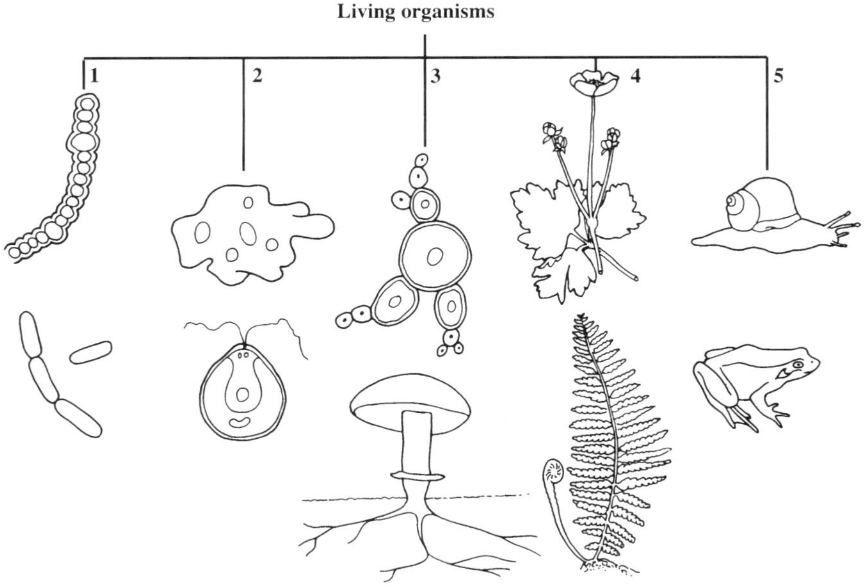

Families of flowering plants

1 Monocotyledons
1a Liliaceae (e.g., tulip)
1b Gramineae (e.g., wheat)
1c Araceae (e.g., Jack-in-the-pulpit)
1d Palmae (e.g., date palm)
1e Orchidaceae (e.g., orchid)
2 Dicotyledons
2a Ranunculaceae (e.g., buttercup)
2b Betulaceae (e.g., alder)
2c Rosaceae (e.g., rose)
2d Fabaceae (e.g., clover)
2e Compositae (e.g., daisy)

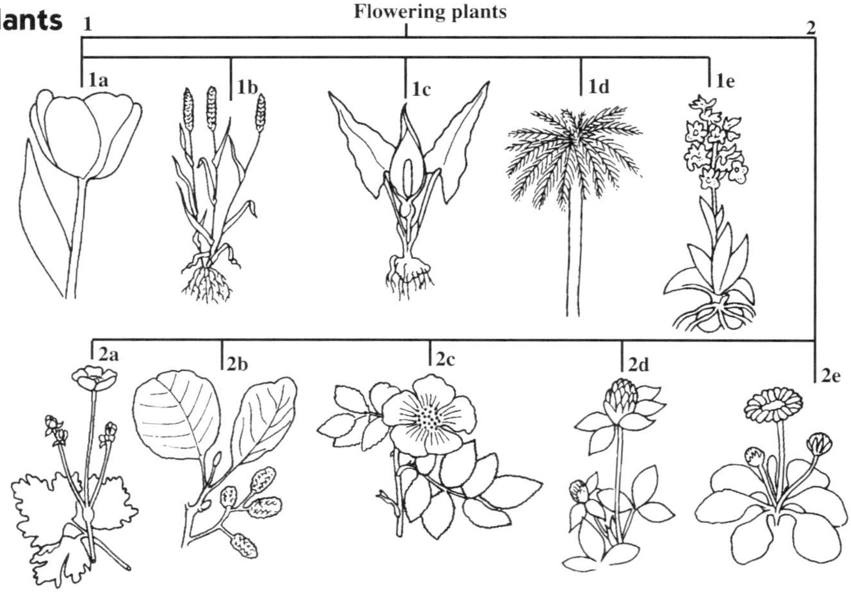

Characteristics of invertebrates

Common name	**Sponges**	**Cnidarians**	**Flatworms**	**Roundworms**	**Segmented worms**	**Mollusks**
External appearance		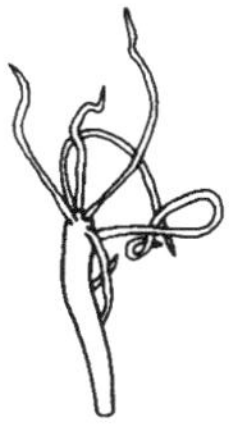				
Locomotion	None	Mostly sessile; free floating	Muscles; cilia	Muscles	Muscles	Muscles
Symmetry	None or radial	Radial	Bilateral	Bilateral	Bilateral	Bilateral
Number of body openings	One	One	One	Two	Two	Two
Number of cell layers	Two	Two	Three	Three	Three	Three
Nervous system	None	Present	Present	Present	Present	Present
Digestive system	None	Present	Present	Present	Present	Present
Excretory system	None	None	Present	Present	Present	Present
Circulatory system	None	None	None	None	Present	Present
Respiratory system	None	None	None	None	None	Present
Skeletal system	Spicules, no true system	None	None	None	None	Hard outer shell

Phyla
1 Porifera
2 Cnidaria
3 Platyhelminthes
4 Nematoda
5 Annelida
6 Mollusca

Characteristics of vertebrates

Class	**External appearance**	**Integument**	**Body temperature**	**Limb structure**	**Gas exchange**	**Fertilization**
1 Agnatha		Slimy skin	Ectotherm	No	Gills	External
2 Chondrichthyes		Scales	Ectotherm	2 pairs of fins	Gills	Internal
3 Osteichthyes		Scales and slimy skin	Ectotherm	2 pairs of fins	Gills	External
4 Amphibia		Slimy skin in most forms	Ectotherm	2 pairs of legs, no claws	Gills; Lungs	External
5 Reptilia		Dry, scaly	Ectotherm	2 pairs of legs, claws	Lungs	Internal
6 Aves		Feathers, scales on legs	Endotherm	1 pair of wings, 1 pair of legs, claws	Lungs	Internal
7 Mammalia		Hair	Endotherm	2 pairs of legs, claws in most forms	Lungs	Internal

1 Jawless fish (lampreys, hagfish)
2 Cartilaginous fish (sharks, rays)
3 Bony fish (cod, perch)
4 Amphibians, frogs, salamanders)
5 Reptiles (lizards, crocodiles, turtles, and snakes)
6 Birds
7 Mammals

Classifying a plant

Plants are classified in successively larger, less closely related groups. The smallest unit shown here is a species. Members of one species normally cannot interbreed with those of another, but many garden plants are hybrids of varieties of one species.

Read upward, this diagram shows that the tea rose (*Rosa odorata* **8**) is one of many species in the genus *Rosa* **7**, one of many genera in the family Rosaceae **6**. That family is one of a number in the order Rosales **5**, one of many orders in the class Dicotyledonae (dicots **4**). Dicots form one of two classes in the subdivision Angiospermae (angiosperms or flowering plants **3**). Angiosperms are one of two subdivisions in the division Spermatophyta **2**, one of the 10 divisions in the Plantae (plant kingdom **1**).

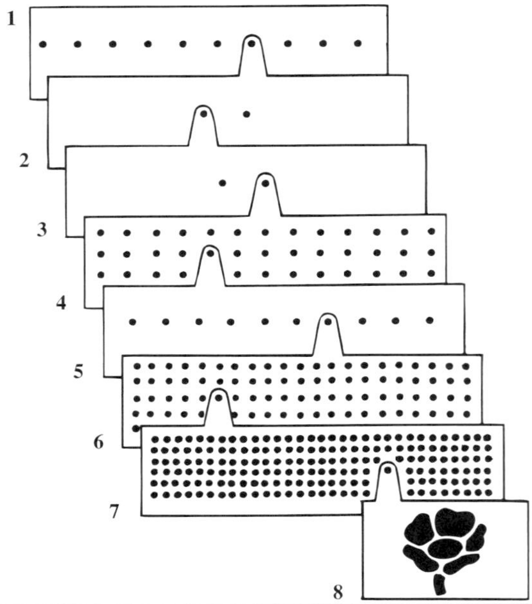

Classifying an animal

Animals also are classified in successively larger groups, with successively less close anatomical relationships. The smallest unit usually used is the species. Members of one species normally do not interbreed with members of any other species.

This diagram shows (reading upward) that the lion (*Panthera leo* **8**) is one of several species in the genus *Panthera* **7**. In turn, this genus is one of four genera in the family Felidae **6**. That family is one of seven families in the order Carnivora **5**. This order is one of 17 orders in the class Mammalia **4**. The class Mammalia is one of seven in the subphylum Vertebrata **3**. Vertebrates belong to the phylum Chordata **2**, one of nine phyla making up the Animalia or animal kingdom (**1**).

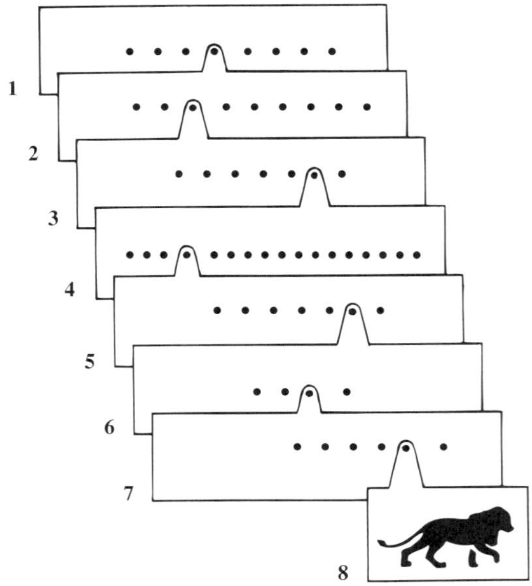

Tree of life

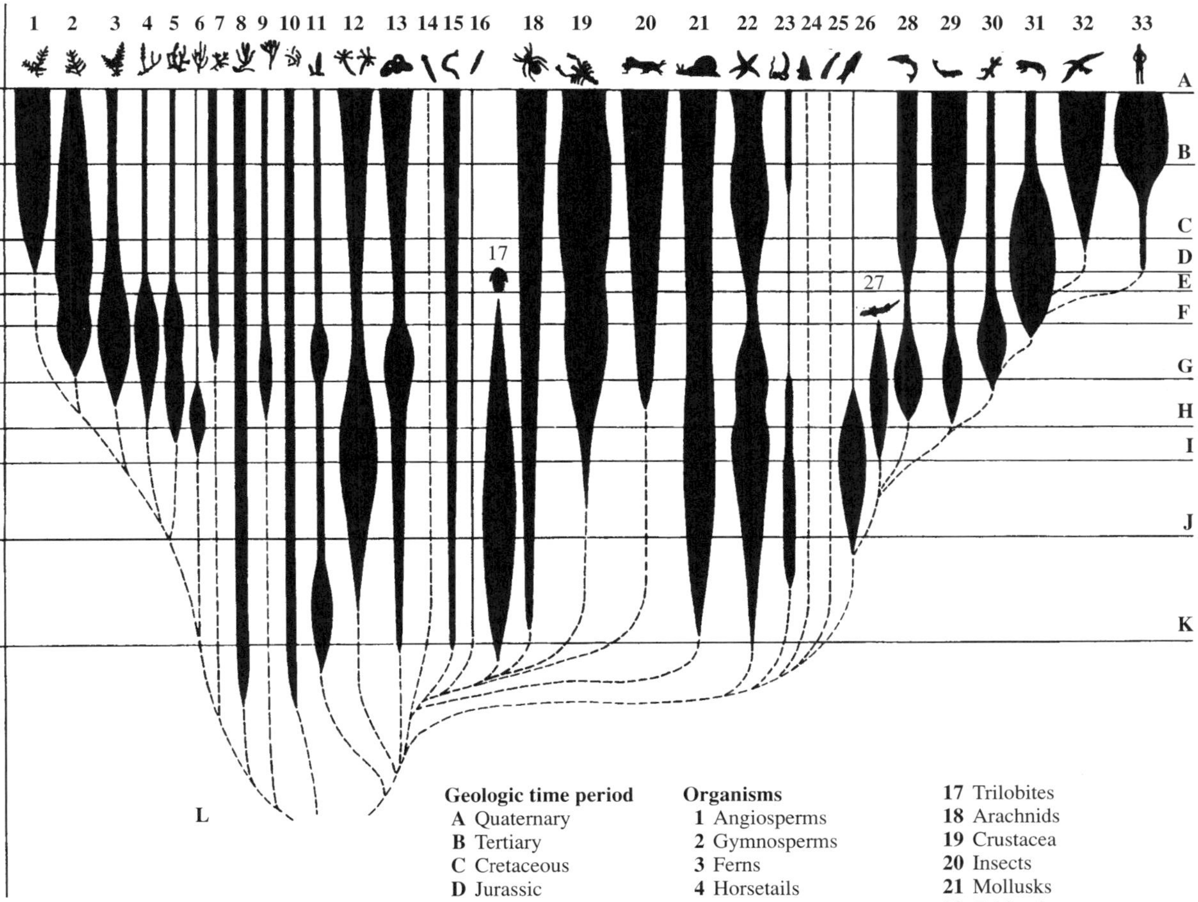

The chart shows how our current organisms evolved. The width of the line indicates the population size and the dotted lines show how organisms evolved from other groups. Time flows from the bottom to the top of the chart.

Geologic time period

A Quaternary
B Tertiary
C Cretaceous
D Jurassic
E Triassic
F Permian
G Carboniferous
H Devonian
I Silurian
J Ordovician
K Cambrian
L Proterozoic

Organisms

1 Angiosperms
2 Gymnosperms
3 Ferns
4 Horsetails
5 Clubmosses
6 Psilopsides
7 Bryophytes
8 Algae
9 Fungi
10 Bacteria
11 Sponges
12 Cnidarians
13 Protists
14 Flatworms
15 Annelids
16 Onychophora
17 Trilobites
18 Arachnids
19 Crustacea
20 Insects
21 Mollusks
22 Echinoderms
23 Hemichordates
24 Urochordates
25 Cephalochordates
26 Agnatha
27 Placoderms
28 Cartilaginous fish
29 Bony fish
30 Amphibians
31 Reptiles
32 Birds
33 Mammals

Biochemical cycles

Oxygen cycle Oxygen plays a vital part in the respiration of animals and plants.
1 Oxygen in air
2 Oxygen breathed in by animals
3 Carbon dioxide (a carbon-oxygen compound) breathed out by living things as waste
4 Carbon dioxide absorbed by plants and used in photosynthesis to make carbohydrate foods
5 Surplus oxygen released into the air by plants as waste

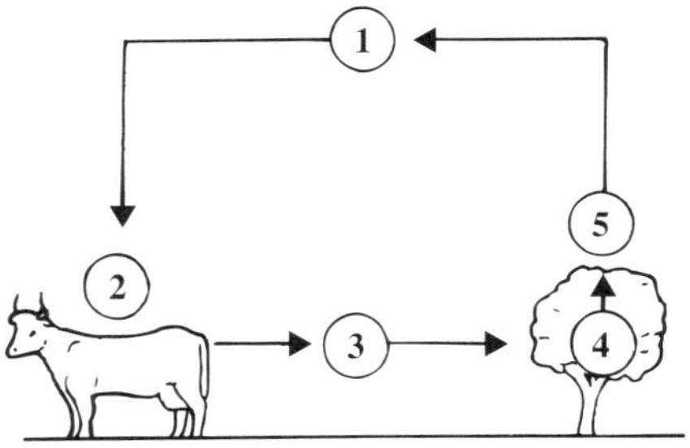

Carbon cycle Plant material is a valuable source of carbon. Oxidizing carbon compounds provide energy for animals and plants.
1 Carbon dioxide (a carbon-oxygen compound) in air
2 Carbon dioxide absorbed by plants for making food
3 Plants eaten by animals
4 Carbon dioxide waste breathed out by animals and plants
5 Dead organisms broken down by bacteria
6 These give off carbon dioxide waste
7 Remains of long-dead plants and microscopic organisms forming hydrocarbon fossil fuels: coal, oil, and gas
8 Carbon dioxide released back into the air by burning fossil fuels

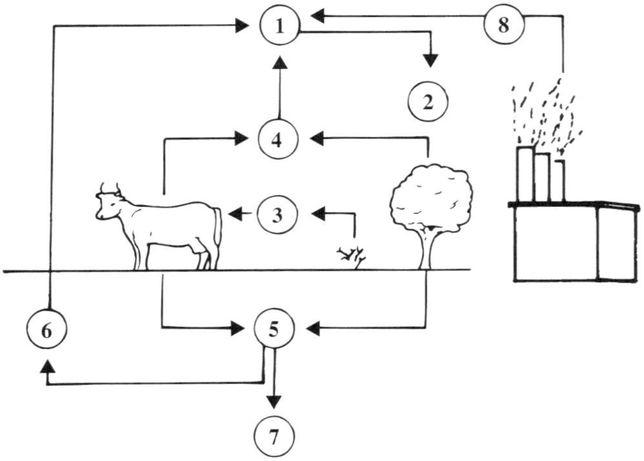

Nitrogen cycle As an ingredient in proteins and nucleic acids, nitrogen is vital to all living things.
1 Nitrogen in air
2 Atmospheric nitrogen trapped by some plants' roots
3 Nitrogen used by plants for making proteins
4 Plant proteins eaten by animals
5 Proteins in dead organisms and body wastes converted to ammonia by bacteria and fungi
6 Ammonia converted to nitrate by other bacteria
7 Nitrate taken up by plant roots

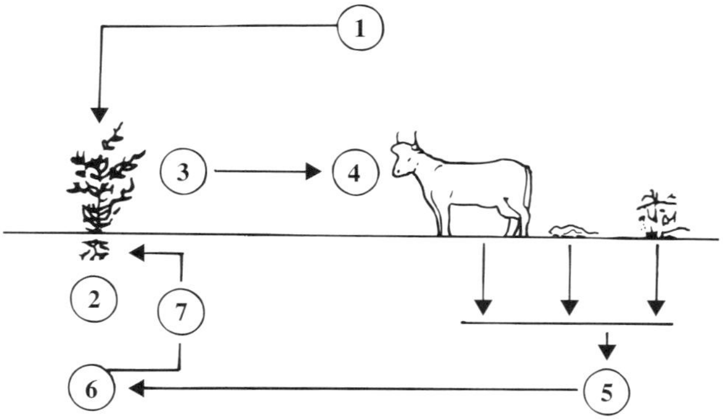

Sulfur cycle Sulfur is in two of the 20 amino acids that are used by the body to make proteins.
1 Sulfates (sulfur-oxygen compounds) absorbed by plant roots
2 The oxygen in the sulfate is replaced by hydrogen in a plant process that produces certain amino acids
3 Plants eaten by animals
4 Sulfur-containing amino acids of dead plants and animals broken down to hydrogen sulfide (which gives off a rotten egg odor) by decomposer microorganisms
5 Sulfur extracted from sulfides by bacteria
6 Other bacteria combine sulfur with oxygen, producing sulfates

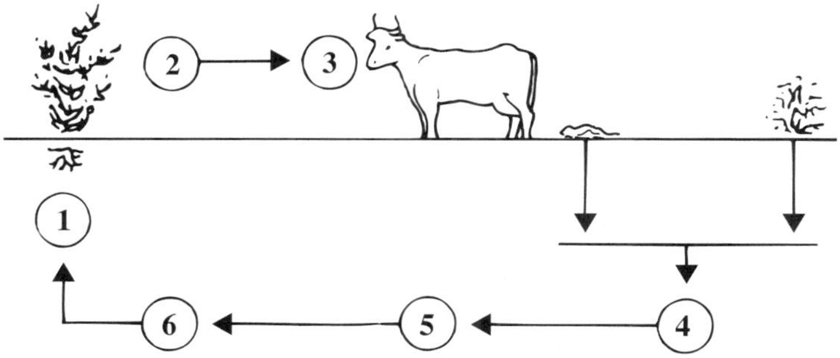

Phosphorus cycle Phosphorus is a vital ingredient of proteins, nucleic acids, and some other compounds found in living things.
1 Phosphates (compounds of phosphorus, hydrogen, and oxygen) absorbed by plant roots
2 Phosphates used by plants in making organic phosphorus compounds
3 Plants eaten by animals
4 Compounds in dead plants and animals broken down to phosphates by microorganisms

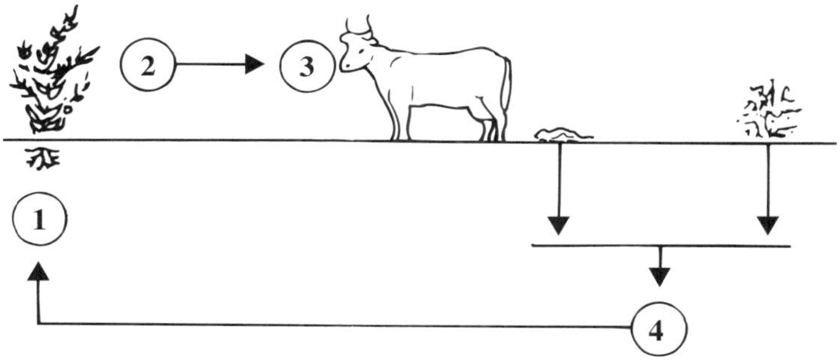

Krebs cycle The Krebs or citric acid cycle is the second stage of aerobic respiration in which living things produce energy from foods. It requires oxygen; enzymes (proteins that promote but are not used up in chemical changes) create successive compounds, thus transforming pyruvate to carbon dioxide and water and releasing energy.
1 Acetic acid combines with . . .
2 Oxaloacetic acid to form . . .
3 Citric acid. Later changes produce . . .
4 Aconitic acid
5 Isocitric acid
6 Ketoglutaric acid
7 Succinic acid, carbon dioxide, and energy-rich ATP (adenosine triphosphate)
8 Fumaric acid
9 Malic acid

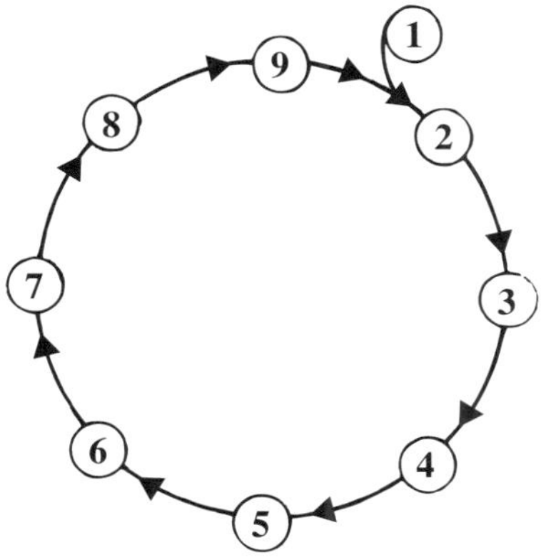

Digestive system in humans

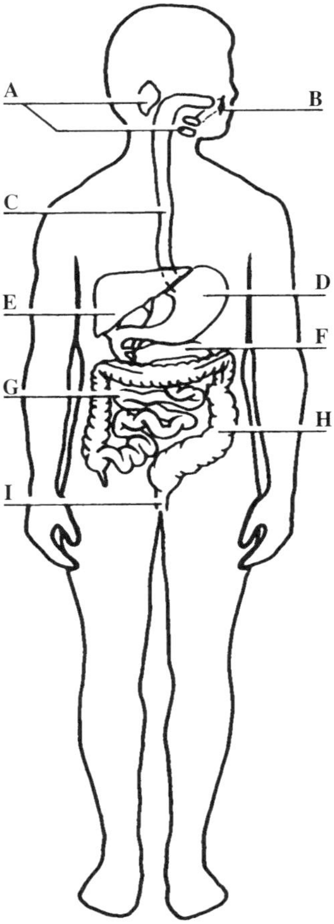

Part	Function	Secretion	Substance acted on	Products of action
A	Saliva secretion	1	Starch	Maltose
B	Mechanical digestion			
C	Carry food to stomach			
D	Food storage and protein breakdown	2	Pepsinogen	Pepsin
		3	Proteins	Polypeptides
E	Bile production and transport	4	Large fat droplets	Small fat droplets
F	Pancreatic juice production	5	Starch	Maltose
		6	Fats	Fatty acids and glycerol
		7	Proteins	Polypeptides
G	Digestion and absorption	8	Starch	Maltose
		9	Polypeptides	Amino acids *
		10	Disaccharides	Monosaccharides *
		11	Fats	Fatty acids and glycerol
H	Absorption of water and salts			
I	Excretion of waste			

* indicates a molecule small enough to be absorbed

A–I Parts of the digestive system
- **A** Salivary glands
- **B** Mouth and teeth
- **C** Esophagus
- **D** Stomach
- **E** Liver
- **F** Pancreas
- **G** Small intestine
- **H** Large intestine
- **I** Anus

1–11 Major secretions
- **1** Salivary amylase
- **2** Hydrochloric acid
- **3** Pepsinogen (pepsin)
- **4** Bile salts
- **5** Pancreatic amylase
- **6** Lipase
- **7** Trypsinogen (trypsin)
- **8** Amylase
- **9** Peptidase
- **10** Carbohydrase
- **11** Lipase

Endocrine system in humans

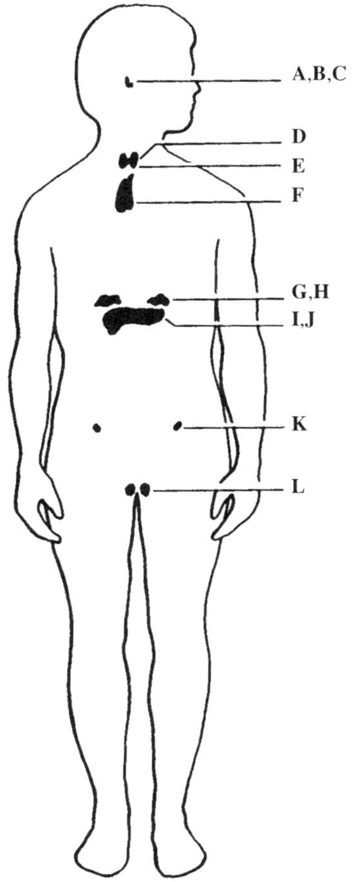

Gland	Hormone	
A	1	Controls growth
	2	Stimulates thyroid gland
	3	Stimulates adrenal cortex hormone formation
	4	Stimulates mammary glands to produce milk
	5	Stimulates ovaries (female) and testes (male)
B	6	Stimulates melanin production in skin
C	7	Causes contraction of uterus during birth
	8	Controls water reabsorption by kidneys
D	9	Causes calcium to be released from bones
E	10	Controls metabolic rate
	11	Causes calcium to be deposited in bones
F	12	Related to T-cell and antibody formation
G	13, 14	Stimulates formation of carbohydrates from protein
	15	Regulates salt levels
H	16	Prepares body for "flight or fight"
	17	Maintains high blood pressure and vasodilation
I	18	Reduces blood glucose level
J	19	Increases blood glucose level
K	20, 21	Secondary sexual features and menstrual cycle
L	22	Secondary sexual features and sperm formation

Endocrine glands

A–C Pituitary
- **A** Anterior lobe
- **B** Midlobe
- **C** Posterior lobe

D Parathyroid (behind thyroid)
E Thyroid
F Thymus
G–H Adrenal
- **G** Cortex
- **H** Medulla

I–J Pancreas
- **I** cells
- **J** cells

K Ovary (female)
L Testes (male)

Hormones

1 Growth
2 Thyroid-stimulating (TSH)
3 Adrenocorticotrophic (ACTH)
4 Prolactin
5 Gonadotrophic, follicle-stimulating (FSH), luteinizing (LH)
6 Melanocyte-stimulating (MSH)
7 Oxytocin
8 Antidiuretic (ADH)
9 Parathormone
10 Thyroxine
11 Calcitonin
12 Thymosin
13 Corticosterone
14 Hydrocortisone
15 Aldosterone
16 Epinephrine
17 Norepinephrine
18 Insulin
19 Glucagon
20 Estrogens
21 Progesterone
22 Testosterone

Cells

Types of cells
The main features of an animal cell (**1**) and a plant cell (**2**):
a Cytoplasm: a transparent, jelly-like substance.
b Cell membrane: a "skin" around the cytoplasm.
c Nucleus: denser and acting as cell's control center.
Note that **a**, **b**, and **c** are present in both plant and animal cells. Plant cells have three additional structures:
d Cell wall: surrounding the cell and made of cellulose, a nonliving substance.
e Plastids: units involved in the making and storing of food.
f Vacuoles: cell sap maintains turgidity.

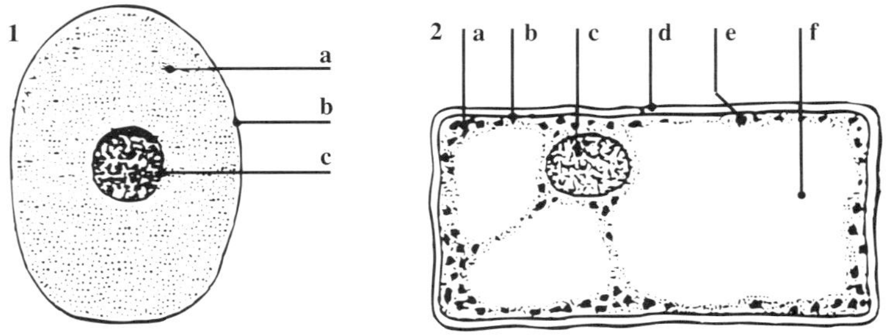

Cell variety
Cells have different shapes and perform different tasks. Examples of types of cell:
1 Food-conducting plant cells joined by perforated walls.
2 Sperm cell: a male sex cell, which lashes its tail to swim toward a female sex cell.
3 Nerve cells to conduct nerve impulses.
4 Red blood cell (erythrocytes) to transport oxygen.
5 White blood cell (leukocytes) to fight disease.
6 Blood platelets to help blood-clotting.

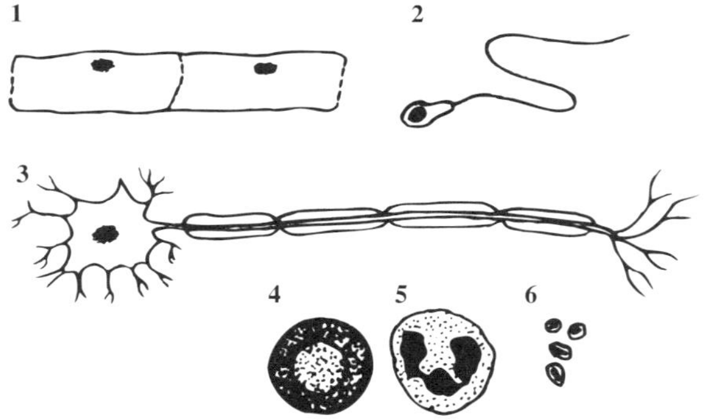

How cells divide
The five steps of mitosis, or cell division:
1 A single cell before mitosis.
a Cell nucleus
b Nuclear membrane
c Chromosomes
d Centrioles
2 Chromosomes divide into chromatids.
3 Nuclear membrane fades and centrioles diverge, producing fibers.
4 Chromosomes line up in cell center and chromatids pull apart.
5 New cell membrane divides cell into two; chromatids become chromosomes of new cell.

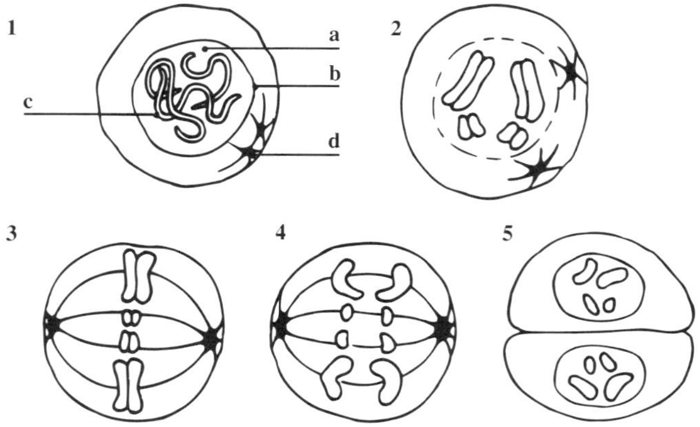

Levels of organization of living creatures

The body is a single organism (living creature) made up of many different substances and structures. These can be arranged into levels of increasing complexity called levels of organization, beginning with the most basic.

1

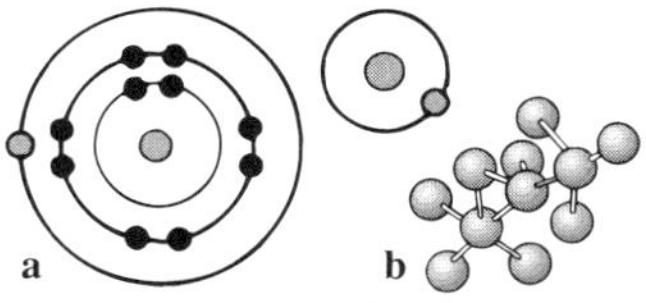

Chemical level
Atoms (**a**) and molecules (**b**) make the substances that are the building blocks (for example, water and protein) for all the other levels.

2

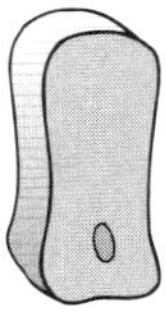

Cells
Cells are the smallest living units of the body.

3

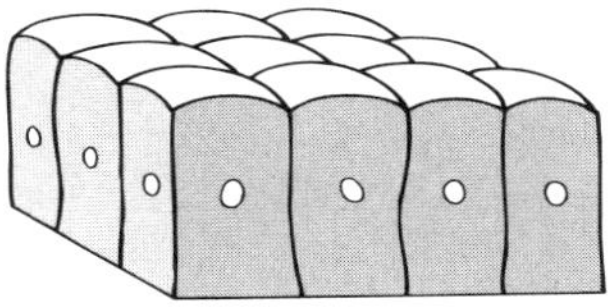

Tissues
These are formed by groups of cells with similar structures and functions (together with other substances).

4

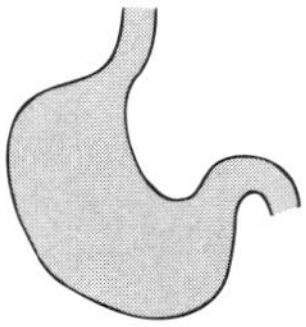

Organs
These are formed by tissues.

5

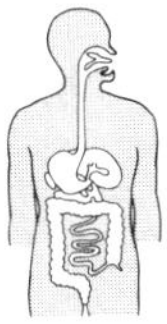

Body systems
These result from various organs working together.

6

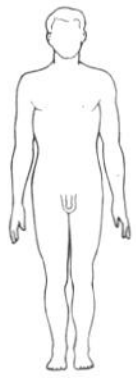

The body (organism)
This is the sum of all the levels existing and operating together.

Types of cells in living organisms

Although there are many different types of cells–each with its own unique structure and function–they all share certain features.

Typical cell structure
a Cell (plasma) membrane is the cell's "skin."
b Cytoplasm (transparent gel-like substance) contains the cell's basic living materials.
c The nucleus controls the working of the cell.

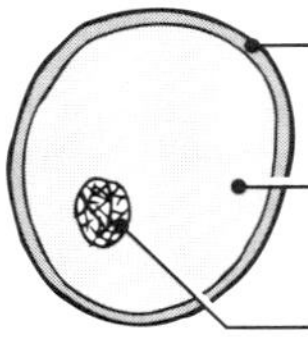

	Example of cell	Description	Location	Functions
	**Adipocytes**	Each contains a droplet of fat that pushes the nucleus and cytoplasm to the edge of the cell	• Deposited under the skin and around the heart and other organs as fat	• Store energy; • cushion body parts; and • provide insulation.
	**Chondrocytes**	Large and circular	• In cartilage (semirigid connective tissue)	• Maintain cartilage • and in their immature form, chondroblasts, make cartilage.
	**Epithelial cells**	Three main types: flat, cuboidal, and columnar	• In the coverings and linings of the body	• protect; • absorb; • secrete; • filter; and • allow stretching.
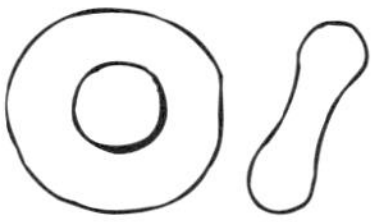	**Erythrocytes**	Disk-shaped red blood cells that have no nuclei	• In the bloodstream	• Transport gases around the body.
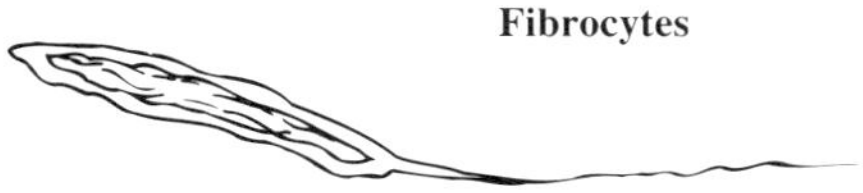	**Fibrocytes**	Long, flat, and branching	• In the connective tissues	• Maintain fibers and in their immature form, fibroblasts, • make fibers.
	**Leukocytes**	White blood cells of various shapes and sizes, larger than the red blood cells	• Throughout the body	• Fight and destroy invading germs and bacteria.
	**Neurons**	Nerve cells with extensions called dendrites and a longer axon	• In the brain and spine	• Transmit electrical impulses.
	**Osteocytes**	Mature, circular bone cells	• In bones	• Maintain bones and in their immature form, osteoblasts, make bones.

SECTION SEVEN ASSOCIATIONS

BIOLOGICAL

American Association of Anatomists

Professional body for biomedical researchers and educators focusing on anatomical form and function.
9650 Rockville Pike, Bethesda, MD 20814
Tel. 301-634-7910
http://www.anatomy.org

American Biological Safety Association

Professional association formed to "promote biosafety as a scientific discipline."
1202 Allanson Rd., Mundelein, IL 60960
Tel. 847-949-1517
http://www.absa.org

American Institute of Biological Sciences

Organization dedicated to "advancing biological research and education for the welfare of society."
1444 1 St., N.W., Washington, DC 20005
Tel. 202-628-1500
http://www.aibs.org

The American Ornithologists' Union

Oldest U.S. organization devoted to the study of birds.
1313 Dolley Madison Blvd., McLean, VA 22101
Tel. 703-790-1745
http://www.aou.org/

American Society for Cell Biology

Professional organization of cell biologists dedicated to advancing scientific knowledge, increasing public awareness of the importance of biomedical research, and guiding national policy on the education, training, and career development of biomedical researchers.
8120 Woodmont Ave., Bethesda, MD 20814
Tel. 301-347-9300
http://www.ascb.org

American Society for Photobiology

Organization that "promotes original research in photobiology, facilitates integration of different disciplines in the study of photobiology, promotes dissemination of knowledge of photobiology, and provides information on photobiological aspects of national and international problems."
P.O. Box 1897, Lawrence, KS 66044
Tel. 785-843-1235 ext. 216
http://www.pol-us.net/ASP_Home/index.html

American Society of Ichthyologists and Herpetologists

Professional society "dedicated to the scientific study of fishes, amphibians and reptiles... to increase knowledge about these organisms, to disseminate that knowledge... and to encourage and support young scientists who will make future advances in these fields."
Florida International University, Biological Sciences, 11200 SW 8th St., Miami, FL 33181
Tel. 305-348-1235
http://www.asih.org

American Society of Mammalogists

Society formed to "promote the study of mammals and provide information for public policy, resources management, conservation, and education."
810 East 10th St., PO Box 197, Lawrence, KS 66044
Tel. 785-843-1235; 800-627-0629
http://www.mammalsociety.org/

American Society of Naturalists

Society formed to "advance and diffuse knowledge of organic evolution and other broad biological principles."
c/o University of Chicago Press, PO Box 37005, Chicago, IL 60637
Tel. 773-753-3347
http://www.amnat.org/

American Society of Plant Biologists

Organization formed to "promote the growth and development of plant biology, to encourage and publish research in plant biology, and to promote the interests and growth of plant scientists in general."
15501 Monona Dr., Rockville, MD 20855
Tel. 301-251-0560
http://www.aspb.org/

American Society of Plant Taxonomists

Association promoting research and teaching in the taxonomy, systematics, and phylogeny of vascular and nonvascular plants.
University of Wyoming, Department of Botany 3165, 1000 E University Avenue, Laramie, WY 82071
Tel. 307-766-2556
http://www.aspt.net

Association of Biomolecular Resource Facilities
International society "dedicated to advancing core and research biotechnology laboratories through research, communication, and education."
2019 Galisteo St., Bldg. I, Santa Fe, NM 87505
Tel. 505 983-8102
http://www.abrf.org/

Botanical Society of America
Not-for-profit membership society that promotes botany, the study of plants, their uses, and their interaction within the biosphere.
PO Box 299, St. Louis, MO 63166
Tel. 314-577-9566
http://www.botany.org/

The Entomological Society of America
"Largest organization in the world serving the professional and scientific needs of entomologists and people in related disciplines."
10001 Derekwood Lane, Lanham, MD 20706
Tel. 301 731-4535
http://www.entsoc.org/

Federation of American Societies for Experimental Biology
Coalition of independent member societies that serves the interests of biomedical and life scientists, particularly those related to public policy issues.
9650 Rockville Pike, Bethesda MD 20814
Tel. 301-634-7000
http://www.faseb.org

Herpetologists League
"International organization of people devoted to studying the biology of amphibians and reptiles."
Biological Sciences, Box 4050, Emporia State University, Emporia, KS 66801
Tel. 316-341-5606
http://www.inhs.uiuc.edu/cbd/HL/HL.html

The Human Anatomy & Physiology Society
Organization founded to promote excellence in anatomy and physiology education.
8816 Manchester, Suite 314
St. Louis, MO 63144
Tel. 800-448-4277
http://www.hapsweb.org/

International Marine Mammal Association, Inc.
Association "dedicated to the conservation of marine mammals and their habitats worldwide, through research and education."
1474 Gordon St., Guelph, ON, Canada N1L 1C8
Tel. 519-767-1948
http://www.imma.org

Marine Conservation Biology Institute
Organization dedicated to protecting ocean life through science and conservation advocacy.
2122 112 Ave. NE, Suite B-300
Bellevue, WA 98004
Tel. 425-274-1180
http://www.mcbi.org/

National Association of Biology Teachers
Professional association for life science educators.
12030 Sunrise Valley Dr., Reston, VA 20191
Tel. 703/264-9696; 800/406-0775
http://www.nabt.org/

National Human Genome Research Institute
Government agency supporting "genetic and genomic research, and investigation into the ethical, lega,l and social implications surrounding genetics research."
National Institutes of Health, 31 Center Drive, MSC 2152, 9000 Rockville Pike, Bethesda, MD 20892
Tel. 301-402-0911
http://www.nhgri.nih.gov/

National Wildlife Federation
Conservation group, "uniting individuals, organizations, businesses, and government to protect wildlife, wild places, and the environment."
11100 Wildlife Center Dr., Reston, VA 20190
Tel. 703-438-6000
http://www.nwf.org

Society for Conservation Biology
Professional organization dedicated to "promoting the scientific study of the phenomena that affect the maintenance, loss, and restoration of biological diversity."
4245 N. Fairfax Dr., Arlington, VA 22203
Tel. 703-276-2384
http://conbio.net/

Society for Economic Botany
Professional society encouraging "scientific research, education, and related activities on the … uses of plants."
P.O. Box 1897, Lawrence, KS 66044
Tel. 785-843-1235; 800-627-0629
http://www.econbot.org/home.html

Society for Industrial Microbiology
"Professional association dedicated to the advancement of microbiological sciences, specifically as applied to industrial materials, processes, products, and their associated problems."
3929 Old Lee Highway, Fairfax, VA 22030
Tel. 703-691-3357
http://www.simhq.org

Society for Integrative & Comparative Biology
Organization formed to "integrate the many fields of specialization which occur in the broad field of biology."
1313 Dolley Madison Blvd., McLean, VA 22101
Tel. 703-790-1745; 800-955-1236
http://www.sicb.org/

GENERAL SCIENTIFIC

American Association for the Advancement of Science (AAAS)
Organization formed to "further the work of scientists; facilitate cooperation among them; foster scientific freedom and responsibility; improve the effectiveness of science in the promotion of human welfare; advance education in science; and increase the public's understanding and appreciation of the promise of scientific methods in human progress."
1200 New York Ave., N.W., Washington, DC 20005
Tel. 202-326-6400
http://www.aaas.org/

Association for Women in Science
Organization formed to "achieve equity and full participation for women in science, engineering, technology, and mathematics."
1200 New York Ave., N.W., Washington, DC 20005
Tel. 202-326-8940
http://www.awis.org/

Association of Science–Technology Centers
Organization of science centers and museums dedicated to "furthering the public understanding of science among increasingly diverse audiences."
1025 Vermont Ave., N.W., Washington, DC 20005
Tel. 202-783-7200
http://www.astc.org

The National Science Foundation
An independent agency of the U.S. government whose mission is to promote the progress of science; to advance the national health, prosperity, and welfare; and to secure the national defense. It is a major source of research grants and funding in the sciences.
4201 Wilson Blvd., Arlington, VA 22230
Tel. 703-292-5111
http://www.nsf.gov/

National Science Teachers Association
Professional organization dedicated to "excellence and innovation in science teaching and learning for all."
1840 Wilson Blvd., Arlington, VA 22201
Tel. 703-243-7100
http://www.nsta.org

Society for Amateur Scientists
Collaboration between world-class professionals and citizen scientists to "remove the roadblocks that prevent ordinary people from participating in scientific adventures of all kinds."
5600 Post Rd., East Greenwich, RI 02818
Tel. 401-398-7001
http://www.sas.org/

SECTION EIGHT
WEB SITES

BIOLOGY

Access Excellence
National Health Museum Links to resources in biology, biotechnology, and health issues.
http://www.accessexcellence.org

ActionBioscience.org
Bioscience Productions Articles on biodiversity, environment, genomics, biotechnology, evolution, and other cutting-edge topics.
http://www.actionbioscience.org

Anatomy of the Human Body
Gray's Anatomy Online version of the classic book—over 13,000 entries and 1,200 images.
http://www.bartleby.com/107

Animal Diversity Web
University of Michigan Museum of Zoology Database of natural history, distribution, classification, and conservation biology.
http://animaldiversity.ummz.umich.edu

Animal Physiology
Teachnet.ie Clear, concise presentation of animal classification and physiology.
http://www.teachnet.ie/farmnet/Animal_physiology.htm

Ask a Biologist
Arizona State University, Life Sciences Visualization Group ASU faculty and staff answer e-mail questions for students grades K–12.
http://askabiologist.asu.edu/pages/about.html

BBC Nature-Wildfacts
Information on the distribution, habitat, diet, and conservation of hundreds of animals.
http://www.bbc.co.uk/nature/wildfacts

Biology Online
Richard Lees Tutorials, a dictionary of biology, and links to other sites.
http://www.biology-online.org

The Biology Project
University of Arizona Resources in biochemistry, cell biology, developmental biology, human biology, genetics, and molecular biology.
http://www.biology.arizona.edu

Biotech Life Science Dictionary
University of Texas at Austin Over 8,000 terms deal with biochemistry, biotechnology, botany, cell biology, and genetics.
http://biotech.icmb.utexas.edu/search/dict-search.html

Brains Rule!
University of Nebraska Information, interactive games, and lesson plans on the human brain; includes "Ask the Brain Expert" and "Meet a Neuroscientist" features.
http://www.brainsrule.com/index.htm

Cells Alive
James A. Sullivan Devoted to cell images and processes.
http://www.cellsalive.com/

DNA-Interactive
Cold Spring Harbor Laboratory Information on the history and science of DNA research.
http://www.dnai.org/index.htm

Dr. Saul's Biology in Motion
Leif Saul Animations, interactive activities, and cartoons "designed to make learning biology a richer, more engaging experience."
http://biologyinmotion.com/

Evolution
Public Broadcasting System Animations, simulations, dynamic timelines, conversations with experts, news bulletins, and links on evolution.
http://www.pbs.org/wgbh/evolution/

The Franklin Institute Online: BioPoint Hotlist
Links to hundreds of excellent sites on a wide variety of biology topics.
http://sln.fi.edu/qa97/biology/biolist.html

Froguts.com
Virtual frog dissection using photos of frogs recycled from schools.
http://www.froguts.com

The Geee! In Genome
Canadian Museum of Nature Information on genes, stem cells, cloning, and the diversity of life; also educational resources, ethical debates, interactive games, and opinion polls.
http://nature.ca/genome/index_e.cfm

Genetic Science Learning Center
Eccles Institute of Human Genetics, University of Utah Activities and information on topics in genetics, genetic disorders, and genetics in society
http://gslc.genetics.utah.edu/

Go Ask Alice
Columbia University Question and answer service on physical, sexual, emotional, and spiritual health issues.
http://www.goaskalice.columbia.edu

HHMI's Biointeractive
Howard Hughes Medical Institute Virtual labs, activities, and interactive demonstrations on many subjects related to the human body and health.
http://www.biointeractive.org

Human Anatomy On Line
INTELLIMED International Corporation Over 100 descriptions, animations, and anatomy images.
http://www.innerbody.com

Kimball's Biology Pages
John W. Kimball Online biology encyclopedia.
http://users.rcn.com/jkimball.ma.ultranet/BiologyPages/

Learning Programs for Biology
BioMedia Associates Images, animations, organism identification quizzes, teacher resources, and information on videos and CD-ROMs.
http://www.ebiomedia.com

MicrobeWorld
American Society for Microbiology Portal to three Web sites on microbiology: for students, for educators, and for general audiences.
http://www.microbeworld.org/home.htm

NASA Astrobiology Institute
Explores the origins of life on Earth and the possibility of life in space; contains an "Ask an Astrobiologist" feature.
http://nai.arc.nasa.gov/index.cfm

Red Gold: The Epic Story of Blood
PBS, Thirteen/WNET, New York Describes blood production and function; discusses facts and myths about blood and its impact on everything from religion to commerce and popular culture.
http://www.pbs.org/wnet/redgold/about/index.html

The Tree of Life
David R. Maddison, ed. Information about the diversity of organisms on Earth, their history and characteristics.
http://tolweb.org/tree/phylogeny.html

The Virtual Cell Web Page
The Virtual Cell Web Project Interactive, animated exploration of the cell with virtual textbook.
http://www.ibiblio.org/virtualcell/index.htm

World Biodiversity Database
ETI Bioinformatics Taxonomic database and information system documenting and disseminating information on all known species.
http://www.eti.uva.nl/Database/WBD.html

GENERAL WEB SITES

American Association for the Advancement of Science (AAAS)
Information on scientific developments and education programs for all ages.
http://www.aaas.org

Exploratorium
Experiments, exhibits, and sound and video files exploring hundreds of different topics.
http://www.exploratorium.edu

How Stuff Works
HSW Media Network Individual tutorials in Earth science, engineering, physical science, life science, and space.
http://science.howstuffworks.com

National Science Digital Library (NSDL)
National Science Foundation Giant database of links to quality resources and services supporting science education at all levels.
http://nsdl.org

NOVA: Science in the News
Australian Academy of Science Information on scientific principles and concepts in the headlines.
http://www.science.org.au/nova

Quiz Hub
Schmidel & Wojcik Learning center with quizzes, homework help, resources, and interactive games.
http://quizhub.com/

Science Learning Network (SLN)
Links to an international group of inquiry-based museums and Web sites and educators' hotlists.
http://sln.fi.edu/org/

Science News for Kids
Science Service Suggestions for hands-on activities, books, articles, Web resources, and other useful materials for students ages 9–13.
http://www.sciencenewsforkids.org

Scientific American.com
Latest news in science as well as an "Ask the Experts" feature.
http://www.sciam.com

Society for Amateur Scientists
Hotlists for a variety of disciplines, as well as for science hobbyists, science suppliers, science education stores, scientific organizations, also science books, magazines, and newsletters.
http://www.sas.org

ThinkQuest: Library
Oracle ThinkQuest Educational Foundation
Links to hundreds of scientific sites on the Web.
http://www.thinkquest.org/library

TEACHER RESOURCES

Biology Lessons for Prospective and Practicing Teachers
San Diego State University Approximately 20 lesson plans for teachers grades K–8.
http://www.biologylessons.sdsu.edu

Curriculum Center: Discoveryschool.com
Discovery Classroom activities supporting core curriculum topics.
http://school.discovery.com/curriculumcenter

Education World: The Educator's Best Friend
Lesson plans, practical information for educators, links to educational Web sites, and information on how to integrate technology in the classroom.
http://www.education-world.com

National Association of Biology Teachers
Professional association for U.S. biology teachers provides support and materials, including the journal *American Biology Teacher*.
http://www.nabt.org/sup/resources

National Science Teachers Association
Information on the teaching of science, including links to teacher recommended Web sites.
http://www.nsta.org

Science NetLinks
Provides a wealth of resources for K–12 science educators, including lesson plans and reviewed internet resources.
http://www.sciencenetlinks.com/

EQUIPMENT SUPPLIERS

Carolina Biological Supply Company
Online catalogue of science equipment and teacher resources.
http://www.carolina.com

Fisher Science Education
Online catalogue of science equipment and teacher resources.
http://www.fishersci.com/education/index.jsp

Frey Scientific
Online catalogue of science equipment and teacher resources.
http://www.freyscientific.com/index.jsp

NSTA's Suppliers Guide
National Science Teachers Association
Suppliers of textbooks, reference works, computer programs, curriculum kits, and lab equipment.
http://suppliers.nsta.org

ScienceLab.com, Inc.
Discount supplier of science education materials and laboratory equipment.
http://www.sciencelab.com

Ward's Natural Science
Supplier of materials for high school- and college-level biology and geology classes, as well as life, environmental, Earth, and physical science studies in grades 5 through 9.
http://www.wardsci.com

INDEX

The A–Z Glossary and other thematic Sections provide direct access to information. The Index offers supplementary access to Sections 2 to 6. Page numbers in **bold** type indicate the main biographical note on individuals.